"AI is a constellation of technologies that allows machines to sense, comprehend, act and learn. Like any powerful technology, AI entails responsibilities that need to be understood, communicated and addressed. I can only applaud the valuable contribution of this book and advocate for using AI+DLT to guarantee the 'trustlessness' of next-gen platforms: contexts where trust in parties is unnecessary because the system itself guarantees validity veracity and integrity of data and predictions."

Laura Degiovanni, Founder and CEO, TIIQU

"As a GDPR EU representative, I work exclusively with companies that move personal data across borders. Because that data comes from various sources located in multiple countries, it enables AI systems to uncover patterns, make connections and manage risk. These international data flows are crucial to grow the use of AI in financial services."

Jane Murphy, EDPO

"AI is changing financial services beyond recognition. This is a timely and excellent handbook on the subject and should be compulsory reading for all in the financial services sector. It treats in straightforward terms the complexities, major challenges but importantly also sets sight on the abundance of opportunity AI offers. The editors have gathered an impressive array of market commentators, practitioners and AI experts to produce the AI reference book of 2020."

Kieran Rigby, Global President, Claims Solutions, Crawford & Company

"AI is a new world for most of us, but it is developing fast so the more insight and transparency we bring to the topic the better for everyone. AI presents a fantastic opportunity for our profession to do things much quicker, more rigorously and with more personalization than has ever been possible before. But we need to embrace this and share experiences. This is why *The AI Book* is super helpful."

Sian Fisher, CEO, Chartered Insurance Institute

"The UK remains a global leader in Insurance. Brokers are integral to this, as is the commitment to fully understand and embrace the risks and opportunities of Innovation, especially in Technology, and fast-moving areas like AI. On beh
members, BIBA remains actively
digital upskilling, and Insurtech, f
support ambitious projects like *T*
accessible ideas and experience
not just Insurance, so that we can continue to deliver the best outcomes for customer."

Steve White, CEO, British Insurance Brokers Association

"As an AI practitioner, I truly believe the AI technology to be only valuable in real-world applications. *The AI Book*, written by technology and business experts, is a great tool for busy executives both in China and abroad who would like to learn more about AI and how it may impact their businesses."

Dong Li, PhD and MBA, CTO, Sunshine P&C Insurance Company

"*The AI Book* is a much-awaited cornerstone to holistically applying artificial intelligence to finance while highlighting the importance of trust, transparency and ethics. AI brings transformative changes for economies and societies in the world, and these changes need to benefit all people. *The AI Book* demonstrates how we can harness the potential of AI for financial services by putting our human values at the heart of it. The book written by great AI experts globally can guide and inspire you to think further into the future. A must read."

Gülser S. Gorat, Director, UNESCO

"Artificial intelligence is the stealth disruptor of the financial services industry and its impact is being felt in every corner, from risk modelling and compliance to chatbots and roboadvisors. But with such transformational power comes legal, regulatory and ethical issues. *The AI Book*, crowdsourced from leading industry experts, provides important insights into the use of AI in financial services, as well as the debates surrounding its application."

Joy Macknight, Managing Editor, The Banker

"As a major financial services company we are already experiencing on a day-to-day basis how transformative, and disruptive, AI can be for our business, from trading, risk analysis, research, and wealth management to even straightforward processes such as client identification and KYC reporting. This book has proved to be an invaluable guide to these many different applications for AI in finance and how it can benefit businesses, and where it may not. In sum, a very timely and helpful contribution to understanding the real world implications of AI in finance."

Miranda Carr, Managing Director, Research, Haitong International (UK) Limited

"Technologies are meant to solve business problems. Artificial Intelligence is no exception. It can help make decisions and predictions by analysing huge amount of data in real time. The highly computerized and data-rich financial services industry is a key industry that is very suitable for AI applications. AI can help in many financial service scenarios such as credit decisions, risk control, asset allocation and portfolio rebalancing. You will find all these interesting topics in *The AI Book*, written by global AI pundits and industry insiders. I highly recommend it."

Ning Tang, Founder, Chairman and CEO, CreditEase

"Artificial Intelligence has been transforming the world digitally, bringing limitless potential to push us forward to enormous business opportunities and social wellbeing. Contributing US$15.7 trillion to the global economy by 2030 according to PwC's research, AI should also go hand in hand with proper governance and responsible framework. A good read of the AI Book to help harness the power of AI in an ethical and responsible manner. Responsible AI starts with responsible leaders!"

Elton Yeung, Vice Chairman, PwC China

"AI is an emerging technology and *The AI Book* is required reading by professionals in trade finance and working capital markets globally. AI is being increasingly harnessed in a variety of applications, starting with invoice data capture, credit assessment and pricing, to fraud and money laundering mitigation in suspicious transactions. Check out *The AI Book* for the all the latest in AI and machine learning tools."

Walter Gontarek, CEO and Chairman, Channel Capital

"In financial services, the harvesting of data and wrangling of it to unlock its power for Artificial Intelligence and Machine Learning is proving to be the lifeblood of the industry. As we progress into the future, Machine Learning in financial services will continue to lead the pack and allow us to solve increasingly complex problems that would otherwise be impossible without harnessing the power of AI. *The AI Book* is packed with information from leading experts on how AI is used and impacts the financial services industry."

Shuki Licht, Chief Innovation Officer, Finastr

"AI will undoubtedly impact every stage of the insurance value chain, from customer acquisition and customer experience, to underwriting, product development, pricing and ultimately through each stage of the claims settlement process. Few other technologies have the potential to impact the industry so significantly as an enabler to innovation in a changing world where information underpins every decision. Insurance organizations ignore or limit the application of artificial intelligence at their peril; utilizing and understanding data to the benefit of the ultimate customer will always be a successful business strategy and a competitive advantage. This book will help leaders and executives understand more about how to get that done."

Ruth Polyblank, Vice President, Insurance, Mastercard

"From the early days AI for the financial industry, to Deep Blue, invented by Ron Coleman at IBM, the AI chess game that beat Kasprov in 1997, these were all incremental steps that have lead us to the most significant and profound changes that will reshape the financial markets. Today, we are seeing many platforms emerge, and free open source code from the biggest players like Google, and it will be several years before we know who will emerge as the tech AI victors. But one thing is certain, we are in the exploratory services phase of AI, where banks are learning from service providers who know how to piece the correct AI components together to solve real problems. Within two to three years, we will witness an AI boom no different from the Internet craze of the 1990's. If you plan to be in the AI game, strap yourself in, read *The AI Book*, and this will guide you and shape your thinking on how you can take advantage of the forthcoming AI wave."

Steven O'Hanlon, CEO, Numerix LLC, NYC

The AI Book

This edition first published 2020

Registered office

John Wiley & Sons Ltd, The Atrium, Southern Gate, Chichester, West Sussex, PO19 8SQ, United Kingdom

For details of our global editorial offices, for customer services and for information about how to apply for permission to reuse the copyright material in this book please see our website at www.wiley.com.

A catalogue record for this book is available from the Library of Congress.

A catalogue record for this book is available from the British Library.

ISBN 978-1-119-55190-4 (paperback) ISBN 978-1-119-55186-7 (ePDF)
ISBN 978-1-119-55192-8 (ePub) ISBN 978-1-119-55196-6 (Obook)

10 9 8 7 6 5 4 3 2 1

Cover design: Wiley

Cover image: pkproject/Shutterstock

Set in 10/13pt Helvetica Lt Std by Aptara, New Delhi, India

Printed in Great Britain by TJ International Ltd, Padstow, Cornwall, UK

The AI Book

The Artificial Intelligence Handbook for Investors, Entrepreneurs and FinTech Visionaries

Edited by
Susanne Chishti
Ivana Bartoletti
Anne Leslie
Shân M. Millie

Contents

6. Capital Markets

7. Trust, Transparency and Ethics

8. Legal Risk and Regulation

9. The Future of AI in Finance

Preface

Artificial intelligence (AI) is changing our lives. It has never been more important to have a clear understanding of what AI is and the ramifications of its mass adoption, particularly in the financial services sector. However, the inherent complexity of the topic is often intimidating to non-specialists, and the absence of a broad-based dialogue on the topic of AI is hindering business decision-making. *The AI Book* explains what exactly artificial intelligence is; how is it being used in financial services; what is at stake; who are the major players; and what lies over the horizon?

AI and Deep Learning have broad ranging applications in deposits & lending, insurance, payments, investment management and capital markets. Deep learning solves the classification problem by letting the machine learn by itself. Similar technologies are used in assessing the right premiums for insurance markets and making predictions about stock market prices based on a large number of variables, which can then be used for automated trading.

Deep Learning is now used in finance to make connections between large numbers of seemingly unconnected events and variables to make predictions for fraud detection, insurance pricing and trading stock.

However, data needs to be unbiased, or otherwise the machine will learn the bias that is inherently embedded in the data. It is a known fact that many facial recognition algorithms work well with certain races but much less reliably with other races and gender. So there are many ethical issues associated with the use of AI in finance, particularly issues linked to privacy and the use of personal data.

AI is the new electricity, and with great opportunity comes great responsibility. AI is not perfect and therefore it is crucial for all of us in finance to fully understand how AI can be used properly.

The AI Book is the first crowd-sourced book globally on the future of artificial intelligence in the financial services sector – a book that provides food for thought to FinTech newbies, pioneers and well-seasoned experts alike. The reason we decided to reach out to the global AI, machine learning and FinTech community in sourcing the book's contributors lies in the inherently fragmented nature of the field of AI. There was no single author, group of authors or indeed region in the world that could cover all the facets and nuances of AI in finance in an exhaustive manner. What is more, by being able to reach out to a truly global contributor base, we not only stayed true to the spirit of FinTech and the AI community, making use of technological channels of communication in reaching out to, selecting and reviewing our would-be contributors, but also made sure that every corner of the globe had the chance to have its say. Thus, we aimed to fulfil one of the most important purposes of *The AI Book*; namely, to give a voice to those that would remain unheard, those that did not belong to a true FinTech and AI community in their local areas, and spread that voice to an international audience. We have immensely enjoyed the journey of editing *The AI Book* and sincerely hope that you will enjoy reading it, at least as much.

More than 140 authors submitted 142 abstracts to be part of the book. We asked our global FinTech and AI communities for their views regarding which abstracts they would like to have fully expanded for the book. Out of all contributors, we selected 74 authors who have been asked to write their full chapter, which has now been included in this book. We conducted a questionnaire among all our selected authors to further understand their background and expertise. In summary, our selected authors come from 20 countries. More than 75% of our authors have postgraduate university degrees (78%) (see Table 1), have strong domain expertise across many fields (see Table 2) and 87% of our finalist authors had their articles published before.

Table 3 and Table 4 show that more than 40% of our finalist authors are entrepreneurs working for FinTech startups and scaleups (many of them part of the founding team), 10% each comes from established financial and technology companies and more than a third from service providers such as consulting firms or law firms servicing the financial services sector.

Table 1: What is the highest educational qualification of our finalist authors?

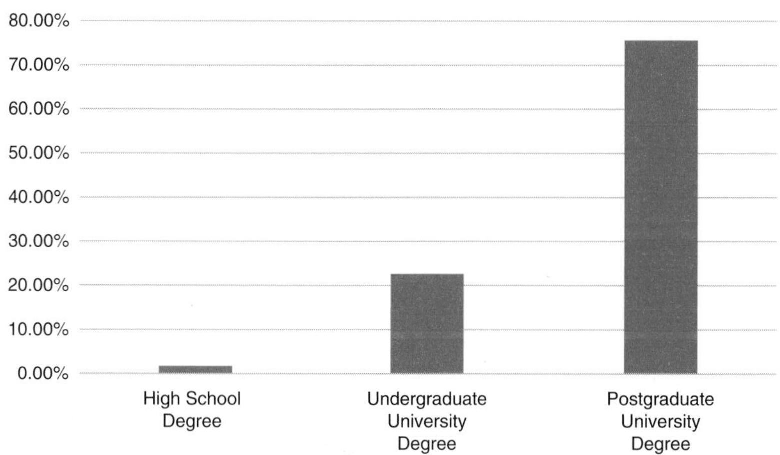

Table 2: List all areas our authors have domain expertise in; multiple choices were possible

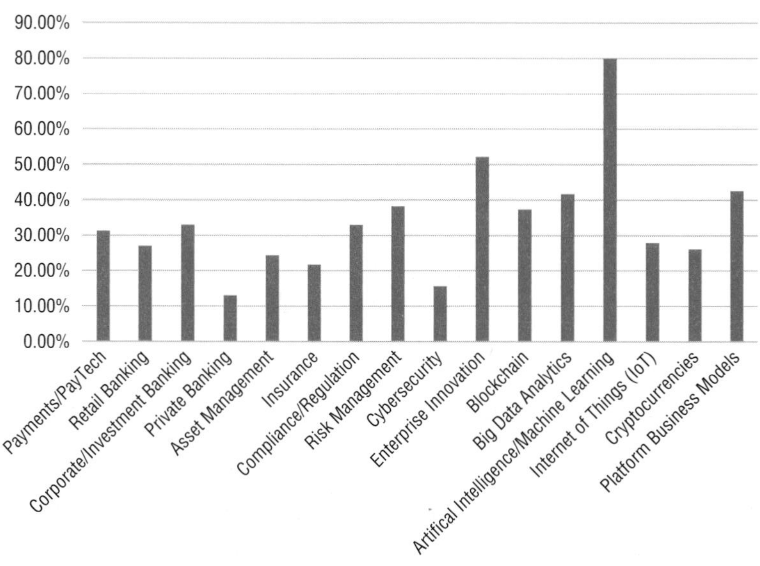

Table 3: Authors selected the type of company they are working in

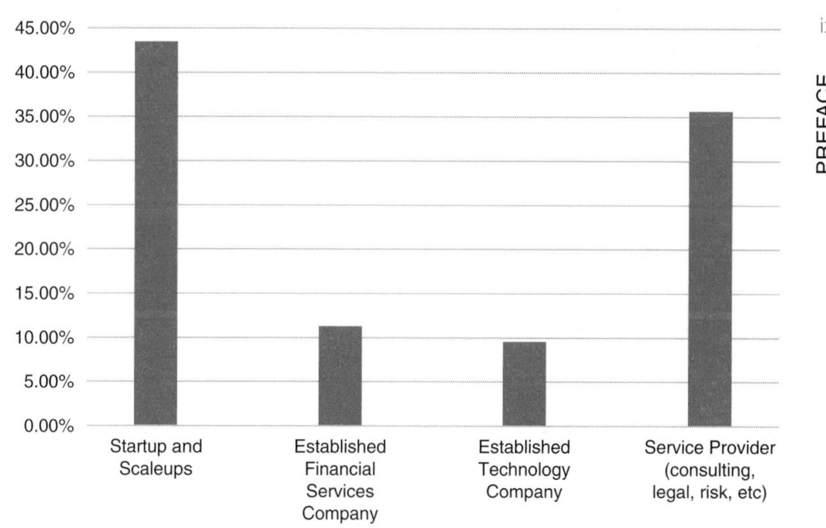

Table 4: Size of companies our authors work for

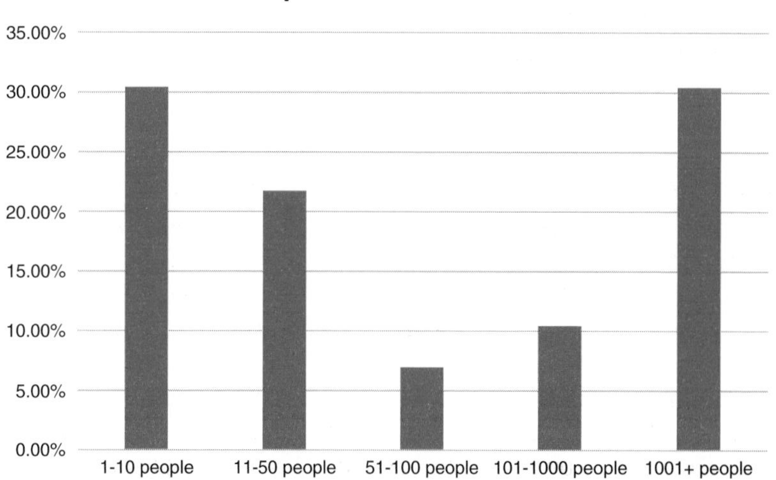

Almost 30% of our authors work for startups with up to 10 people and another 25% for startups/small and medium-sized enterprises (SMEs) with up to 100 people. More than 40% of our authors are employed by a large organization of more than 100 employees.

We are very proud of our highly qualified authors, their strong expertise, and passion for artificial intelligence and FinTech by being either entrepreneurs or often "intrapreneurs" in large established organizations who all are committed to play a significant role in the global FinTech and AI revolution. These remarkable people are willing to share their insights with all of us over the next pages.

This book would not have been possible without the dedication and efforts of all contributors to *The AI Book* (both those who submitted their initial abstracts for consideration by the global FinTech community, as well as the final authors whose insights you will be reading shortly). In addition, we would like to thank our editors at Wiley whose guidance and help made sure that what started off as an idea, you are now holding in your hands.

Finally, I would like to thank my fantastic co-editors Ivana Bartoletti, Head of Privacy and Data Protection at Gemserv; Anne Leslie, Senior Managing Consultant, IBM; and Shân M. Millie, Board Advisor & CEO of Bright Blue Hare. Editing a crowd-sourced book naturally takes several months and Ivana, Anne and Shân were always a pleasure to work alongside with their strong domain expertise and vision for the future of artificial intelligence!

Susanne Chishti
Bestselling Co-Editor, The FINTECH Book Series
CEO FINTECH Circle & FINTECH Circle Institute

About the Editors

Susanne Chishti (Editor-in-Chief)

Susanne Chishti is the CEO of FINTECH Circle, Europe's first Angel Network focused on FinTech investments and the founder of the FINTECH Circle Institute, the leading FinTech learning and innovation platform offering Corporate Innovation Workshops to C-level executives, and providing FinTech courses. She is also the co-editor of the bestselling publications, *The FinTech Book*, *The WealthTech Book*, *The InsurTech Book* and *The PayTech Book* (all published by Wiley).

Susanne has received the following awards:

1. Fintech Champion of the Year 2019 (Women in Finance Awards)
2. Social Media Influencer of the Year 2018 (*Investment Week*)
3. Top 7 Crypto Experts globally 2018 (*Inc. Magazine*)
4. City Innovator – Inspirational Woman in 2016
5. European Digital Financial Services "Power 50", an independent ranking of the most influential people in digital financial services in Europe (2015).

During her MBA, she started her career working for a FinTech company (before the term was invented) in Silicon Valley, 20 years ago. She then worked more than 15 years across Deutsche Bank, Lloyds Banking Group, Morgan Stanley and Accenture in London and Hong Kong. Susanne is an award-winning entrepreneur and investor with strong FinTech expertise. She is a judge and coach at global FinTech events and competitions and a conference keynote speaker. Susanne leads a global community of more than 130,000 FinTech entrepreneurs, investors and financial services professionals globally (www.fintechcircle.com).

Ivana Bartoletti

Ivana Bartoletti is a policymaker, international public speaker and media commentator.

In her day job, Ivana is head of privacy and data protection at Gemserv, where she advises organizations on compliance with privacy legislation, especially in relation to AI and blockchain technology. With an academic background in human rights and law, she has previously worked as adviser to the Minister of Human Rights in Italy and has held senior roles in privacy and information governance at Barclays, Sky and the NHS.

Ivana was awarded "Woman of the Year" (2019) at the Cyber Security Awards in recognition of her growing reputation as an advocate of equality, privacy and ethics at the heart of tech and AI.

In May 2018, she co-founded the Women Leading in AI Network, a thriving international group of scientists, industry leaders and policy experts advocating for responsible AI. Their 2018 report made waves among tech leaders, international institutions and the media, who backed many of their recommendations.

Ivana is a sought-after public speaker and media commentator for the BBC, Sky and other major broadcasters and news outlets on headline stories where technology intersects with privacy and data law and politics. Ivana's own book, focusing on the socio-economic impact of AI, will be released by Indigo Press.

Anne Leslie

Anne Leslie is a senior managing consultant at IBM Security where her focus is on security intelligence and operations consulting, specializing in cyber talent management. She has spent her entire career at the intersection of financial services, regulation and technology, in pivotal roles in both sales and advisory. Prior to joining IBM, Anne was managing director of a blockchain startup specializing in digital identity and online privacy, after leading the France-Benelux RegTech practice at BearingPoint where she was engaged in complex data governance, regulatory transformation and cloud migration programs for systemic banks, global insurers and supervisory authorities. As co-author of *The RegTech Book* recently published by Wiley, Anne is passionate about responsible technology. She believes that technological innovation should be the result of a human-centred design process that serves the ethical and social purpose of enhancing human well-being for the many and not the few. She is a fervent advocate of inclusive dialogue and multidisciplinary engagement in order to have crucial conversations that count about topics that matter.

Originally from Ireland, Anne has lived in France for over 20 years and today lives happily in Paris with her three children and her partner. She participated as Co-Editor in a personal capacity.

Shân M. Millie

Shân M. Millie specializes in practical innovation, supporting firms and high-performing individuals in value proposition design and incubation, business storytelling, and brand generation. Primarily focused on the insurance sector (since 2008), her work includes board advisory, training, facilitation, and 121 coaching. "I create value for individuals, teams and firms by engineering process and internal creativity, to unlock insight, shape purpose and convert intent into successful outcomes," she says. Drawing on 25+ years of corporate leadership and brand-building, she works with corporate intrapreneurs, startups and scaleups alike. Clients include the leading insurance organizations in the UK – Association of British Insurers, Chartered Institute of Insurance and British Insurance Brokers Association – established firms including Lloyd's of London, and leading InsurTechs, including digital claims specialists, RightIndem. Shân founded Bright Blue Hare in 2016, and is a founding associate of multidisciplinary London market consultancy, Green Kite. She is co-editor of the bestselling *The InsurTech Book: The Insurance Technology Handbook for Investors, Entrepreneurs and FinTech Visionaries* (Wiley, June 2018). Passionate about brilliantly run insurance as a social necessity, she serves as sector expert for the UK Disability Champion's Access to Insurance Taskforce, and as board member, Insurance United Against Dementia.

Acknowledgements

After the global book launch events of *The FinTech Book*, *The WealthTech Book* and *The InsurTech Book*, we met thousands of FinTech entrepreneurs, investors and financial services and technology professionals who all loved the books and wanted to learn more how artificial intelligence and machine learning will impact the financial services sector and our world overall.

We came up with the idea for *The AI Book* and spoke to our FinTech friends globally. Entrepreneurs across all continents were eager to share their powerful insights. They wanted to explain how AI is poised to disrupt lives, businesses, whole economies and even the geopolitical world order and of course, how it will improve the world of finance. FinTech investors, "intrapreneurs", innovation leaders at leading financial and technology institutions and thought leaders were keen to describe their embrace of the data and AI revolution.

The global effort of crowdsourcing such insights was born with *The FinTech Book* which became a global bestseller across 107 countries in 10 languages. We continued this success with *The WealthTech Book*, *The InsurTech Book* and *The PayTech Book*. We hope that with *The AI Book* we can satisfy the appetite for knowledge and insights about the future of artificial intelligence applied to the financial services sector.

We are aware that this would not have been possible without the global FINTECH Circle community and our own personal networks. We are very grateful to more than 130,000 members of FINTECH Circle for joining us daily across our website www.FINTECHCircle.com, our Twitter accounts and our LinkedIn group. Without the public support and engagement of our global FinTech and AI communities this book would not have been possible.

The authors you will read about have been chosen by our global ecosystem purely on merit; thus, no matter how big or small their organization, no matter in which country they work, no matter if they were well known or still undiscovered, everybody had the same chance to apply and be part of *The AI Book*. We are proud of that, as we believe that artificial intelligence will drive the world of finance. The global AI community is made up of the smartest, most innovative and nicest people we know. Thank you for being part of our journey. It is difficult to name you all here, but you are all listed in the directory at the end of this book.

Our publisher Wiley has been a great partner for The FinTech Book Series and we are delighted that Wiley will again publish *The AI Book* in paperback and e-book formats globally. A special thanks goes to our fantastic editor Gemma Valler. Thanks to you and your team – we could not have done it without your amazing support!

We look forward to hearing from you. Please visit our website https://fintechcircle.com/ai-book/ for additional bonus content from our global AI community! Please send us your comments on *The AI Book* and let us know how you wish to be engaged by dropping us a line at info@FINTECHCircle.com

Susanne Chishti
Twitter: @SusanneChishti
Anne Leslie
Twitter: @AnneLes1ie

Ivana Bartoletti
Twitter: @IvanaBartoletti
Shân M. Millie
Twitter: @SMMBrightBlueH

AI: Need to Know

1

AI has been in use in Banking and Finance since its inception in the 1950s and today's successful AI transformations are being driven by visionary leaders

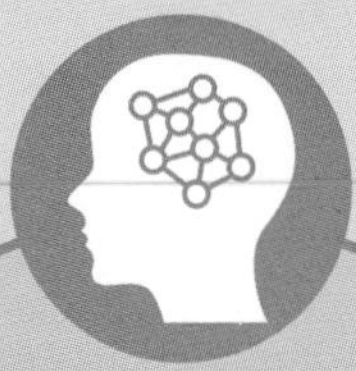

AI encompasses everything from rule-based technologies and probability-based methods that detect fraud, through to primitive neural networks for optical recognition and automatic stock and option trading. These technologies automate processes that were previously undertaken by human beings, often improving accuracy and efficiency

McKinsey & Co. estimates the technology will generate $13 trillion of revenue over the next decade and approximately 5,154 AI startups have been established globally during the past five years

AI nonetheless has limitations. These limitations can present themselves in the form of implementation challenges, unintended consequences and ethical issues

43% of banking executives see data quality as the biggest hindrance to benefiting from AI

Artificial intelligence (AI) is poised to disrupt lives, businesses, whole economies and even the international geopolitical order. As such, it has never been more important to have a clear understanding of what AI is and the ramifications of its mass adoption, particularly in the financial services sector. However, the inherent complexity of the topic is often intimidating to non-specialists, and the absence of broad-based dialogue on the topic of AI is hindering business decision-making related to its application.

What exactly is AI; how is it being used in financial services; what is at stake; who are the major players; and what lies over the horizon?

In Part 1, we will explore all these questions and more. By delving into the detail behind the hype, readers will gain a firm understanding of the different type of technologies that fall under the more general, and somewhat opaque, "AI" heading. We will have the opportunity to look at how nation states are jostling for position and international competitive advantage relative to their peers through their national AI strategies and action plans. We will also have a chance to learn about tried-and-tested recommendations for successfully embedding AI into the daily operations of financial services firms, while avoiding the myriad pitfalls that still unfortunately get in the way of firms reaping the full advantage of their AI investments.

Finally, we will take a close look at the "human" aspects of AI and examine the reasons why, in the face of the growing sophistication of algorithmic systems, the exercise of sound human judgement, governance and control has never been more important. We will look at the role of boards and directors in the formulation and execution of AI strategy within firms, and we will see how artificial intelligence systems that complement human cognition have the potential to deliver maximized value.

The Future of AI in Finance

By Chee-We Ng
Venture Capitalist, Oak Seed Ventures

How will artificial intelligence (AI) transform finance? What can AI do and how can we get it to work? What do we need to do to regulate AI in finance? These are questions at the forefront of many minds as we try to investigate the future of finance.

AI, a loosely defined set of technologies that try to mimic human judgement and interaction, has been in use in banking and finance since its inception in the 1950s. AI encompasses everything from rule-based technologies and probability-based methods that detect fraud, through to primitive neural networks for optical recognition and automatic stock and option trading. Collectively, these technologies automate processes that were previously undertaken by human beings, often improving accuracy and efficiency. One might argue that none of these traditional AI technologies is truly intelligent; AI merely automates what was previously performed manually.

The Promise of Deep Learning

The recent excitement around AI has tended to be linked to deep learning in its various forms. To understand why deep learning technologies simultaneously inspire excitement among researchers (who believe that deep learning is the breakthrough in AI everyone has been waiting for), and fear among tech leaders and politicians, it is important to place deep learning in the context of what its component technologies have achieved in the past 6 years.

The most recent wave of deep learning began in 2012 when Geoffrey Hinton and his students used deep convolutional neural networks (CNN) to tackle image recognition, a problem that has baffled scientists and engineers for many years. By achieving significantly higher detection rates and smaller false positives without having to write complicated code, Geoffrey Hinton was able to teach computers how to classify images just by showing many labelled samples, hence the term "machine learning". AI was taken to new heights in 2017, when Google's AlphaGo, and subsequently AlphaGo Zero, beat the world's best Go player, Hanjin Lee. Using reinforcement learning, AlphaGo Zero learnt how to play by playing against itself without having been provided any instruction on how to play. Not only did it teach itself Go strategies humans had developed over hundreds, and possibly thousands of years, it developed strategies that no human had ever conceived of previously.

Meanwhile, recurrent neural networks (RNN), and variations like long short-term memory (LSTM), improved machine translation significantly, while generative adversarial networks (GANs) succeeded in restoring colour photographs from old black and white ones, creating cartoons and oil paintings from photographs and even making fake videos and photographs. In a matter of years, deep learning has demonstrated, at least under certain conditions, that it can learn better than humans (without being taught) and be capable of mimicking humans themselves.

Business Applications in Finance

Today, AI and deep learning have broad ranging applications in deposits and lending, insurance, payments to investment management and capital markets. Deep learning methods are now better than probability-based methods in fraud detection. Like image recognition, fraud detection is a classification problem. Instead of creating static rules which struggle with keeping up and are not sufficiently discerning at times, deep learning solves the classification problem by letting the machine learn by itself. Similar technologies are used in assessing the right premiums for insurance markets and making predictions about stock market prices based on a large number of variables, which can then be used for automated trading.

Just like how AlphaGo Zero taught itself strategies of Go that humans haven't discovered, deep learning is now used in finance to make connections between large numbers of seemingly unconnected events and variables to make predictions for fraud detection, insurance pricing and trading stock. With strides in natural language processing (NLP) achieved by deep learning, chatbots are also used in banking and finance to do preliminary sales and improve customer service, replacing human customer service agents.

Time for a Reality Check

Despite having made significant breakthroughs, deep learning nonetheless has limitations. These limitations can present themselves in the form of implementation challenges, unintended consequences and ethical issues. In order to implement deep learning technologies well, large quantities of labelled and clean data are often required. Picking the right neural network architecture and the number of layers is largely an art today and performance and robustness varies with architecture. To obtain large volumes of clean labelled data often requires significant effort on the part of firms in consolidating, fusing and cleaning large volumes of source data.

Data needs to be unbiased, or otherwise the machine will learn the bias that is inherently embedded in the data. It is a known fact that many facial recognition algorithms work well with certain races but much less reliably in other races and gender. It is also known that language models today are sexist or discriminatory because of biases engrained in the training data. When such biases exist in finance, it means that certain races or gender may be subject to lower approval rates for loans, or higher interest for mortgages or higher premiums for insurance.

Furthermore, because deep learning is essentially still a "black box", it can fail catastrophically in unexpected ways. Studies have shown how when noise imperceptible to the eye is added to images, deep learning can recognize a panda as a cat with high confidence. It has also been demonstrated that deep learning algorithms used in autonomous cars to recognize road signs can be easily tricked.

As deep learning learns patterns and correlations without understanding causality, its classification result may be based on the wrong features, or features that are only temporal, or even features that coincide but actually do not mean anything. When deep learning is applied to finance, it can mean that loans could be rejected unfairly for a reason that is hard to decipher and explain to customers. Meanwhile, it is also plausible that a smart attacker could fool a deep learning model used to detect fraudulent activity.

Safeguards and Systemic Risk

When AI is used in isolation, the impact of major failures could be large but contained. However, as AI is being used more and more in connected systems such as in the stock market for automated trading, unexpected catastrophic failures could lead to the widespread failure of entire systems. We don't need to go very far back in history to recall how credit default swaps caused the financial crisis of 2008 and the valuation of Russia's ruble led to the 1998 crash of Long Term Capital Management (LTCM) – a $126 billion hedge fund – that subsequently required a bailout from the US Fed. Will the use of more AI in financial markets lead to similar catastrophic failures in the future?

Finally, there are ethical issues associated with the use of AI in finance, particularly issues linked to privacy and the use of personal data. For example, do insurance companies have the right to use data related to places customers go to frequently, or their DNA profile, to optimize the pricing of insurance premiums? Other issues are linked to questions of fairness. Today, insurance premiums and mortgage rates may already be biased for people of certain ethnic origins; however, with the use of deep learning to discover connections between multiple sources of data, we may end up faced with quotes and premiums that depend on factors that we would typically consider unfair and unjust from an ethical perspective.

The question is, will AI cause our moral compass to shift course?

AI is the new electricity, and with great opportunity comes great responsibility. AI is not perfect and can be harmful if used improperly. What it certain is that AI will expose us to immensely challenging questions related to ethics and accountability, and we will need to leverage the very best of our humanity if we are to find the answers we need.

What Is AI and How to Make It Work for You

By Terence Tse
Co-Founder and Executive Director, Nexus FrontierTech

Mark Esposito
Co-Founder and Chief Learning Officer, Nexus FrontierTech

and Danny Goh
CEO, Nexus FrontierTech

Let us start with a fact: there is really no intelligence in "artificial intelligence" (AI). If anything, the term has been so overused recently that the hype is reminiscent of the dot-com boom in the late 1990s. The problem back then – as now – was that many companies and opportunists were making exaggerated claims about what technology can really do; so much so, that a recent study found that a staggering 45% of companies in Europe claiming to do AI actually operate businesses that have nothing to do with AI.[1]

Sure, machines can solve problems. Yet, while they can perform complicated mathematical calculations with a speed that no human can match, they are still unable to do something as simple as visually distinguishing between a dog and a cat, something that a 3-year-old child can do effortlessly. Viewed from this vantage point, AI can at best solve clearly defined problems and help with automating time-consuming, repetitive and labour-intensive tasks, such as reading standard documents to onboard new customers and entering customer details into IT systems. Furthermore, the term "machine learning" is somewhat misleading, as machines do not learn like human beings. They often "learn" by gradually improving their ability and accuracy so that, as more data is fed into them, they guess the right answer with increasing frequency. Through such training, they can come to recognize – but not understand – what they are looking at and are still very far away from comprehending the nuances of context. This is like when we text on our smartphones: often the "right" words will be presented for us to choose from. While "remembering" what we have typed in the past, our smartphones can guess the right words to complete a sentence to a reasonably accurate degree; this doesn't imply that our phones actually understand the meaning of the words or sentences we type.

So, all in all, and for the moment at least, AI resembles much more a "mindless robot" and much less a "thinking machine". This, in turn, means a bit of presence of mind is required when leveraging AI in business activities. The following five action points can help.

1. Be Narrow Minded

AI is currently most effective in dealing with very narrow tasks in well-defined circumstances. It is therefore important to narrow your scope when thinking about what you would like to use AI to achieve in your business. It is also paramount to know the exact business objective you want to achieve. Labour-intensive and time-consuming standardized tasks are particularly ripe for automation using AI.

2. Weigh the Risk

When it comes to AI, humans need to get comfortable with the idea of relinquishing some control. Once you implement AI in your business, it is important for everybody – human and machine – to stay in their respective "lane": there are certain things people will be responsible for and certain things that will be best left to the machines. One of the biggest issues that people have with AI is the idea of letting machines make decisions for them. It can be a scary prospect, but it doesn't have to be all or nothing. If the

[1] Olson Parmy, "Nearly Half of All 'AI Startups' Are Cashing In On Hype", Forbes.com, 4 May 2019: www.forbes.com/sites/parmyolson/2019/03/04/nearly-half-of-all-ai-startups-are-cashing-in-on-hype/#61d8a348d022.

decisions are minor, and the machine can improve its accuracy over time, then the risk is minor, and the best path is in letting the machine continue autonomously. However, if the decisions have major repercussions, then it is probably advisable to have humans involved in the decision-making, with AI assisting by processing data in a way that helps inform those decisions.

3. Get the "Last Mile" Right

Even if 99% of a job is automated, there will always be 1% that needs to be handled by humans. There are three main reasons why it is important to think through this "last mile" carefully and the manner in which it should be integrated into workflows and procedures. Firstly, it remains important to have a human checking the work of machines, particularly those that carry potentially large financial risk. The second reason is that while certain tasks can be automated, there are still a lot of tasks that are best left to humans, such as customer-facing work that involves selling complicated financial products. Thirdly, there are tasks that machines are simply unable to take over from human beings, particularly the many physical activities still requiring human intervention, such as quality control.

4. Consider That Less Data May Mean More

Contrary to what many people believe, the idea of "the more data the better" is often a misconception. Not all goals need to be achieved with 100% accuracy. The important thing to understand is the minimum level of accuracy needed to do a job. If this baseline level is low, then less data would be needed to train the AI models. While there are times when 100% accuracy is not needed to solve every problem, at other times problems can be so complex that not even a machine can solve them with perfect accuracy. In this case, no matter how much data is available, it will not help reach the objective. By contrast, where the task is easily definable and straightforward, it is possible to achieve near 100% accuracy even with only a small training set. Furthermore, machine models decay over time because data sets evolve and become outdated. If a firm has a massive store of data on selling mortgage products, for example, the same huge set of data will not be of much help in making an AI model to improve the selling of insurance products.

5. Do Your Homework

If we take as a given that there is only so much AI can actually do, then that means that firms must take on the burden of effort involved in laying the groundwork for putting AI to work. Executives often do not know what they really want or only have an abstract idea of a goal they would like to set for their business. They may know, for example, that they want to reduce costs, but they do not know how to go about doing so. It is important to know that AI is not built to serve abstract purposes. To get results, firms need to have a very clear idea about what it is they want to achieve. Another must-do piece of homework is to map out current workflows and processes. This is because technology must be supported by the robust workflows and processes to maximize its potential. In turn, the workflows and processes should be backed by broad-based staff buy-in, both managerial and IT. While this may sound like stating the obvious, it is often surprising to see people's enthusiasm in taking on AI wane as soon as they are asked to plot out the existing workflows and processes they seek to improve.

It is easy to be overwhelmed by the sheer possibilities offered by AI. Many companies make the mistake of thinking too big when the scope of impact of AI is, in fact, quite small. They overgeneralize and exaggerate the impact AI could have on their company. The unassailable truth is that AI is most effective in narrow, well-defined and specific circumstances. When approaching the question of implementing AI in your company, it is important to stay grounded in the overarching goals and missions of your business. AI cannot define or replace your business strategy. "AI for AI's sake" is neither useful nor cost efficient; however, employing AI strategically to help advance your business can be a boon for everyone.

Getting to Day Zero: Let's Get the Foundation Right

By Matt Allan
Founder, Fintech Sandpit

Artificial intelligence (AI) is new, exciting…and difficult. McKinsey & Co estimates the technology will generate $13 trillion of revenue over the next decade, affording global GDP over 1.2%.[1] New use cases consistently promise not only efficiency improvements but also deeper experiences for customers. However, the road to AI adoption is windy, unmarked and filled with potholes of resistance. Herein lies the root of the problem. Banks have traditionally placed themselves at the centre of their own universe, while the customer came second. The customer only had access to the bank during opening hours, and always had to play by the bank's rules. This is incompatible with a successful deployment of AI, which requires an obsession with customers, their data and its quality.[2] Many banks are missing fundamental aspects of reliability, scalability and security within their existing architectures, and yet are committing to build AI systems that promise to be reliable for customers, adaptable for the future and secure for data. We must grow legs before we can crawl, walk or run, and banks must create a firm digital foundation before they rush to deploy AI. This chapter teases out some of the challenges that firms must overcome and the opportunities available to maximize the value of artificial intelligence.

Challenge 1: A House Built on Sand

As customers began to demand new forms of interaction via internet and anywhere/anytime mobile banking, the requirements placed on legacy core banking systems grew exponentially. Instead of renewing these systems, most banks layered additional products on top of the base system to satisfy new business demands, creating additional layers of operational complexity, cost and risks. Core technologies were expanded to do things they were never designed to do. From a cost perspective, this means most banks today spend between[3] 80% and 90% of their IT budget simply to keep the lights on. Some banks still use core banking software purchased 30 or more years ago. Forcing these systems to support real-time mobile banking or open banking application programming interfaces (APIs) creates a massively complex architecture that is extremely fragile. Advisory firm KPMG[4] suggests that the status quo is slowly changing, and that CIOs are becoming more proactive in solving their data access and operational resilience problem. They know that in order to take advantage of technologies like AI, there is an urgent need to revitalize legacy systems, move workloads to the cloud and open their core for collaboration.[5]

Challenge 2: The Digital Transformation Dilemma

Banks are struggling to adopt AI because they have not traditionally placed customer data at the centre of their operations. Digital transformation is an attempt to rid themselves of the constraints of their legacy technologies and to re-establish the customer as their primary focus. However, undergoing a full technology refresh while continuing to serve millions of customers is like trying to replace the engines on an airplane while 30,000 feet in the air. Banks are stuck in a classic catch-22 dilemma: their ongoing commitment to serve their customers is preventing

[1] www.mckinsey.com/featured-insights/artificial-intelligence/notes-from-the-ai-frontier-modeling-the-impact-of-ai-on-the-world-economy.

[2] www.forbes.com/sites/willemsundbladeurope/2018/10/18/data-is-the-foundation-for-artificial-intelligence-and-machine-learning/#13a77be751b4.

[3] www.bobsguide.com/guide/news/2019/Jun/5/banks-marooned-by-mainstream-technology-development/.

[4] https://assets.kpmg/content/dam/kpmg/nl/pdf/2018/sector/banken/banking-systems-survey-20172018.pdf.

[5] www.fintechfutures.com/2019/06/core-modernisation-is-essential-for-truly-digital-banking/.

them from succeeding in the timely deployment of emerging technologies (such as AI), that would ultimately improve how effectively they can serve their customers. Above all else, customers value service availability and want unfettered access to their money at every second of every day. To complicate matters further, banks must continue to support the needs of an increasingly diverse customer base. Challenger banks have started their businesses with a greenfield approach and are unencumbered by the maintenance burden of old products (like cheques) or legacy account structures. Unfortunately for themselves, incumbent banks do not have that luxury.

Banks operate in a web of social friction that they must skilfully navigate during their deployment of emerging technologies like AI. The best example of this is in the debate of whether to close brick-and-mortar branches. Despite declining utilization and significant cost, closing branches in rural towns often escalates to a social or political issue.[6] Despite the resistance, banks must continue to overcome the challenges that prevent their digitalization. The applications of artificial intelligence discussed in later chapters will only be realized if banks can successfully navigate this transition successfully.

It's time to take advantage. Although banks are playing catch-up when it comes to laying a firm foundation for AI, there are several opportunities banks can take advantage of today in order to prepare for tomorrow.

Opportunity 1: Share Your Data with the World

Banks with an open attitude to data sharing will realize much more value from AI than those who seek to lock their data away. Banks who have adopted an open data or platform strategy like Starling, a UK challenger bank, are generating much more revenue from their data than those who remain closed. Starling's developer APIs go well beyond that mandated by open banking and PSD2, which enable FinTech companies to solve problems for their users and integrate directly with their platform. Accenture[7] found that 71% of banking practitioners believe that organisations that embrace open banking will reduce their time to market, streamline their operational costs, and offer better experiences for their customers. Banks who prioritize their data openness will be in a much better position to consistently leverage AI as opportunities arise.

Opportunity 2: The Alternative Data Revolution

Never before have firms had access to so much contextual and supplementary data about their customers as they have today. Unstructured data contained in news articles, broker research and/or written documents is becoming much easier to ingest in automated systems due to advances in convolutional neural networks. Firms that can synthesize and mobilize the information contained in health, geographical, transaction, credit and social media data sets will be at a significant competitive advantage. To benefit from data availability, banks must pay close attention to improving data quality. Refinitiv,[8] a banking consultancy, found that 43% of banking executives see data quality as the biggest hindrance to benefiting from AI. When it comes to machine learning, the adage "garbage in, garbage out" has never been more pertinent. As future chapters will explore, alternative data alongside AI will be the catalyst to streamline back-office processes for legal and compliance purposes. Banks must keep

---

[6] www.theguardian.com/business/2018/may/01/rbs-to-close-162-branches-with-loss-of-800-jobs.

[7] www.accenture.com/_acnmedia/PDF-71/Accenture-Brave-New-World-Open-Banking.pdf#zoom=50.

[8] www.refinitiv.com/en/resources/special-report/refinitiv-2019-artificial-intelligence-machine-learning-global-study.

asking how they can become more efficient, and then use the data available to execute.

A Bright Future

> *It is not the strongest of the species that survives, or the most intelligent, but the one most adaptable to change.*
>
> *Charles Darwin*

AI is an incredible set of technologies, yet most banks are still unable to fully realize its potential. Most are trying desperately to move faster, yet the complexity and cost of "keeping the lights on" continue to hold them back. In nature, as in business, those most responsive to change will survive. Financial institutions that are proactive in taking advantage of alternative data and understanding their own data will be better positioned to capitalize on the new and exciting opportunities presented to them.

At Fintech Sandpit, we are helping financial institutions securely work with fintechs to realise the potential of their data. Banks use our digital sandbox to do proof-of-concepts in order to find the best partner to work with. Get in touch to instantly test any fintech on our marketplace.

Navigating a Sea of Information, News and Opinion with Augmented Human Intelligence

By Andreas Pusch
Founder and CEO, YUKKA Lab AG

We are drowning in an endless sea of new information. Google reported that the number of web pages has grown from 1 trillion in 2008 to a whopping 130 trillion in 2016.[1] Even though a majority of these might be irrelevant to your or your company's interests and operations, it is equally true that well-informed decisions will have a major impact on the success of any project or investment. While the amount of information is growing, the human ability to read and digest information has stayed rather stagnant in absolute terms, and even decreased in relative terms. Research has shown that an average professional reads 5–15 articles per day from 1–3 sources. Not only is this a negligible amount compared to the actual volume of news published each day, but there is also an undeniable information bias driven by personal preferences and valuable time lost reading nonsense. It is thus easy to get lost in this growing sea of information, which leads to wasted time and prevents well-informed decision-making.

But what if we could be one step ahead? What if we could objectively analyse hundreds of thousands of articles from thousands of professional sources within a matter of minutes? This would not only give us the opportunity to understand an industry, a firm or another entity in greater depth while minimizing information bias. It would also enable us to save multiple hours per day that are otherwise "wasted" reading news or researching disclosures from a company. The solution to this exact problem can be found in augmented human intelligence and specifically in two key underlying techniques, which can be used to increase process efficiency in many information driven industries, such as financial services and management consulting.

Making Sense out of Complex Text through Natural Language Processing (NLP)

In order to extract the most value out of incoming data for it to be useful for future purposes, we need to first analyse and make sense out of it. Here, NLP comes into play and performs a linguistic analysis of the text at different levels of increasing complexity. At the lowest level, NLP performs actions to make sentences and words digestible, understandable and comparable. Initially, information is used to obtain a syntactic-semantic representation of the sentences (a representation of their meaning). The ultimate goal is for the system is to gain a deeper understanding of individual words and sentences (similar to a child learning to speak). Furthermore, NLP needs to be able to detect entities that are mentioned implicitly through pronouns or general expressions (such as "the company"). Building upon this, an application-dependent analysis can be performed such as through sentiment and target recognition, which allows the NLP system to detect the polarity of sentences (positive, neutral, negative) and the respective target entity. This entity recognition not only expands to company names, but also to C-level executives, subsidiaries, etc., as discussed in the next section.

In so doing, deep learning and neural networks set the baseline for this type of next-generation machine learning. Neural networks can almost limitlessly expand their learning capability without requiring significant pre-processing, since they are able to learn language structures from sentences and their context alone. The readily available and continuous data flow from numerous news organizations enables the algorithm to make use of a vast resource pool.

[1] https://searchengineland.com/googles-search-indexes-hits-130-trillion-pages-documents-263378.

Ontologies Link Entities and Thus Create Valuable Connections

As previously discussed, it is not enough to merely sort and analyse data according to their explicitly named entity. In this context, ontologies are used to extract an exhaustive set of meaningful and valuable information. Ontologies represent a working model designed to provide classification of the relations between various concepts in a particular knowledge domain. Ontologies are all around us and are not only used by major firms (such as Amazon, to classify products into categories) but are also wired into our understanding of language. For example, if a person mentions "Mount Everest" the first thing that pops into your mind is probably "mountain" or "high". Similarly, for "iPhone" this is likely to be "Apple" or "smartphone". In essence, this reflects the simple fact that our brains have a tendency to categorize raw information, so that we can remember it and draw connections between certain subjects. Writers make use of this: a headline stating "Sales forecast for Model X lowered" is enough for us to assume that this is bad news for Tesla. AI ontologies replicate these connections and use them to understand relations to the same extent as we do.

How Augmented Human Intelligence Will Change the Way We Read News and Inform Ourselves

NLP and ontologies, along with several other related techniques, will have a huge impact on how we process daily information. AI allows businesses to gain both an information and time advantage, as news articles are analysed, categorized and updated in real time. Up until now, getting an overview of the current situation of an entity was a labour-intensive task. Simultaneously, feeling like you were always up to date with the latest trends was near impossible due to the rapid inflow of fresh information. Completing these tasks with the help of an augmented human intelligence offers the benefit of staying on top of the news while simultaneously freeing up time and making better informed business decisions.

While previously "getting an overview" meant reading the first 2–3 articles in the newspaper, in the future it means looking at insightful visual analytics such as Tag Clouds, trend signals or data networks. Important information can be spotted within seconds, while still offering the capability to delve deeper into topics of your interest. Information bias is minimized, as keywords and sentiments are curated and computed from thousands of trusted, global sources and insights can be explained and shared more easily. All of this is possible within minutes, since as humans, we tend to remember and recall information better when it is presented visually rather than through plain black-white walls of text.

While augmented human intelligence can have an impact in many verticals, the most profound impact will be in research-intensive sectors. In these verticals, much time is spent trying to assess companies' past operations and spotting trends going forward. If this time can be saved and thus reallocated from less repetitive work to more high-value, unstructured business processes, there will be a measurable increase in productivity for the individual user and for the company.

Augmented human intelligence thus acts as a technology compass, helping firms reach their goals in the most efficient manner, free from any unnecessary information distractions along the path.

The Seven Deadly Sins of AI

By Luis Rodríguez
Chief Product and Innovation Officer, Strands

Quoting Andrew Ng (Co-founder of Coursera and Adjunct Professor of Computer Science at Stanford University), "Artificial intelligence is the new electricity". And just like electricity, AI has the power to transform every industry and it is already transforming financial services. However, the use of this new "electricity" does not come free from the risk of electrocution and other implementation difficulties. Just like any other technology, AI can be both beneficial and harmful. Whether you are already using AI or just thinking about it, you need to be aware of the potential pitfalls and, most importantly, plan a course to avert them by setting your organization on the right path towards a sound and ethical use of AI. Let us look at "the seven deadly sins of AI" that can stop us from reaching AI utopia, and how to best avoid them.

Data

There is no AI without data, and yet data availability is not as clear-cut a topic as it may seem. Organizations tend to have systems that aren't designed to easily share data, or which are siloed, making it difficult to aggregate information across multiple sources. While big data technology is rapidly evolving to ease this pain, firms who are contending with data aggregation are already playing catch-up in the AI stakes. Data availability should always be front of mind when acquiring or designing IT systems, regardless of their genre. Secondly, chances are that you are not gathering all the data that you need for certain use cases and it is very important to encourage *UX design teams to think about data. An even better approach is in placing a data analyst directly inside your design teams*. It is easy to capture and store data points that may turn out not to be useful in the future, but it is very difficult to travel back in time to find data points that turn out to be missing at a future date. That said, we need to ask ourselves carefully not only if we can collect such data, but also if we should. The line between provision of value and privacy invasion is very thin. Thirdly, where are the data labels? Most current AI models are trained through supervised learning which means that humans must label and categorize the underlying data; a notoriously tedious and error-prone task.

Finally, even if you have all the labelled data you need, your teams, especially in a highly regulated industry like financial services, might not be able to get their hands on it for reasons linked to privacy. Anonymization of data is a painful and costly process and can destroy important features of your data or fail to properly secure the data set. *Our advice: make sure that you have a robust synthetic data strategy from the get-go!*

Research Failure

Resilience should be an intrinsic part of any organization or project, but even more so in the case of AI projects. AI projects are fundamentally research projects, meaning they do not come with a guarantee of success. Firms may discover that the data they have cannot answer a specific question, or that the performance of the new AI-based system they acquired is not as much of an improvement to current processes as they had hoped. Organizations need to realize that *AI is not a silver bullet*, and it will not compensate for underlying corporate flaws and inefficiencies.

Bias

Can algorithms and machines have bias? The short answer is "yes". The most frequent sources of machine bias come from:

Our data: Data reflects our imperfect world, which is full of bias coming from traditions and practices laced with inequality. AI can aggregate and assess vast quantities of data but contentious societal issues don't disappear merely because machines take over certain recommendations or decisions.

Our teams: Humans play a fundamental role in every aspect of machine-learning and AI, from data assembly and annotation to algorithm development and beyond. They bring their culture and their point of view into the process and therefore it is important to ensure that the team composition reflects different genders, age groups and origins, and is as balanced as possible.

Despite the technical advances in detecting and eliminating bias, the best and perhaps only way to avoid bias is the collaboration of multidisciplinary human teams drawing on the social sciences, law and ethics with as much support as possible from technical tools and statistical definitions of fairness verifying the results of the algorithms. By forcing us to define what it is fair, perhaps AI will push us towards a better position with regards to the removal of bias from our human decision-making processes.

Explainability

Not every decision made by AI needs to be explained but having an opaque model may be unacceptable in certain cases, and explainability becomes even more important as we seek to identify and eliminate intrinsic bias (be it data or algorithmic). Until explainable AI (XAI) can remove the mystery from AI predictions, the best strategy is to make sure that robust governance controls are in place to safeguard decisions around why certain methods are used instead of others, with due consideration given to the trade-off that balances performance with explainability.

Emotion

Human machine interfaces powered by AI will soon be the norm. We need to realize that humans are not binary creatures characterized by zeros and ones and, as such, emotional communication anchored in empathy remains crucial to all our human interactions. That said, we will need to define corporate values in such a way that AI can both comprehend them and behave in accordance with them. *Your "voice of the customer" will be an AI; think about it for a moment…*

Ethics

The crucial point is to realize that AI, despite not being sentient, does have targets fixed for it by humans, such as maximizing advertising revenue or taking passengers to the airport as fast as possible. Once we recognize that AI can have targets, it becomes evident that there must be ethical limitations put on the way those targets can be achieved. Despite all the efforts made at the technical level, human intervention and monitoring are key to ensure ethically proper applications. *AI will only be as ethical as your organization requires and allows it to be.*

Organizational Readiness

Humans are key for the successful use of AI in an organization. Think of it as raising a child: AI needs continuous care and guidance. Experts with deep machine learning knowledge and good business judgement are just like good parents; and the more of those people there are in your organization, the better the results will be. It is important to propagate this understanding throughout your organization in order to remove management resistance and employee fear. Now more than ever, companies need employees with exceptional business acumen allied with a strong ethical and moral compass.

Conclusion

The potential of AI in financial services is enormous, but with great power comes a heavy onus of responsibility. In an industry which is highly regulated, and where huge amounts of sensitive data about people's lives are generated, the improper use of this data can have massively detrimental impacts on both customers and on offending organizations. Following the moral roadmap provided in this chapter will help readers navigate through the reality of implementing AI, avoiding being caught in its deadly sins whilst still realizing the huge transformational potential of these technologies in a financial services context.

A New Internet, Data Banks and Digital World War

By Lubna Yusuf
Founder, La Legal

We are surrounded by warnings of a media dystopia, led by artificial intelligence, which will disrupt the way we perceive the world and ourselves. The boundaries between real and virtual realities are fast diminishing and the sci-fi movie scenarios of our youth no longer seem so far-fetched. With algorithms making decisions for us and data systems constantly monitoring us, where will machine learning and deep tech lead human cognition? Are we destined to lose our learning capabilities, with machines programmed to do all the "thinking"? If future decision-making is based more upon results of data analytics than on human reasoning, a whole new concept of human intelligence is set to evolve. The future that awaits us is the human-AI convergence: a whole new interdependence between ourselves, machines, data and numbers.

The Future of Artificial Intelligence

In recent times, Google pulled out of a Department of Defense contract and called on the US government to formalize rules on the use of AI and Amazon joined Microsoft in calling for regulations on facial recognition. While seemingly significant now, corporate stances of this kind may soon be nothing more than a relic of the past, if privacy becomes a lost concept as the commercialization and trading of data become more commonplace.

In much the same way as blood and sperm banks exist today, it is likely that in the future there will be data banks stocked full with data (such as biomedical data and human behaviour patterns), to fuel sophisticated analytics in a vast array of fields. People will be able to knowingly and freely deposit their human data in these banks for research and deep learning performed by machines. It will also be possible to sell and earn revenue from personal data transactions. However, it will be interesting to observe how the data collected will be segregated and classified according to the race, region, economic and educational background of data sellers and donors, and the uses to which the data will be put.

What privacy laws shall prevail? What will be the quantum of ethics used to demarcate the rules of engagement with these data banks? Such are the questions raised by the use of data and AI in the new internet world.

Reinventing How We Invent

AI lacks all five human senses of sight, smell, touch, hearing and taste. Nonetheless, today AI already decides which advertisements appear in your newsfeed, which song to play next, which direction to take and your next meal. Human intelligence and our sense of compassion separates us from other species. Our sense of smell is the strongest link to our memories. However, our future memories will be strongly manipulated by AI-driven systems being fed with data to increase consumption by consumers. AI may be disrupting the world around us, but some things never change: the underlying commercial objective is always and forever to sell more of everything and anything. The fine line between popular influence versus AI-generated influence will be diminished and our individual decision-making will be largely impacted by the data that will have been fed into the system.

In a world of growing social media influencers and pop "Insta-celebs", the most influential "influencer" will be the analytics-driven AI itself, which will decide for us before we can decide for ourselves. Online surveys interpret our motivations and desires to take us to advertisements for our next holiday, and that sweater we browsed on Amazon keeps flashing on every tab we open, even when we browse from a different device. Worryingly, almost 90% of apps and extensions lack an approved privacy policy, signalling that the people behind the creation of these apps and extensions either don't understand or don't care about the concept of privacy, and there is a lacuna of internationally harmonized regulations and laws to define data privacy norms.

In this context, who decides "how much AI is too much AI" and when is that likely to happen?

AI Neural Network

A team from Columbia University has already developed a system that combines deep learning with a speech synthesizer that translates one's thoughts to words. As our cognitive capabilities are increasingly heavily influenced by data-driven AI, our perception of the world around us will also be impacted. With the huge influx of apps, bots and ever-increasing connections across the world, we are already witnessing a rise in the number of people feeling "disconnected". However, perhaps this phenomenon is not so surprising if we place it in the wider context of deteriorating mental health and depression. Instead of it causing further deterioration on our social fabric, could AI possibly be a step towards the creation of a technology to decode people's thoughts for their own benefit? There is already a huge change in the order of the realities as we know them, with major changes in the interdependency of the virtual world on our real-world happiness and emotional quotient.

We are "happy" if we get liked or loved on social media; we create virtual worlds for ourselves and our well-being is influenced all day every day by strangers, as we share feelings in this virtual space through emoticons and emojis, rather than through actually smiling or speaking in the real world. People are increasingly dependent on such virtual spaces for personal validation, relationships and even sex. This has significantly decreased our faculty for language and facial expression as a means of communication. The human mind has learnt a whole new language of the internet, with symbols replacing words as the primary means of expression, communication and manifested emotion. This is both fascinating and alarming because we are possibly the last generation to experience both the internet and non-internet worlds of communication.

Will future generations come to use their opposable thumbs to only type on mobiles? Will writing and drawing on paper become entirely obsolete?

The Human API and Digital War: World War III

Humans have memories and up until this century, all of mankind's history had been preserved through cave writings, books and audiovisual formats. However, with the advent of the internet we have a new medium of data transfer and storage that makes data destruction exceptionally complex and its multiplication potentially infinite. APIs are currently connecting anything to everything. In the future, this may have irreversible consequences. Wealth and power will be wielded through the ownership of and access to vast quantities of data. In this context, how safe is anyone's data and who bears the risks and responsibilities for its use and protection? Beyond the GDPR, we can expect a further raft of data-related laws to emerge. In the future, data theft may actually be the cause of a major international conflict, with a "data war" being used to destroy economies through the mass manipulation of advanced biometrics, bank details and the sensitive personal data of a nation's population.

To live consciously, think rationally and interact emotionally is what makes us human; and we must ensure that, as humans and in spite of any AI-induced interference, we retain control of our cognition. Anything less, and we may end up being the very last of the Homo sapiens, particularly if we stop learning and evolving, and delegate our agency by default to machines for them to do the learning and thinking for us.

AI: A Cross Country Analysis of China versus the West

By Bonnie Buchanan
Head of Department of Finance and Accounting and Professor of Finance, Surrey Business School, University of Surrey

Artificial intelligence is impacting industries ranging from IT to financial services, healthcare, education, surveillance and regulation. Approximately 5154 AI startups have been established globally during the past five years.[1] A 2019 PwC report[2] estimates that AI could add as much as $15.7 trillion to the global economy by 2030, and claims the greatest gains will be experienced in China and North America. Between 2012 and 2016 the US invested $18.2 billion into AI compared with $2.6 billion in China and $850 million in the UK.[3]

There are two main explanations which account for AI's rapid growth. Firstly, exponential advances in computing power have led to declining processing and data storage costs. Secondly, data availability has increased on a massive scale. AI is now a national priority, but approaches vary. China, the United Kingdom (UK) and the European Union (EU) have adopted a government-led approach to AI. The United States' (US) AI strategy has been dominated (and self-regulated) by big tech companies like Microsoft, Facebook and Amazon. Singapore's AI structure emphasizes a more "human-centric" approach that includes explainability, transparency and fairness to establish public trust in AI. The Chinese strategy is also based on a very different financial market model. Whereas the economies of the US, UK and Singapore are based on an English common law model (which emphasizes strong shareholder and creditor protection), China's market model is best described as being in the primary stage of socialism, which is to say, the state controls access to capital, influences investment decisions and stock market listings and thereby combines state power with capitalist tools. At the local government level, there are financial incentives to encourage AI-related innovations.

In 2017, the Chinese government announced the "Next Generation Artificial Intelligence Development Plan" with the goal of China being the AI world leader by 2030. The Chinese government presented a timeline where it expects companies and research facilities to be at parity with the US by 2020.[4,5] In 2017, the Chinese government also announced plans to set up an "intelligence industry zone" near Tianjin to support the AI industry. Historically, the US has dominated the AI landscape, but this pattern is now shifting. There were 3033 AI startups in the US between 2000 and 2016, accounting for 37.41% of the global total. Since 2016 the proportion has decreased, dropping to under 30% for the first time.

In 2017, China surpassed the US in terms of AI startup funding,[6] accounting for 48% of the global total. The US is also losing its global AI equity deal share, decreasing from 77% to 50% of

---

[1] B. Buchanan and C. Cao (2018) Quo Vadis? Fintech in China Versus the West. Working Paper. Available at: https://swiftinstitute.org/wp-content/uploads/2018/10/SIWP-2017-002-_Fntech_China_West_BuchCao_FINAL.pdf.

[2] Sizing the Prize: What is the real value of AI for your business and how you can capitalize. PwC Report, 2019. Available at: www.pwc.com/gx/en/issues/data-and-analytics/publications/artificial-intelligence-study.html.

[3] "Britain Urged to Take Ethical Advantage in Artificial Intelligence", John Thornhill, *Financial Times*, 16 April 2018. Available at: www.ft.com/content/b21d1fb8-3f3e-11e8-b9f9-de94fa33a81e.

---

[4] www.nytimes.com/2017/07/20/business/china-artificial-intelligence.html.

[5] The exact timeline is 2017–2020: Chinese companies need to keep pace with the world's leading AI technologies and breakthroughs. In 2020–2025, Chinese companies are expected to make AI breakthroughs and achieve global leadership by 2030.

[6] CB Insights (2018) Top AI Trends to Watch in 2018. Available at: www.cbinsights.com/research/report/artificial-intelligence-trends-2018/.

equity deal share over five years.[7] During the same period China accounted for 68.67% of Asian AI startups and corresponding AI funding was 60.22% of the Asian market. Many Chinese cities and provinces dominate other Asian countries. In terms of the number of AI companies, there are 1387 in Beijing, 792 in Guangdong and 154 in Shanghai, compared with 57 in Singapore and 283 in India.[8] Beijing has attracted $1387m in AI funding, followed by Guangdong ($792m) and Shanghai ($154m), the total exceeding that of Japan ($436.81m) and the UK ($1251m).[9] Between 2012 and 2016 the compound growth rate of AI patents was 33.2% per annum. Currently the US and China hold over 50% of all AI patents (35,508 in US and 34,345 in China, respectively) but patents are being filed at a much faster pace in China. The US holds 32% of machine learning patents and 26% of natural language processing patents, followed by China with 23% and 14%, respectively.[10]

Currently China dominates the machine vision patent category (55% of 150,000 patents globally). Machine vision describes object and facial recognition and is useful in public security, healthcare, e-commerce and autonomous driving. China outpaces the US in terms of both deep learning and AI-related patent publications (by a factor of more than five), and the gap is closing for machine learning-related patent publications. Cross-border investment is on the rise but not in an equal manner. There are now more Chinese investments in AI startups in the US, rather than vice versa. What explains the increasing dominance of China in the area of AI? Firstly, many machine learning techniques require vast amounts of data, and China has the scale. China's online population of 730 million people is almost twice the size of the US, with the WeChat platform alone accounting for over a billion users. Secondly, there are two prominent technologies fuelling the drive, namely facial recognition and AI chips.[11] Both the US and China compete heavily in AI chip technology. Chinese corporations such as Baidu, Tencent, iFlytek and JD.com invest heavily in AI, both domestically and abroad.

Chinese and American "big tech" firms also differ in terms of their AI focus. Microsoft, Google and IBM focus on machine learning, speech recognition and speech synthesis, whereas Tencent, Alibaba and Baidu focus on AI searching and facial recognition.[12] Deep neural networks applications need to supplement central processing units (CPU). AI chips draw on graphic processing units (GPU) technology which is then applied to AI, machine learning and deep learning problems.

From a corporate perspective, Alibaba is aiming to have its first AI chips on the market in 2019. Ant Financial already uses facial recognition for payments at Alibaba-owned retail stores. In 2016, Ant Financial, Foxconn and the city of Hangzhou partnered for the "City Brain" project using AI data from social feeds and surveillance cameras. Additionally, 55 cities participate in the "Sharp Eyes" project whose surveillance data could end up in the nation's Social Credit System, a measure to gauge citizens' "trustworthiness". Three big techs, Baidu, Alibaba and Tencent, are also privy to what consumers buy, where they travel and who they chat to online. In fact, Baidu has shifted its business strategy from "mobile first" to "AI first".

[7] Ibid.

[8] B. Buchanan and C. Cao (2018) Quo Vadis? Fintech in China Versus the West. Working Paper. Available at: https://swiftinstitute.org/wp-content/uploads/2018/10/SIWP-2017-002-_Fntech_China_West_BuchCao_FINAL.pdf.

[9] Ibid.

[10] www.chinamoneynetwork.com/2017/09/14/china-may-hold-artificial-intelligence-patents-us-year-end.

[11] "China takes the crown in AI Funding", Louise Lucas, *Financial Times*, 21 February 2018.

[12] www.chinamoneynetwork.com/2017/09/14/china-may-hold-artificial-intelligence-patents-us-year-end.

Internationally, there is progress to adopt a more coherent cross-border AI governance network. In May 2019, 42 countries signed an accord which committed to common AI principles. Even though China did not endorse the principles, it is developing its own framework. The UN, OECD and Council of Europe have all formulated their own AI goals. In April 2019, the European Commission published AI guidelines. Growth in the EU AI market has been dominated by the Nordics, France and Germany, but overall is more fragmented because of heterogeneous resources and regulation.

Today, global political leaders have choices to make. It will be interesting to see which countries continue to adopt an inward-looking, and almost protectionist, nationalistic stance with regards to building AI capability compared to other countries which may be more inclined to leverage the existing institutional framework for international cooperation. Regardless of the stance adopted, the geopolitical landscape is sure to be heavily impacted by national AI strategies, although the future consequences of today's decisions are far from clear.

The AI Advantage: Near-Term Workforce Opportunities and Challenges

By Barbara C. Matthews
Founder and CEO, BCMstrategy, Inc.

Backdrop

Periods of profound technological transformation traditionally trigger at least as much angst as excitement. Recent efforts to make sense of how advanced technology will disrupt and reformulate our societies draw from the nineteenth century by referencing *The Second Machine Age*[1] and the "Fourth Industrial Revolution".[2] This is not just hype. Rapidly accelerating process automation from artificial intelligence (AI) systems will generate economic dislocations even as they improve materially how people think and work.

Policymakers are reacting strategically. At their June 2019 summit, the Group of Twenty (G20) embraced these changes in their Osaka Declaration[3] and issued non-binding AI Principles[4] to guide policy development. G20 leaders thus seek to *accelerate* the rate of AI adoption within economies while committing to "empower people with the skills for AI and support workers for a fair transition".

Companies and policymakers must act now to help people benefit from the enhanced cognition delivered by AI systems.

[1] http://secondmachineage.com/.

[2] www.weforum.org/centre-for-the-fourth-industrial-revolution.

[3] www.g20.org/pdf/documents/FINAL_G20_Osaka_Leaders_Declaration.pdf.

[4] www.oecd.org/about/secretary-general/2019-g20-leaders-summit-digital-osaka-june-2019.htm.

Enhanced Cognition: The Good News

"Enhanced cognition" refers to the improvements in analytical functions from the machine–human interface. The premise is simple: computers perform repetitive tasks (information acquisition, organization and visualization), delivering outputs that provide a more advanced entry point for humans to conduct higher-order analysis.

Early technology delivered enhanced cognition through printouts, followed by digital spreadsheets with automatic calculations and automated data visualizations (charts, graphs, etc.). AI systems extend the frontier by automating basic reasoning and generating predictive analytics.

Two parallel technological advances are now revolutionizing how knowledge workers operate. Firstly, innovations in hardware and processing mechanisms (neural networks, cloud computing), expand the availability and capacity of automated analysis. Secondly, natural language processing (NLP) and smart, connected devices are exponentially expanding the amount of data available for use in AI systems.

For example, NLP makes it possible to convert unstructured verbal data into structured data. This data can be used by AI systems to identify correlations (pattern recognition) across concepts faster and better than humans. This pushes the perimeter of process automation into analytical tasks currently performed by knowledge professionals.

The promise of enhanced cognition is real for those ready to embrace it. Knowledge professionals are today able to perform more interesting and creative analytical functions. The result is a substantial increase in the velocity of insight formation by humans, as well as operational efficiencies due to decreased time spent acquiring information.

Considerable economic gains will accrue particularly to early adopters. Increasingly, AI-as-a-service is delivering advanced insight formation to mid-sized companies seeking advanced insights to help drive internal productivity and efficiency enhancements, as well as superior customer service and even public policy risk analysis.

Macro-Trend Analysis of Workforce Challenges

But reality is not tidy at the margins of this virtual, AI-enhanced world. Rapid job creation within the technology sector expands the skills mismatch, redistributing jobs (and joblessness) in the economy. This places pressure on (i) older professionals and (ii) younger unskilled individuals who are unable – or unwilling – to adapt.

This dynamic has been a fixture of the modern economy for decades, as process automation reached critical mass in advanced economies. Structural shifts hit unskilled labour first. Secretaries and typists, automobile mechanics, and assembly line workers were next. The AI revolution today places comparable pressure on knowledge professionals. Bookkeepers, stock analysts, and economists are currently on the front line of process automation. It is unclear where the disruption will stop.

Cross-border connectivity and globalization will drive dramatic shifts in trading relationships and job distribution, further fuelling concerns regarding economic dislocations. Fear of the unknown often fuels counterproductive, emotional backlash, as the current trade policy landscape illustrates.

Pragmatic Suggestions for a Way Forward

With governments seeking to accelerate the transition to a digital, AI-powered economy, companies and policymakers should focus on policy priorities that empower individuals to keep pace with – and better understand – the opportunities presented by AI technology.

1. Investments in Lifelong Learning

In order to retain talent and innovate internally, companies must expand investments in educational benefits for *all* employees.

The last significant technological shift in the workplace for knowledge workers occurred in the 1990s, when information processing became ubiquitous. Employers at the time financed training to teach employees how to use word processors, spreadsheets and email.

Some executives grumbled about being asked to perform secretarial tasks. But they adapted. Secretaries were asked to perform more interesting work, like database management and executive assistant functions. A similar investment in on-the-job training is needed today.

Rather than feed fears of being replaced by AI systems, companies should train employees on how AI systems function. These employees – who know the data and the business far better than any AI system – will be poised to deliver enhanced value and new insights when working with (rather than against) AI.

Such on-the-job training need not be disruptive or expensive. As the International Finance Corporation (an arm of the World Bank) highlights here,[5] online courses like Udemy are partnering with companies to provide relevant offerings to workers on their own schedule as well as more formal in-person training.

[5]www.ifc.org/wps/wcm/connect/26ea104c-e872-4fc6-9d1f-fe900fadbb4c/Education+Newsletter_issue+2_Final_web_2.pdf?MOD=AJPERES&CVID=muFpk4J.

The key is to empower professionals to experiment with how AI can enhance existing skill sets and job functions. Meaningful training should be interdisciplinary. Subject matter experts should become familiar with coding and neural networks. Professionals with expertise in coding should take higher-level courses to accelerate their ability to operate AI systems.

Low-skilled adults require different – but no less important – training. For example, the European Union in 2018 launched an "Upskilling Pathways"[6] initiative to fund education for low-skilled adults to acquire minimum levels of literacy, numeracy and digital skills. As Germany's apprenticeship system illustrates, multiple avenues for skills enhancement exist beyond the educational system.

Retraining is good for business. Companies that invest today in upskilling their workforce will receive early mover informational advantages and operational efficiencies. Just as importantly, they will increase retention rates from employees eager to explore new horizons within a corporate environment that invests in their skills.

2. Coding as a Second Language (CSL)

Equipping people for success starts in school. Much has been written about the importance of teaching creativity and problem-solving. However, sales and marketing staff, operations management and strategy analysts must be proficient in the language of coding and the structure of AI systems in order to deploy creativity and problem-solving skills effectively.

[6]https://ec.europa.eu/social/main.jsp?catId=1224&langId=en.

From elementary school and up, instruction and experiential learning involving coding languages and computer processes should exist across the curriculum. This would equip the next generation to understand the strengths and limits of AI-powered processes, while providing the foundation for the next round of innovation.

Policymakers remain focused on strategic evolution. For example, in 2018 the United States Congress passed bipartisan legislation (the "Strengthening Career and Technical Education for the 21st Century Act") providing federal funding and other support for state and local government programmes delivering career development and technical education.

Private entities are also taking leadership roles. Organizations like Girls Who Code as well as innovative partnerships (see this partnership[7] between the Panasonic Foundation and the Hispanic Heritage Foundation in the United States) are delivering technology skills training to underserved communities.

Conclusion

AI solutions will revolutionize business analytics in the same way that word processors and spreadsheets revolutionized business processes. The responsibility for meeting the challenges and opportunities presented by this technological shift is shared by individuals, companies and governments alike. How we choose to shoulder this responsibility will determine the rewards we reap.

[7]https://thejournal.com/articles/2019/04/22/coding-as-a-second-language.aspx.

The Art of Involving Boards in Embracing AI

By Dr Sabine Dembkowski
Managing Partner, Better Boards Ltd

Successful AI transformations start with visionary leaders who understand how to deploy technology as part of a broader strategy to future-proof their organizations. It is clear that organizations need to be prepared or face inevitable decline. Boards are being challenged to play their part in providing oversight and governance of the efforts involved in defining and delivering an AI strategy, along with the accompanying organizational transformation. Analysts and experts are clear: boards "must", "should" and "have to" embrace AI.

But are they doing so?

The Art and Science of Board Dynamics

The reality is that AI seldom makes it onto the agenda of traditional, legacy organizations. The call to embrace AI is far from being the only demand placed on boards these days. They are also grappling with the ever-increasing complexities of governance, environmental and social issues, and the integration of a diverse set of stakeholders, geopolitical risks and challenges. The agendas of boards are not merely full; they're overflowing.

Being a board member is so much more than a job and is often part of the overall identity of the individuals who serve on boards. The preservation of this identity takes centre-stage and will be defended under any circumstances, and at any cost. The smallest perceived threat to that identity can trigger the fight-or-flight response.

As people, we are hard-wired to preserve the concept we have of ourselves by defending the boundary and justifying and reinforcing what's inside the boundary of the concept-of-self. This is true both at the individual and group level; the principle is the same. And while it might not always be obvious to those with a digital mindset, AI is a big threat for those that sit on the boards of legacy organizations.

Few members of boards of legacy organizations have deep insights and understanding of state-of-the-art AI solutions for all the working processes within their organizations, and fewer still will be able to claim that they have provided oversight and governance of the development and implementation of a successful AI strategy. AI challenges all known conventions; nothing less than a complete process and reorganization around AI will do.

The Challenge of AI for Boards

Embracing AI means that board members need to be willing to challenge everything they themselves have contributed to within their industry. Embracing AI means that members of boards will need to ask, learn and rely on the experience and expertise of a generation that is beyond the confinements of their professional networks.

The fear of falling into the same traps as their peers who burned their fingers with ad hoc, opportunistic and ill-conceived AI initiatives has to be weighed against the need to expose themselves to the unknown, and to the risk of failure and public criticism for having approved budgets for something they cannot fully grasp. In short, it's a tall order.

The fight-or-flight response manifests itself in a vast array of behaviours, not all of which are logical. As a result, any demands couched in terms of "must", "should" and "have to" are unlikely to convince members of legacy boards that the time to embrace AI is right now.

An action plan for encouraging boards to embrace AI

What can be done to encourage boards of traditional, legacy organizations to embrace AI? Legacy boards who have successfully embraced the AI call to action tend to focus on a 5-Point Action Plan.

Work with Strength-Based Management Techniques

Essentially, this involves focusing on, and continuously developing, the innate strengths of board members and by so doing, minimizing the negative effects of any perceived weaknesses. Strength-based management techniques are at the heart of leadership development programmes around the globe, yet, curiously, remain underleveraged in the boardroom. Once individual board members understand which strength they can bring to the table, specific board roles and responsibilities can be shaped, and the result is an increased openness and willingness to discuss specific knowledge gaps on the board.

Design and Provide Special Educational Programmes for Board Members

Directors need to understand how AI solutions can add value at all levels of the organization. Ideally, the programmes should be practical and led by practitioners who provide insights into what has worked in different contexts.

Chairmen and company secretaries are often reticent about asking their non-executive directors for additional time to attend special educational programmes, yet non-executive directors almost unanimously welcome such initiatives and happily make time for them.

Dare to Change the Composition of the Board

When talking about the composition of the board, people immediately think about women on boards, but it is so much more than a gender issue and goes to the heart of ensuring that boards are really diverse in their thinking – embracing different thinking processes, as well as digital and technical expertise. Once core members have understood the strength and resources diversity and inclusion bring to the table, there is frequently an increased willingness and openness to really change the composition of the board.

Establish an AI Council

An AI Council can provide the board with the know-how and expertise it needs to effect organizational transformation. The AI Council is an advisory body[1] with a board-level mandate to ensure that company strategy actively anticipates, and keeps pace with, AI advances. The AI Council also drives AI acumen and foresight in the organization, drives efforts to establish clear and adequate governance of AI development and application, safeguards against any risks and ensures that AI practices are ethically and fiscally responsible. The overarching goal is to ensure that shareholders, customers, employees and society overall benefit as fully as possible from the company's strategy to embrace the benefits of AI. The AI Council is also a good incubation facility for future board members.

---

[1] www.asaecenter.org/resources/articles/an_plus/2015/december/the-basics-of-board-committee-structure.

Create a Communication Campaign

When a board starts to embrace AI, it will have a ripple effect throughout the organization. Any steps a board takes – and the perceived benefits of such undertakings – are worth being integrated into the organization's overall communication campaign.

Embracing AI is a tall order for members of boards of legacy organizations. AI is perceived as a threat that can trigger a fight-or-flight reaction in many board members. Simplistic arguments that place demands on boards in the form of "must", "need to" and "should" imperatives with regards to embracing AI unfortunately are not always enough to elicit the desired response and behaviour.

The 5-Point Action Plan outlined in this chapter is a demonstrated safe route for setting boards of legacy organizations on the right course for successfully embracing AI.

Internationally, there is progress to adopt a more coherent cross-border AI governance network. In May 2019, 42 countries signed an accord which committed to common AI principles. Even though China did not endorse the principles, it is developing its own framework. The UN, OECD and Council of Europe have all formulated their own AI goals. In April 2019, the European Commission published AI guidelines. Growth in the EU AI market has been dominated by the Nordics, France and Germany but overall is more fragmented because of heterogeneous resources and regulation.

Today, global political leaders have choices to make. It will be interesting to see which countries continue to adopt an inward-looking, and almost protectionist, nationalistic stance with regards to building AI capability compared to other countries which may be more inclined to leverage the existing institutional framework for international cooperation. Regardless of the stance adopted, the geopolitical landscape is sure to be heavily impacted by national AI strategies, although the future consequences of today's decisions are far from clear.

Deposits and Lending

2

Today over 2.5 billion people are still unbanked, meaning that 38.5% of the global population is fully deprived of banking services, and only 42% of the banked population is labelled as eligible for lending

AI is being used across the spectrum of deposits and lending to solve data asymmetry problems, improve speed and reduce costs in underwriting, improve the robustness of decision-making and reduce risk

The utilization of alternative data is playing an increasingly key role in deposits and lending

AI will be able to help with personalizing savings products as well as with loan approvals and with reducing defaults

At this stage, we can reasonably consider the application of AI in deposits and lending as complementary to existing tools and not yet as a replacement

Banking, and the core activities of deposit-taking and lending, have been around for many hundreds of years, offering individuals and businesses the opportunity to manage their financial affairs more safely and efficiently, and expand their horizons.

However, it is only quite recently that the banking landscape has begun to evolve significantly. Technology is empowering new entrants to the market and stiffening the competition facing incumbents. Today, legacy institutions are under immense pressure to overhaul their product and service offerings in order to remain relevant in the face of changing customer expectations.

Part 2 takes readers on a sweeping *tour de force*, looking at the role of technology in banking from today through to tomorrow's world. In examining the value chain of deposits and lending, we explore the societally important underbelly of these critical services and the way they contribute to the well-being of citizens and the functioning of our economies.

We take a look at how the availability of large quantities of high-quality alternative data is enriching credit-scoring models and facilitating the extension of responsible credit to borrowers in underserved market segments, who otherwise would find themselves excluded from traditional bank lending because of being judged "too risky".

We also see how AI is being used by banks and FinTechs to personalize new offerings for increasingly demanding customers. We discuss the pervasive role that chatbots are playing, particularly in the retail segment, and how they are creating value for customers through innovative approaches to creating customer intimacy, through financial coaching for example.

Lastly, we revisit the theme of financial inclusion and gain an understanding of the vibrant dynamic in the African financial sector, where AI and related technologies are improving access to secure financial services by offering people in local markets pragmatic and useful solutions that are adapted to their situation.

AI in Lending

By Joshua Xiang
CTO and SVP, CreditEase

Overview

The financial services industry is one of a few highly computerized industries. IT systems have automated all aspects of financial services processes and have thereby accumulated huge amounts of data. To many, artificial intelligence is yet another IT tool to help increase efficiencies and reduce costs. But to some industry pundits, AI is more than just another technical tool. It represents a paradigm shift – a new way of solving problems with human-like intelligence.

In many cases, such as customer engagement or telemarketing, AI's lack of emotion is probably a disadvantage. For example, lack of empathy and sympathy makes a customer service chatbot unfriendly and unpopular. But in many other cases, lack of emotion turns out to be an advantage. For example, if AI is underwriting a loan or making an investment decision, it will do so purely based on hard data, without any bias towards a particular loan applicant.

As an important vertical in financial services, lending is a massive business which directly and indirectly touches almost everyone's life and all parts of the economy. As of May 2019, consumer debt in the United States was just over $4 trillion. Credit card debt accounts for roughly $1 trillion, student loans around $1.6 trillion, and car loans around $1.1 trillion. In addition, total value of mortgage debt is over $15.5 trillion. Lending is clearly big business.

With tens of millions of Americans holding loans worth trillions of dollars, any technology that can make even a small improvement in a company's returns on the loans they hold, or that can improve their share of the market, would be worth a significant amount of money. That is why both established banks and FinTech companies are constantly looking for ways to innovate – and AI might allow for just that.

Lending is essentially a big data problem, and therefore is naturally suited to machine learning. Part of the value of a loan is tied to the creditworthiness of the individual or business that took out the loan. The more data you collect about an individual borrower and how similar individuals have paid back debts in the past, the better you can assess their creditworthiness.

Use Cases

AI has been used in many lending scenarios. Here are some common use cases.

User Identification

In the old days, when people applied for loans, they went to banks or met with loan agents. Their identities and documents were easily verified and processed on the spot. In recent years, applicants with good credit records and completed documents can also apply for loans and sign loan documents electronically, without having to meet lenders in person.

But for borrowers who have less optimal credit scores and insufficient supporting documents, their chances of getting loans are reduced, and that's without even talking about getting loans online. Today, AI technology is able to help. Those with urgent needs for relatively small loans can provide their personal ID and take live pictures and videos to identify themselves. AI models and facial recognition technology can instantly make creditworthiness decisions and verify user identities during the online loan application process.

Credit Decisions

The value of a secured loan is tied to assessments of the value of the collaterals – e.g. car, home, business, art collections – the likely level of future inflation, and predictions about overall economic growth. AI theoretically can merge and analyse all of these data points from various sources to make a holistic decision. For these reasons, "creditworthiness" is highlighted as one of the most common AI applications.

Thanks to companies like FICO, which create the well-known credit ratings used to determine creditworthiness, lenders have a common standard to screen loan applications. FICO uses machine learning both in developing FICO scores, which most banks use to make credit decisions, and in determining the specific risk assessment for individual customers. MIT researchers found that machine learning could be used to reduce a bank's losses on delinquent borrowers by up to 25%.

An AI-powered credit decision process is shown in the following diagram.

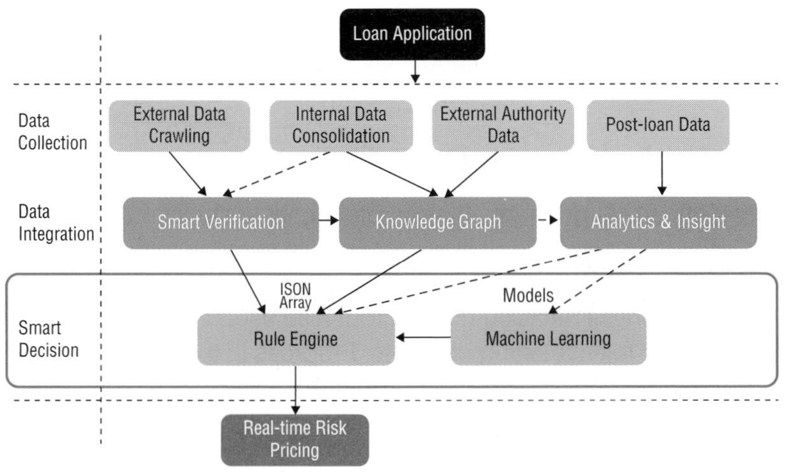

Figure 1: AI-powered real-time credit decision

Fraud Prevention

How can a financial institution determine if a transaction is fraudulent? In most cases, the daily transaction volume is way too high for humans to manually scrutinize each transaction. Instead, AI creates systems that learn what types of transactions are fraudulent. Some companies are using neural networks to predict suspicious and fraudulent transactions. Factors that may affect the neural network's effectiveness include recent frequency of transactions, transaction size, transaction location, transaction type and the kinds of merchants involved.

Now let's look at several examples of how AI is being used to help lending in China.

Consumer Lending: Proprietary Risk Management Based on Big Data

Compared with America, China's credit system is relatively new. PBOC (People's Bank of China) credit scores are not as accessible and comprehensive as credit scores offered by FICO and other US credit bureau agencies.

Whenever you apply for a loan or credit card, the financial institution, especially online lenders, must quickly determine whether to accept your application on specific terms, e.g. interest rate, credit line amount, etc. If someone doesn't have good PBOC credit scores, will lenders reject his or her loan application? Banks may do just that. But other inclusive finance firms may still approve the loan, if they have the following risk management system based on big data.

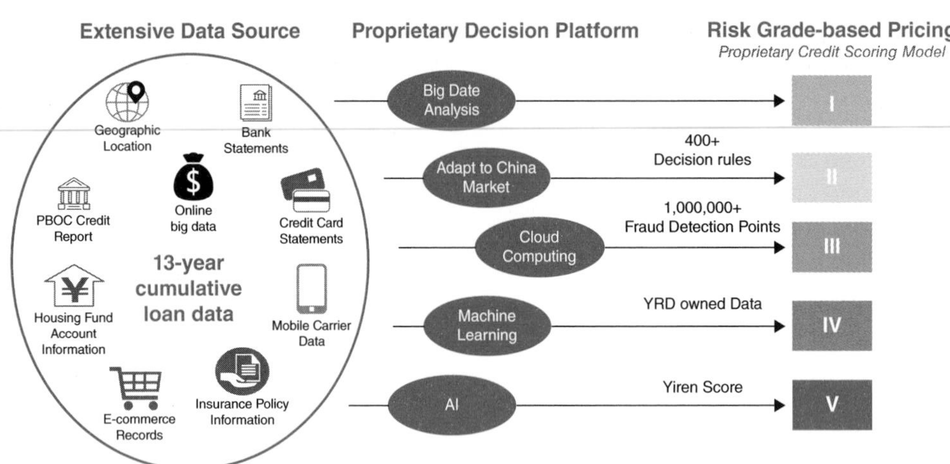

Figure 2: **Consumer lending: risk management based on big data (courtesy of CreditEase)**

Credit Decision Powered by Knowledge Graph

Knowledge graphs can be used in lending to screen qualified loan applicants and identify fraud. Loan applicants' personal ID, telephone number, device ID and home and work addresses are extracted and mined from various data sources, and fed into a loan applicant knowledge graph. The knowledge graph system processes and correlates a large number of unstructured data, forming a structured graph database that is ready for real-time query, mining and decision-making for creditworthiness and fraud detection purposes. The nodes (entities) and their attributes help make underwriting decisions. The links disclose valuable insights that assist with fraud detection.

SME Lending: Unsecured Loans Backed by AI and Machine Learning

Like their counterparts in the rest of the world, small and medium-sized enterprises (SMEs) are financially underserved in China. By working with cashier system and payment providers (e.g. 2DFire, PayPal) and e-commerce platforms (e.g. Amazon) via API (application programming interface), financial firms can get and analyse business data of SMEs (e.g. restaurants and online merchants) and provide unsecured loans to them accordingly. The creditworthiness decision is based on such data as business transactions, profitability, reputation, pricing, operational stability and cost, leverage, debt situation, growth, liquidity, shareholder background, etc.

Chatbots Used in Debt Collection

Chatbots are AI programs that simulate conversations with people via voice or messaging. It is widely seen in many human–computer interaction scenarios. Knowledge graphs are not only used in creditworthiness decision-making, but also used in customer service and telemarketing chatbots. Progress in the knowledge graph-based question answering (KGQA) area is making chatbots smarter and even more effective.

Let's take a look at another chatbot use case: debt collection. Debt collection chatbots are more effective than human collectors in simple collection scenarios, such as informational and reminder phone calls. They can simultaneously "speak" to as many customers as desired, always politely and professionally, without becoming emotional in tense situations. Here is how a debt collection bot works:

TTS: Text to Speech
NLP: Natural Language Processing
ASR: Automatic Speech Recognition

1 Upload call list
Upload call list to bot platform

2 Grouping
Group users by risk levels. Apply different call models

3 Policy setting
Apply different collection paths, strategies, tactics, and wordings based on different call groups

4 Making calls
Make calls based on call policies

5 Dialogue
Make conversations using ASR, TTS, NLP technologies, collecting feedbacks

6 Data feedback
Generate reports/feedbacks after calls

Figure 3: **Debt collection chatbot (courtesy of CreditEase)**

Suggestions to Lenders

According to James Manyika, chairman and director of the McKinsey Global Institute (MGI) (speech at AI Frontier Conference, 11/3/2017), 30% of companies are uncertain about AI's importance in business; 41% of companies are uncertain about AI's benefit; 28% of companies are unable to put together an AI team; and only 1% of companies understand AI and are actively executing an AI strategy. Tech, telecom and financial companies are early adopters and pioneers of AI. Things have been improving since then. But lenders, like many financial firms, still face a steep learning curve to fully understand and benefit from AI.

For those financial firms that are embarking on an AI journey, some suggestions are worth considering.

Have a clear understanding of AI's potential and limitations. Educate the management team and set the right expectations.

In layman's term, AI is a computer system that is able to perform tasks that normally require human intelligence, such as visual perception, speech recognition, language translation, automobile driving and many other decision-making activities.

The key decision in the lending business is to decide on creditworthiness of a loan applicant and the loan terms. Like any new technology, or revived technology as in the case of AI, it usually generates a lot of hype at the beginning and takes quite a lot of time to mature. Business leaders in the financial services industry need to understand AI's potential, limitations and applicability within their enterprises.

Unlike typical IT systems introduced in the past that automate business processes, AI assists (or even replaces) people to do things in an automated manner. While its potential and impact will be significant, it needs to be trained iteratively to reach a satisfactory level.

Clearly understanding and communicating AI's power, uniqueness and limitation to key stakeholders is the No. 1 task for all of us. We should wholeheartedly embrace AI, but be realistic and patient, and set the right expectations to key stakeholders.

Engage with business groups. Understand their pain points. Evaluate and introduce AI technologies that deliver immediate business values.

Technologies are meant to solve business problems. AI is no exception. Unlike other IT technologies that essentially hard-code business logic in computer systems or customize a standard solution in various deployment scenarios, an AI system is more self-learning and evolving.

A simple configuration, customization or implementation of a shrink-wrapped software system is not enough. A process called "feature engineering" is needed. It involves selecting the right set of features based on existing data, training the model and then using the model to predict the future. This is a lengthy process that takes in a huge amount of real business data and gradually learns to generate better results.

This requires frequent and deep engagement with business groups that provide real training data, such as bad loans and frauds. By engaging with business groups, lending institutions can identify tedious data-intensive and error-prone tasks such as customer services, loan underwriting and auditing and debt collection, and use AI to improve efficiency and customer satisfaction. It is always wise to focus on solving immediate business problems by engaging with business groups early.

Bring in industry leaders and train internal teams to become AI savvy. Hire and train AI product managers who are the key to success of AI implementation.

Financial institutions, especially those without strong in-house technology expertise, desperately need AI expertise and talents. At the same time, AI technology providers need application scenarios and real business data to polish their AI models and algorithms. AI tech companies have a strong incentive to work with businesses that have real data and significant problems to solve.

Lenders that lack AI expertise can form joint labs with leading AI research institutions and technology providers. Besides recruiting a few full-time AI experts such as a chief AI scientist or chief AI officer, they can hire advisors and consultants on a part-time basis. With the help of those AI experts, companies can then train and grow internal AI engineers and especially AI product managers to successfully implement AI solutions in multiple application scenarios. It is a simple borrow and grow approach.

Financial Technology and China's Inclusive Finance

By Jianxiong Lei
Director, Jingdong Digital Technology Big Data Decision Science Center

The development of financial technology is in the ascendant compared to the traditional financial services model. Digital competitors, such as P2P companies, online micro loan companies, consumer finance companies and wealth management companies as well as major internet companies such as BATJ (Baidu, Alibaba, Tencent, Jingdong) are on the rise and threatening the status quo. The traditional banking industry is standing at the gate of the digital age.

McKinsey & Company predicts that 10–40% of the bank's top five retail businesses will face competitive threats by 2025 and 20–60% of profits might disappear as a result of digital competitors. In response to the pressures and challenges coming from these "Barbarians at the Gate" the banking industry urgently needs to embed digital technology into daily financial services and open its doors to digital revolution.

At present, China is undergoing a vigorous revolution in inclusive finance. The technology of big data and artificial intelligence has broken through the obstacles in respect to data availability both in terms of breadth and accuracy in the traditional personal credit system based on China's Central Bank's credit information system. Therefore, financial institutions can use the behaviour data left by customers when using the internet to identify their risk profile and preferences accurately.

On the basis of such detailed information, financial institutions can develop and design differentiated financial products. In this way, more ordinary people, small and micro business owners can enjoy the products and services that traditional financial institutions were not willing to provide to them, such as micro loans, financial management, electronic payments, insurance and so on.

In this chapter, we briefly introduce how artificial intelligence technology empowers the retail credit sector by helping financial institutions identify accurate risks and improve the efficiency and quality of customer service.

First of all, artificial intelligence technology can help effectively identify true customers and eliminate fake and fraudulent applications. In the past, when financial institutions accepted customer loan applications, they needed to manually compare the relationship between the applicant and the documents held by them. This not only refers to the operational risk that comes as a result of customer identification with the "naked eye" but includes other risks such as stakeholder collusion during the client onboarding process.

In mobile banking and on other online terminals, financial institutions traditionally relied on password identification, but this is increasingly easily cracked because of customer password disclosure, equipment loss or cybersecurity attacks. For safety reasons, financial institutions often take measures to strictly manage the process and impose various restrictions.

It is something of a Catch-22 situation: on the one hand, financial institutions are still not efficient in screening high-risk customers, but on the other hand, more stringent screening will seriously affect the onboarding experience of normal customers, reducing their willingness to apply, and resulting in the loss of customer flow and potential business opportunities.

In this respect, the technical advantage of artificial intelligence is immense: the customer is neither required to provide additional proofs of identification, nor do they need to enter the ID card or address information, repeatedly enter the password, identify the image, or perform further actions to complete the financial institution's human–machine identification and personal identity confirmation.

Financial institutions can distinguish applicants from photos and video recordings by means of biometrics such as human face, eye and fingerprint recognition, so as to quickly lock specific applicants and confirm their true identities during the application process. For frequent risk points, financial institutions can optimize rules in the identification process.

Secondly, artificial intelligence technology can help connect data and solve the problem of missing or fraudulent data. One of the biggest risk assessment challenges often encountered by financial institutions is the lack of customer data, especially for young customers, customers whose main salary is transferred into the bank account or other new customers who have been financially excluded so far, banks lack effective data that can assist in decision-making as to whether these types of customers are creditworthy or not.

In addition to the fact that the personal credit system mentioned above is not perfect as a whole, there are also internal challenges such as irregular data retention processes in financial institutions, organizational silos and the fact that data of each line of business is separated, such as banks' retail business data and banks' commercial business data, wealth management data and personal loan data, and credit card data.

Financial institutions have accumulated a lot of feedback in the daily interaction of each contact through their bank branches, front-line personnel and customer service personnel, but this unstructured data has not been well retained, excavated and applied. In addition to the problem of compliance, some financial institutions try to collect and purchase external channel data, but also have the challenge of how to make full, effective use of the data from different sources.

In this respect, the enabling value of artificial intelligence lies in merging silos of data and judging the truth and accuracy of the data. Data sources come from financial institutions and the Central Bank's credit system, as well as a number of public service systems, including the industry and commerce bureau, taxation bureau, customs, justice, social security, provident fund and so on, to form a comprehensive judgement of a single applicant.

While making up for "holes" in customer financial data, AI can also provide the cross-verification between a number of data sets. In China, some young customers are separated from the financial system, even the public service system, but they end up with communication records, as well as records of geographical positioning and access to public networks, as well as content, chat, likes, voice records and text records formed in the interaction of various applications. These behavioural data and social relationship data sets can also be used to determine the risk level of customers and their overall risk profile.

Thirdly, AI technology can help monitoring the due diligence process of the credit personnel. In the past, in China, financial institutions carried out small and micro-credit business assessments by generally requiring account managers and risk managers to visit the office address of small and micro enterprises to understand their office environment, employment situation, operating conditions and so on.

The credit approval process requires account managers or outsourced promoters to see the applicant himself. If the interview process takes place at the bank site, audio and video recordings are mandatory as required. If it happens at the client's site, employees are often required to take pictures with the location of the business, the corresponding applicant, and even the location information in the photo, and the newspaper information of the day, to prove that they did go to a specific place and meet a specific person at a specific time. This kind of management process is obviously not intelligent enough, and tends to be expensive, rigid and formalistic in practice.

In this regard, artificial intelligence can be deeply embedded in every step of the personal credit pre-loan assessment to ensure the effectiveness of the due diligence process.

Fourthly, artificial intelligence technology can help loan approvals online, standardize and optimize the logic of loan examination and approval. Loan examination and approval benefit from "economies of scale". The centralized examination and approval by the head office is better than that of the main branches, and the centralized examination and approval of the main branches is better than that of the smaller branches.

The problem is that for many branch applications the direct contact with the customer is in the branch with the ensuing complication of how to effectively transfer all collected materials, information, etc. to the approvers. When the volume of applications reaches a critical mass, the question is, how to manage the approval process efficiently? How to prevent stakeholders from seeking "regulatory arbitrage" when there are differences in the quality, efficiency and credit scoring standards among different branch managers?

We can use big data, cloud computing and machine learning technology to reduce information leakage, standardize and optimize the internal logic of the examination and approval process. In the information transmission step, OCR (optical character recognition), document anti-counterfeiting, text recognition and other technologies can reduce manual input and improve the efficiency of information collection and distribution.

Fifthly, artificial intelligence technology can monitor the changes of post-loan data in real time and implement dynamic controls. Traditional financial institutions also have their own post-loan management requirements, but objectively speaking, resources are relatively limited which means the ongoing due diligence is often lagging, and it is difficult to achieve real-time early warning signals based on customer behaviour to trigger intervention and prevent the actual occurrence of default.

In this regard, the use of artificial intelligence can do a good job of profiling risk events with prejudgment for preventive intervention. For example, the requirement of regular customer data submissions can be changed into the process of automatically collecting customer data from multiple sources, including the financial data mentioned earlier, public service data and other online and offline behavioural data, so as to detect and dispose of "cancer cells" early before customers default on loan payments. All changes of individual data or the deviation of merged data, such as the increase of large transfers and withdrawals, the decrease of fund retention, abnormal fluctuation of related personal account balances and so on, can be compared and analysed in an early warning monitoring dashboard, comparing it with the customer's historical data in order to try to predict and/or verify customer behaviour.

If early warning signals increase their probability and the "abnormal behaviour" occurs again, it can be concluded that the customer is most likely a credit risk and emergency action is required, such as restrictions on transactions, quota freezing, pre-emptive disposal of collateral and so on, so as to avoid losses for the financial institution.

Lastly, artificial intelligence technology can provide intelligent customer service, so that financial institutions and customers are more closely linked. Customer service is the core link between financial institutions and customers, and it is the channel through which customers can provide feedback. With the rapid development of social media and network platforms, customer service can cover more and more channels, such as WeChat, Weibo, email, telephone, mobile app, web, and a variety of instant messaging (IM) tools. In the current environment, the most important application of artificial intelligence in customer service centres is to reduce costs and enhance the customer experience:

In terms of improving the customer experience, the most important application is the upgraded version of "voice navigation". Voice navigation under artificial intelligence technology should be called an "intelligent voice" solution, as it is no longer the kind of bad experience that is limited to key words within the set range but can ask users open prompts.

In terms of interaction, the user can interrupt at any time, state his/her requirements naturally, the system can recognize and understand the natural language, and leverage the installed voiceprint recognition technology to obtain the customer identity authentication results silently during the conversation, so that the communication between the user and the system is faster and natural.

In terms of service, the system can also predict the needs of users by analysing the key semantics in the natural dialogue of users and combining with the analysis of customer data, so as to provide the most appropriate information or service. With these leading technologies, voice self-service applications can provide a more natural interactive experience, bring higher customer satisfaction and achieve a higher level of automation.

Secondly, AI can directly reduce the demand for manpower. There are four main types of application scenarios in this area:

1. The customer service robot replaces the artificial online customer service and uses semantic analysis technology to directly answer customer questions online;
2. Speech quality inspection instead of manual quality inspection, using speech semantic recognition technology for recording quality inspection (these two are the most extensive and mature applications);
3. Intelligent calling instead of real person calling, through the intelligent call system which can carry out three to four rounds of questions and answers to carry out satisfaction surveys, and other highly standardized external call items, such as customer maintenance, customer marketing and other personalized external call items for customer screening;
4. Intelligent assistants improve the processing efficiency of customer service personnel, use real-time speech recognition and semantic analysis technology to push matching answers to current customer questions, shorten the time for customer service personnel to search for knowledge, or directly generate customer call records, reducing the post-processing time of customer service personnel.

In summary, with the continued development of mobile, big data, cloud computing, artificial intelligence and other emerging digital technologies, China's inclusive financial strategic goals will be achieved faster. These technologies will also greatly change the current mode of economic operation and social life, and enhance existing economic and social environments, giving birth to new finance, new manufacturing, new retail, new agriculture and other forms of continuous innovation and evolution.

The Future of Deposits and Lending

By Anindya Karmakar
Business Head – Digital Lending, Aditya Birla Finance Ltd

It is believed that the word *bank* comes from the Italian word *banco*, meaning a long bench. These benches were placed in open markets or near places of worship, where people used to get loan services and currencies from bankers. While banking has evolved since then, it is really only in the last five or six decades that it has undergone a dramatic change, driven by the emergence of better technology and data management. Today, "banking" as provided by traditional banks is not considered to be the best way to bank by most young consumers. Anyone who can make it easy to pay, invest and get credit and is able to bring convenience to the most common banking needs will take the lead; and the reality is that it may not be a traditional bank.

Technology has moved banking to the fast lane. Mainframes have given way to cloud. Application programming interfaces (APIs) have become the norm. Challenger banks, with the knowledge of legacy issues and an eagerness to correct the situation, have appeared on the horizon. However, the two factors that have contributed the most to the disruption are consumers becoming more digitally savvy, with access to the internet wherever they go, and a surge in smartphone usage which has created an abundant supply of data. Traditional banks are at risk of becoming utilities operating behind the scenes, offering deposits and lending as commodities, losing control to players which can create customer-focused products. Core banking systems have become technological relics of the past which, with their monolithic structures, are unable to decompose into multiple capabilities required to meet the consumer demands of modern banking.

Money is ingrained in our lives and society. While money can be kept in cash, there are two key drawbacks – it's not safe and its value diminishes over time due to inflation. To address this problem, bank accounts were invented. Bank accounts give an efficient solution to store cash safely and earn interest in return. Bank accounts could only be opened from bank branches, and this simple fact helped the expansion of bank branches across the world. But, over the last few years, banks have started to close many of their branches. Many analysts and observers call this trend alarming. But what's driving it?

The concept of banking anywhere and everywhere, but never at a bank, has started to take deep root in the minds of consumers. A major share of banking now happens on mobile and internet platforms. There have been significant disruptions in the three main areas of banking – payments, investments and credit – ensuring that customers never have to visit a branch.

Value Stores

Branches are expensive to run, and increasingly anachronistic in the face of the changing dynamics driven by technology and smart devices. Bank accounts are value stores, a safe place for saving and enabling money movement. But they have ceased to be the only value store. Customers now have a wide choice of value stores available locally on their smartphones. Think about the last time you used your Starbucks app to make payment for your coffee. It's not a banking app, but a substantial fraction of the total payments made inside Starbucks is done using this app. Starbucks now boasts more users, more deposits and more transactions than many established banks across the world. There are a whole host of other value stores. iTunes, PayPal, Alipay, PayTM, Samsung Pay are all value stores, all residing in our smartphones. They have a customer base larger than the customer base of the top banks in the world. The value of money stored in these apps and the number of transactions are getting larger by the day. These numbers are all set to surge further in the coming years. And the traditional modes of payment (cash, cheque) have started to decline and (in some cases) disappear from economies.

But that's not all. Original equipment manufacturers (OEMs) are bringing out refrigerators, cars, robots, smart mirrors, vacuum cleaners and toasters which can connect with one another and communicate. They are becoming capable of making transactions on our behalf. They will have a value store (or multiple value stores) of their own and do not need a bank account to transact. The owner (or owners, in case of distributed ownership) can authenticate the transaction(s) using a biometric method (fingerprint, voice, iris scan, face recognition, heartbeat) and leave the devices to take care of the transactions themselves.

Future of Deposits

With the future headed towards value stores on smart devices and with choices aplenty on that front, bank accounts will cease to be the primary place for deposits for the bulk of transactions. Banks will be slow to adapt to the changing dynamics. They will become backend utilities with the customer-facing apps creating the experience and interactions and providing the value store for the transactions. Smart devices connected with one another will buy and sell services and square off the payments on their own with authorization from their owners. Artificial intelligence will supplement this ecosystem and algorithms will keep getting better through learning loops, allowing for better decisions and safer transactions. Bank accounts will be relegated to maintaining the larger deposits.

Access to Credit

Vast swathes of the population, including those who have bank accounts, don't have access to credit. And for those who have, it comes after a considerable wait due to the paperwork needed and the presence of fragmented data, legacy processes and systems in the banks and lending institutions. But for an economy to grow and for people to prosper, access to credit for the creditworthy, at the right time, is no longer a privilege, it has become a right.

Abundance of data, advances in machine learning and innovative operating models are changing the way people access credit.

Changing Expectations

The new age digital borrower expects money to be available on demand, as he/she goes through the experience of buying a product or a service. The context in which the loan is availed and how quickly it is made available is driving innovation and disruption. Be it an unsecured personal loan, or a loan for purchase of a car or a home, the majority of customers have moved online when applying for the loan.

For straightforward personal loans, the end-to-end experience (from application to disbursal), necessitates simplicity and seamlessness. For car loans, the buyer expects her bank or financial institution to let her know before she leaves the showroom whether her loan is approved, and even disbursed. And for the home buyer, the digital application process must be combined with the physical advisory process (at the closing stage) to provide a well-stitched online-to-offline experience.

Data Deluge

There are three key decisions to be made before giving a loan – establishing the identity of the borrower, estimating their income and repayment capability and detecting fraudulent intent. Technology-led innovations in these areas have shortened the lending time. Electronic "know-your-customer" (eKYC) systems are being enabled by many governments; optical character recognition (OCR) technology has enabled extracting information from scanned documents; advanced machine learning algorithms are enabling matching of information and photos in documents with self-provided information; anomaly detection algorithms are helping prevent identity frauds; and data from credit bureaus, alternative data from SMS, apps, social media, payment gateways, e-commerce, telecom companies, wallets and psychometric surveys is improving the prediction power of underwriting algorithms and drastically reducing the decisioning time.

Post loan disbursal, data and AI models have ensured that servicing, cross-selling and collections have become more cost efficient, faster and better, enabling lenders to offer customized solutions at scale.

Future of Lending

Armed with these, lending companies are creating innovative products and plugging into online journeys to take advantage of the context in which financing is needed. Unique lending products for travel, healthcare, education, buying electronics on e-commerce sites, microlending to underbanked segments and new-to-credit segments are surfacing. Players who own an ecosystem are on a roll. The likes of Alibaba, Amazon, PayPal, Flipkart and Square are leveraging the data they own about their buyers and sellers to advertise and deliver personalized offers in real time.

Toyota's "just-in-time" production revolution, which propelled it to dominate the auto industry, has emerged as a new paradigm in lending models. The future of unsecured lending will adapt to individual purchases, making the loan specific to the context and enabling the lenders to price dynamically based on the risk profile of the customer and the transaction. All this will happen in real time without friction and delivering a customer experience which incumbent banks will find difficult to match. Large ticket loan advances will be transformed by integrating into the client's data sources and using predictive algorithms to anticipate the borrowing needs and then disbursing funds in real time. More complex situations are being solved by extracting relevant data from financial documents through natural language processing tools and using advanced analytics to customize underwriting.

Bill Gates once said, "We need banking, but we don't need banks anymore." Banking in the future will be built around people and will be delivered where they are and when they need it. It will be connected to myriad things, all at once, and will be driven by data and technology. It will be there working for us as we work, travel, shop, play or relax. We may never have to do banking at a bank again.

The views and opinions expressed or implied herein are my own and do not reflect those of my employer, who shall not be liable for any action that may result as a consequence of my views and opinions.

Applications of AI in Deposits and Lending

By Pouya Jamshidiat
Leader in Product Management, Pioneer Minds

Artificial intelligence (AI) works best in the company of humans, and not on its own. The key power of AI is to provide people with insights and knowledge so that they can make more informed decisions about their finances and then act accordingly. The business of lending works primarily based on one key piece of information: the credit scoring. This is a key measure that shows a person or organization's ability to repay a loan, which is crucial for lenders in order to price and grant any financial product. The priority for lenders is to avoid or minimize the risk of borrowers defaulting, which is assessed by analysing their repayment histories. And this implies that borrowers need to have an existing credit history. But in the absence of any credit history, such as for students or new businesses, how can lenders judge their creditworthiness? Should they just miss out on this customer segment?

Not any more.

Alternative Data

The utilization of alternative data is playing an increasingly key role in deposits and lending. Alternative data refers to any additional data points or real-time information that can be collected in order to help lenders build a realistic and more granular picture of a borrower's profile. Alternative data can encompass:

- Digital footprint, which refers to customers' online presence (including mobile data).
- Financial transactions and patterns.
- Lifestyle data, such as data from activity trackers or smart homes and smart cars.
- Deposits and cash flow that show how people are spending their money and how much they earn.
- Psychometric data from social networks, showing personality and attitudes, and how you tend to think, feel and act.
- E-commerce transactions.
- Geolocalization data.
- Social and economic environment data.
- Sales on e-commerce or platforms for small or new businesses.

By feeding large quantities of alternative data from various sources into machine learning models, lending applications can foresee financial patterns and infer certain behaviours or psychological traits that correlate positively with borrowers' attitudes towards loan repayments. This also leads to the creation of a rich knowledge base that gradually learns over time and adjusts its outputs.

Value Chain

Now that we know the importance of the alternative data, let's look at how it can impact the lending value chain, by streamlining the process and compressing the time required for the processing of applications from a few days or weeks down to a few minutes.

Origination and Onboarding

At this stage, lenders identify eligible customers and onboard them as potential borrowers. Assuming the knowledge base is in place and the underwriting machine learning model is already trained, predictions and insights about various customer segments can be provided to marketing campaigns in order to offer borrowers personalized lending conditions. Once a prospective borrower begins the onboarding journey, APIs (application programming interfaces) can be used to integrate borrower data into KYC (know-your-customer) systems, which themselves use machine learning models to verify that customers are who they say they are. KYC systems are also supported by biometrics and facial recognition technologies that utilize AI.

Underwriting

Once borrowers are onboarded and additional information about them is captured, the knowledge base is used to reinject real-time information into further machine learning models. Lenders can then predict the risk and future repayment behaviour of potential borrowers. Additionally, this helps lenders to better assess the customer segments that have been traditionally categorized as "at risk" and can potentially reduce default rates significantly. The machine learning model used in the underwriting stage can also detect anomalies and understand complex patterns that can flag potentially troubling financial behaviour, which may not be humanly visible to a loan expert.

Eventually, by applying the human-in-the-loop model, this type of output from the machine learning model can augment the capability of human loan experts to make the final judgement on affordability and risks.

Financing and Contract

When a loan is approved, a contract then needs to be created and sent to borrowers for them to accept and sign before the funds are made available. This process can be automated by either RPA (robotic process automation) or blockchain technology, or a combination of both.

Servicing and Payment Collections

In the last stage of the value chain, machine learning is used to continuously monitor the financial behaviours and patterns of the borrower in order to flag any future risk of potential default, and proactively inform the customers and lenders in advance.

Imagine!

Now following a responsible lending comes Transaction Monitoring and Money Management in order to keep borrowers on track with their finance.

With the introduction of open banking, customers can now choose to share their financial information with other banks or regulated FinTech companies with banking licences. This information includes their current and savings accounts, existing financial products, regular payments, account transactions and account features and benefits. What this means is that, in addition to the knowledge base of alternative data, there is a great opportunity for lenders to aggregate this additional information (with customers' consent), in order to feed into machine learning models and obtain deeper insight on their borrowers' financial behaviour and pattern.

But insight is not enough. Actions matter.

Imagine if we all had a virtual advisor that was always on hand to advise us in our natural language, text or voice, on the best course of action for each of us? Imagine a virtual advisor that can learn faster and know where our finances are heading better than we do; a personal advisor always in your pocket.

Based on all the insights generated by machine learning, a personal advisor can proactively provide customers with guidance on their finances. It can help them monitor their budget and make real-time spending adjustments or provide early signals of moving to default or missing any payments. The virtual advisor can also provide recommendations and help with budgeting, savings goals and expense tracking, providing customers with what they need, when they need it and in the channel of their choice.

So far, the value chain has followed a smooth and happy path. But surely there exist some tough challenges?

How Much Data Is Enough?

You may think the more the merrier. And to some extent that is indeed correct, but not entirely. The more *high-quality* data the merrier. Be wary of making the mistake of assuming that simply having data lakes means that obtaining great results with AI is a pre-ordained certainty. Normally, most alternative data is unstructured and messy, such as data from social media (which can also be heavily biased). This means that it's important to first understand the data collected, conduct extensive data cleansing (such as finding incorrect labels or missing values), label data, and then take a sample of the data to train the models and observe the results. Furthermore, this should be an iterative process until both the models and the training data are in good shape. The success of a machine learning algorithm depends on the quality of the input data and, of course, on choosing the right algorithm.

Remember the old adage: garbage in, garbage out.

How Much Information Do You Store About Your Customers?

And of course, there will always be the challenge of managing sensitive personally identifiable information (PII). It is important to ensure all customers' information is respected and that they are aware of what information you possess on them. Remember: people's privacy is not negotiable.

Is What You Are Doing Transparent, Ethical and Fair?

Before launching, it is important to conduct an ethical impact assessment to evaluate the impact of your lending model on both the society and the wider economy. Does it make both better or worse? The outcome of any AI-powered lending application must be fair, ethical and transparent. Identifying risks and assessing impacts is an iterative cycle and should be conducted continuously as new sets of data are fed into the model.

Machines do not intrinsically know what is fair and what is not. They don't know what discrimination means either. However, human beings do, which is why AI must be supervised by humans. Furthermore, machine learning models applied in lending will be responsible for making economically significant decisions and if they turn out to be very successful, then it is likely that the systems will be subject to adversarial attacks. In practical terms, this means that malicious actors will try to fool machine learning models by injecting biased data. Just like in the context of fake news, we will need to be exceptionally vigilant.

Last Word

At this stage, we can reasonably consider the application of AI in deposits and lending as complementary to existing tools and not yet as a replacement. In spite of its undeniable added value, the application of AI is not yet a silver bullet and existing mechanisms based on past payment histories are still the most reliable way to evaluate customer creditworthiness and anticipate future borrowing and saving behaviour.

Showcase and Customer Service: Leveraging Chatbots in the Banking Industry

By Yvon Moysan
Academic Director, IÉSEG School of Management

Brief History

According to Andrew Leonard, a bot is "an autonomous computer program supposed to be smart, endowed with a personality and which most of the time, gives a service". The term "personality" is justified by the level of anthropomorphism of the bot. The assumed intelligence of the bot brings us to the notion of Artificial Intelligence (AI) proposed by Marvin Minsky and which consists in "creating machines that can make human tasks which require intelligence". One of the well-known examples of this kind of AI is Siri, the numerical vocal assistant of iPhone developed by Apple. When this bot interacts on platforms such as Facebook Messenger or WhatsApp, we then talk about "conversational agent" or "chatbot" (a combination of "chat" and "robot").

Chatbots aim to improve interactions with customers. Gartner already predicts that, across all sectors, 25% of mobile interactions will be conducted via conversational agents by 2020.[1] Moreover, Gartner predicts that by 2020, individual customers will have more conversations with a bot than with his or her significant other.

The Expansion of Chatbots

Considering the advantages of chatbots and the positive predictions of development, combined with the current growth of mobile utilization, firms are tending to use more and more chatbots as part of their suite of customer relationship management tools and channels. Whether it is assistance for a purchase, managing a booking or answering a question, chatbots are used day and night with the aim of delivering an automated and personalized experience.

More and more banks are exploring the opportunity to let virtual assistants manage some of their customer support services, by providing extended availability at lower costs. For the banks, it is an opportunity to reduce the overhead related to call centres and, if needed, to redirect the customers to human advisors, when the questions are too complex or if they require a deeper level of expertise.

According to Juniper Research, chatbots will generate savings in excess of US$8 billion (EUR 7.3 billion) each year by 2022, against US$20 million in 2017, with the health and bank sectors being the first to benefit from these new customer service possibilities.

Juniper Research estimates that the average time per question will be reduced by over 4 minutes compared to a comparable call centre interaction, which translates to a saving of between 50 and 70 cents per interaction. This maximal average level should be reached by 2022 for the banking bots based on messaging. Juniper Research expects the success rate of bots' interactions (without the help of a human operator) will exceed 90% in 2022 in the bank sector, and more than 75% in the health sector.

The long-term goal for banks in terms of positioning will most likely be the progressive increase of the use of voice assistants such as Amazon Alexa, at the expense of imbedded IM (Instant Messaging) in existing desktop and mobile digital experiences, which will face a parallel decline in usage.

Banking Applications

The advantage for banks in these intelligent systems which can learn from their mistakes is evident: they enable them to answer customer requests via a straightforward communication channel,

[1] www.gartner.com/en/newsroom/press-releases/2018-02-19-gartner-says-25-percent-of-customer-service-operations-will-use-virtual-customer-assistants-by-2020.

7 days a week, 24 hours a day, and they can also expect a reduction of customer dissatisfaction by lowering operational costs.

Non-Banking Services

French banking giant Société Générale offers customers who visit their Facebook Fan Page "par amour du rugby" (for the love of rugby) the possibility to interact with their chatbot. All Facebook Messenger users can now instantly access the daily match schedule program for the French Rugby Championship and the rugby match results as well as other exclusive contents. The goal of the bank is to test the potential of this new technology, especially this kind of relationship channel considered as easier, more personalized and instant.

Money Matters

In the same spirit, Société Générale established a partnership with JAM, a startup specialized in student guidance, which has designed an automated instant messaging application like "Artificial Intelligence for the good things in life", based on tips to simplify the daily life of young people.

The goal of this partnership for the bank is to better understand the needs and expectations of people under 30. Being on first name terms, the chatbot will have the goal of redirecting young prospects to Société Générale for the bank to answer any questions these young people may have about money, with a target baseline for the accuracy and relevance provided by the algorithm.

Information and Banking Operations

At this point, some banks have entrusted part of their customer service to conversational robots to answer customer questions. Among them, the Royal Bank of Scotland (RBS) announced, in September 2016, the launch of a system with IBM to provide 10% of its customers with the services of a chatbot.

The purpose of this system is to ease the workload of the bank's call centres by taking care of routine questions regarding matters such as address changes or credit card activations, and to redirect the customers towards advisors to take care of the more complex questions.

Spanish bank BBVA also offers its first "chatbot" (reachable by Facebook Messenger and in Telegram), which essentially allows customers to check the balances of their accounts and credit cards. BBVA also offers a second chatbot, available in all messaging tools using a personalized keyboard, which allows customers to send money to a contact in a very frictionless manner.

Considering that verifying account balances currently represents more than 90% of access to banking applications, and payments among friends are frequently used, banks of all sizes and profiles clearly need to be able to respond to these common use cases in an efficient and cost-effective way.

Financial Coaching

Bankin', the FinTech company specialized in banking data aggregation, launched a chatbot running on Facebook Messenger in September 2018. This particular chatbot enables customers to obtain information on their account balance and their last transactions, as well as acting as a financial coach by suggesting, for example, that the customer save some of their available cash balance.

Conclusion

Overall, even though initiatives have proliferated in recent months, banks are still quite cautious, mainly because costs and time associated with implementing chatbot infrastructure are significant.

In addition, for some customer interactions, chatbots are still unable to provide 100% accuracy, with the most frequent errors being linked to off-topic responses or simply being unable to answer.

It is important to be aware of the customer frustration such interactions may cause, and the potential consequences in terms of image for the bank.

Through these examples, we can observe two approaches of chatbots in the banking sector: "showcase" chatbots, whose main purpose is to create visibility around a brand, and "customer service" chatbots. There is still a long way to go but, based on progress so far, it is reasonable to expect an increasingly pervasive use of chatbots in the banking customer service arsenal of tomorrow.

The Power of AI to Transform the Global SME Credit Landscape

By Nadia Sood
CEO and Founder, CreditEnable

Bill Gates once said that people always overestimate the effect of technology over two years, but completely underestimate its effect over ten. While it is doubtful that he was referring to SME lending, in few sectors could his comments have been more appropriate. Across the world, the introduction of AI into the SME lending space is producing improvements in the most dysfunctional credit market of all: the US$4.5 trillion gap between what creditworthy SMEs need to grow and the finance that banks and other finance providers want to extend to them but cannot, because it has been too difficult for the two parties to transact.

The global market for SME credit stands at a staggering $8.1 trillion.[1] In emerging and developed economies alike, roughly two thirds of the working population are employed by SMEs. Providing finance into this sector is critically important for GDP growth, yet historically it has been a slow, costly and difficult process for banks to underwrite these small companies.

That dynamic is now changing because of the introduction of AI. AI is being used across the spectrum of SME lending to solve data asymmetry problems, improve speed and reduce costs in underwriting, improve the robustness of decision-making and reduce risk. The innovation is coming from both FinTechs that are "leapfrogging" banks as well as from companies that are working with banks, and from banks themselves, who are approaching niche segments in entirely new ways with data-driven products.

Identifying More Creditworthy SMEs

While banks can draw on decades of historical data to determine to whom they can extend credit, their lending models have traditionally only factored in a narrow range of data points. Machine learning (ML) can help make sense of the vast amount of data a bank holds on its customers. As well as improving the loan approval process, data can flag signs of trouble far more quickly than was previously possible, often identifying shifts in parameters that enable a lender to head off a problem before it happens, ensuring the loan remains safe and the lender remains profitable. Chinese firm JD Finance is helping mainstream banks make use of the data they have to make better decisions. JD uses AI to recognize and analyse 30,000+ risk control variables, 300m+ user credit evaluations, 500+ models and 5000 risk strategies with which to help institutions better analyse risk. Another well-known marketplace for small business loans is Lendio. Its platform surveys 40 unique data points, including time spent in business and monthly revenues, to match the best loan product to an SME applicant. Its successes include boosting acceptance rates by 20% and, crucially, shrinking approval times.

Speed Is of the Essence

The inordinate waiting period for a loan to be approved is often a make-or-break factor for a small business. After waiting for an initial response, an SME often must carry on waiting for anything from a few days to a few weeks for a decision, and the eventual distribution of the loan. Once again, ML streamlines the process with dramatic effects, creating happier customers, at a lower cost and generating higher profits for lenders. In the UK, Esme Loans

---

[1] www.smefinanceforum.org/sites/default/files/Data%20Sites%20downloads/MSME%20Report.pdf.

(an SME unit of NatWest Bank) has reported that it has hit over £50m of lending to UK small businesses two years after its launch. Its loans over the last 12 months have jumped more than threefold compared to the year before. Esme has partnered with Microsoft to use AI to speed up customer applications and provide AI chatbots to answer common customer questions during the application process, to make faster and better targeted lending decisions and improve customer experience. Alibaba's FinTech affiliate Ant Financial takes AI in SME lending to new heights. Ant Financial's entire model depends on AI, using deep learning and advanced algorithms to harvest data. By tracking and analysing spending habits and histories, it determines lending rates and extends credit online through MYbank. Crucially, it also shares its tech with traditional financial firms to improve their own credit offer, boosting loan-making and risk-taking efficiencies across the whole financial services industry.

Problem Solving, Sector by Sector

Not only are no two companies the same, neither are the sectors in which they operate. Location, industry, market forces and demographics are examples of the variables that ML can integrate to improve the outcomes of loan applications and proactively identify new opportunities. By monitoring customer behaviours within sectors, ML can predict the best time to approach a specific SME in a given sector with a specified amount of credit. Certain companies, such as CreditEnable, build integrated AI solutions which combine automatic data capture, data mining, algorithms, rule-based and statistical anomaly detection, random forest model ML, and Bayesian and neural-network-based natural language processing (NPL), to objectively categorize the creditworthiness and trustworthiness of SMEs that that do not have credit scores or ratings. These companies can then help lenders identify SMEs that match their lending criteria, have a high appetite for debt, can repay the debt and are trustworthy in a matter of seconds, thereby reducing the time it takes to pre-qualify an SME from 3–4 weeks and significantly improving the quality of lender loan books.

The Power of AI to Shift Capital

In the fullness of time, AI will not only be able to help improve the speed of loan approvals but also reduce defaults because it can instantaneously correlate market events that may cause problems to borrowers caught up in economic cycles. AI lenders and borrowers both stand to gain from the added insight and foresight that is key to avoiding situations that lead to defaults.

SME lending is a tailor-made example of where AI can be applied, adding incredible value for borrower and lender alike, just as it has for doctor and patient, traveller and destination. Success in SME lending depends essentially on the lender's ability to make informed decisions about a company's future financial performance. What better realm could there be to introduce AI than here were the integration of large data sets not only improves decision-making but also helps create opportunities for lender and borrower. Even social media and utility information is being captured by AI systems that can contextualize loans against market conditions and a lender's bespoke risk parameters. For example, MyBucks is a Luxembourg-based FinTech that provides loans in seven African countries as well as in Poland and Spain. The company compares the applicant's social media feed against the information in their mobile wallet. They look at behavioural traits in order to make sure the information on the customer's cell phone and their social media accounts tie together coherently.

Today, the concern for established lenders should be how quickly niche FinTech providers will be able to use their technological capability to expand both horizontally and vertically.

Established lenders who shy away from AI would be well advised to remain mindful of the trajectory of the formerly humble online bookseller that is now the world's largest company.

The promise of AI in SME lending is not merely one of technological advances, but of shifting assumptions and convictions: a shift that is allowing rapid and robust decision-making to occur in the service of delivering credit as a way of fundamentally improving the health of entire economies for the benefit of all.

Using AI for Credit Assessment in Underserved Segments

By Mihriban Ersin Tekmen
Co-Founder, Colendi

Today over 2.5 billion people are still unbanked, meaning that 38.5% of the global population is totally deprived of banking services, and only 42% of the banked population is labelled as eligible for lending.[1] The credit scoring models used by the banking system are still based on the same dynamics as when the banks were built, way back during the industrial revolution. The technical innovations of today still depend on the models as they were when first built. This explains why, in most traditional credit scoring models, the potential borrower is required to have a sufficient amount of historical credit information available to be considered "scorable". And, in the absence of such information, the potentially creditworthy borrower often gets denied access to credit, as the credit score cannot be generated.

The main obstacle here is that the credit scoring model can only calculate a score if the potential borrower is already in the financial system, meaning that the borrower is considered to be uncreditworthy if they are unbanked. There are many reasons for people being unbanked and being unbanked or underbanked shouldn't mean that a potential customer gets "blacklisted" by default, even if this is how the traditional credit system continues to label them. Even with the rise of FinTech, while people can access banking services without having to be a customer of a full-blown bank, the credit models of loan providers still rely on the borrower's transaction history and payment details from financial institutions.

Even for the banked population, traditional models calculate the credit score from the limited amounts of structured data provided to them by tools like regression, decision trees and statistical analysis. Banks build their financial scores based on the track records of their customers, which hinders the process of discovering the real characteristics of a potential borrower. Since they cannot freely access the necessary private data of the potential customers (such as the digital footprint or psychometric profile), their degree of freedom is limited to their own databases. In an effort to widen the data capture net, the traditional credit system forces potential borrowers to try to prove their creditworthiness through excessive amounts of burdensome paperwork which makes the borrowing process time-consuming, frustrating and tedious. Even if databases of customer data can be aggregated into greater data pools to forge a more pertinent metric of creditworthiness, this type of effort cannot match the level of inclusiveness and dynamic analysis proposed by machine learning (ML) and AI. The core tenet of the traditional approach is based on what the borrower can *prove* through previous transaction records rather than their actual capacity and willingness to repay.

What we are observing is that AI technology is creating financing opportunities for new segments of previously underserved individuals and businesses. This is accomplished by evaluating complementary and distributed data segments of users with the help of AI-based credit scoring technologies. AI can mimic the way a human brain would work, which means setting up complex patterns and rules and analysing the outcomes of these rules to update the underlying models and make predictions. All available sources of alternative data can be consumed by AI, whereas in the traditional system only a predetermined list of data is considered relatable.

The data set used by AI models for prediction-making purposes can be expanded and new rules are formed with every new data point that is included. For example, transaction histories are very valuable tools in assessing creditworthiness, as steady purchase habits over time may reveal stability and regularity that imply higher probabilities of on-time payments and therefore lower probabilities of default. Transactions can be leveraged to score creditworthiness across sectors and industries, from simple

[1] www.cashmatters.org/blog/globally-2-billion-people-are-unbanked.

hardware stores to global shipping companies. They share certain common attributes such as date of purchase, amount, descriptions of items, and involved parties. With AI this kind of purchase history obtained from alternative sources is converted into rules for individuals as well as businesses, and acts as an important element in innovative credit calculation models.

Another way alternative data sources and AI systems are used to assess creditworthiness without the need for any financial history is through the use of mobile phone data. Such data is obtained from location services, communication patterns and social media activities, for example. By extracting the seemingly unrelated characteristics of people from their phones through the data sharing process, it is now possible to create a credit score on the basis of sample digital footprints. One of the main data types collected from mobile phones is location services. The weekly and monthly cycle of the previously visited places can indicate a salaried income and settled house and family. For example, an individual visiting the same place five days a week from 9 a.m. to 6 p.m. typically indicates a stable job, and if the same person has a regular nightly location it is considered to be indicative of a steady home. As AI has the ability to constantly improve and expand the data it uses to determine the credit score, personality and willingness to repay, and event pictures shared through social media can help to determine the potential borrower's personality. For example, posting pictures of a pet may positively correlate with the level of commitment the individual is willing to make as well as the ability to care for a living being other than themselves.

Today, with the help of alternative data sources and the power of AI, the prism of evaluation used to establish creditworthiness can be enhanced and extended. For example, lenders can now arrive at credit decisions by assessing the ability and willingness to repay, something that had earlier been an impossible task to achieve.

As we have seen, one of the newest and most exciting ways AI is being used in lending and deposit is to determine creditworthiness, particularly for those without credit histories, as well as to streamline the lending process. Through the power of AI, lending decisions can now be accelerated to take as little as a couple of minutes, compared to the previously lengthy wait of weeks or even months. By reaching underserved customer segments and delivering benefits to both customers and banking service providers, AI is already showing huge promise as a driver of a value-creating win-win paradigm in lending.

Watch this space!

Why Video Games Might Help You Buy Your First House

By Ben Gilburt
AI Ethics Lead, Sopra Steria

Skyrim, an award-winning video game, reimagines the open-world fantasy epic, bringing to life a complete virtual world open for the players to explore. Hoarding was the unfortunate consequence of the 2012 update to the video game. This expansion allowed players to own a plot of land and build a home. And, as it turned out shortly after, fill it up with mountains of junk from around the game that players just couldn't bear to get rid of. It might be a silver plate that could sell for a few hundred gold, or a cosmetic item that might look cool on their character at some point, but the hoarding got out of control for some players. There is a problem building up in our financial services industry, specifically related to mortgages, and I think these people might just have the solution. Rich new sources of data from some surprising places can be used to make first mortgages safer and easier.

The Problem

We have two opposing forces growing in our mortgage market. One relates to house prices, and the other problem is data.

- Property prices
  The ONS reports that house prices in the UK grew by between 5–10% each year between late 2013 and 2016; this compares with 0–2% average inflation in the UK over the same period and wage growth of around 2% average per year over that time. The UK is only just beginning to see the growth rates realign once more, which may be a result of Brexit and political "uncertainty", though we're not seeing prices fall, just stall. This problem is seen repeated elsewhere in the world and is particularly noticeable in big cities.
- Data
  The second problem is diminishing data on historical lending. With properties costing more and wages not keeping pace we can expect people to apply for loans which are both bigger in actual terms and as multiples of their income. For our banks to be able to make safe and reasoned decisions on when and how much to lend they need more and better data. It's easy to think that we live in a world where data is in abundance, but this is not the case for the financial services industry.

Historically, banks have had something like a lending ladder which they can climb at the same time buyers are going up the property ladder. They start purchasing at a comparatively young age, with a smaller property that is a small multiple of their income. As they grow older their needs change, they might have more possessions, need to move to a more expensive area, they might have a family or children who need rooms of their own. As these things change their mortgage requirements change too, but at each step the banks have the historical data to rely on – evidence that this person was able to steadily pay back their loan.

Rising property prices are seeing younger people wait for longer than ever before to buy a property; people under 30 are becoming known as "generation rent", continuing to live with their parents or moving into rented accommodation until far later in life. This often means the needs of buyers change when they are able to consider buying their first property. They may have a family, with children who need rooms of their own, or they may simply have amassed more possessions over this time which mean they need more space than they would have at a younger age. More space means more cost, further driving up the income multiples and amount lent. Even if people are unable to afford a truly suitable home they are likely to stretch to the absolute limits of their affordability to get the closest thing to what they need. Our situation is that higher property prices mean people are applying for larger mortgages, but also making them less likely to move or afford starter properties, meaning banks lack a key piece of data, prior lending history, to be able to make safe and informed decisions on these large loans.

How Do We Bridge the Gap?

Whilst the banks are receiving fewer data on historical lending to make decisions on mortgage applications, there has been a whole host of other available data that they can make decisions on. Banks can make use of publicly available data in their decision-making algorithms including social data, depending on your privacy settings. They may also analyse historical transactional data, making inferences from the times, places and amounts spent in transactions to understand more about that customer, including potentially what stage of life they are at and their personal motivations. The important factor here comes under Article 22 of GDPR, that suitable measures should be put in place to "safeguard the subject's right and freedoms and legitimate interest", and there must be a lawful basis to make these informed decisions in the first place. Banks, therefore, are very careful to ensure the data they use and the algorithms that they train are unbiased, and do not weight lending decisions more or less likely depending on any "sensitive variable", such as age, gender or race, that would unlawfully discriminate against certain applicants.

Though this data is better than nothing, it still pales in comparison to the data available to big tech companies. We have seen a shift in recent years to payment services being facilitated by tech companies, notably with Google Pay and Apple Pay adding contactless payment to people's phones, but these services really act as a proxy for the existing banks – setting up a process where Google or Apple use an intermediary account to bill your actual bank account, with no facility for saving or lending in these services. This might be about to change, with the Apple Card being released in 2019, issued by Goldman Sachs. Though Apple does not issue the card this is clearly a step closer to the big tech companies being able to make use of their incredibly rich data sets to make decisions. One key thing to note here is that people would need to give explicit consent for these tech companies to use their data in this way, and the direction both in consumer sentiment and policy is towards greater transparency. The direction is towards businesses taking responsibility for ensuring each and every user, especially those who are more vulnerable, understand what data is being used, how it impacts them and what the service would be like if they withdrew or refused to provide their data. This sentiment can be seen particularly clearly in the EU with the "Trustworthy AI" model gaining significant traction.

For this to work, users need to understand why their data is important, and how it can be used lawfully, to serve their legitimate interest. If they do, maybe we could imagine a world where video game hoarding is no longer seen as a problem. Maybe we will start to look at players who save items carefully, holding on to single use potions to use them at a time when they have a high probability of giving an even greater benefit to that player than they cost in the first place, or significantly reduce the chance of a greater loss. Maybe we could learn to understand if and how this data from playing games relates to their probability of repaying a loan.

Maybe house prices in our cities will drop. Maybe…but until that happens, we need to keep our eyes open for the data we can use to make safe lending decisions on huge mortgages. We need to make sure customers know what they are signing up to when they consent to their data being used, and we need to take great care in ensuring this data does not create biased decisions and that we understand how a decision is being made.

AI Opportunities in the African Financial Sector: Use Cases

By Charlette Desire N'Guessan
Co-Founder, BACE Group

It is no secret that the African continent is full of opportunities. In the last ten years alone, the business environment has become eminently more attractive, and international investors are investing significant amounts of capital in startups targeting the African market. In 2018, According to WeeTracker's report, African start-ups raised a record $725.6 million in 458 transactions. FinTech startups received the most investments in the same year with financial technologies accounting for 40% of total funding, as well as five of the top ten deals.[1] This data shows the size of the market and the opportunities that make the financial technology industry attractive. This chapter highlights some of the challenges facing financial institutions and the efforts of African startups in the digitalization process of financial services, and finally, points to several innovative solutions that are leveraging Artificial Intelligence (AI) as a means of further developing the African financial sector.

Two Significant Challenges: Financial Exclusion and Cybercrime

According to the latest statistics published by the World Bank, Africa is still among the most underbanked regions in the world. Unfortunately, traditional banks are still struggling to reach the unbanked in Africa. The result is that a very large number of Africans lack access to financial services in both rural and urban areas, whereas what they need are accessible low-to-medium-cost solutions adapted to their needs. In terms of digital services, the issue of security is hampering adoption, development and growth. Figures reported for 2017 indicate that cybercrime cost African economies $3.5 billion,[2] and since then Africa has been one of the fastest growing regions in terms of cybercrime activity. In 2019, the issue of security is absolutely front-of-mind when it comes to providing online services and conducting online transactions.

The solutions widely used in African FinTech ecosystem

Today, the most popular and innovative solutions seek primarily to address the issues highlighted above. The main players in the FinTech ecosystem are traditional banks, startups and mobile operators. The services provided by these actors aim to provide secure payment infrastructure, facilitate savings and facilitate access to credit in order to ensure greater financial inclusion of the currently unbanked. Traditional banks have reluctantly deferred from serving many Africans because of the costs associated with the physical expansion of their branches, and the risks associated with serving low-income people. By leveraging mobile phones, however, banks, mobile operators and startups have been able to develop mobile solutions to expand the breadth and depth of the financial services offered. In Côte d'Ivoire for example, the mobile penetration rate already exceeds 100%[3] (a situation which occurs when people have multiple phones), and it is undoubtedly not an accident that the country is also one of the largest mobile money markets in West Africa.

Furthermore, given the proliferation of online services available to consumers (including digital payments), merchants and commercial companies have understood that consumers expect them to be able to accept payments from multiple providers (even if it is costly to do so) as consumers frequently are not in a position to make cash payments. The relative rarity of cash is one of the primary explanations for the high number of online payment solutions and electronic money transfers in the African market.

---

[1] https://weetracker.com/2019/01/04/what-a-year-the-state-of-venture-capital-in-africa-2018/.

[2] www.serianu.com/downloads/AfricaCyberSecurityReport2017.pdf.

[3] http://www.artci.ci/index.php/Telephonie-mobile/abonnes-service-mobile.html.

AI at the Heart of Innovation FinTech Solutions

Given the trajectory of economic growth, the demographic scale and the commercial opportunities offered throughout the African continent, there is no better place to exploit the potential of AI than in Africa.

> *Africa has many challenges where the use of AI could be beneficial, sometimes even more than elsewhere.*
>
> *Moustapha Cisse, Head of Google AI (Ghana)*

In this regard, Google recently opened its first AI centre in Africa. The centre is based in Accra, Ghana, and aims to create a collaboration between local and international researchers on AI to develop content and solutions tailored to the specific issues of the continent, where the source code will be open to all. This is an example of a very beneficial initiative that shows that the time is right for the full range of African stakeholders to get involved in leveraging the power of AI for the benefit of local populations all over the continent.

Some of the most interesting solutions based on AI are found in the African financial sector. Indeed, regional developers have already found success in the application of AI to problems related to FinTech. My company is developing a facial recognition technology that uses AI in the identity verification process, for example when opening bank accounts remotely, performing online financial transactions or when trying to detect fraudsters. On a more macro level, we are seeing that banks in particular are benefiting from the use of AI technology in their efforts to stay compliant with different forms of regulation, such as anti-money laundering (AML) and know-your-customer (KYC).

The Use of Chatbots

A further use case concerns chatbots, which are increasingly used by financial institutions for their customer interactions. What smarter way to engage and retain customers than the use of AI?

Certain African startups are developing intelligent chatbots, using either machine learning or Natural Language Processing (NLP), which adapts to the needs of banks. These 'smart' bots offer instant connectivity and drastically reduce the workload of customer service managers. Their ability to process large quantities of data and perform context-based operations in the manner of a personal assistant is powerful and impressive. For example, African banks are already using smart bots to answer simple questions from users of a personalized banking application and redirect them, if necessary, to the bank's website or customer care agent. Direct and basic transactions, such as opening or closing an account, transfer of funds among others can be done by chatbots. Furthermore, including a multilingual capability inside customer care bots to reflect the diversity of local languages in Africa is proving to be a powerful lever of differentiation of firms who are looking to set themselves apart in the market.

Looking Ahead

Data generated within the FinTech ecosystem is increasing exponentially as more financial processes are digitized. This is creating immense opportunities to apply AI and machine learning to this growing pool of diversified data with the aim of performing deep-dive analytics and spotting patterns and correlations to make better decisions for better outcomes. An understanding of the insights that can be extracted from this data will help enterprising firms to create even more products and solutions that customers would love to use. There are already numerous AI-based solutions available today that offer a great fit to customer needs, and help financial services companies generate new revenue streams by improving transaction accuracy and enhancing the efficiency of internal management. The next step in the AI journey will be for financial institutions to start offering their African customers AI-driven tools that create a better banking experience by allowing customers to gain autonomy in managing their money.

The opportunity is there for the taking. The time is now.

Insurance

3

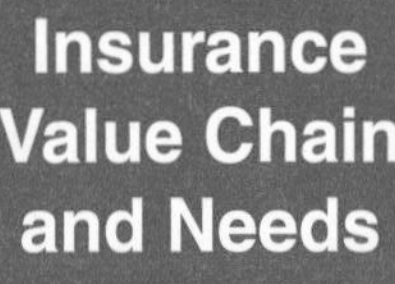

Indicative uses:
- voice technology to detect fraudulent indicators at FNOL
- algo-enabled analysis of disparate, large data sources to identify predictive indicators at policy inception

Indicative uses:
- real-time behavioural premium pricing using e.g. telematics
- real-time usage-based (on-demand) offerings using e.g. sensors

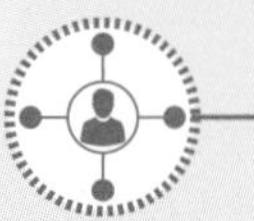

Indicative uses:
- sentiment analysis + big data for personalized, swift customer on-boarding
- chatbot-enabled policy recommendation

Indicative uses:
- digitalized FNOL, triaging, and settlement
- validation e.g. property loss through use of drones and computer vision

Indicative uses:
- post-onboarding e.g. enabling digitalized communications between medical practitioner and patient
- personalized care programme and preventative check-ups

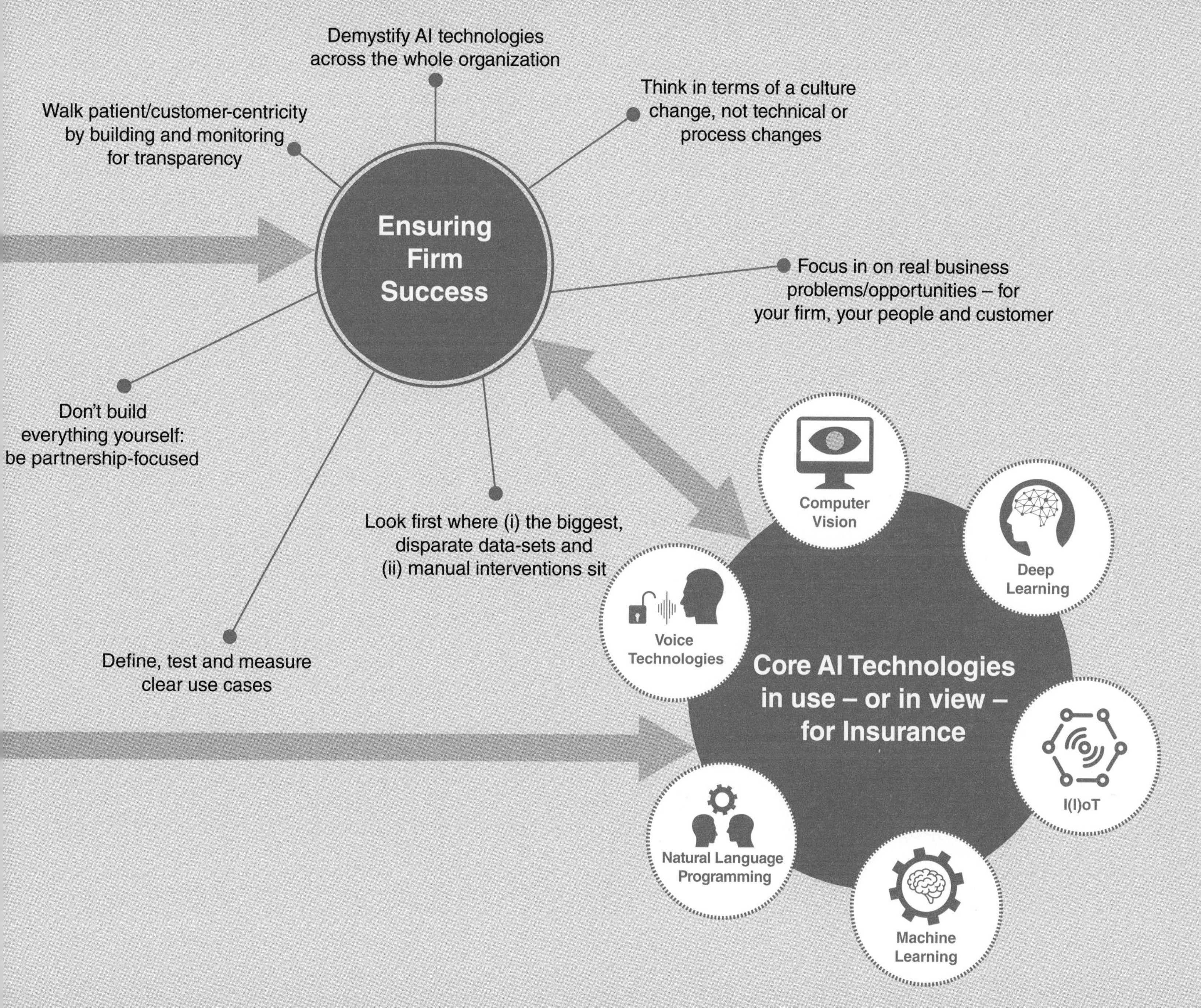
Demystify AI technologies across the whole organization
Think in terms of a culture change, not technical or process changes
Walk patient/customer-centricity by building and monitoring for transparency
Ensuring Firm Success
Focus in on real business problems/opportunities – for your firm, your people and customer
Don't build everything yourself: be partnership-focused
Look first where (i) the biggest, disparate data-sets and (ii) manual interventions sit
Define, test and measure clear use cases
Computer Vision
Deep Learning
Voice Technologies
Core AI Technologies in use – or in view – for Insurance
I(I)oT
Natural Language Programming
Machine Learning

Part 3 looks at key questions being asked – and answered – as this data-rich sector navigates what one author refers to as AI's new "eternal springtime". Read on for:

- How "algocratic insurance" is being built, consciously and unconsciously, as we speak, and why and how regulators – and firms – need actively to put in place the means to ensure its "moral compass".
- An assessment of health insurance use cases, including a 4-step process for firms to find the right starting point, and from there develop a route map to deliver optimum benefits.
- A deeper look at health insurance and the socio-economic drivers for all stakeholders, public and private, that constitute a pressing need to make best use of AI, not least to tackle escalating costs and inefficiencies that create big issues for the insurer, and suboptimal customer experience
- The case for the opportunities for commercial insurance underwriters to empower their expert humans, and concretely to deliver better experiences to their customers, from SME to corporate.
- An analysis (including use cases and results to date) of how commercial insurance firms are *already* transforming underwriting using AI technologies.
- An explanation of AI-powered policy life cycle management that can take fraud detection and management back to policy inception – and through claims, to renewal.
- A detailed dissection of opportunity areas for insurers deploying AI technologies from products to capital management.
- A survey piece presenting a view of current adoption in computer vision, NLP, voice and IoT, illustrating core principles for the next steps that will result in the successful leveraging of AI being the most important differentiator for firms.

Presenting a range of views from the range of perspectives, this part offers ideas and resources that technologists, data experts, function heads and business leadership will find informative, stimulating and challenging.

Insurance and AI: Choices in Leadership, Purpose and Trust

By Shân M. Millie
Founder, Bright Blue Hare

Let's say you've skipped to this section of the book because you're in (re)insurance; maybe you're an executive on the board, or an independent non-executive/external director, or leading a critical function in the firm. Almost certainly you've grown up in insurance, and are technically adept in underwriting, finance or actuarial. This is a business that (a) productizes data-driven insights, measurement, tracking and mitigation, and (b) specializes in imagining and quantifying risks that have not been invented yet. Technology is constantly on the board agenda in one way or another…so, no-one can say that your data and technology foundations are shaky. But technical literacy means something different in the 2020s, and as an insistence on individual accountability for leaders across financial services strengthens,[1] this matters to individual leaders.

So to a long agenda of "everyday" issues – results; COR; analysts' ratings; economic, political and social turbulence; investment returns and the rest – insurance executives must now add the requirement to develop, articulate and (increasingly) defend decision-making on that cluster of technologies labelled "artificial intelligence" and on algo-driven business. This chapter will not list use cases, or survey scenarios (covered thoroughly in this section). Instead, it tries to sit where you're sitting and consider the questions to ask yourselves and the firm, to go beyond "response", to leadership.

[1] Exemplified in the UK by the Senior Managers and Certification Regime. www.fca.org.uk/firms/senior-managers-certification-regime/insurers.

Insurance: Too Important *Not* to Lead on AI?

Insurance has been a primary funder of InsurTech from the outset, and an enthusiastic investor, incubator and funder of AI technologies, startups and scaleups. That's not leadership, it's a business strategy. And it's not enough for insurance, mainly because of how very important it is. Insurance's role as a social protection mechanism cannot be overstated. If it didn't already exist, a system to recover from the stuff we really cannot control – illness, accident, death, natural disasters – would have to be invented.

Insurance:

- provides financial security and peace of mind to individuals, households and businesses, and the guarantees that enable business – and whole verticals, e.g. life sciences – to operate;
- is a major contributor to GDP, and very often a significant local employer;
- remains a vital source of patient capital, providing long-term investment and a key component in the stability of the global financial system.

When you think about what insurance firms do at the most basic level – organize capital, resources and experts to be there for the customer on their worst day (or at least a very bad one) – it's much easier to compare it to a health or emergency service than to, say, a wealth manager. Whether the customer is a shipping firm, a factory owner, or an individual wanting to protect their health and family, insurance participates in highly charged and critical moments of vulnerability. In health insurance, this can even mean life and death. The very importance of insurance means that different, arguably higher, standards apply, as these examples illustrate:

(a) **Life Insurance and Genetic Testing**
Civic society has decided to limit the use of powerful genetic testing technologies by insurers for life insurance. Moratoria on insurers using genetic information are in force in Australia, the UK and in some European Union member states if the sum assured is below a certain threshold. Canada's 2017 Canadian Genetic Non-Discrimination Act imposes a complete ban on underwriting based on the results of any disclosed genetic test results.[2]

(b) **Household Insurance for Flood Risk: The Flood Re Solution**
Super-accurate, personalized property risk ratings (and premia) developed by UK household insurers using proprietary data sets, sophisticated modelling and predictive analytics created a situation of effective exclusion: the people who needed the protection most were being priced out – or not priced at all. Society, in this case, the UK government, decided this was not acceptable. UK Insurance created Flood Re, a scheme whereby every household policyholder in the UK pays a small extra premium each year towards a reinsurance pool, which then allows others deemed to be in areas of high flood risk to be offered insurance at normal rates.

So, insurance plays such a vital role, what's expected is different; further, its toxic reputational legacy amplifies and energizes legitimate scrutiny with suspicion, often at the heart of brand storytelling new players use to differentiate themselves. At the time of writing Swedish property insurance startup Hedvig is making headlines with a million-dollar funding round and its "Nice Insurance" meme, further described as building a "modern full-stack Insurance company" by "not being inherently greedy".[3] My professional experience is that insurance is full of skilled, empathetic, and conscientious people. But, euphemistic jargon like "dual pricing" and "loyalty penalty" really doesn't wash outside our professional bubble, does it? Insurance is starting from such a dire position of "non-trust" generally, hyper-vigilance is required on AI.[4]

Your Job as Leaders (1): Get the Reality Check

The confident prescriptions for your firm's success (or imminent demise) dependent on "enthusiastic adoption" of AI coming at you from all directions belie an inconvenient truth: we're at the very beginning of getting used to life and business with widespread AI. There is no blueprint, even "professional disagreements" amongst AI technologists, debating with each other vociferously on definitions and the timing of "the singularity" (the hypothesized future merger between human intelligence and machine intelligence to create something bigger than itself).[5] There *is* general agreement that having experienced two "AI Winters" (see AI milestones timeline at the end of this chapter), and despite deal velocity and mind-boggling valuations echoing dot.com bubbles past, we're now at a tipping point where algo-driven activities are embedding into and affecting every area of human life. It is erroneous (dangerous, even) to think that (a) AI is a source of absolute and totally predictable "truth", and (b) its design and control is no-one's

[2] https://ccla.org/genetic-non-discrimination-act-overview/.

[3] Sweden's Hedvig raises $10.4m led by Obvious Ventures to build "nice insurance", TechCrunch.com, 27 August 2019.

[4] For more detailed and expert insights in trust and related issues, see the chapter by Bonnie Buchanan, "AI: A Cross Country Analysis of China versus the West", in this volume.

[5] The Singularity: A Talk with Ray Kurzweil, The Edge, www.edge.org (2001).

business except the technical AI builders and specialists. These two quotes alone should hammer home why that really is not good enough:

> Programs are not products; they are processes and we will never be sure what a process does until we run it – as occurred recently when Amazon's facial recognition software misidentified 28 members of Congress as criminal suspects.
>
> *David Fisk, Emeritus Professor Imperial College, Centre for Systems Engineering and Innovation, Imperial College*[6]

> Many AI techniques remain untested in financial crisis scenarios. There have been several instances in which the algorithms implemented by financial firms appeared to act in ways quite unforeseen by their developers, leading to errors and flash crashes (notably the pound's flash crash following the Brexit referendum in 2016).
>
> *Bonnie G. Buchanan, PhD, FRSA, Artificial Intelligence in Finance, Alan Turing Institute*[7]

Insurance leaders in the 2020s need to have a working understanding of AI technologies that is sufficient to confidently ask – and answer – the business-critical question: *Just because we can, should we?*

Your Job as Leaders (2): Question the "Absolutes"

Let's look at three examples common in insurance as food for thought:

[6]Letter to the FT, www.ft.com/content/48f3b01e-94e4-11e8-b747-fb1e803ee64e.

[7]Artificial Intelligence in Finance, Bonnie Buchanan, The Alan Turing Institute, April 2019.

Behavioural Analytics – The Predictable Human

Insurance has enthusiastically adopted behavioural analytics techniques for predictive and habit-changing purposes as a core competency and business process, notably in auto and health insurance**.** It turns out that humans may not work that way after all: in a recent study, researchers analysed the data of 382 Singapore residents who, in the hope of getting an insurance discount, agreed to let an app monitor and rate their driving. So far, so "run of the mill". The research found that driving scores were noticeably *worse* on trips people took right after reviewing their ratings, compared to trips taken when people hadn't reviewed them. What's going on here? The research concluded that "the best approach is to provide individualized feedback because no single approach is going to work well for everybody."[8]

Customers Don't Care About Their Personal Data If It Means Getting a Better Deal

For a while, one could have been forgiven for thinking that, or even confidently making this assertion, and in public forums (as I've personally seen insurance leaders do). How times change. There is a clear and powerful shift ongoing in public and civic society: the novelty of bartering personal data in return for utility – on Google, social media, or with other commercial entities like insurers – is wearing off. Data privacy, discrimination and cyber risks have entered common discourse, for many reasons including legislation (e.g. General Data Protection Regulation) and informed advocacy.[9] The more we experience algo-driven activities in

[8]Professor Masha Shunko, University of Washington et al, HBR Reprint.

[9]For more detailed and expert insights on privacy, legislation and related issues, see the chapter in this volume.

action – election campaigns, recruitment, facial recognition used for repression – the more "information asymmetry" changes from acceptable business "advantage" into discrimination and control. The lasting consequences of being on the wrong end of that imbalance become clear.

Personalization Is the Future of Insurance

In the search for that game-changing "killer app", personalization has been held up as both what insurance should be built around, and what customers really want. The Flood Re & Genetics in Life Insurance examples mentioned earlier illustrate how highly accurate models create "risk pools of one": your challenge sat at the board table is, when does personalization (or "positive selection" or "natural segmentation") become architecting exclusion? Insurance ethics expert Duncan Minty[10] is clear:

> *I believe the future shape of insurance will not be formed around personalisation because it is a solution that ultimately serves the market far more than it serves the consumer. It involves too much push, and not enough pull. It's built upon inherent partiality, and will progressively feel exclusionary, rather than complete and inclusionary. Therein lies its fatal flaw.*

Your Job as Leaders (3): Help the Firm Get Purposeful

AI is not a plug-and-play piece of "kit" and leadership here should not be measured by the size of your data science team, yet boards routinely insist on using this type of "prove we're doing something" approach. The World Economy Foundation's (WEF) New Physics of Financial Services report[11] prescribes the following:

1. Workforce engagement is critical to the large-scale deployment of AI.
2. Institutions must balance their competitive impulses against collaborative opportunities.
3. Time, energy and resources must be committed to resolve outstanding regulatory uncertainties.
4. AI development must serve the needs of customers and remain in the best interest of society.

Taking the last point first, this speaks to being able to articulate your purpose as a business, your "Why (are you)?". You and your people are there for a reason, and, ultimately, that reason is the customer. It's not a trivial matter to pinpoint and describe; it's even more arduous to live it, because that requires defining exactly how your firm lives its purpose. Without the detail, all you have is a slogan, not an authentic promise and ambition around which your organizational culture is built and nurtured and that inspires outstanding performance from your people, and which flows through decision-making everywhere in the firm. According to the FCA, "A focus on culture is the responsibility of everyone in the firm. It should be a collaborative effort, by all areas and at all levels – and industry must take responsibility for delivering the standards it aspires to."[12] Codifying purpose – clearly and transparently – tells you where you stand on AI. Addressing all four of the WEF's action areas, questions to ask include:

- How is your purpose enabled by what you invest in (institutional investment, corporate venturing, incubators)?
- Who will you partner with, buy or choose as vendors?

[10] Duncan Minty, Data Analytics: Six Fundamental Challenges for Insurance Ethics and Insurance, 15 July 2019.

[11] New Physics of Financial Services, World Economy Foundation, August 2018.

[12] Transforming Culture in Financial Services, FCA, 2018.

- What constitutes "value" and "fairness" in your products, processes and customer dealings?
- What will (or won't) you countenance in data provenance, usage and commercialization? Would you use (or invest in) techniques to monitor and use propensity for mental health and stress in your business processes, such as in acceptance, premiums or excesses? What's your position on facial recognition?
- How much importance is given (and supported) to eradicating algo-bias (from whatever source – your model's or someone else's), e.g. insisting on diverse project teams?
- Where does proactive guardianship of your firm's ethics sit? Do you have a formal position on AI Ethics?
- Are you actively contributing to the bigger effort to resolve regulatory issues?
- If you want "workforce engagement", can you explain why, what and how?
- What will you – or won't you – insure?
- In a world of monetized or "licensed" (personal) data, where you were paying the data subject for use, how would that change what you collect and what you do with it?

Your Job as Leaders (4): Bring AI Ethics to the Boardroom

If ethical design and explainable AI (XAI) haven't made the agenda yet, it's only a matter of time. Whether you're developing a leadership position or not, I believe the requirement for organizations to meet codified standards on their use of AI explicitly addressing design, transparency (in use) and accountability (use, effects and results of programmed algorithms) will be commonplace by 2025, manifested in kitemarks, mandatory audits and all the mechanics of insurance-specific regulatory oversight and accountability. Corporate carbon emissions reporting via greenhouse gas protocols may well be the blueprint here, with much faster progress to "Scope 3" equivalents for corporate use of AI – i.e. accountabilities going beyond internal operations but deep into your entire value chain including partners and investors. Below are selected and non-exhaustive lists of (a) definitions, and (b) key developments in ethical design.

(a) Selected Definitions

AI Ethics	A set of values, principles and techniques that employ widely accepted standards of right and wrong to guide moral conduct in the development and use of AI technologies.
Ethically Aligned Design/ Ethical Design*	**Ethics by Design:** The technical/algorithmic integration of ethical reasoning capabilities as part of the behaviour of an artificial autonomous system. **Ethics in Design:** The regulatory and engineering methods that support the analysis and evaluation of the ethical implications of AI systems, as these integrate or replace traditional social structures. **Ethics for Design:** The codes of conduct, standards and certification processes that ensure the integrity of developers and users as they research, design, construct, employ and manage artificial intelligent systems.
Explainable AI (XAI)**	A developing subfield of AI, focused on composing complex AI models to humans in a systematic and interpretable manner to increase the transparency of black box algorithms by providing explanations for the predictions made.

**Source:* Dignum, V. Ethics Inf Technol (2018) 20: 1. https://doi.org/10.1007/s10676-018-9450-z.

**See the chapter "Introduction on AI Approaches in Capital Markets" by Aric Whitewood, for more detail.

(b) Selected Design, Certification & Standards Initiatives

ECPAIS	Ethics Certification Program for Autonomous & Intelligent Systems	Certifications & processes for autonomous and smart systems (e.g. smart homes, companion robots, autonomous vehicles).
OCEANIS	Open Community for Ethics in Autonomous and Intelligent Systems	Awareness-building platform focused on algos, sensors, big data, ubiquitous networking and technologies used in autonomous and intelligent systems across all industry sectors.
EAD	Ethically-Aligned Design	A manual created by the IEEE of practical recommendations for policymakers, technologists and academics to advance public discussion and establish standards and policies for ethical and social implementations
—	AI Commons	Non-profit, made up of AI practitioners, academia, NGOs, AI industry players, entrepreneurs, and others. Connects "problem owners" with "solvers".
CXI	Council on Extended Intelligence	Joint IEEE/MIT Media Lab initiative comprised of individuals who "prioritize people and the planet over profit and productivity."
FEAT	Monetary Authority of Singapore: Fairness, Ethics, Accountability, Transparency	Principles-based guidelines for data use and data protection, introduced in 2017.

Final Thoughts: Architects of Exclusion — or Enablers of Protection?

Insurance at its best blends data, tech and human judgement and applied empathy to produce responsive, relevant, cost-effective solutions to some of the most challenging situations in life and business. If it chooses, purposeful, meaningful leadership on AI could be the answer to our sector's deeply tarnished reputation with the customer, repositioning insurance as an "agent of trustworthiness" par excellence. You have a choice: instead of organizing your firm to help prevent that "worst day", and certainly help cope and recover from it, how much of your resources will you countenance to be directed at explaining why NOT?

VERY Selected Further Reading

Dignum, V., "Ethics in Artificial Intelligence", *Ethics Inf Technol* (2018) 20:1: https://doi.org/10.1007/s10676-018-9450-z.

Marcus, Gary and Davis, Ernest, "How to Build Artificial Intelligence We Can Trust", *NY Times Opinion*, 6 September 2019.

Max Tegmark, Life 3.0: Being Human in the age of Artificial Intelligence, 2017.

The IEEE Global Initiative on Ethics of Autonomous and Intelligent Systems. Ethically Aligned Design: A Vision for Prioritizing Human Well-being with Autonomous and Intelligent Systems, First Edition. IEEE, 2019.

Leslie, D., *Understanding Artificial Intelligence Ethics and Safety: A guide for the responsible design and implementation of AI systems in the public sector*. The Alan Turing Institute, 2019: https://doi.org/10.5281/zenodo.3240529.

Drifting into Algocratic Insurance?

By Srivathsan Karanai Margan
Insurance Domain Consultant, Tata Consultancy Services

Artificial intelligence (AI), powered by the concurrent and converging in global connectivity, explosion of data, growth in memory capacity, and increasing computing power, has entered an "eternal springtime". An invigorated AI is seemingly capable of devouring all types of data, and demonstrating rejuvenated capabilities, for example in image and speech recognition; natural language processing (NLP), understanding and generation; pattern recognition and anomaly detection; and automated decision-making.

Furthermore, growth in the Internet of Everything (IOE) will spike a mega data deluge that is beyond the capability of human faculties to analyse. Only AI systems guided by codes and algorithms (algos) will be able to perform fast-data analytics in real time to generate actionable insights. The complete human dependence on algorithms and ensuing algorithmic dominance will create seismic shifts in the business landscape, and eventuate the genesis of new business models, products and services.

Welcome to the binary world of the algocracy!

Algocracy implemented with benign motives and strict ethical principles might result in a kind of benevolent dictatorship, because more informed, efficient and faster decisions are made. However, algos are *not* born neutral. They reflect the opinions, prejudices, biases and inaccuracies of their creators. Algos created with a purpose to optimize speed, accuracy, and cost, will focus only on these goals and consequently compromise on the ethical aspects. Considering the complexities involved, it will be a Herculean challenge to keep the algo's moral compass functioning, and functioning well.

AI and Insurance – A Natural Partnership

Insurance thrives on its capability to predict the probability of a future risk event. To achieve this, insurers categorize customers into homogenous risk segments; assess the possibility, probability and severity of a risk event occurring in the large segment within a specific period; and calculate an actuarially fair averaged premium for the covered risk. This process has evolved over the years from calculated guesswork, to univariate and multivariate analyses.

The functional requirements of insurance vis-à-vis the capabilities of AI make them natural partners. Currently we see insurers experimenting with AI in the business value chain to leverage its capabilities across three AI dimensions – insights, automation and (customer) engagement.

The immediate focus is to automate routine tasks and analyse the existing data to gain deeper actionable insights. This somewhat cautious approach is explained by data challenges, unquantifiable return on (necessarily significant) investment and regulatory constraints.

So, use cases are primarily oriented towards improving customer experience, followed by reducing operational cost and increasing the accuracy of prediction. Whilst important, these use cases are skewed more towards peripheral operational areas, rather than towards core functions such as product design, pricing, reserving, capital modelling, exposure management, and asset and liability management (see Table 1).

Insurance turning Algocratic

The dawning age of data super-abundance will change the concept of homogenous risk pooling and the law of large numbers. The focus will shift to granular risk categorization, and the so-called "segment-of-one". The generalized linear models that are widely prevalent today will turn ineffective. Insurers will require non-linear, non-parametric and non-statistical models to discern data associations. As the insurers reinvent themselves algorithmically, every model, product, service and process that has been traditionally accepted as an industry norm will be revisited and re-cast.

Algorithmic wrangling of mega-data could unearth convincing associations on which risk assessment, categorization, pricing, acceptance, service and claim settlement decisions are based. With ginormous data, **correlation gains superiority over causation**. Algorithmic determinism could be meted out based not on any explicit classifications such as demographic lines, but on digital shadows, complex proxies, inexplicable (maybe spurious?) associations and invisible patterns.

A connected insurance ecosystem will enable **risk surveillance** in the name of real-time monitoring for risk prevention. Consequently, the terms and conditions could be surveilled and stringently enforced during every micro-moment of the contract. Unforgiving algorithms could enforce risk recidivism penalties on genuine inadvertences, which themselves did not even result in a risk event.

The advancement of open insurance will atomize risk, enable the creation of real-time, risk-based pricing models and turn insurance into an autonomous, parametric and algo-driven offering. With the use of AI spreading from peripheral to the core, the models that are experimented in silos today will become symbiotic, eventuating into autonomous orchestration of processes with one algorithmic function segueing into another.

As decisions get hyper-automated, processes will start to resemble a robotic factory assembly line. In this scenario, every decision made across the insurance value chain becomes automated and autonomous. This is when insurance will transform into an algocratic dominion.

If left unchecked, algocracy could perpetuate bad faith practices such as price optimization, voided coverage after a loss, unaffordability or even denial of insurance coverage. Algos could not only discriminate against customer segments but also treat the **same** customer in a different way at different times – what might be called "niche discrimination".

Such niche discriminations done behind the mask of automation, touch-free transaction, contextualization and personalization, will go entirely unnoticed – until and unless there are unacceptable consequences for the customer. The important lesson to be learned and adhered to is to follow the precautionary principle. While designing their AI strategy, insurers would be well-advised to think, "Just because we can, should we?"

Regulating the Algocracy

Regulation has always lagged behind any new technology. Regulators have traditionally preferred an ex-post approach instead of ex-ante, so that they do not stifle innovation, and to allow space for a clear image of the impact to emerge.

However, regulating AI could be an altogether different exercise. The possibilities of what all AI could do traverses into uncharted dimensions and regulating it by following an ex-post approach could be too late. The need to regulate algorithmic supremacy has become a global concern, with governments and professional bodies propounding overarching principles to be considered for developing AI systems.

To govern algos that influence every sphere of the human realm, regulators will have to adopt a collaborative law-making process and follow a multi-level nested governing structure. The regulator's palette to govern AI should contain a mix of every hue, such as guidelines, standards, self-regulation, moratorium, compliance filing and audit. Complementing any overarching principles, insurance sector regulators need to publish guidelines addressing industry-specific areas. They need to cover aspects such as:

- Data sources and data sets to be considered for building models
- Types of algo allowed
- Norms for fairness, accuracy and transparency
- Learning models to be adopted
- Tolerable range of results
- The periodicity for algorithm refresh.

Insurance regulators must classify the algos that are put to use as core or peripheral, and rank their importance depending on their financial and societal impact. While the scrutiny of high-priority algos is done by regulators themselves, those of medium priority could be decentralized to authorized AI audit firms. For low priority algos, self-regulation could be sufficient.

Regulatory approval should be required for exploring the use of algos in a new business space, repurposing an existing algorithm, or to include new data sources and data sets in the existing models. Insurers should maintain a history of the input and output records for conducting a periodic algorithmic audit.

Regulating algocracy is a wicked problem that requires monitoring a network of algorithms throughout their entire life cycle to ensure its conformance to ethical and legal principles. Governing primary algos may get easier, either with the emergence of explainable AI (XAI) that describes its purpose, rationale and decision-making process to users, or AI-fuelled "counter-intelligence policing" algos. While the growth of XAI is yet to gather momentum creating policing algos is still a niche area of research and the challenges around policing them will open another Pandora's box in its turn. Until such algorithmic alternatives emerge to assist humans for performing the prerequisite task of regulating the coming algocracy, it will continue to be human-driven and a regulator's nightmare.

Table 1: Indicative use cases for AI in insurance

	Insurance Value Chain		
	Proposition	**Distribution**	**Operations**
Insights	• Insurance company's portfolio risk analysis • Glean information from financial documents and provide insights to portfolio managers • Hyper-personalized risk assessments	• Micro segmentation of customers • Identify customers with high propensity to buy	• Calculate customer lifetime value and return on investment • Detect claims fraud in real time • Customer churn prediction for early intervention

AI Dimension	**Automation**	• Analyse financial impact of cyber risk • Catastrophe liability analysis • Predict potential cases with high probability of litigation • Predict supply chain disruption and quantify impact • Claim reserve estimation	• Scan social media and online data mining to understand customer needs and calculate risk scores • Hot lead identification using NLP and sentiment analysis	• Issue policy quotes based on images of auto and home contents • Facial image analysis to determine biological age, body-mass index and smoking status • Cognitive vision to assess severity of damage and estimate claim cost • Optimized triaging of sales, underwriting and claims processes • Automation of claims by validating claims against conditions and coverage limits in the policy contract • Convert unstructured - typewritten and handwritten data into digital format • Robotic/Intelligent Process Automation
	Engagement	• Real-time driver risk analysis from telematics data • Robo-advisory and investment management	• Context-aware hyper-targeted sales based on profile, location, context and behaviour • Cross sell and upsell marketing • Consolidate all insurance policies of customers and analyse over/under insurance	• Chatbots to answer product and service-related queries and for processing transactions • Biometric authentication

Acknowledgement: The author thanks Chris Logan, Manager, Deloitte and Suresh Aranala Krishnamurthy, Insurance Domain Consultant, Tata Consultancy for comments and suggestions.

Moving the AI Needle: Strategies for Health Insurers to Put AI into Practice

By Hendrik Abel
Consultant, Roland Berger

and Dr Ulrich Kleipaß
Partner, Roland Berger

What's the Problem with AI in Health Insurance?

The healthcare sector is one of the biggest digital data providers, accounting for one third of global digital data volumes. Insurers in particular have acquired unique and elaborate customer data sets. Leveraging this data through the use of AI applications can enable new ways of generating profound impacts on both customer experience and provider efficiency. Data-based forecasts allow, for example, for the better identification of individual risk profiles and customer inclusion in special preventive check-ups and suitable care programs.

However, insurers struggle to adequately develop use cases and use their data. Decentralized data management, paper-based patient data, legacy IT systems and stringent regulatory boundaries make it hard to apply modern data analytics solutions. At the same time, big digital incumbents such as Apple and Samsung have recognized the power of AI in digital health, and smaller startups are entering this space with disruptive use cases, for example Berlin-based ADA Health and their symptom checker apps. This chapter aims to identify relevant AI use cases that really move the needle for health insurers and give an overview on key strategic imperatives to derive an AI strategy that can best utilize their untapped data treasures.

AI Use Cases That Can Move the Needle

A wealth of use cases for AI have emerged that are gaining increasing traction both outside and inside health insurance. These use cases will become relevant at different stages of a company's journey towards AI as they require varying competency levels of the incumbent. In general, use cases can be classified into three different levels (see Figure 1):

1. Standard AI solutions
2. Tailor-made AI solutions
3. Explainable AI solutions.

They differ by implementation complexity, but also have the potential for increased business impact.

Level 1 – Standard AI Solutions

As a sub-discipline of AI, machine learning (ML) algorithms were developed to solve narrow sets of problems and replace rule-based methods. This proved to be especially helpful in the support of routine processes to overcome time-consuming and costly inefficiencies. Over time, this has evolved to several industry-agnostic, standardized use cases that have proven successful over and over again and are thus comparably easy to implement into an organization's existing processes. A great example of streamlining routine processes are chatbots. By training a chatbot with existing Q&A forms and helpdesk reports, a significant amount of customer interaction can be automated. ZhongAn, China's largest insurance company, for example, is already showing strong improvements in their customer communication through the utilization of a chatbot. When consumers reach out to ZhongAn to apply for coverage, check their benefits or file a medical claim, 97% of the time they interact exclusively with an AI chatbot, which has significantly improved the company's operational efficiency.

Generative use case model for health insurers (with exemplary use cases)

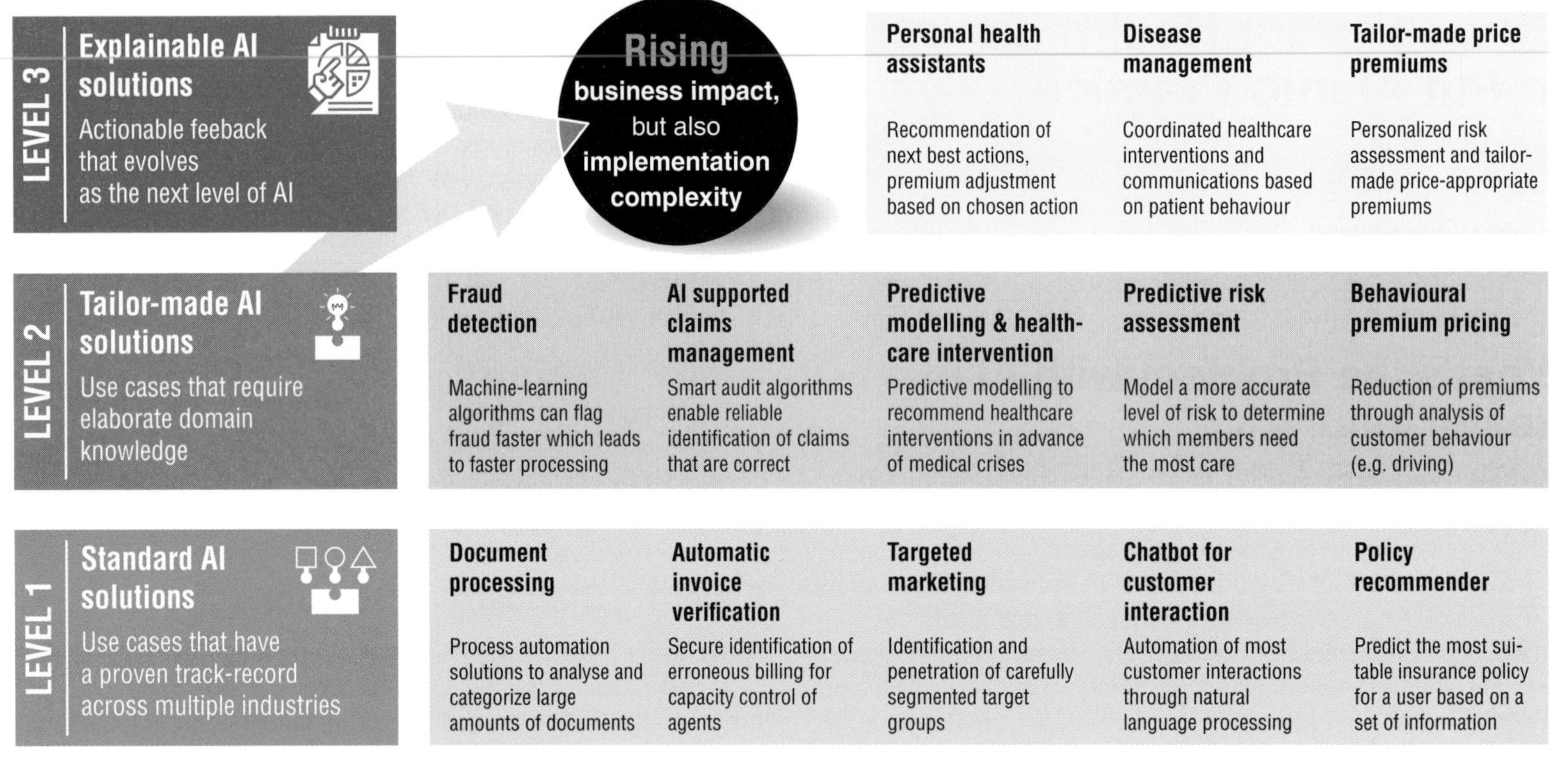

Figure 1: **AI use case model for health insurers**

Level 2 – Tailor-Made AI Solutions

This second level of AI is shaped by tailored classification and prediction use cases. Unlike the previous level, these use cases require a much deeper understanding of the respective industry and its underlying processes and mechanisms. Risk assessment is one example. NYC startup Prognos is using AI to predict a more accurate level of risk to determine which members need the most care and will drive the highest cost, so insurers can expend their resources towards these beneficiaries. By using a lab registry of 18 billion clinical records on about 175 million patients they can determine risks for beneficiaries who recently enrolled and can therefore let the insurers know which members may need disease management.

Level 2 use cases are subject to much greater complexity, due to issues such as the need for sophisticated data privacy handling concepts and the full potential of AI only being accessible through sophisticated human domain knowledge.

Level 3 – Explainable AI Solutions

The third level of relevant use cases is enabled through a discipline of AI called "explainable AI" (XAI). Instead of working with a "black box", where even the designers cannot explain why the AI arrived at a specific decision, XAI can be more easily trusted and understood by humans. This has a noticeable impact on improving actionable feedback, as it allows for better judgement of the reasoning of the algorithm. Personal health assistants with recommendations of next best actions for a health insurance premium adjustment, or an AI-supported disease management are just two of the examples we have seen in our consulting projects and highlight the far-reaching impact of Level 3 use cases.

How to Get There – Strategic Imperatives

With often little experience and limited internal expertise, it is important for organizations to start learning about AI by implementing use cases now. There is no right or wrong approach; however, health insurers need to start treating AI as a strategic asset that can help them in achieving their overall strategic goals. But with little experience, limited internal expertise and an overwhelming number of increasingly powerful AI solutions, the difficulty is knowing where to start and how to set up a feasible AI strategy. The following four-step approach can help decision-makers find the right starting point, and to plot a way forward.

Define Clear Use Cases and Demystify the Topic of AI

Especially in its later stages, AI is more than just a technology to be implemented for random use cases – it is a mindset that makes data the DNA of a company. This makes it more important to start with feasible, standardized use cases that help encourage a culture shift across the organization.

Intelligently Integrate Partners Instead of Developing Everything Internally

Along all stages of the AI journey there are opportunities to jointly work with smaller challengers and/or startups on transferring their technology, knowledge or way of working to the incumbent.

Focus on Solving Real Business Problems

AI is at its core a technology that can help to deliver real value to the end customer and the organization. This is important to consider, so that use cases don't merely perish as proof-of-concepts but are designed to evolve to functioning solutions.

Value Patient Centricity and Gain Patients' Trust by Ensuring Transparency

Transparency is a key component in gaining the patient's trust. As insurance digitizes and uses techniques more familiarly found in commerce – like online processing or individualization – putting the customer at the heart of every product and understanding the implications of adjacent industries will become increasingly important.

With big data, cloud computing and machine learning advancing at an unprecedented pace, health insurers might see their business threatened by new, digital players much faster than they expected. To remain competitive, they must act just as quickly, and begin working on a dedicated AI strategy to really move that AI needle.

AI and Healthcare: Doctor Will FaceTime You Now!

By Parul Kaul-Green
Head of AXA Next Labs Europe, AXA

In mid-2019, the *Financial Times*[1] reported that National Health Service waiting times were an abomination. Only 38% of NHS trusts were meeting the 62-day waiting time limit for cancer patients to begin treatment after an urgent referral. Meanwhile, the waiting list for elective, or non-urgent, care had increased by 1.5 million in March 2013 to 4.2 million in November 2018. This situation is not unique to the UK; health systems in Europe face the challenge of ageing populations, an increasing burden of chronic disease (representing nearly 77% of health expenditure) and non-demographic factors such as the emergence of new, and often expensive treatments.

The *Health at a Glance: Europe 2018* OECD report[2] which analysed health systems in 28 EU member states set out some warning signs. Gains in life expectancy have slowed down in many EU countries, and growing income inequality is a major contributor.[3] The report also estimated that up to one fifth of the health expenditure within the EU is wasteful, primarily due to unnecessary treatment and hospital admission.

Additionally, the public health response to preventable risk factors such as obesity, smoking and alcohol consumption is inadequate and, in many instances, ineffective. The report postulated that up to 1.2 million lives could be saved with more effective and timely healthcare. However, it also noted that unmet healthcare needs are generally low in the EU, and that the emergence and adoption of new digital technologies has the potential to achieve more people-centred care.

AI and Healthcare Now

One of the most fundamental and profound drivers of these vaunted new digital technologies is accessible health data. The quantity, velocity and diversity of health data has dramatically increased. While it took ten years to obtain the first human genome sequence in 2003, the same result can now be achieved in a few hours.

Public health authorities and researchers are analysing data collected from many sources to estimate the incidence and prevalence of different health conditions, as well as related risk factors. The digitization of consumer/patient health records is also fuelling the democratization of health data insights.

Consumers/patients are now engaged with the wider healthcare system in more complex forms of information sharing. More people are using digital devices, from smartwatches to internet-connected insulin pumps, to monitor and manage their health. Increased mobile connectivity and the popularity of wearable devices is also helping clinicians better understand the differences in individuals and populations to diagnose and deliver personalized healthcare,[4] and to better plan to implement preventive and therapeutic measures.

Finally, tangible benefits are being witnessed in care coordination,[5] where AI is used to process personalized data, to elicit patient

---

[1] https://www.ft.com/content/c85c4d84-8c50-11e9-a24d-b42f641eca37.

[2] https://read.oecd-ilibrary.org/social-issues-migration-health/health-at-a-glance-europe-2018_health_glance_eur-2018-en#page1.

[3] On average within EU, 30-year-old men with university education live up to 8 years longer than those with low education. The difference in life expectancy in women in similar conditions is 4 years. Source: Health at a Glance Europe 2018, OECD Report.

[4] Personalized healthcare is an approach for disease management that considers individual variability in the environment, lifestyle and genes for each person.

[5] Care coordination is deliberate organization of patient care activities between two or more participants involved in a patient's care to facilitate the appropriate delivery of healthcare services.

preferences, to help patients (and families) to participate in the care process and connecting patients with information beyond those available within their care setting.

Not surprisingly, the strongest boost to AI in healthcare adoption is coming from the consumers/patients themselves, and through mHealth apps on smartphones and wearables. There are more than 318,000m health apps available on the market – nearly double the number of apps available in 2015 – with more than 200 apps being added each day. The majority of these apps are general wellness-related. However, the number of condition management apps are increasing rapidly, now representing 40% of all health-related apps.[6] The global mHealth app market is expected to grow from US$28 billion in 2018 to US$102.35 billion by 2023.

The Economic Opportunity

The question that remains is about the size of economic opportunity – both in terms of potential cost savings to health systems, and investments in AI. McKinsey Global Institute estimates that 15–20% of the healthcare market has the potential to be impacted by AI, making it one of the most affected sectors.

Accenture quantifies the total cost of saving from use of AI in healthcare at $150 billion (see Figure 1). It analysed ten AI applications with the greatest near-term impact in healthcare. The top three applications that represent the greatest near-term value were robot-assisted surgery ($40 billion), virtual nursing assistants ($20 billion) and administrative workflow assistance ($18 billion). As these and other AI applications gain more experience in the field, their ability to learn and act will continually lead to improvements in precision, efficiency and outcomes.

The healthcare AI is expected to grow from $2.1 billion in 2018 to $36.1 billion by 2025, at a compound annual growth rate of 50.2%

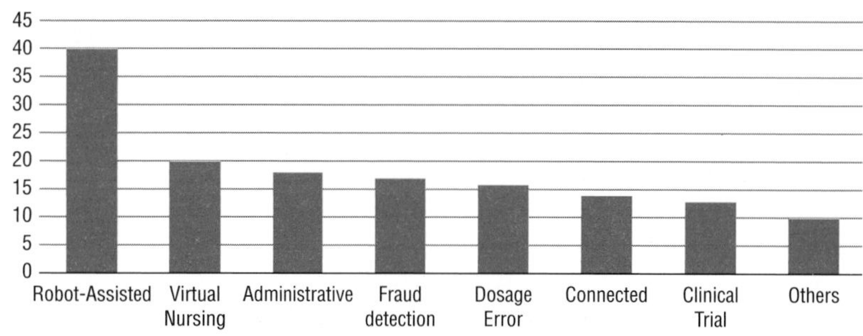

Figure 1: Potential cost savings from AI

during the forecast period. Startups in healthcare AI received $5.8 billion in equity funding from Q1'12 to Q1'19, according to CB Insights data.[7] Increasing investments in AI in healthcare are also coming from tech giants, such as Google, IBM, Intel Corporation and Microsoft.

What Is the Role of Health Insurers in Emerging Healthcare AI Business Models?

You may ask why the healthcare crisis and the economic opportunity presented by AI matter to the insurance industry. The answer lies in how healthcare is financed in many countries.

Compulsory and voluntary insurance are an important source of funding of population healthcare. Insurers[8] as "payers" are important stakeholders in healthcare. And, like public payers such

[6] www.iqvia.com/institute/reports/the-growing-value-of-digital-health.

[7] https://app.cbinsights.com/research/healthcare-ai-smart-money-investments/.

[8] European direct gross written premiums totalled €1213bn in 2017, of which €710bn were life premiums and €132bn were health premiums. https://www.insuranceeurope.eu/sites/default/files/attachments/European%20insurance%20-%20Key%20facts%20-%20October%202018.pdf.

as national health services, they face an acute need to reduce the escalating healthcare costs and improve operational efficiency to hold on to their profits.

This means a shift towards a preventive model of care and leveraging analytics for predictive diagnosis and personalized care. Insurers are utilizing telemedicine for providing remote and convenient care and gradually moving toward a digitally integrated ecosystem that enables seamless and simplified customer experience or moving from just "payer" to "partner" in the consumer/patient health journey.

Among European insurers, AXA has a clear and well-defined strategy to build, partner and invest in digital health capabilities. Padoa, a French startup (incubated in the AXA startup studio Kamet) has developed tools for monitoring the health of employees at work. Another AXA backed startup, Birdie, has developed an AI-powered care technology platform that supports care professionals and families in delivering better and safer elderly care at home. In addition, AXA's venture capital arm has investment in many digital health ventures powered by AI including Biobeats (an employee stress management app) and Annum health (behavioural treatment for alcohol dependence). In teleconsultation, CareVoice, a Shanghai-based InsurTech, has partnered with AXA Tianping and Ping An Health to launch an AI-based voice assistant that enables members to seek information about their symptoms and be guided to the applicable medical specialty.

Health systems are critical to long-term well-being and sustainable development of any country. Europe is lucky to have arguably some of the most well-functioning universal healthcare provisions for its citizens. It is imperative that both public and private players in the European health system work together to deal with challenges of escalating costs and inefficiencies.

AI has a critical role to play. Sometime soon, your next medical appointment may well be a smart-app consultation with your GP, augmented by an AI symptom checker and NLP-powered GP notes. Doctor will FaceTime you now!

Using Artificial Intelligence in Commercial Underwriting to Drive Productivity Growth

By Hamzah Chaudhary
Director of Product Management, Cytora

Insurance is a product that has remained unchanged almost since its inception. This filters through to the way in which it is transacted today. The majority of commercial insurance is still done in person or over the phone. Although a lot of personal lines insurance (e.g. car insurance, life insurance) is now sold online in a fast and automated way, the same changes have not been adopted in commercial insurance.

There are a number of factors that play into why this should be, but the major one is that commercial risks are often seen as far more heterogeneous than personal lines, even at the smallest business level. Insurers therefore require human underwriters to be involved in understanding the true nature of the business, and to price accordingly.

However, as customer demands change, this system is no longer acceptable to the end user. As individuals, we expect fast and frictionless processes, and this is something that is currently not supported by the insurance infrastructure in place for commercial underwriting. Consumers expect all transactions to be simple and automated, regardless of whether they are buying a car insurance policy or a policy for their business. This means that commercial insurers must change how they do business to meet customer demands.

Also, underwriting decisions today are often made using incomplete and outdated information. Paired with legacy systems that make it difficult to automate processes, it is easy to see how the commercial insurance workflow today is far below the expected standard. It also means that the frictional cost of operating in these markets is extremely high for insurers, and often the cost of change can be even higher.

Like many sectors, insurance has also seen some companies already attempt to incorporate artificial intelligence applications into parts of their business. This article walks through a few specific use cases that AI can enable to transform the customer experience and drive productivity growth. The focus is on applications that exist today, rather than future possibilities dependent on technological developments.

At a high level, there are three near-term use cases powered by AI that are within the grasp of implementation by insurers today, and that impact different areas of the underwriting value chain:

1. Using AI to structure incoming submissions from brokers and customers to help teams prioritize their work.
2. Using advanced matching algorithms to link external data, as well as advanced modelling techniques to gain a more holistic risk profile of a customer.
3. Leveraging data collected from connected devices within machine learning models to provide advanced and tailored risk management to customers.

Using AI to structure incoming submissions from brokers and customers to help teams prioritize their work. The majority of commercially underwritten policies are intermediated transactions, often with a broker between the customer and the insurer. Typically, brokers will fill out a submission form containing relevant information which is then sent via email to an underwriter. Underwriters must go back to the broker if they have questions on the submission or require any extra information. This can often mean it may take days to get a price back to the customer. It is also an extremely unoptimized process, as underwriting teams must go through each submission manually to understand if it is within their business appetite.

Using computer vision and natural language processing (NLP) technology, information can be automatically extracted and structured from broker submissions and put into a queue for underwriters. Underwriting managers can then easily prioritize these submissions around the kind of business they want to write. This means that brokers get faster responses, and underwriters focus their time on business that is most relevant to them.

Use advanced matching algorithms to link external data as well as advanced modelling techniques to gain a more holistic risk profile of a customer. Using advanced matching algorithms to link disparate data sources helps leverage the power of alternative data to gain a more holistic risk profile of a customer. Leveraging external data sources not traditionally used also means data can be accessed that the customer may not even know about themselves. As an example, when insuring properties, fire can be a major hazard, so looking at the distance to the nearest fire station may be beneficial. Pairing these new data sources with advanced machine learning modelling techniques can provide a much more accurate price for an individual customer.

This helps create a fairer risk price, using comprehensive, contextualized data, avoiding biases and discrimination. This also means a future where the user journey is more frictionless than today, while still ensuring customers are properly understood by the insurer.

Leverage data collected from connected devices within machine learning models to provide advanced and tailored risk management to customers. Risk management is about realizing changes that a customer can make to their insurable property and advising them on the best way to rectify this. Often, this can result in a lower premium for customers due to the reduced probability of a claim. However, this process is mostly manually carried out by risk engineers who have to conduct on-site assessments, and it just isn't economically viable for most insurance companies to carry out these assessments on smaller customers.

However, with the data collected from new connected devices, the power of advanced risk management can be available to all customers. Take the example of connected smoke alarms: if a customer's smoke alarm goes off a few times in a week, the insurer can send them a notification with tips on how to reduce these false alarm incidents to avoid a fire.

Collecting data directly from customers like this means that insurers have information that is directly relevant to the assets they are insuring. Over time, they can train machine learning models on data from connected devices that allow them to serve up relevant and real-time risk management information to all customers. This can help avoid claims and save money for customers.

There is a sliding scale of how AI can help commercial insurers through different classes of risks. In the smaller end of the market – known as SME businesses – it can help to achieve full automation of the underwriting process, and as risks get larger and more complex, it becomes a tool to augment the capabilities of an underwriting team.

Leveraging the power of AI, insurers can offer their customers effortless access to fairly priced insurance, whenever they need it. AI can be used systematically along all parts of the underwriting value chain to achieve this. The future of insurance has to be one where underwriting teams are empowered by AI-driven tools.

The Digitally-Enabled Underwriter: How AI is Transforming Commercial Insurance Underwriting

By Ron Glozman
Founder and CEO, Chisel AI

Investment in InsurTech by commercial insurance companies has long lagged behind personal lines. According to *Insurance Business Magazine,*[1] over the past decade, InsurTechs focused on personal lines saw $5.8 billion worth of investment versus just $1.3 billion for InsurTechs focused on commercial lines. For every dollar that personal lines spent on InsurTech Innovation, commercial insurers invested a mere 22 cents.

It is no surprise that commercial insurers have some catching up to do when it comes to technology innovation. What *is* surprising is the extent to which artificial intelligence (AI) has become a catalyst to accelerate their digital transformation. While commercial insurance has habitually been among the last industries to embrace new technologies, AI is proving the exception to the rule.

Why AI, Why Now?

Kevin Kelly, founding editor of *Wired*, coined a famous phrase that captures the flux that commercial insurance finds itself in today: 'The future happens very slowly and then all at once.' A perfect storm of massive volumes of unstructured data, slow and cumbersome back-office processes and years of underinvestment in technology has created a commercial insurance industry that is ripe for disruption – and also finally ready to embrace it.

In the era of Amazon, commercial insurers are grappling with the on-demand expectations of a new breed of customer and a new business paradigm based on instant gratification. Customers expect the same high level of engagement and responsiveness in their working lives as in their personal lives. While purchasing commercial insurance may never be as easy as ordering dinner on Uber Eats, commercial insurers are under pressure to provide higher levels of customer engagement, a high degree of personalization and much faster response times – and to do it all digitally.

This is where AI comes in, offering insurers the opportunity to solve age-old challenges standing in the way of customer responsiveness and growth. Nowhere is this truer than in the back office, where cumbersome, high-volume, high-touch underwriting processes create significant bottlenecks.

A Deluge of Data, A Drought of Insights

Commercial insurance underwriting is data-intensive. Making sense of policy-level data is critical for risk mitigation, pricing, decision-making and growth. But getting at the data that underwriters need to thoroughly assess and price risk has become more difficult with the exponential growth of enterprise data stores and data lakes.

Much of this data is trapped in digital documents of various types and formats – policies, binders, quotes, submissions, loss run reports, statements of value, etc. – and most of it is unstructured. Older technologies and approaches can't keep pace with the ever-growing volumes of data; nor is it sustainable for insurers to outsource or hire more people to manually process and re-key it.

Advances in artificial intelligence are providing new ways to address the industry's data dilemma. AI can help brokers and carriers interpret massive amounts of data and identify correlations that would otherwise be invisible to the human eye.

[1] "The insurtech bandwagon", *Insurance Business Magazine*, 11 February 2019.

The AI revolution is being driven by InsurTechs offering solutions designed specifically for insurance. These solutions use natural language processing (NLP) and machine learning to extract, read and interpret data in digital documents the same way humans do, only hundreds of times faster.

These purpose-built solutions typically employ named-entity recognition to identify and classify insurance-specific data types, such as premiums, limits, deductibles, types of coverage, exclusions and endorsements. Rather than simply recognizing page and layout patterns like optical character recognition (OCR), AI solutions are able to comprehend the context of the data they extract with a high degree of accuracy. Put another way, these solutions understand the language of commercial insurance.

Use Cases for AI in Commercial Insurance Underwriting

As profit margins shrink and customer expectations rise, it's more important than ever for insurers to find new ways to automate high volume, repetitive, error-prone underwriting processes. By extracting unstructured and structured data in real time and outputting the data in insurance industry standard formats like ACORD, AI solutions allow insurers to ingest actionable information and put it to use in ratings engines, core insurance systems and analytics platforms. By allowing ready access to policy-level data, AI powers intelligent automated workflows, enabling a range of transformative use cases, such as:

- Application Intake – speeding up the submission intake process by automatically reading submissions and applying rules to auto-route them to the right department, based on type, line of business, geography etc., or auto-declining submissions that don't meet the insurer's criteria and risk appetite.
- Checking Policies – digitizing and standardizing the process of checking an application, submission, quote and binder against a policy. Automatically identifing inconsistencies, errors and omissions in seconds to accelerate quote to bind, ensure contract certainty and mitigate E&O risk.
- Submission Prioritization – achieving straight-through processing by automatically ranking submissions based on key performance indicators, such as projected profitability, probability to bind, broker experience, line of business and acceptability of risk.

Insurers can no longer afford to ignore inefficient underwriting processes. As Senior Analyst Greg Donaldson of the Aite Group writes,[2] "Carriers that do not explore ways to integrate AI into their underwriting processes will fall behind their competitors."

The Rise of the Digitally-Enabled Underwriter

AI is, first and foremost, an enabling technology. According to *Entrepreneur Magazine*,[3] a report from *Harvard Business Review* found that firms achieve the most significant performance improvements when humans and machines work together: "The ideal AI-human arrangement is one in which AI technology drives the lower-level, repetitive processes associated with completing a task, while human oversight ensures the timely and accurate completion of that task."

Human underwriters are unlikely to be replaced by AI. A more likely scenario is that AI will augment underwriters with superhuman powers. By digitally transforming high-touch workflows, AI will enable underwriters to focus on more accurate risk predictions, new distribution strategies, deepening customer relationships, offering bespoke services, and growing and shaping their book of business.

---

[2]Greg Donaldson, "P&C Underwriting: Changing the Global Dynamics With AI", Aite Group, 18 June 2019.

[3]Tom Livne, "Why AI and Humans Are Stronger Together Than Apart", *Entrepreneur*, 27 February 2019.

We Are Still at the Beginning

With all the hype, it's worth remembering that we are still in the early days of AI. The initial pilots have come and gone, and we are now seeing production deployments, but there is still work to be done to scale up and scale out AI across geographies and lines of business. The types of results that commercial insurers have seen so far include:

- 50% increase in underwriting capacity without adding staff
- 2X increase in quoting capacity with no additional headcount
- Billions of dollars in potential E&O exposure identified and averted.

In his book *Behind the Cloud*,[4] Marc Benioff, founder of Salesforce, writes that, "In all industries, especially the technology industry, people overestimate what you can do in one year, and they underestimate what you can do in ten."

It is safe to say that in ten years' time commercial insurance is going to look a lot more like personal insurance. Brokers and their customers will no longer have to wait days or even weeks for an answer to their quote request, and carriers won't lose business because back-office bottlenecks prevented them from responding fast enough. Underwriters – freed from mundane manual tasks – will spend more time listening to and responding to customers and focusing on high value work. And AI will have made this digital transformation a reality.

[4] Marc R. Benioff and Carlye Adler, *Behind the Cloud: The Untold Story of How Salesforce.com Went from Idea to Billion-Dollar Company—and Revolutionized an Industry*, Wiley-Blackwell, 2009, p. 256.

Improving Policy Life Cycle Management with AI and Data Science

By Jeff Manricks
Sales Director UK Region, Shift Technology

and Dan Donovan
Head of Customer Success, Shift Technology

There is no argument that fraud is a huge problem plaguing the global insurance industry. Millions of dollars are lost each year to fraudulent claims, ultimately raising the cost of insurance for everyone involved. To combat the problem, the industry is already doing some interesting things when it comes to using artificial intelligence (AI) to root out fraud within the claims process. Spotting the potential for fraud at first notification of loss (FNOL), and therefore *not* paying out for non-meritorious claims, is already generating tremendous benefits for many insurers around the world.

But what if we could do more? What if we could apply AI much earlier in the process? What if we could identify the potential for fraud at the point of sale, i.e. at the very beginning of the underwriting process? And perhaps even more ambitiously, what if we could apply AI to achieve better policy life cycle management, improving the process for insurers and the insured alike?

The good news is that we absolutely can, but only if we begin thinking more holistically about the insurance policy itself – from underwriting, policy amendments, claims and agency audits, all the way through to renewal.

So, what does not only detecting but also preventing and managing risk, leakage and fraud across the life of a policy look like? What needs to be part of an insurer's strategy to make this a reality? Can it even be done? Yes: but certain things need to be in place to make it happen, and this chapter sets out to paint that picture.

One of the biggest challenges to true policy life cycle management is that anything that even resembles a current approach is bifurcated between the underwriting process and the claims process (including fraud detection). Yet, usable data that can be applied to identifying risk, leakage and fraud are generated at all critical milestones in the policy life cycle.

Take, for example, data that could be used to identify risk at time of application. Ideally, this information is available at the time the customer signs up for a policy, influencing the underwriting process. But depending on when the data is obtained, perhaps at FNOL, it could also be leveraged to retroactively validate information submitted on the original application for insurance. What is exciting is that all of the relevant processes related to policy life cycle management can all be supplemented with external data.

AI-Supported Policy Life Cycle Management: Point of Sale

Effective policy life cycle management begins at the point-of-sale/underwriting. Spotting the potential for fraud before the policy is even bound can help ensure that bad policies simply do not get written. Since most agents have direct access to the application system and the binding authority to approve new policies at the point of sale, any "propensity for fraud score" needs to be delivered near instantaneously.

Using an auto policy as an example, the data an insurer is looking for here is information related to the proposed policyholder's driving history, prior policies, vehicles covered by those policies, known addresses associated with the applicant, other members of the household, prior number of claims and potentially even past premium information. At the point of sale, the internal and public record data outlined above can be used to validate the information supplied by the potential customer on their application and determine if it's accurate.

Continuing the theme of using external data sources to support policy life cycle management, can you tap into information about the vehicle being insured to validate whether it has ever been classified as a total loss vehicle? Does the vehicle have pre-existing damage? Are there photos available that may accurately represent the current vehicle condition or indicate if it's likely being used for commercial versus personal use? Is there data available from publicly accessible social media sites that show the proposed policyholder racing cars or indicate the potential for underage drivers in the household?

Turning back to data the insurer may already have, look for multiple vehicles being insured for the household but all for only a single driver. This may be a strong indicator that the insurance will ultimately be covering an underage driver, an unlicensed driver or someone unable to obtain their own policy. Using AI to develop a comprehensive picture of the proposed insurer at the point of sale is the first stage of effectively managing that policy.

Re-Scoring and Re-Evaluating the Initial Application after a Claim Has Been Submitted

In the case where a policy was written and accepted, AI can still be used to understand the legitimacy of the original application during its term. When a claim is filed, a whole new set of data is made available and from which new connections and correlations can be made. What we're looking for here is any new information obtained from the claim that doesn't match what was provided on the application.

For example, was the driver at time of loss underage or an unlisted driver? Do the vehicle damage photos at time of appraisal show the vehicle is being used for business purposes when it's insured as a personal use vehicle? Is the vehicle garaging location accurate, or does the claims data indicate the insured may really reside in a different state or a different part of the state, where annual premiums would be significantly higher? Was the condition of the vehicle misstated at time of application?

Taking an AI-driven approach to policy life cycle management allows insurers to truly know their customers and make better decisions about current claims and even the policy going forward. Can the current claim be denied – even if legitimate – because the insured materially misrepresented critical information at the time of application? Should the insurer not renew the policy? Or is it more advantageous to renew the policy under a new premium rate?

These decisions can best be made only when all the information is available, and the connections and correlations between data points made.

It's Not Just about Fraud

Effective policy life cycle management is not simply about fraud. It is about knowing your customer through data and information. It is about applying that knowledge to a policy and determining if it is a likely candidate for premium leakage – a condition marked by missing or erroneous underwriting information leading to lower premiums. It is about breaking down information silos and then arming highly trained sales agents, underwriters and Special Investigations Unit (SIU) teams with unrivalled insights derived from all of the data available, applied at scale and in real time.

Policy life cycle management is also about using AI to track and understand how data may change throughout the life of the policy and effectively using these data points at the time of claim or renewal to go back and confirm the veracity of the information first submitted at the time of the policy application and help identify risk and take appropriate action.

There is a lot of talk in insurance circles related to AI and its role in the claims process. These conversations typically focus on fraud detection and more recently claims automation. Interestingly, the same attributes that make AI so appealing in these areas also make it ideal for managing the overall life cycle of the policy, from underwriting to renewal, and for helping insurers know as much as they can about their customers, improving the experience for everyone involved.

Disrupting the Insurance Value Chain

By Abhineet Sarkar
FinTech and Innovation Lead, India

Like banking, insurance is an age-old method of securing one's life, wealth and health for the future. However, insurance seems to be the *only* industry where innovation can be embedded in each and every part of the value chain.

Generally thought to be a "grudge" purchase or "push product", unlike investment products, for example, continuing year-on-year premium growth globally indicates ongoing demand. Insurance is not going away – and the opportunities to embed AI, and fundamentally change the way things are done, are huge.

This chapter proposes a practical approach to imbibe an AI strategic framework into insurers' existing culture, focused on driving specific use cases.

The following is a comprehensive Action List covering:

1. Product
   a. Sales and distribution
   b. Product management
2. Customer Onboarding
3. Underwriting
4. Customer Services
   a. Customer Support
   b. Policy administration
5. Claims and settlement management
6. Capital management.

Products

Sales and Distribution

- Enterprise analytics using all existing data, and predicting sales behaviours, taking into account various media, social, demographics and third-party resources.
- Real-time predictive analytics on various risk parameters, e.g. to identify customer profiles for upsell or cross-sell.
- Real-time conversational bots, e.g. for agents to address a client's current and future needs, and for selling of policies on the platform.
- Gamification, e.g.to create relevant customer profiles and propose targeted policies.
- Sales and agent AI analytics dashboards, e.g. to track real-time telecallers and salesforce effectiveness, customers' funnel analysis, calculate real-time premiums.

Product Management

- Behavioural premium pricing using telematics, connected health and other Internet of Things (IoT) devices (also can be connected to actuarial processes) to monitor and determine premiums based on usage, and other on real-time data feeds.
- Building up and customizing *real-time insurance products* based on immediate incidents such as, e.g. natural catastrophe and proposing dynamic premiums accordingly.
- Using *AI drones* to provide *real-time feedback* about a property to provide an instant bespoke premium at the quote stage.
- Creating peer-to-peer (P2P) products by analysing referrals of existing policyholders and creating a pool of products to recommend to relevant customer profiles.

Customer Onboarding

- Natural language processing (NLP)-based voice tech and/or chatbot to, e.g., explain and recommend products, authenticate customers, validate documents, collect payments and issue policies seamlessly.
- Real-time document uploading using intelligent character recognition (ICR) and verification from source, and proceeding into workflows (based on initial checks for underwriting).
- Advanced image recognition and connecting various geographic and social data of customers to onboard them quickly with no manual intervention.
- Electronic know-your-customer (KYC) with biometric authentication to automate lengthy form-filling procedures.

Underwriting

- Pre-onboarding: Using alternate resources and existing data to create financial and risk profile of the customer to onboard, *before* recommending products.
- During onboarding: Using facial analytics to predict certain health characteristics and habits of customers such as BMI, drinking habits, age.
- Post-onboarding: Tonal and context polygraphic analysis of calls between digital medical practitioners and customer to enable voice-based underwriting once required documents are submitted for onboarding.
- Using alternate data, financial statements and referral data to create risk ratings.

Customer Services

Customer Support

- Chatbots and email bots help to bucket queries and requests, draft responses based on the intent and context of queries and respond without any human interventions.
- Understand call transcripts using call records from call centres made to customers and predicting persistency of premium payments.
- Identify existing customers using voice recognition and authentication (in different languages) to welcome and capture unstructured policy issues and escalate for effective, efficient resolution.

Policy Administration

- AI-based segmentation for, e.g., timely renewals by triggers based on real life events.
- Product sophistication achieved by testing different risk tolerances with the customer during the policy for e.g., collecting various real-time feed from home tech and other sensors, connected car devices and the like.
- Behavioural analysis of existing customers using voice and/or chatbot-based Q&As to predict the lifetime value (LTV) and churn rate.
- Extract and enrich data from different websites and other resources to understand competitor strategy.
- *Conversational chat- or voice-based bots* to enable self-servicing for policy issuance, policy endorsements and cancellations for the customers.
- Facial, fingerprinting, voice and PIN-enabled recognition systems to enable *digital signatures* on policies.

Claims and Settlement Management

- Using drones and video analysis to check on the status of property during natural calamities, fires, theft, etc. to process claims instantly.
- Remote scanning of vehicles using image analysis to confirm on the claim amount for instant settlement and payout.

- NLP-based data mining techniques to help in extractions of subrogation and litigation indicators from contracts.
- Predicting early warning signals to prevent or identify fraudulent claims and calculated claims correctness forecasting before disbursement of claims to the customers.
- Real-time money transfer to customer accounts.

Capital Management

- Predicting patterns for unclaimed policy benefits against cost of write-offs and policy terminations cost.
- Timely triggers and augmentation of regulatory reporting.
- Predicting expenses of marketing, product development and claims paid as percentage of premium.

Cutting to the Chase: Mapping AI to the Real-World Insurance Value Chain

By Nigel Walsh
Partner, Deloitte

and Mike Taylor
Director, Deloitte

AI's (re)arrival is hailed by some to be the fourth industrial revolution, and its impact on insurance is no exception. In this chapter we don't attempt to reach consensus on the various definitions of AI. Instead, we seek to explain the applications of AI in insurance through the various layers of AI applications and logic, as illustrated in Figure 1. There are a number of functional capabilities that AI can deliver that mimics, or augments, human capabilities:

1. **Computer Vision:** analysis that enables the classification and tagging of objects within a video, image or any sensor reading. An example of this is the identification of an individual from a picture of their face or facial recognition.
2. **Natural Language Processing (NLP):** this encompasses both the understanding of written text and the generation of new text, for example, the understanding of questions and generation of text responses within a chatbot.
3. **Voice:** the transcription, enrichment and analysis of audio data, invariably resulting in NLP but with the additional information available during speech such as emotional tone.[1] An example of this is the augmentation of a chatbot to support spoken questions and responses.
4. **Internet of Things (IoT)**: processing of any sensor information from a network of devices connected through the internet. This category might include visual and voice data, so overlapping with (1) and (3), but also other data types, like temperature readings, and smells.

Enabling and Applying AI

AI has been around for more than 60 years, but its successes tend to be forgotten, or taken for granted. In fact, as soon as a task is credibly solved by AI it typically ceases to be considered "true AI" and efforts are focused on new areas.

Take optical character recognition (OCR): a vibrant area of AI research in the 80s, it is now typically relegated to a straightforward API call within software solutions that automates the digitization of forms, claims and other submissions, be it text or handwriting, with ever-increasing accuracy to import data more efficiently. Today, ImageNet Large Scale Visual Recognition Challenge (ILSVRC) submissions – a yearly benchmarking of computer vision systems – now easily outstrip human capabilities.[2]

AI is being cautiously integrated into a range of processes, with progressively greater autonomy enabled as the outcomes demonstrate greater reliability. At the trivial end of the spectrum is the purely deterministic (clearly defined and logical) robotic process automation (RPA) solution, but, as the quality of AI outputs improves, greater autonomy could be achieved.

[1]General audio data, as it pertains to non-verbal sounds such as music requires similar techniques but has not been included in this analysis owing to their relative lack of importance within insurance.

[2]A competition that required tagging of image data with multiple labels, for example the presence of a cat in a photo, where the progress in this benchmark was so impressive that in 2017 the completion was ended, with a new 3D image task and natural language generation now considered as appropriately difficult.

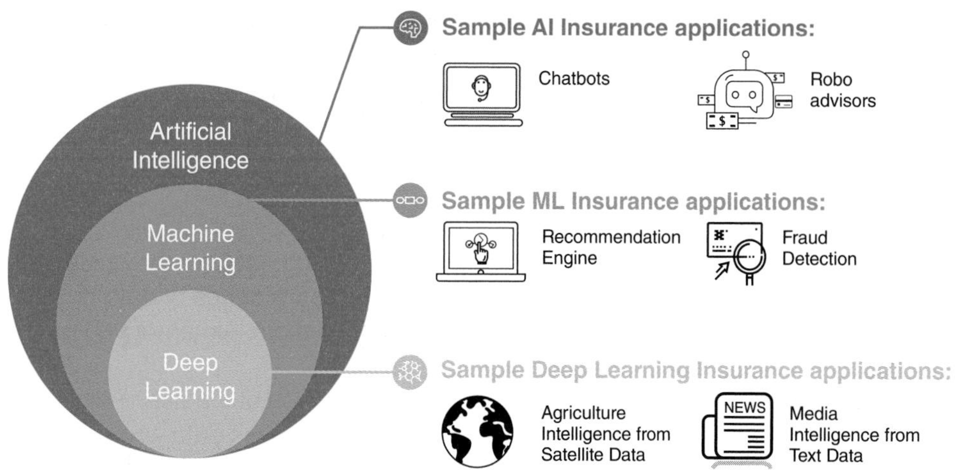

Figure 1: **The interrelation of various aspects of AI from an application perspective**

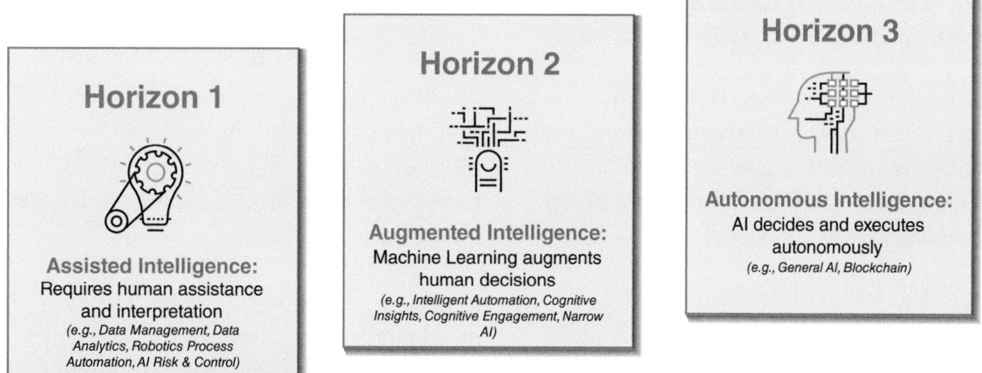

Figure 2: **The maturity progression of enterprise AI is illustrated by three distinct and progressive horizons**

As a next step there is assisted intelligence, the proposal of optimal decisions to human agents who make the final decision.[3]

Next is augmented intelligence, where algorithms are empowered to make decisions of which they are confident, but also defer to human agents where they are uncertain. Finally, there is autonomous intelligence, be it in a traditional machine learning model, or one enabled by reinforcement learning, where AI decides and executes autonomously. This is illustrated in Figure 2.

[3]It should be noted that Google's ubiquitous search engine is an example of decision support with the best matching websites proposed in rank order, but not decided upon by the search engine's algorithms (unless of course you count the "I'm feeling lucky" button).

Insurance is a highly regulated sector; this, coupled with the significant ethical and reputational risks posed by "rogue AI" implementations, explains the somewhat slower uptake of AI, especially in fully autonomous applications. Whilst this relatively cautious approach contrasts starkly with emergent big tech trendsetters, careful application and progression will ensure that AI is integrated safely within insurance; and combining insurance's proven existing models and approaches with new features derived from AI could show enormous promise.

History vs Present

Historically, insurers have been big users of quantitative or statistical applications. They have relied upon traditional and linear statistical modelling techniques and these models have mainly been used for pricing and calculating risk scenarios based on a series of human judgements, and including the relative maturity of GLM[4] based models used today.

However, on the flip side, a traditional insurer has built their business models on having onerous processes and legacy applications situated directly between the actual product, and the customer. This creates considerable friction and prevents incumbents from being able to deliver a seamless "click and buy service".

Insurance products retain a brand value of "protection", and so many customers remain willing to spend time answering detailed questions regarding their lifestyle, health conditions or the circumstances of their claims. This is despite the advent in the UK of price comparison websites and their quote engines turning multiple quotes in seconds.

Change is happening as we witness the ubiquity of data available through personal devices, and insurers embracing AI to disrupt their own processes, and indeed the route to market. Will this be quick enough to stop some of early disrupters like Lemonade and Metromile rebranding what insurance is for newer consumer generations? We believe insurers *can* disrupt their own value chain and offer a truly frictionless customer experience.

To start the process of identifying and applying AI in areas with the potential to transform the business, the key question to ask is, where are high volumes of data being consumed, managed and controlled by more human-driven processes and algorithms?

The key adoption of the use of cloud computing has also allowed the collation of mass data which has resulted in the ability of high levels of computation to be executed in seconds. Analysing masses of structure and unstructured data using these techniques makes it possible to exploit data sources that previously were too costly to harness at scale.

The key benefit to the use of AI is the reduction or removal of the need for humans to input or interpret these data streams such that they can be analysed algorithmically. This change radically alters the return on investment (ROI) of data capture making highly granular ground truth data available at a fraction of the previous cost.

However, until the application of AI can truly be "truly human", and regulation permits the placing of more trust in such applications, the use of more traditional stochastic modelling will work hand in hand with newer AI disruptors.

Meantime, insurers are increasing the awareness of the use of AI disrupters amongst their teams. We are also seeing more of a cultural change in the business and coming from the leadership level, rather than as technical or process change.

Aviva's Quantum Team, for example, are looking to create a global team of data scientists and provide the environments and training to nurture the best talent to build a deep, data-driven

---

[4] General linear model, a family of traditional statistical techniques that rely upon linear combinations of variables; examples include logistic regression and ordinary least squares regression.

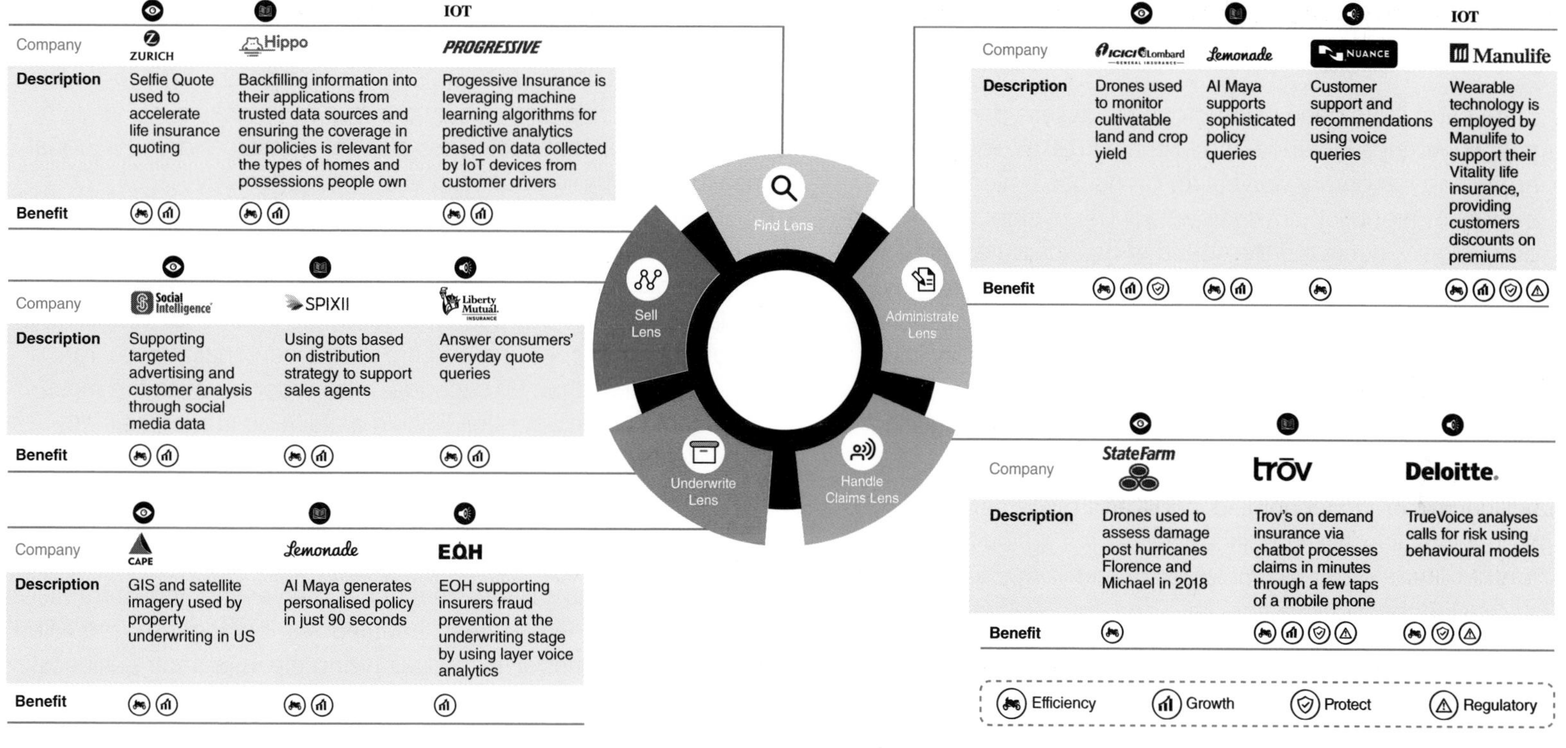

Figure 3: Example of AI in action across the insurance value chain

understanding of their customers. As Figure 3 shows, insurers around the globe are employing AI-curated data at an unprecedented pace.

Below we explore a sample of these use cases in more detail, comparing and contrasting the historic information-gathering processes with the modern approaches.

Computer Vision

Establishing the "ground truth" is critical for underwriting and claims process; site surveys have been a mainstay for insurance risk engineers. Historically, these tasks were performed manually, a costly and often dangerous activity. The advent of drone[5] and computer vision technology supports information gathering at unprecedented speed, accuracy, granularity and safety.

In place of scaling ladders to inspect a property, or treacherous travel to and through disaster zones to assess damage, a remote control drone can be employed from the safety of an engineer's

[5] According to Goldman Sachs, the easing of drone regulation in the US by the FAA in 2016 has been followed by a significant increase in the number of insurers adopting this technology, with an estimated 17% of commercial drone usage associated with insurance activities in 2018.

vehicle, perhaps even hundreds of miles away. Example applications of this technology:

1. State Farm have been using drones to assess damage post hurricanes Florence and Michael in 2018, with the FAA approving temporary waivers for drone use beyond the line of sight of the "pilot". This temporary line of sight waiver dramatically increased the speed of data capture, with as-the-crow-flies reconnaissance from drones capable of rapidly obtaining data on event severity, in turn improving resource allocation and finally customer outcomes. This facility is of particular importance in natural disasters, where damage to local infrastructure (e.g. flooding) compounds the logistical challenge of capturing data at scale.
2. ICICI Lombard have applied drone and computer vision technology in India, specifically within the agricultural insurance market. Here, drone technologies provide rapid and unbiased assessments of cultivatable land and crop yield achievable. In a country where droughts and flood are commonplace, the speed and responsiveness of claim adjustment teams is a massive differentiator.
3. Skyglyph (formerly known as Daterion) and Cape Analytic, InsurTech ecosystem players, provide image-based intelligence for Insurance. By using a combination of drone technology, satellite image and GIS (geographic information systems) techniques they provide data for the entire insurance value chain, primarily supporting underwriting and claims processing. Their entrance into the market supports access to data that would have previously been unthinkable for smaller players, eliminating the barrier to entry that would typically exist for such sophisticated technology.

Voice and NLP

Reducing the cost of interactions with customers has long been a business goal – let's address our expense ratio! Chatbots represent the next stage of this evolution, conferring several key benefits over traditional human agents. A chatbot is available 24/7 and able to scale effortlessly, dramatically reducing the risk of customer wait times while simplifying load balancing efforts. This is particularly relevant in the more mundane tasks such as data capture, a task that customers and call operators dread in equal measure. Example applications of this technology:

1. Lemonade have made extensive usage of AI-powered chatbots to simplify and expedite the insurance process with brokers; claims agents have been replaced with bots. Their Maya bot is capable of processing and creating a personalized insurance policy in less than 90 seconds, a tall order for even the most diligent human operator. Should a claim be made, their Jim bot reviews claims, using an ensemble of over 18 anti-fraud algorithms to assess risk. Simple claims are approved and paid out in seconds; more complicated claims are handed over to the company's human team for review. While a substantial number of these claims still require manual intervention, this progressive automation of the process, coupled with Lemonade's simplified subscription model, is revolutionizing the insurance business in the US.
2. Allstate uses a chatbot called Allstate Business Insurance Expert (ABIE, pronounced Abby)[6] to provide real-time access and insight into insurance products relevant to small business owners. Originally developed for Allstate agency owners in 2015, it was used with great success as an assistant in the quoting and issuance of insurance products.

   In 2018, it was extended to support Allstate's wider customer base where it has been an unqualified success. In a large part this is down to the platform's scalability, with a dynamically evolving knowledge base that is updated via ABIE's experience with small business owners. This knowledge base comprises

[6] www.prnewswire.com/news-releases/allstate-business-insurance-shares-an-innovative-resource-to-help-small-business-owners–consumers-with-top-of-mind-questions-300653033.html.

a taxonomy of key concepts and terms, curated and tagged to support rapid searches.

3. SPIXII is a dedicated chatbot platform to help insurers improve interactions with their customers, for example Zurich's "Zara", and allowing agents to focus on important client interactions.

Internet of Things

The availability of near-unlimited new sources of data is radically altering how insurers and their customers interact. The Internet of Things (IoT) is a suite of technologies that provide real-time monitoring of environmental variables, ranging from telemetry from a vehicle to an Apple watch's monitoring of human movement and heart rates through to insights and performance of machines and buildings.

Information that would previously have been considered absurdly impractical, obtrusive and even invasive is now readily accessible, benefiting customer and insurer alike. Why pay a premium for something that might be true about you, as opposed to your actual habits? Example applications of this technology:

1. Manulife was amongst the first insurers to start to incorporate behavioural economics-based nudges into their insurance processes, based on telemetry provided via IoT devices. Their Vitality programme, launched in 2016, has allowed customers to save substantial sums of money on their premiums by pursuing healthier lifestyles; for example, the monitoring (and encouraging) of the walking and running they perform. They have even gone as far as to reward users with a coveted Apple watch, with users able to "earn" back the watch through the pursuit of such activity, all the while being monitored by the watch.
2. Progressive Insurance has taken a similar approach, but with a focus on auto insurance. Previous insurance models were built upon inference, with the higher premiums charged based not on actual driving habits, but on inference thereof. For example, the gender of a driver has little credible effect[7] on their risk, but has served as a surrogate for the driving habits of the individual. Instead of relying upon such outdated measures, Insurers can now analyse data and use it to encourage drivers to improve their driver behaviours. Via their Snapshot mobile app, Progressive have collected over 14 billion miles of driving data, with information such as speed, acceleration, usage frequency and turning motions, creating a rich and personalized view of a drivers' habits for translation into a competitive, but risk-appropriate, premium.

Conclusion

The insurance sector is fiercely competitive – and the race to best apply AI will only perpetuate this. New features made possible by a disrupted information value chain enabled by AI present extraordinary opportunities to insurers, improving not only the efficiency of data capture but also the breadth, precision and personalization of the information. This new information value chain might resolve the historical conflict of enhancing customer experience and retention, whilst simultaneously satisfying the market's demand for ever-lower prices. But however you look at this, we are looking at the tip of the iceberg: the future differentiator that matters for insurance will be between those that have successfully leveraged AI, and those that have not.

[7] Nor can it be legally used, based on a European Court of Justice ruling in 2011.

Payments

4

PAYMENTS

Global volume of online payments setting to increase by 11% a year between 2015 and 2020

Consumers want seamless experiences and AI can bring invisible banking and payments, including guided by voice thanks to conversational AI

Opportunities:

- Fraud prevention and detection
- Smart re-routing as a business drive for efficiency and error reduction
- Better know-your-customer insights

Payments: from cost centre to a defining factor for business success

The payments industry is constantly evolving and Part 4 looks at how AI can revolutionize it at a time when people are no longer bound by borders or time zones. We know from our daily life that goods and services are purchased from across the globe, and at any time of the day. Research shows, for example, that night-times are when a lot of people shop online, especially for clothing and food.

For this reason, the old school system to detect fraud is no longer efficient: right now, what AI can help provide is real-time fraud detection to support the round-the-clock/round-the-globe payment sector. This part offers solutions and ideas around this dramatic shift, and the challenges and opportunities it presents.

The key issue is that as so many transactions happen at every moment, it is proving impossible for humans alone to provide oversight and control to ensure errors and fraud incidents are kept at a bearable level. This is where machine learning comes into play, as it allows the monitoring of activities and the early detection of anomalies to act on.

Furthermore, as AI is transforming the payments industry, consumers are increasingly pushing for more seamless experiences. If you add open banking and the PSD2 Directive, it becomes apparent that consumers will want to be able to safely and quickly make payments via their devices and across platforms without having to experience frictions.

Again, this is an area explored in this part with fascinating insights about the intersection between digital identity, security and privacy necessary to provide customers with the frictionless experience they are seeking.

And there are other ways AI is reshaping the payments industry. At a time of great competition for the retention of customers, AI can be used to provide recommendations about wise spending and savings by analysing the payment history of a client – this is a service that would be welcomed by clients if done in compliance with high privacy and transparency standards.

And, finally, great benefits can also involve the wider supply chain if, for example, an AI system were able to assess the likelihood of an invoice being settled right after it is issued. For companies, this would mean a massive step up in their logistics and overall efficiency across the supply chain.

This part explores all this, and beyond. This valuable knowledge can be a source of learning and understanding of the possibilities ahead of us.

Artificial Intelligence: The Next Leap Forward in the Payments Revolution

By Tamsin Crossland
Senior Architect, Icon Solutions

The financial payments sector is undergoing a revolution, leading to an increase in the volume of digital payment transactions across the world. In emerging markets, especially in Southeast Asia, this is due to a rapid increase in smartphone ownership and improved internet access. In Europe and the USA, the development of new technologies driven by open banking in the European Union, along with the growing use of contactless payments and e-wallets are leading to ever-increasing numbers of digital transactions.

This rise in digital transactions is further increased by artificial intelligence, with both virtual assistants and recommendation engines generating additional sales. Additionally, the emergence of faster payment technologies enables settlements to be performed within seconds. This increase in payment volume and speed means that existing manual labour-intensive fraud detection processes are proving inadequate.

Meanwhile, machine learning is finally becoming commercially viable, and has the potential to revolutionize fraud detection. Although machine learning has existed since the 1950s, the technology has only recently become commercially viable due to the increase in processing power of computers predicted by Moore's Law and the emergence of big data.

Machine learning is a technology built using artificial neural networks that are based on the internal structure of the brain, which consists of interconnected neurons, individual cells that receive signals from other cells via the dendrite (the input) and then pass them through the cell body which may pass the signal to other neurones via axons (the output). Within artificial neural networks, neurones are modelled by interconnected "nodes", which trigger an output signal when a certain value is reached.

With machine learning, patterns of behaviour can be created by adjusting the weights within an artificial neural network; for the first time since the creation of Babbage's Analytical Engine, a human-built machine can learn behaviour without having been given precise instructions on how to behave. Instead, machine learning "learns" behaviour by adjusting the weights given to nodes within an artificial neural network as data is loaded. In fraud detection, this ability to detect patterns from a data set can lead to detection of previously-unknown fraud techniques and much faster detection of new fraud techniques.

There are two main techniques for machine learning:

- Supervised learning
- Unsupervised learning.

Supervised learning is the most commonly used technique in machine learning. With supervised learning, an artificial neural network will be "trained" using multiple sets of inputs and outputs (results). As each set of input and desired output is loaded, the weights within the neural network are adjusted.

Let us consider the following example which is based on the old Western movie tradition of "goodies" wearing white hats and "baddies" wearing black hats.

The first set of input and output is shown in Figure 1.

The input is an image of a person with a white hat and the desired outcome is the first output, a "goodie". In order to load the image, it would be converted into an array that represents each pixel with a numeric value. This array for the image would then be loaded into the leftmost row of nodes, the input layer. On the rightmost row of nodes, the desired result would be that the first node (the "goodie") is triggered.

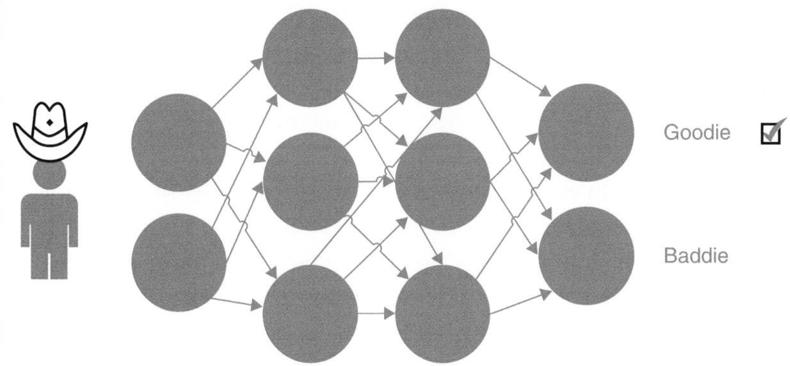

Figure 1: Training a Machine Learning model with an image of a "goodie"

The learning process involves the neural network adjusting the weights (in Figure 2) so that the input results in the desired output.

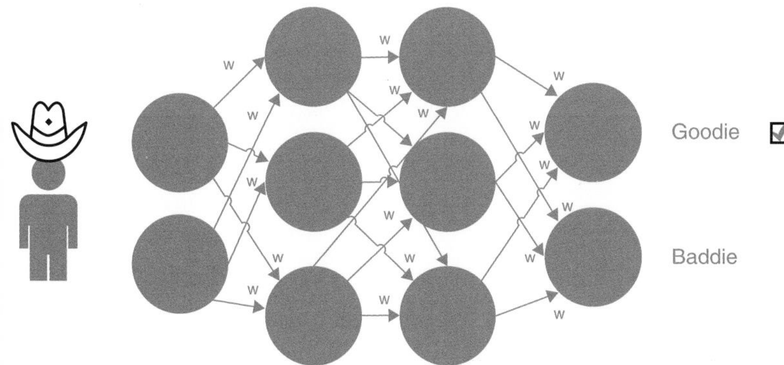

Figure 2: Adjustment of weights during the learning process

As more sets of inputs and outputs are loaded during the learning process, the weights will be further adjusted and the accuracy should improve.

Figure 3 shows another set of inputs and outputs that includes an image of somebody wearing a black hat and that the desired outcome is to return the second value ("baddie").

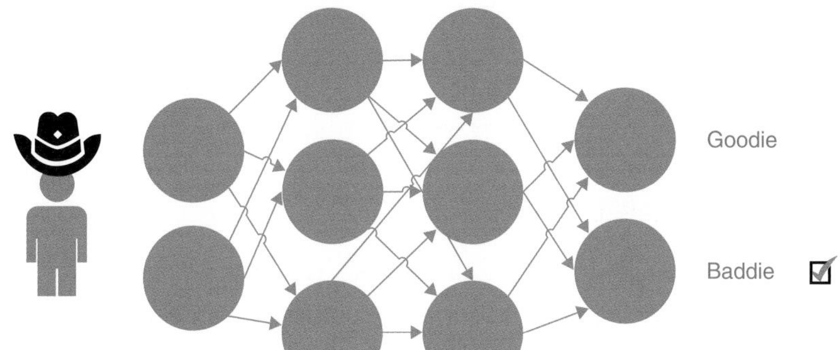

Figure 3: Training a Machine Learning model with an image of a "baddie"

With sufficient training, the weighting configuration should be such that the neural network determines that a black hat means the person is classified as a "baddie", whilst a white hat means the person is a "goodie".

It should be noted that the neural network has not been given specific instructions on what a hat or a person is; the network is only learning its behaviour by adjusting its internal weights according to combinations of numeric representations of the pixels that constitute an image along with the desired outcome.

This simple example illustrates one of the advantages of using machine learning in fraud detection: patterns can be detected that may not have been noticed before, in the same way that there may be people that have not heard of the tradition in Western movies of "baddies" wearing black hats. A neural network may thus be able to detect a new fraud technique faster than human analysis.

By contrast, in unsupervised learning the outcomes are not specified; in the example the outcomes of "goodie" or "baddie" are not supplied. Instead the unsupervised system would group together related items. In the example, the unsupervised system should highlight the hat as a grouping criterion.

In addition to detecting fraud, machine learning can be applied to the know-your-customer (KYC) and anti-money laundering (AML) processes, to spot inconsistencies and patterns undetectable by manual processes, especially when there are highly complicated links with ultimate beneficial owners (UBOs), politically exposed persons (PEPs) or prohibited states.

The ability to rapidly detect patterns from big data can also be used as an upselling tool, to suggest customer requirements and identify when there is the risk of losing a customer.

While the ability to learn from data is extremely powerful, there is a risk that the data may contain biased data which could result in prejudiced behaviour. For example, there have been cases where an organization has historically been more inclined to recruit candidates of a specific race or gender; in that case, machine learning would be at risk of inheriting that bias from the data. Given this risk and the difficulty of analysing weights within a neural network compared to inspecting code, testing needs to include ensuring that the system does not display bias.

With the ability to detect previously unseen patterns of fraud and to detect new patterns of fraud more quickly, the advantages of deploying machine learning are now accepted in most financial organizations. This ability to detect patterns can also be applied across the financial sector whether it is to identify new sales opportunities or to detect customers that are at risk of moving their business to another organization. At a time when the payments industry is seeing ever-increasing volumes of digital payments and the emergence of faster payments, machine learning is emerging as a highly beneficial technology to the payments revolution.

Frictionless Payments: If or When?

By Theodore Lloyd
Innovation Consultant, Axis Corporate

Amazon Go represents a step change in how payments are handled at point of sale, and provides a revolutionary customer experience. You can enter the store, pick up any product and leave, knowing your account will be charged. No need to fumble with cash or cards. The payment is entirely invisible. Invisible payments as a business model are expected to be worth $78 billion by 2022,[1] but to achieve this – and to truly impact the payments market – the key issue of security needs to be overcome. Customers' primary concern when making payments is ease of use (the reduction of friction) as we have witnessed by the rapid increase in contactless payments. Security is certainly a major concern, but it consistently comes afterwards. It is the payments providers that face the regulatory burdens, thus bearing responsibility to maintain security. Truly frictionless payments require advanced security systems, systems that can authenticate a customer and their payment method without causing friction in their customer journey. This requires a fundamental rethink in how we authenticate and secure payments, moving from static to dynamic data, and from event-based authorization to continuous assessment.

Today's Security Paradigms Will Not Suffice Tomorrow

Security systems for payments are built around the concept of multifactor authentication. The user needs to combine two of the following: "what I know", i.e. password or PIN; "what I possess", i.e. card or device; "who I am", i.e. biometrics; and, increasingly, "where I am". There are, of course, exceptions to this rule. Contactless card payments, which rely solely on "what I possess", represent a risk, as a stolen card could be used by anyone. To mitigate this risk, contactless payments are capped.

Card payments above the contactless threshold are secured through PIN numbers – the card is "what I possess", the PIN "what I know". While this offers more security than traditional card signatures, it is a point of friction. The customer must present their card, insert their PIN and wait for their payment to process. The PIN number must be memorized, and it is vulnerable to fraud and theft by over-the-shoulder attacks.

E-wallets have been mooted as a means of reducing friction in a secure way. Contactless payments can be made with a device that is secured by biometrics. While this would in theory speed up the payment journey, in practice e-wallets are still limited by contactless payment limits. Furthermore, biometrics are vulnerable, as they use static data which can be stolen or mimicked. Moreover, static data requires a specific "authorization event" – a customer looks into a facial scanner, or touches a fingerprint reader. This still inserts significant friction into the process – for example, consider how frustrating e-passport gates are, or unlocking a phone with a wet finger.

Ultimately, biometrics are little different to using passwords – secure, but not foolproof, and still cause friction in the payment journey – with one additional caveat, and that is that we cannot change our biometrics should they become compromised.

Invisible, Precise, Highly Robust Authentication

So, how do we create secure and frictionless payments channels? The answer lies in dynamic authentication, the best example of which is behavioural biometrics.

[1] www.iotm2mcouncil.org/juninvis.

Behavioural biometrics is the measurement and use of human behavioural patterns as a means of identification and authorization. This can take many different forms, from gait to typing style. This data is dynamic – detection of pressure across a screen over time, as opposed to an image of a fingerprint; or looking at angles made by a leg while someone walks, as opposed to a facial image.

The strength of behavioural biometrics comes from the continuous analysis of vast amounts of behavioural metadata. The number of parameters measured is limited only by the sensors used, and the sophistication of the algorithms that learn from and decipher this data. This complexity in the data sets underpinning behavioural biometrics makes it extremely difficult for an outside agent to compromise – the patterns identified in data sets with so many dimensions are impossible for a human to identify, and there is no way to train a working algorithm without access to the specific user's metadata.

It is only through machine learning that we can unlock the possibilities of behavioural biometrics. The algorithms used are complex, as they cannot be pre-trained to identify patterns: to identify a specific user, they must analyse that user specifically. As such, behavioural biometric algorithms must continuously train on the same data they are using for identification.

A simple example of how a behavioural algorithm can work might look like this:

- Select behaviour that is to be analysed (e.g. typing data).
- Break up the behaviour into its component parts (e.g. key precision, weighting, general typing speed – this will typically encompass a very wide range of data points).
- Determine the frequency/value for each determinant for the specific user.
- Combine these results in a user profile.
- Apply a similarity measure between the generated profile and current behaviour.
- Determine a threshold value for generating an alert.
- Verify user based on current behaviour against the profile, accounting for the threshold value.

As this simple model shows, there are multiple algorithms working, each underpinned by different machine learning methods. First, a user profile is created – this is a form of unsupervised learning, taking the relevant user meta-data, identifying patterns, and building a profile. The type of unsupervised algorithm best suited will vary depending on the behaviour being analysed, as different behavioural metadata can vary significantly in terms of type and relationship. This profile can be trained continuously, and as such the more the user interacts with the relevant device, the more precise the user profile can become. Secondly, current usage data is analysed – this is still through unsupervised learning, but differs from user profile generation in that the data is time-limited. Patterns must be identified from current usage data – which means that these will never have the degree of precision of the user profile. Thirdly, a similarity measure is applied – this means analysing both the user profile and the current usage data to determine a functioning margin of error. Just as the patterns within the metadata are complex and vary significantly from individual to individual, so also does the margin of error. As such this must also be generated dynamically for each user. Finally, the user profile is analysed against current usage data to authenticate the current user. This algorithm takes into account the margin of error that has been determined to create a probability of the user being correct. This probability is used to determine whether an alert should be generated.

The strength of this model is continuous assessment of a user, both in terms of authenticating based on current device usage/ sensor exposure, and also in terms of refinement of the user profile authenticated against. This happens entirely in the background and requires no authentication event to interrupt the user's purchase journey.

While it takes time to generate a precise user profile – requiring other security measures in the interim – once a precise enough user profile is available, behavioural biometrics offers a means of authentication that is invisible (it requires no authorization event), is precise (very low likelihood of false positives), and is highly robust (an almost negligible likelihood of false negatives – i.e. security breaches).

Rethinking Authentication

Unlocking secure frictionless payments requires a rethink in how we approach authentication. Static authentication introduces friction and insecurity. Passwords, PINs and fingerprints will need to give way to constant analysis. Security based on limited parameters that can be mimicked (physically or digitally) must be replaced with complex data sets that generate highly individual and complex relationship groupings. This requires the utilization of extensive behavioural metadata created by the devices and sensors we constantly interact with.

Not all static security measures will be rendered obsolete – devices, or non-intrusive biometrics (e.g. facial recognition) will be key to spotting which user is to be identified by the behavioural algorithm. And even passwords, PINs and fingerprints will have their place, albeit relegated to a secondary measure, used if the dynamic authentication algorithm cannot make a positive match within the accepted margin of error.

Frictionless payments are still far from becoming the norm. Before they can be rolled out extensively we will need significantly more connected devices that can collect the requisite metadata. The area where behavioural biometrics currently operates is principally in device security, where it is already possible to collect extensive usage data. However, with precipitously declining sensor costs, and the rapid growth in IoT devices, the next decade will see an exponential increase in access to behavioural metadata.

Dynamic authentication use cases now show that truly frictionless payments are not a question of if, but when.

Big Data, AI and Machine Learning: How to Unlock Their Potential in the New Payment Environment

By Omri Dubovi
VP of Product Management, SafeCharge, a Nuvei company

The role of payment and its impact on organizations has evolved considerably over the last few years, from being purely a commodity to becoming a strategic business parameter.

Businesses have realized that focusing on making their payments process life cycle efficient can be extremely profitable, with the global volume of online payments set to increase by 11% a year between 2015 and 2020 (source: Cap Gemini & BNP Paribas report).

While this boom in online payments brings a wealth of opportunity for businesses, it also raises some serious challenges. Merchants now need to worry about increased fraudulent activities as well as increased competition.

In a world where technology is evolving rapidly, it is necessary for businesses to keep up with technological progress in order to stay relevant. Artificial intelligence (AI) and machine learning (ML) are creating new opportunities for businesses in healthcare, IT and even manufacturing. A conscious use of ML and AI in the payments space can be a solution to a wide range of business complexities and a smart tool to fuel further growth.

Payments, a Wealth of Data

Many consumers might not realize, but every transaction made contains a wealth of information for the merchant they are buying from. During an online payment process customers are sharing what they bought, the platform they used, device model, operating system, time zone, general location, delivery address, device ID, mobile fingerprints and more. If businesses input this data into a payment system that uses AI or ML, they can collect this meaningful information, analyse it and produce tangible benefits, such as increased security, better customer experience and more sales.

While there are many benefits from integrating a payments environment with AI and ML, this chapter will discuss four of the most interesting uses with the purpose of showcasing how businesses can leverage the collected data to detect and prevent fraud, design successful payment processes with smart routing, improve customers' user experience and provide deeper intelligence for merchants.

A Tool to Combat Fraud

The increase in online payments brings the unavoidable risk of digital-payment fraud. A traditional rule-based – and largely manual – fraud detection system tries to spot criminal activities by monitoring a range of variables, such as location, the type of merchant and the amount being spent. For example, if a customer suddenly appears to be spending more than usual on a given item with an unfamiliar merchant in a previously unvisited location, this activity will most likely be flagged as a possible fraudulent transaction. However, the problem with the standard fraud detection system is that the rules are too rigid, and in today's highly digitally dependent world, many purchases do not fit into a rigid rule-based model of fraud detection. Using an AI-based system, businesses can perform fraud checks in the blink of an eye. A financial institution that integrates AI and ML modules into its payment infrastructure can not only detect fraudulent activities in real time, but also recognize anomalies and successfully distinguish and predict fraudulent transactions.

The flip side of this, however, is that AI is only as good as the data it receives. When poor data is fed into a system, all that an organization can expect is poor output. Therefore, a high level of due diligence is required to make sure that the data which is being used has been properly governed, otherwise it could incorrectly categorize customers' risk scores, causing a frustrating customer experience, and high chances of fraud.

Most critically, systems can learn from each transaction, constantly improving and becoming more effective. The use of AI can allow payments companies to look at transaction data in new and more effective ways, growing the amount of successful legitimate transactions while shrinking the number of illegitimate ones.

Smart Routing

Payment technology can do more than manage payments. Intelligently designed systems have the ability to not only increase conversions but also provide various ways to optimize the payments journey, resulting in security and business growth. Each transaction on a business platform needs to be approved by financial entities, such as acquiring and issuing banks. A payments system that is integrated with ML and AI technology can use smart routing technology that intelligently calculates various parameters and routes transactions to specific acquirers to maximize approvals. To ensure no transaction loss, soft declined transactions (tech failure, time-out, etc.) are automatically rerouted. For businesses with more than one acquirer, transactions can be routed based on "pricing" or "acceptance rates". The routing rules are designed to meet individual business requirements. ML can maximize card payments acceptance rates by ensuring that transactions will go through the optimal route based on a merchant's payment preferences; efficiency is increasingly improved and processing time for payments can be tangibly reduced, in turn decreasing any human error.

Getting to Know Your Customer

Through ML algorithms, payment companies can analyse data in new and innovative ways to better understand their customers. With AI and ML, payments companies can search rapidly and efficiently through their payments data beyond the standard set of factors like time, velocity and amount. ML can predict customers' behaviour and convert this knowledge into better customer segmentation. Cross-selling and upselling can be optimized by providing a single view of the cardholder data across multiple channels. Payments data – which include point-of-sale data, data collected from Google ads, and merchant sale site data – can all be used to predict trends. Merchants can then better understand what they should sell and how they should set it. For example, Harley Davidson, one of the most popular motorcycle companies in the world, used the AI tool to analyse existing customer data from the company's CRM. On analysing parameters like which customers had completed a purchase in the past, how much time they spend on the website, high-value customers, and so on, the AI tool was able to predict campaigns that would work, and those that wouldn't. By using AI, Harley Davidson was able to increase sales leads by 2930% in a span of three months.

Advanced Analytics for Merchants

Payment providers have been collecting large amounts of data for some time, and businesses are realizing that they can use this data to benefit merchants. ML algorithms can analyse transaction data to find patterns – seasonal dips in revenue, for example – and help business owners plan and compensate. They can also provide targeted marketing capabilities like reward programmes and analytical dashboards to help business owners manage their inventory, capture new sales and optimize their businesses for each consumer. By integrating ML and AI into the payments process, merchants have the possibility of seeing the entire picture, from the shop floor to stock rooms. Merchants can have a better understanding of what the clients want and, therefore, remain more profitable as a business.

Taken as a whole, AI holds many promises for payments technology companies by providing a more powerful payments product, driving consumers and merchants toward more digital commerce opportunities, and by creating a safer and more secure ecosystem. The potential of these technologies and how they transform the payments process and customers' experience will only grow in the coming years. Payments have evolved from being a cost centre to be a defining factor for business success, and the use of ML and AI can put the power back in merchants' hands for the future.

The Rise of Conversational AI Platforms

By Anna Maj
FinTech Leader, PwC

According to Gartner, conversational AI platforms will be the next big paradigm shift in information technology. They predicted that in 2020 the average person would have more conversations with bots than with their partner. Gartner also anticipates that by 2021, 15% of all customer service interactions will be handled solely by AI.[1] This may also hold true for banking and payment services. Voice agents will change the way consumers interact with brands, no matter whether retail, in the form of an enhanced interactive customer experience, or banking ones. The machine learning-based assistants can be particularly effective in the e-commerce domain, driving and enhancing seamless user's shopping experience. How does conversational AI transform payments as well as payment experience then? How do banks, payment companies and other financial players deploy bot technologies to grasp the opportunity of entering the area of voice-guided banking and payment services?

No doubt, bots may become irreplaceable in the service of banking and payments. Conversational AI can definitely improve customer experience, being exactly at the place where consumers, particularly younger generations, want to be – the voice-navigated and messaging platforms. There are a couple of the pain points within the financial industry that can be efficiently addressed by the voice assistants: search for information and waiting time. Consumers will not only be provided with adequate financial guidance, but also the waiting time to get a response to their questions and inquiries will be shortened, since bots can easily handle multiple customer sessions.

[1]Gartner, 2016, www.gartner.com/smarterwithgartner/gartner-predicts-a-virtual-world-of-exponential-change/.

Taking learnings from the Aino use case (a virtual banking agent introduced by the largest bank in Norway, DNB) together with the conversational AI technology provider Boost.ai, we see that consumers want to have a consistent experience across different channels and various interactions.[2] DNB automated 51% of all their chat conversations within six months of launch in June 2018 with Aino.[3] The conversational AI technology provider Lekta.ai is also applying their own NLP (natural language processing) as well as NLU (natural language understanding) capabilities to enhance the customer care experience by introducing complete chatbot solutions to leading banks, utilities and telco companies in Poland.

Response time is critical. It must be immediate. Consumers search for information, seek answers and they want them "now". Customers can't wait too long or can't wait at all. They often prefer and even choose an online chat over an email or phone conversation to interact with a bank, as they expect it to be instant. A human-operated chat is insufficient since it is too slow and not effective then. There is a continuing customer need for an instant response from the bank that can be satisfied by the virtual personal assistant. It automates user traffic as well as handles multiple simultaneous interactions with clients, optimizing and improving the comprehensive customer experience within banking services, making it instant and frictionless, as well as hassle-free. Bots should operate in a channel-agnostic customer care environment creating a solid base for a consistent customer experience within financial services. The concept of omnichannel banking, which has not been fulfilled to date, could demonstrate its full potential, thanks to using a natural interactive interface for communication and interaction, which is ultimately the voice, a new normal.

[2]Boost.ai, May 2019, "How conversational ai can significantly improve customer experience in the financial services industry": https://static1.squarespace.com/static/5c73f03e65019f38b4ba0ebe/t/5d0b5d36e1116b00016aecdf/1567674432904/customer-experience-conversational-AI-Guide.pdf.

[3]According to Boost.ai, February 2019: www.boost.ai/articles/how-norways-biggest-bank-automated-51-of-its-online-chat-traffic-with-ai.

Customer experience in banking will be brought to the next level soon, resulting in payments and other financial transactions becoming invisible. AI-powered bots can perform any type of digital payments: a card transaction, a cross-border transfer or a P2P money transfer, all in a frictionless, secure and fast manner via text or voice-based interfaces. When customers embark on talking to a vocal or chatbot, there are more interactions involved, since AI-powered assistants can lead human-like conversations. Banking and payments services can become more relational and conversational, which in turn puts banks and other financial services providers in front of the challenge to "get the conversation right".

The automation of transactional congestion is definitely of great value, but there is also a new perspective opening up: a move from improving accuracy of, e.g. speech recognition and other programming capabilities towards more interactive and engaging functionalities, such as deep learning and understanding users' moods and emotions. This could become a truly differentiating factor for banks in creating a customer value proposition. By going beyond the accuracy of information rendered as well as automation itself, the next level of customer experience can be unlocked, leading to the decision-making process served by virtual banking agents. The financial advice that is wanted most by consumers in the form of either wealth advisory or personal finance management[4] can be provided by insight-driven chatbots. Bots will also act as advocates to democratize banking services, not only through automation and cost reduction, but primarily thanks to granting access to a range of financial services that are not available for some segments of customers right now. By interacting with a voice agent, consumers will be in position to afford their own VPAs (virtual personal assistant) in the role of a financial advisor or a payment concierge. According to the PwC surveys, 38% of consumers agree that AI can offer a "superior one-to-one personalized experience".[5] That's why a human-like touch is of such importance.

Towards Invisible Banking and Payments

There will be a shift in payments and banking from the traditionally known GUI (graphical user interface), towards the CUI (conversational user interface) that can be navigated by voice, with practically a non-existent front-end. It will be integrated into mobile applications, websites, messaging platforms, but also to connected devices and IoT. Banking interactions will be invisible not only in the sense of applying the intuitive natural interface, but also in the context that the newly created voice or text touchpoints will be integrated in customers' daily life tasks, especially via connected devices and IoT, so they will be unnoticeable and transparent for consumers.

Within the conversational banking paradigm shift the user experience will be designed around a seamless and frictionless (front-end) interface. At the end of the day, customers may not need any screens at all. The proliferation of bots powered by the conversational AI and machine learning technologies will result in a radical change of customer experience towards invisible banking and payment services. We have been witnessing a shift towards mobile so far; and we are in process of shifting from mobile to voice, as an enhanced AI-driven interface transforming the customer journey throughout the financial services ecosystem arises.

---

[4]CBInsights, June 2019, "How can retail banks leverage AI?": https://www.cbinsights.com/research/report/retail-banks-ai/.

[5]PwC, "Bot.Me: A Revolutionary Partnership": http://pwcartificialintelligence.com/.

Two Dimensional Virtual Vertical Integration: Solving the Impossible SC Problem

By Sotiris Melioumis
CEO, SoNiceSoNice UK Ltd

Defining business behaviour is influenced by institutionalized ideas as well as rooted into solutions that previous generations have been deploying to address business problems.

You lack liquidity?...you ask your banker for a loan or a credit line

You experience late payments?...you buy trade credit insurance

You experience disproportional trade risk?...you stop selling on credit

You have high operational cost?...you hire consultants to lean engineer your business

Yesterday's solutions have become today's problems as business profitability is currently below 8%.[1,2,3]

Global insolvencies YOY growth stands at 6%.[4]

Nine out of ten startups will fail in within 10 years of foundation.[5] Same-profession wages inequality varies between $194 and $1864.[6] Institutionalized ideas are driving societies in the wrong direction.

The Cost to the Economy

Asking for a loan to cover your liquidity gap does nothing to correct the root cause of the problem. By using trade credit insurance, you incur cost, reduce your revenue potential and your customer base due to restrictions imposed by your insurer and you fail to address the root cause of the problem. By not selling on credit you will lose between 47% and 85% of your potential customers to your competitors. The way we organized our business processes and our banking systems to cope with transactions, the multiplicity and incompatibility of systems and software we use, the armies of administrators, accountants, financiers, IT engineers, legal teams, debt collectors...deprive the global economy from S43tn/y. This is more than twice the EU GDP.[7]

Businesses are open systems. They affect and are affected by their environments and by each other depending on their degree of exposure. Globalization, WTO rules, shifting societal needs, inflation, legislation, consumer confidence, new trends, technological breakthroughs and more affect performance. And businesses can do nothing about it. You can organize and lean engineer any business as best as you can, but from the moment the equilibrium of the business environment, or supply chain, is lost, the business is powerless to correct unaided. We need to stop thinking in terms of "my business" and "economics" and substitute terms like "our ecosystem" and "socio-economics" if we want to progress.

[1] http://www.aei.org/publication/the-public-thinks-the-average-company-makes-a-36-profit-margin-which-is-about-5x-too-high/.

[2] https://financialrhythm.com/profitability-margins-industry/.

[3] https://csimarket.com/Industry/industry_Profitability_Ratios.php.

[4] https://www.eulerhermes.com/en_global/media-news/news/global-insolvencies-2018.html.

[5] https://startupgenome.com/reports.

[6] https://shenglufashion.com/2018/03/04/wage-level-for-garment-workers-in-the-world-updated-in-2017/.

[7] https://www.imf.org/external/pubs/ft/weo/2018/02/weodata/weorept.aspx?pr.x=68&pr.y=11&sy=2017&ey=2018&ssd=1&sort=country&ds=.&br=1&c=946%2C137%2C122%2C181%2C124%2C918%2C138%2C964%2C182%2C960%2C423%2C935%2C968%2C128%2C939%2C936-%2C961%2C172%2C132%2C184%2C134%2C174%2C144%2C944%2C178%2C136%2C112%2C941&s=NGDPD%2CPPPGDP&grp=0&a=.

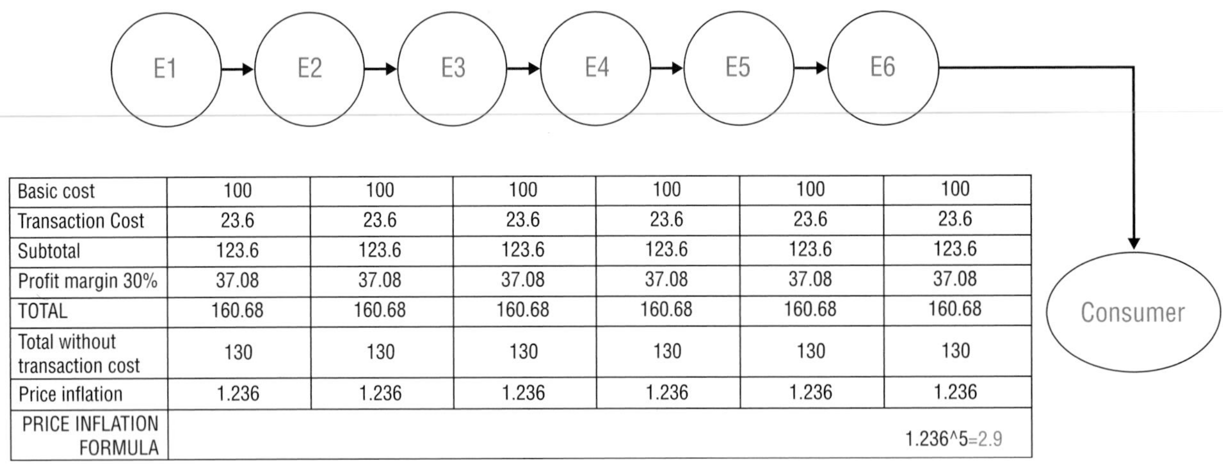

Basic cost	100	100	100	100	100	100
Transaction Cost	23.6	23.6	23.6	23.6	23.6	23.6
Subtotal	123.6	123.6	123.6	123.6	123.6	123.6
Profit margin 30%	37.08	37.08	37.08	37.08	37.08	37.08
TOTAL	160.68	160.68	160.68	160.68	160.68	160.68
Total without transaction cost	130	130	130	130	130	130
Price inflation	1.236	1.236	1.236	1.236	1.236	1.236
PRICE INFLATION FORMULA						1.236^5=2.9

Figure 1: Transaction cost impact on consumer prices

How Do Current Practices Inflate Consumer Prices? An Illustration

If we assume that Enterprise 1(E1) is selling to E2, and E2 to E3 and so on, with E6 selling finally to the consumer, and that the transaction cost between all entities is 23.6%, then the E2E inflation factor is 1.236^5= 2.9, i.e. almost 3 times more than it should be. Absorption of this cost by businesses caused profitability decline to <6%![8]

Introducing 2DVVI

Under 2DVVI, ERPs or accounting software for enterprises E1–E6 are connected to a platform and the existing trade terms between enterprises are coded into smart contracts. Algorithms are then trained to manage the holistic interests of all based on the relative value each is adding across the supply chain (SC). This transforms the previously disjoined SC into a single-entity trust-agnostic shared-interest-based virtual vertically integrated ecosystem. After this stage, when E6 is selling to the consumer, the receivables are redirected to the platform's algorithms that manage the smart contracts. They distribute the receivables across the entire SC. These actions may vary time-wise from instant to Tn. Distribution of receivables continues until the outstanding amount of debt remaining is zero. The system is fed with e-invoices issued and approved by the recipient (see Figure 2).

Equilibrium forms can be monosemantic (i.e. profitability based) or polysemantic (profitability, systemic liquidity, end product price, operational optimization, etc.) AI-based and optionally machine learning (ML)-enhanced. The above approach results in unprecedented benefits: operational optimization that can reach 93%, trade risk reduction of 73%, liquidities up by 300%,

[8] Assuming 25% of the cost is absorbed by the business and 75% is passed over to the buyer.

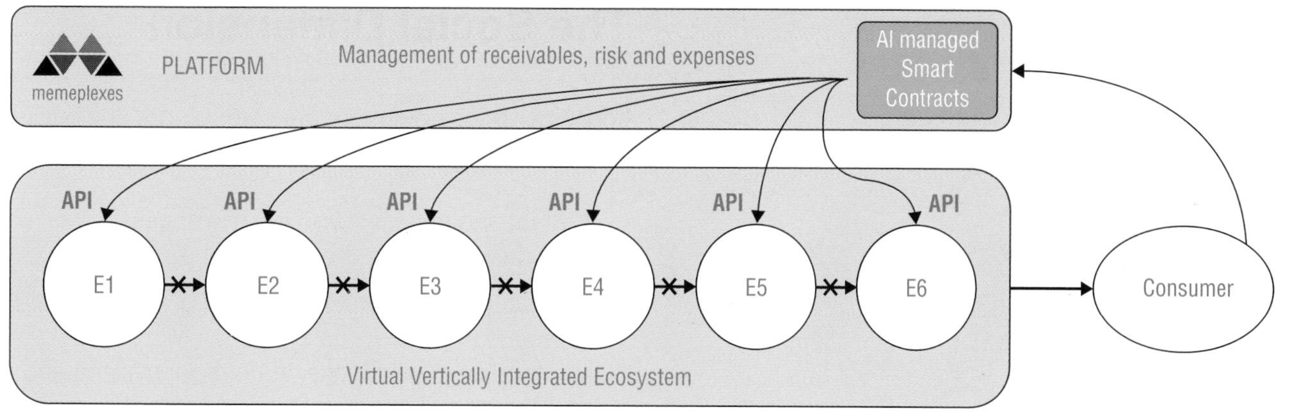

Figure 2: 2DVVI mechanism

profits multiply – problem solved. The virtual integration of just two companies can achieve significant economies of scale with the ecosystem still able to expand both up and downstream.

But It's Not Quite so Simple

Supply chains are mostly two-dimensional complex structures rather than linear. For that reason 2DVVI utilizes a two-step integration process:

- During Step 1, every linear supply chain (black and orange) is transformed into a monodimensional ecosystem. We assign to it algorithms plus ML routines to manage the intra-company smart contracts (see Figure 3).
- During Step 2, because all businesses belong to more than one supply chain, we train AIs to manage the equilibrium state of all interconnected monodimensional ecosystems.[9]

  We use trust-based blockchain structures to record and clear transactions within these ecosystems.[10]

2DVVI favours trust line structures because they can express mathematically the degree of internal or external interdependence between members of the (eco)system which may affect the equilibrium state. 2DVVI can be equally used within an enterprise allowing departments, individuals and stakeholders including non-monetary-based environment-bound ones to be considered parts of the ecosystem!

[9] https://en.wikipedia.org/wiki/Nash_equilibrium.

[10] https://ripple.com/files/ripple_consensus_whitepaper.pdf.

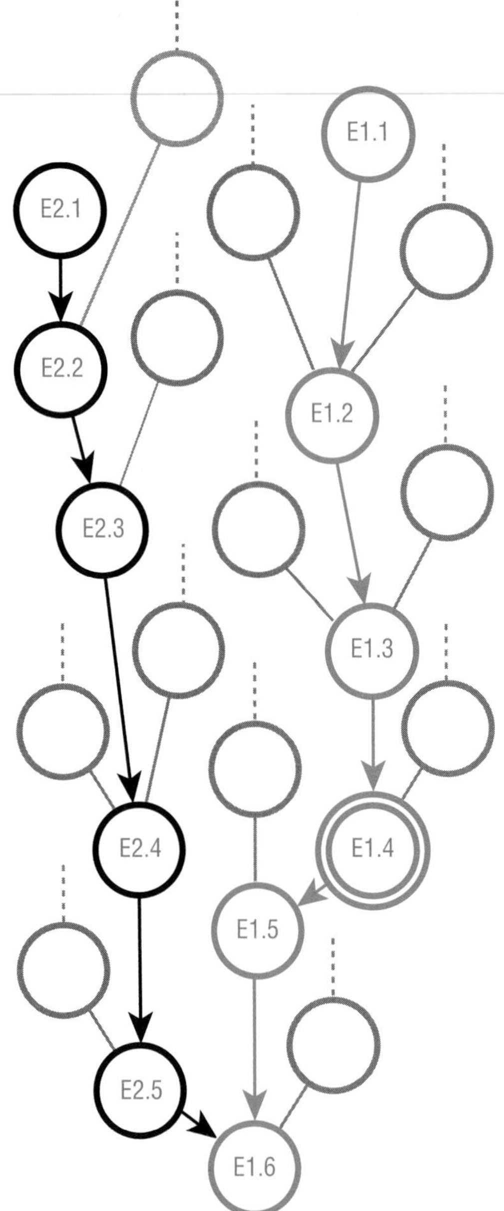

Figure 3: A 2D supply chain

The Social Dimension

2DVVI economies of scale achieve a great deal in deflating consumer prices but there are even bigger implications and benefits that may be derived:

- Product and services will become accessible to more people, lifting millions above the poverty line.
- Bankruptcies and foreclosures will gradually cease to exist.

With enterprises, institutions, state organizations and consumers being parts of one intertwined ecosystem, the value-add (easily defined) could be a route to addressing the pension gap problem. As employment and ownership will overlap, novel forms of start-ups may evolve. Creating an entrepreneurship-friendly environment will allow startups to join existing stable ecosystems benefiting by a ready-made supply chain and a customer base. Cross-border partnerships will allow the creation of novel forms of multinationals "governed" by WTO-level smart contracts. Novel forms of reduced-risk derivatives based on the value of linear or multidimensional ecosystems, trust-agnostic partnerships and the new novel forms of multinationals will appear. Product quality will inevitably improve and we will see a rise in new socio-economic models.

The business dimension will include:

- Enterprises recognized now as parts of a societal value chain and for the first time managed as such!
- Customers and stakeholders will blend into one, creating CRM 2.0.
- Alternative methods of payment, like the forthcoming b-Paid, the B2B2C platform, will eliminate instances of late and non-payments.
- AI-powered socio-economic integration will allow real-time payment of consolidated taxation.
- Trade rules will now be susceptible to lean engineering, allowing novel forms of trade to evolve.

And the banks will now have to choose between alternatives:

- Reduce charges in order to retain their customer base.
- Become the guardians and facilitators of the new ecosystems' processes.
- Create new products and services for the ecosystems or partner with FinTechs.
- Integrate with the ecosystems creating new forms of financial institution.

An AI-powered bright future awaits us all!

Investment and Wealth Management

5

Opportunities (and challenges) of AI in wealth management

AI driven innovation and efficiency:

- investment automation
- back/middle office automation
- content augmentation
- conversational banking

Examples of deployment of machine learning:

- risk profile
- client screening
- client attrition
- product matching

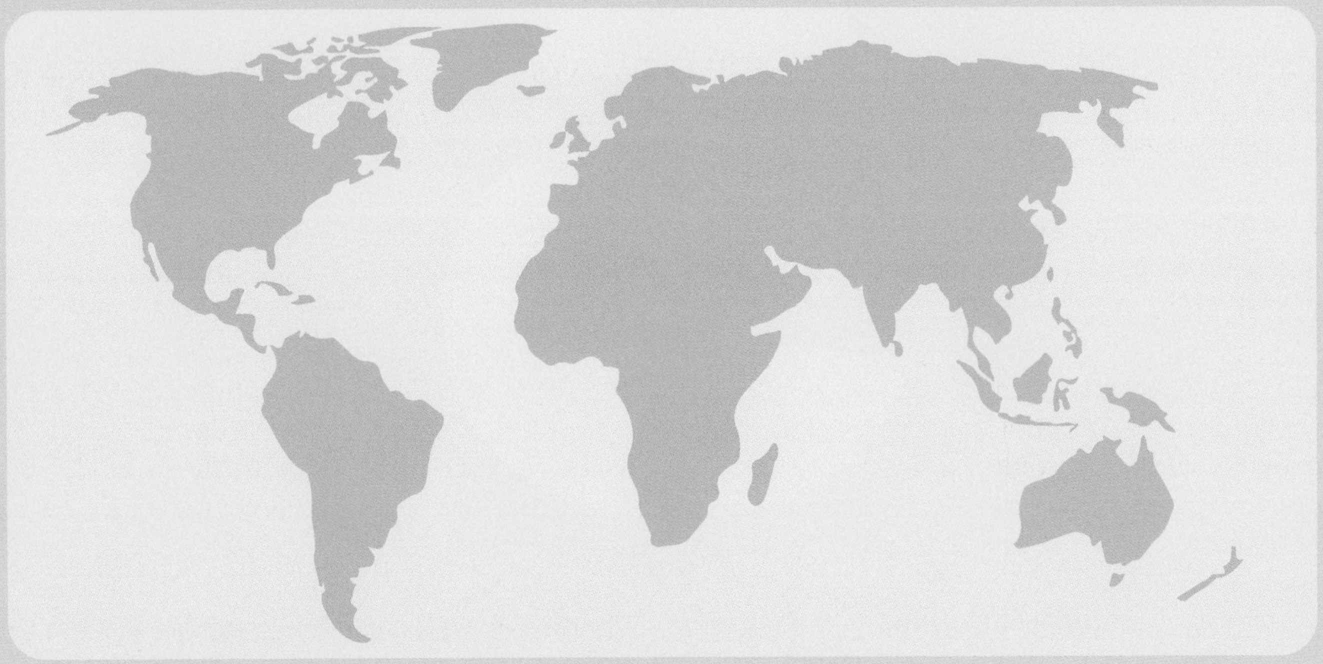

1. Towards responsible social and environmental governance ⟶ can AI support better economic activity?
2. Fluctuations: is there a pattern in the chaos?
3. Quantum computing and AI: what happens with trading at speed of light?

Is AI the future of investment management? Part 5 will present a wide range of perspectives on this topic to help professionals navigate through the promises AI holds.

According to the 2017 Financial Stability Board report, "pure" AI and ML players had about $10 billion in assets under management, but this figure has grown rapidly since then as the scope for the use of AI and ML in portfolio management widened.

This part presents examples of real and possible uses of AI in this field, alongside challenges, risks and opportunities. The reader will be able to navigate through cases of how AI systems can support predictive analytics, trade processing and automate data collection for investment and wealth managers.

The use of AI in predictive analytics is flourishing. These AI systems can provide real help to traders and enable them to make better and faster pricing decisions. Algorithms can also be used to gather and analyse a huge volume of market information to identify better investment opportunities as well as reduce risks.

Key issues remain but do not override the general enthusiasm and positive approaches readers will find in these pages. With AI entering every corner of society, questions around the future of the profession among investment professionals cannot be underestimated. However, a view emerges from these pages, and that is that the deployment of AI will speed up the execution side of activities thus being able to provide answers to investment decisions in a fraction of the time currently needed. With the right digital transformation strategies in the investment management industry, these systems will in the end increase productivity and financial success for investors, investment management companies and private banks as the cost of managing portfolios for institutional, high-net-worth and retail clients will progressively decrease while the returns will increase.

Ultimately, technology will allow customers to have access to data-based decisions and greater insights, and all this will increase confidence and trust. In a sense, and this is what emerges from this part, investment management is an area where cooperation between humans and machines will bring great benefits.

It is certainly true that AI has been used in trading algorithms for years, but the huge amount of research that has now gone into it means AI could reap even greater efficiencies in investment management in the years to come.

The True Value of AI to Transform Push/Pull Wealth Management Offers

By Paolo Sironi
Author and IBM Industry Academy member

Financial services have been in turmoil since 2008 after the default of Lehman Brothers. The most recent years were marked by corporate restructuring, consolidation of regional banks, toughening of capital requirements, more demanding compliance rules, broad simplification of financial products and, last but not least, the emergence of a vibrant FinTech ecosystem fostering digital innovation. Essentially, the cost/income ratios of established firms appear unsustainable when compared to existing and future dynamics of economic, regulatory and digital frameworks. First, interest rate margins (lending operations) don't seem to add a significant contribution to shareholders' value in the Western world after the price for risk. Second, global payments are under continuous digital attack by Chinese technology champions and, most recently, by the Apple partnership with Goldman Sachs and Facebook's Libra. Third, intermediation margins based on wealth management relationships (investment and insurance products) are also suffering from a progressive compression of commissions and embedded fees, affecting capital markets in return.

Many blame digital disintermediation, others artificial intelligence or exponential technologies to be the source for disruption. I honestly believe that this is not accurate. Current commoditization of financial products is primarily a consequence of excessive asymmetries of information that underlined most of the banking trading models with clients. As a matter of fact, the 2008 banking showdown was only the tip of an iceberg whose roots sink deeply into the 1980s deregulation of financial markets and the internationalization of finance, which ignited a process called "financial innovation" (structured products, hedge funds, securitizations) and enabled market players to optimize product-driven economic models to maximize "aggressively" their profit-making with end clients: families, municipalities and small and medium-sized enterprises. The depth of the asymmetry of information was particularly evident in investment management, since end clients tend to be unaware price-takers while banks and financial advisors are undisputed price-makers.

The progressive reduction of interest rate and intermediation margins jeopardized the economic sustainability of many medium-sized transactional banks. Financial services are therefore asked to fight their game by considering two main strategies: one is about volume, the other is about value. Clearly, on one side a strategy based on accelerating volumes requires significant M&A and digitization efforts, knowing that the ultimate competition will not oppose banks to banks or banks to FinTech, but open banking platforms against big technology operators like Ant Financial, WeBank, Amazon or Facebook. Further, on the other side the strategic transformation of business models from *product centricity* to *client centricity* is a true Copernican revolution of incentives and workflows. Therefore, competing on value requires much deeper understanding of FinTech capabilities and clients' biology to craft a suitable hybrid model that can generate differentiating value for clients and higher-than-average margins for financial firms.

Therefore, the digital difference between volume strategies and value ambitions in wealth management is not restricted to front office transformation, that is, frictionless experiences or modern marketing language. Instead, it pertains to the essence of the revenue generating mechanism. Transaction-based investment management is a product-centric model: banks collect embedded commissions and product fees when investors allocate their wealth or roll their investments. In contrast, service-driven wealth management operations require the industrialization of higher-margin relationships by packaging investment solutions into a service called "financial advice". Advice remuneration is progressively disjointed from offered products and clients will be asked to pay for this transparently and happily. Indeed, clients themselves seem to be unprepared to identify real value and assume higher responsibility for investment decision-making.

As such, FinTech and, in particular, artificial intelligence are not the real cause of business margins disruption but an amazing opportunity for financial services to navigate these uncharted waters and reach successfully the new shore of value-based digital banking.

Given the challenges ahead, financial intermediaries seem to be largely unprepared to compete on value-generation for clients. This has resulted in a bigger emphasis on testing FinTech solutions aimed at digitizing distribution channels for investment products, thus competing on cost convenience and frictionless access to digital offers. History has already shown that only hybrid models can help the wealth management industry to move forward, also on volume-driven strategies but most importantly on value-based offers. It is therefore paramount to understand how artificial intelligence can add value into this transformation involving both humans and digital technology.

At a time when the value chain between manufacturers and distributors gets shorter every day, artificial intelligence can primarily add value (or subtract costs) according to the following major use cases:

- Investment automation
- Back/middle office automation
- Content augmentation
- Conversational banking.

The growth of passive investing has accompanied a progressive reduction of embedded commissions, also due to more demanding regulations like European MiFID II enforcing ex-post reporting of costs and charges. As a consequence, investment managers require higher automation of portfolio management techniques to remain sustainable by managing operational costs.

In this respect, FinTech startups are making numerous attempts to infuse AI algorithms inside commoditized portfolio rebalancing techniques. The quest for products differentiation is instead favouring the emergence of AI-based signalling algorithms, aimed at stock picking, promising to trade market news and insights that could not be revealed without parsing on unformatted data with ML and deep learning. We are still at the early stages of a new wave of AI-driven quantitative methods. Yet investment officers will always remain wary of the limitations of the new approaches. AI can certainly provide an enriching perspective on market prices dynamics compared to quantitative finance (based on stochastic models and econometric techniques). However, big data is always a representation of the past, just like traditional risk management time series; since the future is open to uncertainty, even AI can fail to grasp market changes. Therefore, it is relevant to implement AI investment strategies only as part of a larger data architecture, which enables building of the required level of professional interaction and decision-making transparency that divides insightful signals from the insufficient reality of big data and small data.

Regarding process automation, back-office and middle-office activities are where the biggest cost-saving contributions can be harnessed, especially for the activities related to classification and reconciliation of market and contractual data. AI analytics are being deployed progressively to reduce manual tasks, increase time to market and provide point-in-time perspectives of business relationships and event management campaigns.

Robo-advisors have made great efforts to disintermediate human-based investment relationships, focusing on cost convenience and frictionless digital experiences. However, the main obstacle to their success has not been about their investment solutions or imperfect applications. We shall remind ourselves that investing is largely an offer-oriented industry (push economy) while mobile is largely a demand-driven technology (pull mechanism). This is due to the difficulties experienced by the majority of banking clients to become fully self-directed or digitally assisted when it comes to investing money or buying insurance contracts. Wealth management is still a human-driven business, notwithstanding the current level of technology, because of the human emotional aspects behind investment decision-making. The reasons for this gap (which explains the asymmetry of information) are grounded in the biological traits of Homo sapiens, needing relationship-based conversations when making important financial decisions in the presence of fundamental uncertainty. These biological aspects, which need to be carefully understood in the design thinking processes for digital wealth management solutions, are well described in my latest economics and philosophical essay "Financial Market Transparency" (2019).

Therefore, the push/pull gap between digital offers and human demand explains why most robo-advisors had to integrate human assistants and relationship managers to support operations, lower client attrition and make best usage of marketing money to improve onboarding success rates. Yet artificial intelligence can play a key role in making wealth management sustainable by supporting the work of financial advisors with consistent and personalized content to ease the transformation out of product-centric offers towards client-centric solutions. AI-generated content will be a critical factor to allow the reskilling efforts of banking networks, from branches hosting product brokers to centres of financial advice and planning. Whenever possible, AI will also empower end clients to become more pull-oriented (capable of understanding finance beyond push-marketing).

Finally, conversational banking is where AI will make the biggest revolutionary impact. These are the years of the chatbots, which are very basic virtual assistants to engage clients with a captivating level of conversational engagement. The real turning point is expected when AI will become truly and deeply conversational, starting to aggregate trust in e-commerce operations and rolling up into investment management relationships. Voice-powered AI conversations are the main condition which allows us to flip mobile technology from being a pull mechanism to become a push-oriented ecosystem. The time is not yet, but the foundations for this change have being already laid by the AI-driven FinTech revolution.

Machine Learning in Digital Wealth Management

By Patrick Rotzetter
Business Technology Director, EPAM Systems

Artificial intelligence (AI) and its subset machine learning (ML) are becoming part of daily business in all business domains. In this chapter I am going to use ML instead of AI. This seems to be a more appropriate terminology as we have not yet reached *real* AI. Every day, we can see articles claiming that AI can now detect sentiments, create fake news and help build smart applications. Amidst all this media hype, there is little literature on how ML can be specifically applied to the wealth management process and what techniques can be used for that.

ML in Wealth Management

Before looking at the application of ML in wealth management, let us define the context of this article, and what it will cover. Wealth management covers a large area of financial services processes and products. There is no clear definition of what it really encompasses, but in our view wealth management is the end-to-end process of managing the personal wealth of an individual or a set of individuals who want an advisor to suggest actions to take and in which products to invest – in view of the risk appetite of the client and their investment goals. The process starts with the acquisition of clients through advising on investments to servicing clients by providing related banking and security services. The process ends with the transfer or closure of the client account, which we can try to avoid using ML, as we will see later on.

Prospecting and Conversion, Onboarding and Screening

Client conversion is about identifying prospect segments that have a higher probability of converting to clients. In this case we can use different algorithms and data to try and identify segments that will be more likely to be sensitive to wealth management offers. We can take the following unsupervised learning approach:

- Use existing data from existing clients or prospects and try to identify patterns using clustering to identify different groups of prospects.
- Apply clustering to new prospects and identify the clients with a higher conversation ratio and focus on those prospects.

Another supervised learning approach is to use regression to try to predict the conversion ratio and predict revenues with the current set of prospects compared to historical data. This can be done with simple regression techniques as shown in Table 1.

Table 1: **Type of algorithms and their use cases**

Unsupervised Learning
Use Cases
Client segmentation
Risk profiling
Product recommendations
Next best action
Portfolio optimization
Algorithms
k-mean clustering
Self-organized maps (SOM)
Principal component analysis
Recommender systems/ Matrix factorization
Neural network

(*continued*)

Supervised Learning	
Classification	**Regression/Prediction**
Use Cases	*Use Cases*
Prospect conversion	Conversion forecast
Client screening	Revenue forecasts
Client risk profile	Next best action
Client attrition	
Product matching	
Churn prediction	
Anomaly detection (For frauds or AML)	
Algorithms	*Algorithms*
Support vector machines	Linear regression
Decision trees	Polynomial regression
Logistic regression	Support vector machine regression
Neural networks	Decision trees regression
Random forests	Random forest regression
Boosting algorithms	Neural networks
Autoencoders (semi-supervised)	Recurring neural networks

Client experience is also quite key to convincing a potential client to onboard and we can enrich this experience using virtual assistants, either directly by conversing with the client in a natural manner, at least, and collect information that can be reused later in the onboarding process to avoid repetition of the same questions. Virtual assistants can also be used internally to support humans to ask right questions and follow the right process and replace tedious paperwork. Current virtual assistants are currently more focused on questions and answers, but the future is for fully interactive chatbots that can keep the context of the conversation and answer more naturally to unstructured dialogues. Natural language processing comes to the rescue here, trained with domain specific knowledge.

Client Onboarding and Screening

Client onboarding is one of the most discussed topics; the problem is how to automate most of the tasks related to KYC (know-your-customer), risk profiling and client identification. There are many techniques that can support and automate the client screening process. For example, risk profiling does not need to rely on the same simple questions coming out of a form, but can be estimated using classification algorithms, for example where the client characteristics can be used to assess a client risk appetite more accurately than using standard risk questionnaires that are prone to the subjectivity of the answers. Instead using historical data and a simple classification algorithm like a decision tree or a neural network classifier, the result might be less biased than relying solely on questions and answers.

Natural language processing can help analyse unstructured data coming from various sources, such as news articles or companies publications. Extracting entities or summarizing text can be used to get more insights on persons and related companies, for example to determine source of wealth and understand the various involvements a person may have in different industries. Analysing social media using natural language processing can also get useful insights on persons, but that poses the question on how much data can be used and for which purpose. This obviously needs to be transparent to the potential clients. We can analyse social media using a number of natural language techniques, like named entity recognition, to identify people's names, identify the context of the post, and classify the post or article to categories using text classification.

Product Recommendations and Onboarding

When recommending products to clients, financial institutions must go through a suitability assessment, ensuring the product is suitable in terms of risk for the selected client. This is today implemented through rule engines most of the time. Having a ML algorithm can be much more accurate and much more flexible. Using decision trees or even neural networks can indicate the suitability of products for specific clients and hence give a large choice to clients while learning from experience. This would be a major step ahead in terms of advice; instead of relying only on a human advisor, the client would get the best of the experience of other clients in a similar context. We can also use recommender systems based on matrix factorization, for example, pretty much like e-commerce sites that recommend products to you based on other users' experiences. Although this seems simple, this is more complex in the area of wealth management, as a product cannot be simply recommended without checking suitability rules, so one has to be extra careful to take regulatory constraints into consideration when taking this route.

Advisory Process

Current advisory processes are based on questions about financial goals and risk appetite, and based on this an optimal portfolio is derived using well-known risk return algorithms defined decades ago. We can think of advanced advisory processes using ML to learn from the crowd for instance, and use sentiment analysis, an algorithm based on natural language processing, for example. It would also make sense to compile historical data on what has worked and what has not worked for clients and use it as input into the process. So a mixture of portfolio theory and probabilistic predictions can enhance the process and make it more personalized. Personalization of the advisory process will be a winning factor. Similarly to proposing personalized products on e-commerce sites, we can think of proposing investment strategies that are based on what the past has taught us, as well as what comparable clients are doing. This might increase trust in recommendations if based on past experience.

Investment Research and Trading

Although not strictly speaking specific to wealth management, it is quite critical for the advisory process to provide clients with research and trading advice. There is quite a lot of literature on the topic, but we can identify a few areas of interest:

- Finding ideal portfolio weightings through principal component analysis (PCA) and identifying uncorrelated stocks.
- Identifying trading signals using natural language processing to detect positive or negative news for example, or neural networks to find patterns in historical data.
- Predicting trends using sentiment analysis through text mining and classification models.
- Anticipating market movements using social media analysis identifying keywords and contexts
- Trying to find the ideal portfolio with reinforcement learning having the model learning how to invest optimally.

Client Servicing and Support

Client experience can be greatly improved by anticipating client needs or providing personalized advice and service through virtual assistants. Anticipating needs can be implemented with recommender systems for example, where we try to predict the next best action for a customer based on past behaviour. This can, for example, be implemented with recurring neural networks, which keep the context as a way to predict the next sequence of action (like for predicting next word in a sentence).

Another means of support is obviously to implement domain-specific virtual assistants, based on voice recognition as well, to be able to answer calls from clients on a 24/7 basis.

Client Attrition

Avoiding client attrition and account closure is the ultimate objective of any financial institution, so understanding why it happened is quite key. There are simple algorithms that can be used to understand clients at risk and the probability of seeing them leave. Using ensemble learning algorithms (decision tress, random forests or boosting algorithms) usually gives the best result with relatively low complexity. Another way is to use unsupervised learning to try to understand clusters of clients and identify the leavers group, for example. As the problem can become very complex with a lot of different features and very unbalanced data sets (where a category of observation represents the largest majority of observations by far, for example more than 90%), one might think of using algorithms to decompose it into a simpler problem using feature reduction techniques like PCA, or using autoencoders, for example.

Summary of Different Algorithms and Use Cases for Wealth Management

Table 1 shows a summary of possible use cases with related algorithms. This is not an exhaustive list, but includes the main ones addressed in the present section.

There are other algorithms, like reinforcement learning, for example, that do not fall into the above categories, but that for now do not have a lot of practical use in wealth management, in my opinion. Natural language processing is also a class of techniques and algorithms that do not strictly fall into the categories listed in Table 1, but have been discussed in other chapters in this book.

Data Sharing and Confidentiality

One of the key issues institutions might face in implementing ML is related to compliance with data privacy regulations. Regulations are complex and different depending on jurisdictions, making it even more difficult to find general purpose algorithms that can be applied across multiple entities, for example. But ML does not need to know the person behind the data, and using anonymous data sets can be enough to find and train good models. For example, in client segmentation it is not necessary to know the client name or address to train a clustering model, so the data confidentiality issue might be overblown, in my opinion, and can be easily worked around using strictly anonymous data. Also, informing the client clearly that some of his data can be used to train models or to predict some behaviour should also be part of standard agreements nowadays.

Much more critical is the lack of sufficient data or a lack of good data. Large institutions might have access to enough data to train and generalize models, but smaller ones might not have enough data that would be representative enough to train a generalized model. This might come as a surprise when deploying models to production where suddenly the precision and accuracy of the model will drop to unacceptable levels, making the model basically useless. We can also think of monetizing or sharing models between parties; as this is the case with natural language processing models like BERT, we can think of using pre-trained models that we can then refine according to our needs. This is an area largely unexplored except for well-known image recognition or natural language, where it is quite common to reuse trained models available as open source.

Federated Learning

An area that is also worth considering for the future is federated learning, as proposed by Google. The idea is to have a number of models being trained locally on people's smartphones that are then combined to produce a very powerful ML model. We can think of a similar model where smaller institutions want to combine their models in order to gain from the technology advancement without being dependent on other large actors who have much larger data sets.

The Impact of AI on Environmental, Social and Governance (ESG) Investing: Implications for the Investment Value Chain

By Kalyani Inampudi, ACSI, MBA
Independent Consultant (ESG and Sustainability)

and Martina Macpherson, FICRS
President, Network for Sustainable Financial Markets; Visiting Fellow, Henley Business School and Guest Lecturer, University of Zurich

Introduction

There is a great potential for Artificial Intelligence (AI) to contribute towards global economic activity, especially towards Environmental, Social and Governance (ESG) investing. The combination of AI, and other similar Machine Learning (ML) technologies, with industry leading benchmark impact investing metrics can ensure data consistency, reliability and transparency by providing insights into key risks and trends allowing investors and corporations to mitigate their risk while simultaneously optimizing the performance at portfolio and entity level. Building a stronger evidence base will be particularly important for those who are developing practical frameworks and guidelines for AI governance and ethics, including government bodies, legislators, standard-setting bodies and asset owners.

So, what are the challenges and opportunities lying ahead for ESG in this context?

The Impact of AI on ESG

The impact of AI, including unstructured data and ML, on the financial services industry, is an undeniable phenomenon. Currently, several organizations are transitioning towards incorporating a broad range of AI-backed applications across their operations. Hence, it has become imperative for all types of corporate stakeholders to embrace these "twenty-first-century solutions", especially when it comes to serving their tech-savvy and environmentally conscious new millennial customers.

However, with the broad range of new opportunities in AI have also come along key issues, especially around (human) governance, ethics and affiliated concerns. These concerns are integral to an engagement agenda, and the dialogue with regulators, standard setters, investors, employees and the wider supply chain. Ignoring the importance of tech and AI might impact the corporation's reputation negatively ultimately leading to a higher cost to capital and a potential possibility of losing further shareholder value.

Mastering the Data Complexity Challenge with AI

A key challenge is that, every market participant handling complex financial and extra non-financial data must access, analyse and measure vast amounts of data, and must comply with normative and regulatory frameworks. The internet and the explosion of big data is also reshaping the debate about complex financial and extra non-financial data analysis. By implementing ML and AI can enable investment value chain decision-makers and service providers to process vast volumes of information efficiently. It enables them to move from qualitative information to quantitative metrics and to deliver timely, reliable and comprehensible data, analytics and benchmark products. Currently leading AI-centric data providers automatically screen and mine big data and apply AI to their research outputs – to assess, monitor and rate extra-financial data sets such as ESG in the context of e.g. "trends", "risks", "behaviours", "sentiment" and/or "consistency" criteria, in real time.

However, since there is neither just one widely recognized framework nor just one adopted standard, the data complexity around key issues still remains. On the corporate dimension, data disclosure, reporting and inconsistency biases remain on going key issues and disclosures may vary from region to region with some companies in developed economies disclosing more information than companies in emerging economies. Unconventional methods or unstructured data resources are hence key to endeavour for capturing more information. New technologies currently in use include e.g. capturing imagery via satellite for better monitoring and measure the activities and impact from these "black-box" companies.

Engaging The Investor Community to Address AI Concerns

The current investor community has started to look at AI favourably, to leverage its benefits for ESG research, screening and analysis of various factors. However, "there are" and "will be" gaps in terms of analysing corporate's extra-financial information. Existing ESG research models and frameworks can categorize and capture publicly-available information but they often remain qualitative assessments, with biases and inconsistencies. Hence, the asset owners and asset managers are increasingly being asked to look beyond traditional data sets and practices, such as "alternative data possibilities" while keeping an eye on AI solutions.

Investors have also become aware that implementation of AI technology is creating a range of (human) governance and ethical challenges. They are mandating investee companies to consider longer-term risks during and post AI implementation, and to establish a better rigour concerning regulatory oversight.

Here is a brief sample overview of AI and ML questions that we would like to propose which could benefit to the investor community in corporate engagement activities:

(Human) Governance and Ethics

- What initiatives, policies and strategies have you implemented to address/prevent AI governance/ethics issues? Have you already assessed the impact of these initiatives?
- Have your assessments led to alterations and improvements in your policies and strategies and initiatives/transactions? If they have, in what ways has your AI governance strategy altered over time?
- What contingency measures, risk scenarios, mitigation and adaptation strategies have you considered in the context of AI governance, reporting and audit, when it comes to automation, robotics and big data analytics?
- Are you planning to off-shore AI developments to countries with less ethical and regulatory standards and oversight?

Risk/Opportunities and Net Impact

- Have you commissioned any studies to determine which business areas and activities are directly or indirectly affected by your implementation of AI in operations, within your organization's supply/value chain?
- If you have commissioned studies, what were the outcomes? Have you identified business areas and activities most at risk, and what are the financial (and other, reputational, social responsibility, ethical, moral) consequences (cost to capital consideration) in relation to the implementation of AI for your organization?
- What systems are in place already to inform yourselves about AI challenges and enhance ESG risk management in relation to your business (strategy, operations, transactions), including human resources, finance, R&D, and in the context of other (market-related) activities?

- Does your current AI approach ensure that ML technologies are thoroughly researched, and deployed in such a way that enhances ESG goals, human value chain and social justice?
- What might be the possible consequences of rapidly advancing technologies and their impact on your business? Do you have any back up plans to manage these challenges?

Collaboration and Engagement

- Are you engaging, or partnering, with any organization or industry association regarding AI (human) governance and ethics? If so what are the common goals set for these engagements/partnerships?
- Are you engaging with service providers (rating houses/ stock exchanges) and intermediaries (consultants) on AI issues? If so what are the targets, objectives and outcomes of these engagements?
- What practises are set in place to engage companies for disclosing more alternative data and information about their acts and behaviours?
- Would you mind having to retrieve "the big data"? If so are your AI and algorithms efficiently trained for this challenge?

Conclusion

AI and ML will play transformative roles in the ESG arena and various forms of concrete applications are currently being conceptualized, tested and implemented throughout the investment value chain, ranging from institutional investors, to rating agencies, to data service providers to FinTech companies. All of these stakeholders test different applications, including text analysis, GIS (Geographical Information Systems), data scanning, picture analysis or digital document analysis, in order to improve the reliability, volume and speed of identification of material ESG information.

The industry must continue to work with all of these stakeholders to continue the dialogue on better adoption of ESG data and criteria, educating investors about the long-term opportunities and challenges in ESG data management and in AI.

Finally, AI and ML have the ability to reduce the negative effects of human biases on ESG related decisions which can potentially help to better reflect the complexities and the interconnectedness of mega trends and issues in a world in which the reputation, governance and business viability of a company can change overnight.

AI in Indian Investment and Asset Management: Global Perspective

By Nilesh Gopali
International Business Advisor and Strategic Investments

and Hasik Shetty
Machine Learning Engineer and Strategist

India is at a watershed moment with digital explosion and highest economic growth (5–6%) across the world. This has created an emerging middle class with disposable income.

A huge market exists to use AI in the investment management space which is driven by a young population (65% of the population below the age of 35 years), new high-net-worth individuals and significant dead cash with just 18 million investors (around 2% of the population).

Key drivers of the Indian market:

- JAM (Jan Dhan Aadhar Mobile) Trinity: An Indian government initiative which opened 320 million bank accounts post-2014 for low income groups, contributing towards financial inclusion. Bank accounts were opened with the new biometric identification, the Aadhar card.
- Digital India: The Digitization boom in India helped India overtake the US to become the second largest smartphone market, with the cheapest mobile data pack globally.
- Post demonetization (Nov 2016), there has been a significant shift of monies from physical assets to financial assets. The major beneficiary is the mutual funds asset class, which has seen huge inflow.

Inherent Issues in India

The high-net-worth individual (HNWI) end of the market is covered by financial institutions, whilst the investing needs of the emerging middle class is yet to be met. The young generation, smart investors, like to be informed about their portfolio performance. At the same time, they lack trust in financial planners, perceiving them to be no more than an agent. They prefer a digital interaction over face-to-face communication. This is definitely a drastic change from the previous generation who are still very much dependent on their local advisors for investments. The investment strategies provided to them are very generic and product-driven rather than goal-driven. Portfolio optimization is also product-focused instead of client-focused, leading to a mismatch between goals and outcomes. Whilst financial institutions target HNWIs, the advisors are reluctant to onboard these young investors as they have low surplus to invest as compared to older generation clients.

AI in Investment Management in India

AI handles far more data than humans can process, automates repetitive tasks, extracts meaning from data far more quickly, and generates, in several cases, insights from data which didn't exist previously. AI increases the efficiency in a step-change manner rather than just incrementally. AI is also a prediction machine, which by its very nature is perfect for investment purposes, predicting portfolio performance, analysing risk and providing mass personalization which was not possible previously.

Some New Scenarios

1. Account Opening and Personalization

The new biometric identification Aadhar card is used to open investor accounts. Using AI, new data sources could be analysed in real time to holistically understand this investor's preferences and risk profile. With a customer-centric mindset, a holistic view of the customer's financial position could be created, which subsequently is used to generate a customer-specific portfolio.

At the institution level, this amounts to hundreds and thousands of specific portfolios for each of their customers. Each of these portfolios are generated using AI according to customer risk profile and linked with their goals.

2. Alpha Generation

AI is used to predict the portfolio return. Both deep learning and reinforcement learning have shown incredible results when it comes to stock price prediction. Recently Google's BERT model has achieved groundbreaking accuracies in NLP and sequence-related tasks which could be used for fundamental and sentiment analysis. These cutting-edge algorithms can identify previously unexplored pattern and correlation that supports investment decision-making to generate alpha for investors. However, the entire process must not be automated, as AI is still "not explainable", i.e. one can't explain how AI has chosen the strategies behind its decision, especially in deep learning.

Whilst AI improves predictions of future outcomes, currently, as AI is not mature enough, there is a possibility that it may not judge the right outcomes or relate to the correct course of action to be taken because it may not consider all hidden factors. Human judgement, therefore, plays an important role in decision-making. AI prediction must be used as a simple suggestion rather than a decision. Financial experts would interpret AI's suggestion to make the final decision.

3. Advisory

Catering to the young generation of India, every month, a video could be made explaining the portfolio, market growth/decline and reasons for decisions made on each portfolio class.

AI could personalize these videos, at scale, using the advisory script, thereby avoiding the need for a financial advisor for initial explanation of their portfolio performance. An advisory chatbot could be used to answer questions related to portfolio and investments in a natural conversational format.

Emergence of New Business Models

Financial institutions need to reach out to new investors directly, or through pure-play financial product distributors (not advisors) with no increase in current costs, or even at a lower cost, to stay competitive. Some have already adopted passive fund management models to reduce the cost base but we think it is imperative that AI and other technologies are deployed, not just for step-changes in efficiencies but to create the real value that comes from new business models. Management fees have sustained the asset management industry for decades; therefore, a new mindset is required to rise above and beyond the current thinking. A new pricing model for passive funds has emerged that, as "free", could be applied to the emerging middle class and affluent class in India. Active funds could have new tiered or variable pricing structures where a base charge is applied up to a certain level of a fund's performance. Above this performance benchmark, a percentage charge could be applied as an additional bonus.

The jury is out but we think disruption to the Indian investment management sector is imminent. It may be that the "final straw" will come from tech giants like Google and Amazon, working from a high base of inherent trust among Indian millennials. What will the impacts be if they decide to enter into the market?

Reference

The New Physics of Financial Services, World Economic Forum, Aug 2018.

Finding Order in the Chaos: Investment Selection Using AI

By Yaron Golgher
CEO, I Know First

Dr Lipa Roitman
CTO, I Know First

and Denis Khoronenko
Analyst, I Know First

Every Wall Street success story is a combination of a whole variety of factors, but the difference between a successful investor and their peer biting the dust can often come down to one simple question: *How do you pick your investment*? Do you follow the trend and exit just before the bubble bursts? Do you crunch the numbers, meticulously identifying the companies that seem to be undervalued? Or do you just blindfold a monkey, Burton Malkiel-style, and let it have fun throwing darts at a stock page in a newspaper. While all these approaches have their own merits (except for the last one, perhaps), the recent rise of the artificial intelligence industry provides investors with new tools and means to navigate the changing tides of the market. Going through troves of data in real time, smart machines are capable of modelling and predicting the stock price dynamics. This, of course, assumes that markets are predictable, which goes against some of the investment theory – so let us discuss that first before delving into the exciting world of AIs.

Random Walk Through Efficient Markets: Are Stock Price Fluctuations Predictable?

One of the lines of thinking in the debate around investment asserts that the stock prices effectively follow a random walk, changing randomly and unpredictably. This hypothesis was first put forth by French mathematician Louis Bachelier all the way back in the 1900s and was a hot topic in the 1960s. Today, the consensus is that the random walk hypothesis is consistent with the *efficient markets* hypothesis, which, in its turn, postulates that stock prices accurately reflect all the information available to the investors.

Here is how that plays out: in an efficient market, prices are quick to react to any significant update, and since updates are hard to predict until, well, they are actually there, stock prices essentially follow a random course. Accordingly, trying to predict them makes virtually no sense, because you are in fact trying to predict what happens to the greater world out there rather than what happens to the stock market per se.

This approach, however, seems to largely ignore the human factor in trading – and there is ample research on all sorts of tricks that the human mind plays on investors when they place their bets. We humans tend to pay too much attention to the prospect of losses (to the detriment of gains, at times), we tend to over-rely on prior experience, jump on hype trains, overreact to and put too much trust in news reports…Sounds a bit chaotic, doesn't it?

Well, it is.

Bulls, Bears and Butterflies: Markets as Chaotic Systems

Imagine a tornado crushing through a forest. While its arrival may look out of the blue to the woodland critters fleeing its wrath, the reality is different: the disaster was driven by a multitude of quantifiable processes in the atmosphere, with the laws of physics rather than the abstract fury of nature at its engine.

What we just described is a complex chaotic system, one comprising a multitude of drivers and highly sensitive to the initial conditions and relatively small events, which can upset its shaky balance and lead to major changes in the system. The latter is most famously exemplified by a butterfly in Brazil producing a hurricane in Texas just by flapping its wings. These systems are to a degree deterministic and have a semblance of a memory, or, in other words, a self-similarity that produces certain repeating cycles.

Now, if we go back to the point about the irrationality inherent to certain investment decisions and the human bias in trading, and also take into account that the market dynamics are effectively largely created by the decisions made by thousands of investors, large and small, the parallel with chaotic systems becomes clear. There is a randomness to it, granted, as exemplified by cases such as the Apple crash of 2014 or even the famous Flash Crash, but there is also a pattern to be found in all the noise it generates. Just look at the graphs for any stock of your liking, covering a day, a month and a year of trading, respectively. You will see no predictable pattern in the former, the monthly one would also probably be too noisy, but in the yearly graph, you will most likely see the periods where the price is constantly fluctuating around a specific value.

In other words, there is a pattern to this chaos, and patterns are exactly where AI shines.

Best of Both Worlds: Investing With AI-Driven Decision Enhancement Tools

At the core of today's AI technology exist some very advanced statistics backed by the raw computational power of top-notch hardware. The idea is to feed the algorithm a huge trove of data and send it looking for patterns, delivering mathematical functions that would do what the developer wants the AI to do. With neural networks, for example, these would approximate the workings of a human brain, with every "neuron" being a mathematical function of its own, responsible for a specific segment of input. Layer by layer, these nodes would process new data to predict or classify the process it quantifies.

Now, as investors, what we want to do is to get the AI to predict stock price dynamics. Thus, we can train the algorithm on a set of historical trading data (in our case at *I Know First*, it covered 15 years of trading), while drawing on the chaos theory to account for the random nature of the market. We would centre our calculations around a fat-tailed distribution, where evens that are virtually impossible under the assumption of a standard normal curve are seen as way more likely to happen, and use fractal time-series analysis to account for the self-similarity inherent in chaotic systems. Furthermore, to stay in touch with the market, *I Know First* utilizes the so-called reinforcement learning technique, which is essentially about the algorithm recalibrating its models to reflect the current state of events. This helps us avoid a scenario in which the AI falls into the fallacy of over-relying on prior experience in its assessment of a situation where a new pattern is playing itself out.

As a result, what we have is an algorithm that predicts the stock price fluctuations based on fresh and historical data. In doing so, it accounts for all the information that is reflected in the stock prices, but does so without being led astray by emotions running high, with perfect mathematical awareness of the highs and lows of the boom and bust cycle. Now, all it takes is to set the benchmarks for predictability, which can be seen, for example, as a Pearson correlation indicator for past forecasts and actual price movement, and we have a model that can help us pick out the best investment options.

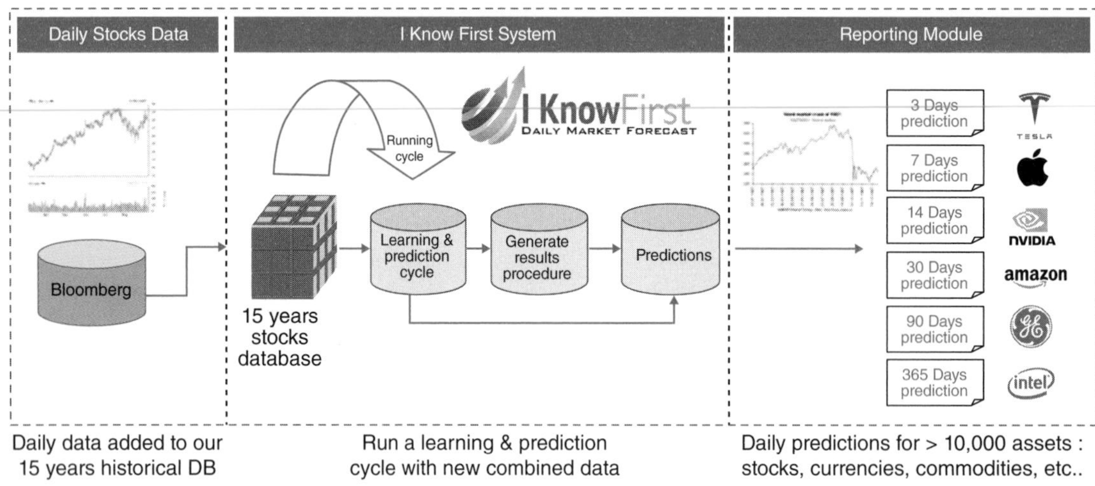

Figure 1: **The running cycle of the I Know First predictive algorithm uses fresh market data and historic trading dataset to model the market dynamics and pinpoint the most lucrative assets for longing and shorting**

Predictive Algorithm Developed by *I Know First*

As we can see, the purely empirical nature of the AI, which goes through quantitative data, allows it to work as a check on the human bias that we touched upon earlier. This makes us believe that AI-driven decision enhancement tools are the most reliable partners an investor may have, working as a safeguard against human biases while leaving ample room for the human mind to strategize – and succeed.

Dispelling the Illusion

By Richard Saldanha
Founder and Managing Director, Oxquant

We are still decades away from a true generalized machine or artificial intelligence but quantitative methods in general can be used far more extensively than most people suppose. Whilst such methods have typically been employed in the search for investment performance, the asset management industry spends far less time considering how quantitative methods can be used to improve profitability through cost savings or better task efficiency. Data-based automation is here now and those firms that fail to understand and embrace this fact will struggle.

Data-Based Automation

One of the biggest hurdles to applying good models with the aim of automatic decision-making is poor data management. The failure to design systems that can share data easily means that much time and effort is wasted wrestling data into the correct format. This assumes that relevant data are available in the first place. Many of the simplest questions posed by boards or risk committees can be difficult to answer because of incomplete data or the failure to collect the right data. Boards should not blame their IT departments for these failings. Instead, they should think in advance about the important questions that might need answering.

Planning carefully, collecting the right data, storing it in an appropriate manner (whether that is in a conventional relational, NoSQL or semantic graph database) and making sure that database can talk effectively to other systems are key elements in implementing any form of automation system. Think of a strong data backbone for the firm. Databases[1] abound and any number of programming languages[2] can be used in conjunction with them.

With the right data infrastructure in place, some form of rules-based automation should be a genuinely achievable goal for all firms.

Front, Middle and/or Back Office?

There has been a tendency to focus AI/ML efforts in the front office. Because of this, the potential for cost savings through better technological efficiency may be much greater in the middle and/or back offices.

Some of the typical tasks undertaken in the middle and back offices and potential automation possibilities are outlined below. The suggestions are in no way the stuff of science fiction. Much can be accomplished with existing computing methods. Quants and IT professionals may find much glamour outside of the front office in the near future.

Middle Office

There are no hard and fast rules as to what functions are to be found where. In general, risk and performance management is found in the middle office. Sales teams dominate client interaction at present but that has already changed for retail-focused firms with a strong outline presence. Thus, elements of client service are increasingly finding their way into the middle office.

---

[1] See DB-Engines' database rankings: https://db-engines.com/en/ranking.

[2] See the PopularitY of Programming Language (PYPL) Index: http://pypl.github.io/PYPL.html.

Table 1: A selection of middle office tasks likely to benefit from automation efficiency

Task	Description and automation possibilities
Client risk appetite, mandate requirements and other guidelines	Encoding of risk appetite, mandate requirements and other guidelines in machine readable form for downstream monitoring and reporting [C, R].
Performance reporting and attribution	Provision of (near) real-time on-demand performance reporting and attribution [C, R].
Risk reporting	Delivery of risk analytics, stress and scenario analyses, capacity and liquidity estimation in a near real-time context [C, R]. Remedial actions or merely suggestions for what action might be taken [ML].
Portfolio modelling	Theoretical portfolio modelling, what-if analyses, associated risk characteristics and provision of relevant commentary [C, R, ML].
Manager reporting	Seamless manager reporting based on relevant holdings [C, R, ML].
Economic insights	Provision of relevant economic commentaries [C, R, ML].
Compliance	Trade costs analysis, mandate adherence [C, R]. Automatic mandate breach signalling and possibly automatic correction [C, R, ML].

Note: The letters inside the square brackets refer to the delivery mechanism, i.e. conventional computing [C] such as server batch processing or on-demand request; event-triggered robotic automation [R] replaces some or all of the actions of a human worker in the same role; machine learning [ML] mechanisms use logic to decide on what action to take based on problem analysis and might consist of anything from a simple regression model used in a predictive manner through to text analysis and natural language processing.

Back Office

No asset manager can function properly without a good back office. In contrast with the middle office, the back office will tend to have plenty of staff and computing resources. It will also receive lots of attention, particularly when errors occur. The key questions centre on back office efficiency.

Table 2: A selection of back office tasks likely to benefit from automation efficiency

Task	Description and automation possibilities
Account setup	Automatic account creation for large clients as well as individuals [C, R]. (Note what FinTechs such as Stripe, N26 and Starling Bank, to name but three, already do now.)
Account compliance	The ability to obtain information automatically from reputable government websites and other trusted sources should allow seamless confirmation for most clients [C, R].
Pre-trade checking	Most investment management firms implement automated pre-trade mandate and other checks. It is merely only the degree of automation, efficiency and intelligence around the rules that typically deserve scrutiny [C, R].
Trade processing	Trade exception reporting should require no human intervention [C, R]. Automated correction should be a key focus for all [C, R, ML].

Trade reconciliation	Reconciliation between broker, custodian and internal books and records should be fully automated [C, R]. Subsequent actions around breaks/exceptions is where intelligent automation can play a big part [C, R, ML].
Post-trade compliance	Automated post-trade and daily close-price monitoring should be achievable for all firms [C, R].
Fund administration	Automated rules-based fund administration is perfectly achievable with the right infrastructure [C, R, ML].
Transfer agency	Much scope exists for transfer agency activity to be fully automated [C, R].
Client reporting	Clients already expect a degree of automated and/or on-demand reporting [C, R, ML]. There is scope for much greater sophistication in this area.

Note: The abbreviations given inside the square brackets are explained in Table 1.

Implementation Strategy

Firms interested in intelligent automation should review their current data-handling procedures as a matter of priority. Typical questions to ask might include:

- Does my firm have the right data?
- How easy is it to get relevant answers from those data?
- Are existing systems integrated, i.e. do data flow freely and easily?
- Do the right people have access to relevant data?

Considering data collection, storage and handling seriously is a necessary first step in any form of intelligent automation. Whilst it may be time-consuming to do this, implementing the right data policy may produce immediate benefits in terms of efficiency. Firms should only then think in terms of

- automation improvements based on existing IT infrastructure;
- more extensive improvements (partial overhaul/redesign of infrastructure); and/or
- building a completely new infrastructure (radical overhaul).

Implications

AI/ML is changing the way investment management services are delivered.[3] Those institutions which understand the power of their data and have learnt to harness AI/ML methods to their advantage can expect to be rewarded.

[3]R.J. McWaters and R. Galaski (eds) (2018) “The new physics of financial services – how artificial intelligence is transforming the financial ecosystem.” World Economic Forum and Deloitte. www.weforum.org/reports/the-new-physics-of-financial-services-how-artificial-intelligence-is-transforming-the-financial-ecosystem.

ETF 2.0: Mega Block Chains with AI

By J.B. Beckett
Author and Founder, New Fund Order

Asset management, as it exists today within the new Western capitalist model, has a very real problem with any notions of social investing, equality or fair distribution of wealth. Indeed the model's foundations are built on the notion of "equality of opportunity" and "inequality of outcome". The American dream. Much of the profits from that model have gravitated to those who provide rather than those who receive. Those who control rather than those who work. How might artificial intelligence change this?

How? The way social networks have changed society cannot be understated and likewise the role social networks could play for asset management. The key is one of engagement, individual control yet without losing the benefits of pooling investors, by creating social investment structures: mega-blocks. We have seen early signs such as "direct-index" exchange-traded funds (ETFs) but we can go much further.

Why? Recall that Karl Marx's *Das Kapital* asserts that workers become disenfranchised in the capital model by capital owners and machines. How true that feels today where the paranoia of "artificial intelligence threatening jobs" pervades all media. The symptoms of that low engagement are a low savings ratio globally, wage disinflation and a lack of alignment (needs matching) between investors and asset managers. Workers typically don't engage with their long-term savings plans until they retire, and too much control remains in the hands of employers, advisers and asset managers. It is why robo advisory is proving so difficult. Asset managers have never been more remote from the workers they are supposed to serve.

Perhaps perversely, that same technology could empower and re-engage workers back into asset management. It could remove the countless intermediaries that suck out the value of asset management. Yet instead, capital flows are being herded into a small number of indices, held in exchange-traded funds (ETFs), controlled by a small number of index providers and supersized asset managers. These ETFs neither accurately match the needs of the investor nor efficiently allocate capital back to corporations. It is groupthink on a multi-trillion scale. It, too, is symptomatic of the problem noted above but is not the solution.

A "New Fund Order" will herald change for the asset industry; Moore's Law is unwavering in this respect. Indeed AI evolution is faster than linear, as Moore suggests. The industry has been in a stupor of old business models, commission, star manager culture, asset concentration, marketing, high costs, low transparency, lavish hospitality and poor fund selection. Asset management is beginning to detox from those heady party days. The party is over but for now the masses remain sedated on the methadone of vast market cap-weighted ETFs.

The reality is that ETFs also face issues. Capable of so much more than how they are being used today, they have been held back by a simple presumption that pooled investing is about cramming masses into a single model, yet somehow each trying to derive their own utility from it. Clearly it hasn't worked, trust in asset management and active managers has never been lower, herding patterns are accelerating, as are the daily trading volumes of index products. The optical value of ETF has become a blunt question of only cost. A huge mistake, but one being driven by the index manufacturers and misplaced academics and pundits. Perhaps in their minds they chose the lesser evil. What started as disrupter is now supposed deliverer.

Meanwhile, concern turns to the asset concentration building among ETFs, as a result of using outdated index construction. In simple terms, the pooling of vast uncontrolled open-ended structures, funnelled into controlled closed-ended securities, is a recipe for Minsky-like commodity bubbles. Earnings, then, do not drive price, the order book does, the equilibrium between buyers and sellers. That may sound fair but as the order book is controlled by brokers motivated by profiteering, not workers, then it falls short. Instead, what we have is a growing index anomaly and a missed opportunity for ETF. I am now even more convinced that we are only at the beginning of ETF evolution. Fully dematerialized fund structures are the future, all others will become obsolete. It is no coincidence that active asset managers are rapidly buying ETF businesses, the potential for active intellectual property through ETFs is huge. This might be summarized as the move to "smarter beta" or codified alpha.

However, I believe ETFs will go even further in the future. I have already begun to structure and codify what "ETF 2.0" might look like. A complete rethink of how ETFs operate, in 2.0 investors will have individual pathways, cross-matching assets for expected return, risk, time horizon and maturity, investors trade through blockchain within the ETF, with fully dematerialized, frictionless trading between investors. The key aspect here is the simultaneous checking of the asset pathway, individual pathway and block pathway – I call this your Asimov test. ETF 2.0 will allow:

- Management of individual investor pathways: for a large neural system, managing thousands of unique investors is achievable with bespoke journeys, targets and risk tolerances within one ETF.
- Matching pathways for inter-block trading. For example, the sale of assets of a retiring member can be matched with the corresponding buys of a younger member without the need to go back through the settlement and delivery versus payment (DvP) process. Such matching could be continuous and occur over thousands of members simultaneously. Such technology already exists on trading and betting platforms.
- Combining automated client risk utility with asset allocation, algorithmic trading and multi-factor systematic investing attuned to each investor, allows continuous monitoring and efficient adjustment.
- Statistical arbitrage: Identifying anomalies within the market, within and outside of the ETF and exploiting them continuously; such algos can also be used to monitor any behavioural anomalies between matching trades or investors within the ETF or the market.
- Restructuring the pooling of the ETF to assign stocks to match different investor time horizons and risk tolerance, moving us away from a one-basket-fits-all mentality that has underpinned ETFs to date.
- Investors may even be able to interact within the block, commingling the wisdom of the crowd; the frameworks needed already exist in the likes of cryptocurrencies and differentiable neural computing like AlphaGo.

"Tech" is full of jargon but safe to say that "blockchain" provides us the necessary infrastructure and AI the ability to manage the block once created. The ETF becomes the centralized clearing agent for all of its investors and trades within the ETF, allowing instantaneous transparent straight-through processing (STP) and DvP, investors still benefiting from novation, fully dematerialized fungible assets and economies of scale (as with current ETFs), but now investor trades are matched inside the ETF, not simply pooled and traded outside on the market. It would make the investors within an ETF a complex adaptive community, trading as a block with other blocks and the rest of the market. Meanwhile ETF 2.0 would communicate continuously with other ETFs, exchanges and trading platforms to ensure correct real-time pricing.

Everyone shares the success of the ETF, assets and returns, weighted to their individual pathway and maturity. Workers become their own capital owners built on the principles of mutuality. The ETF provider deducts one disclosed cost to administer the algorithm, the trades and investors. While this may feel quasi-*ponzi* to some, this is no *fugazi*. The quandary left behind by Bernie Madoff (other than his conceit, deceit and fraudulent behaviour) was that the biggest failing of any *ponzi* is the incorrect estimation of cash flow and matching of assets over time. Eventually they run out of cash. The concept of cash-matching individual investors is itself well supported by liability-driven investing. The technology to match thousands of individuals has been beyond us, until now.

A rapid reduction in friction? Once an ETF is repurposed for individual pathways, rather than aggregated pooled outcomes, then assets are coded for cost, time and risk-matched to investors who need them. ETF 2.0 can trade internally, frictionless through blockchain technology, within the ETF and then only traded externally with the market when in net surplus of cash or assets. In effect we can create mega-blocks of investors, providing efficiencies in turnover costs and accurate investor-matched, risk-targeted allocations. This redesign of mutual investing would require a complete rethink in how asset management is structured today, including advisers, fund managers, fund investors, custodians, exchanges and clearing houses.

Suddenly, passive becomes social, benchmarks become meaningless, replaced by block economies. Each worker can view their own pathway to maturity in augmented reality from the comfort of their own home or on the move. Effectively, we would create a different pooled model and we haven't even begun to think about quantum computing and isotopic algorithms and a hundred other cool bits of jargon that few of us properly comprehend. Science fiction is rapidly becoming a near-term indication of science fact; the lines are blurring.

To some "ETF 2.0" may sound like the onset of techno-Marxism on asset management; for others it is salvation. I explore the concept in detail in my FINTECH Circle Institute lecture and invite ETF innovators and coders to come together to create ETF 2.0 mega-blocks.

Fear and Greed

By Eleftherios Jerry Floros
CEO and Founder, MoneyDrome X

There are two emotions – fear and greed – that guide financial trading and affect the financial markets globally.

Billions of dollars' worth of trades swing back and forth between profit and loss and the only constant is risk.

In finance, emotions should not guide traders, only effective risk management.

And for that reason, investment banks and financial institutions have established effective risk management systems to ensure that trades are based on sound financial decision-making and trading discipline, but most importantly, to prevent losses.

In an effort to enhance trading profits, algorithms have been introduced that are back-tested and deployed as independent trading bots, but the results have been mixed.

Why? Because the algorithm is still designed by a human who is prone to errors.

Artificial intelligence and ML will take financial trading to an entirely new level and with quantum computing, to an entirely new dimension.

Man vs Machine

In the near future, financial trading will be done almost completely devoid of human intervention.

Algorithms designed using artificial intelligence will replace the financial trader as we know them today. Entire trading floors will be replaced by trading bots that will place trades independently, with limited human supervision.

Not only will trading floors fade into history, entire exchanges will become virtual.

And as the transformation from man to machine becomes a surreal reality, the financial industry will go through a profound metamorphosis, one where machines take over from humans.

The mere thought of machines controlling the financial markets is surreal but it is something that will happen sooner than later. The reason for this is that as trading accelerates exponentially, human thinking will not be able to compete with ultra-fast computations of risk assessment and possible outcomes; only superfast computers will be able to process the available market data and execute trades in the financial markets that operate in a lightning fast environment and on hyper-connected networks.

Quantum Computing

The advent of financial trading using quantum computing is simply mind-boggling.

It's not even possible to fathom what will happen to the financial markets across the globe and the prospects are simply unpredictable at present.

Not only has artificial intelligence the power to execute trades; combined with quantum computing, that power becomes exponential.

For sure, humans will not allow machines to take over. By effectively deploying quantum computing and smart algorithms, investors and financial traders will be able to utilize ultra-fast computing to their advantage.

Convergence of Advanced Technologies

Combining artificial intelligence, ML and quantum computing will create an entirely new world in financial trading and investing. A global financial market that will execute trades and transactions at the speed of light without necessarily involving the human factor.

The speed at which financial transactions are executed will simply be mind-bending; it is believed that TPS (transactions per second) will have evolved to nanoseconds, and in doing so, reducing latency to the lowest possible denominator.

High frequency, or low latency trading, as it is also known today, uses powerful computers and complex algorithms to execute orders in fractions of a second with the sole purpose of making a profit within fractions of a second.

By the next decade, sophisticated technologies will accelerate trading exponentially and supercomputers will take out the risk factor entirely, as for each trade, there will be a counter-trade to offset any losses.

Risk management will be governed by smart algorithms instead of humans and that decisive factor will change the financial markets forever.

Automated Trading

It could be argued that humans may view the financial world from a different perspective, immersing real life experiences with long-term trading strategies, and taking into account factors that will not be considered by supercomputers, such as the well-being of company employees and the environment. Other considerations would be ethical and moral standards, factors that a computer can only process if the algorithms have been programmed accordingly. The question then is, by whom and how are these algorithms programmed?

The programmer could be instructed to develop an algorithm where the only objective is profit, regardless of cost, financial or human. In a world of greed, the prospect of "merciless trading" can be discomforting and outright scary. Even today, there's a global debate between experts of all fields about ethical standards and limitations that need to be imposed by humans. The thinking behind this is that advanced technology should be applied to serve mankind and not take over.

Wealth Creation by Algorithm

By harnessing the power of quantum computing combined with artificial intelligence, the financial markets will become significantly more accessible for everyone and the rules of the game will be more equitable. Algorithms that will be programmed to make profits will be available to everyone and access to the financial markets will only be a couple of clicks on a smartphone app.

Using artificial intelligence, investment decisions will be programmed and executed without the involvement of humans, thus reducing the risk factor inherent in human error.

In a global financial market that is equal for all, the benefits can be massive.

By enabling everyone to participate in the financial markets, it will create unprecedented wealth around the world. Presently, this wealth is shared between the banks, financial institutions and the privileged few. Only sophisticated investors reap the benefit of being part of the financial elite that control the markets. Soon this will change through tokenization, which is fractional ownership of real-world assets. As a direct consequence, the financial markets will become more liquid and the number of market participants will increase exponentially, to the point that market manipulation will become increasingly difficult. Tokenization, combined with easy access to the financial markets, will enable retail investors to participate in profits by virtue of fractional ownership, opening the door to mass participation in the financial markets.

Tokenization will be a game changer of epic proportions.

The Financial World of Equals

Today's financial markets primarily serve banks, financial institutions and the rich.

The average person does not have equal access to the money-making machine of the financial markets. Even retail investors that participate in the financial markets rarely make the steady returns that the insiders – banks, financial institutions and the wealthy – do throughout the year. The reason for that is information asymmetry. These insiders know more about any financial trade at any given time than any outsider. By the time that information has reached all investors, the insiders have already cashed out. And the retail investor has most likely made a loss. In the near future, automated trading will level the playing field and make financial trading fair for all concerned. It will allow anyone to participate in the financial markets without the inherent fear of losses. Risk management using artificial intelligence will ensure that losses will be reduced significantly or eliminated completely. And as the risk factor is mitigated or even eliminated, more market participants will be able to enter the financial markets and trade successfully.

Artificial intelligence will benefit all, as opposed to the select few, and tokenization will create an entirely new dimension in financial trading and wealth creation.

The future of finance is already here and tokenization will make it a reality.

Capital Markets

6

Steps to Ensure Firm Success

- Prioritize talent, teams and culture
- Build trust in AI decision-making through ethical design and explainability
- Make data governance and stewardship a priority
- Collaborate more … Bank-2-FinTech, Bank-to-Bank
- Focus on your unique data-sets and insights
- Apply your deep subject/domain expertise
- Design solutions for integration
- Explore 'alt-data' vigorously
- Next-stage data strategy may include the 'meta-quant'

Firms Leveraging AI to…

- give retail traders **parity of information** with banks
- give retail traders **execution control**
- **augment expert humans** in customer services, research, advisory, governance, transactions
- **cut** inefficiencies, remove cost and reduce risk

Enhanced Regulatory Capabilities

- **NLP for bad actors** e.g. trader communications for collusion
- **Augmented regulator**
- **Digital dashboard** of financial stability
- **Real-time stress-testing**

86%
increase in AI-powered quant funds, 2010-2017

$512bn
revenues from enhanced automation for FS firms by 2020

10%
average amount of data held by firms that's actually used

70%
of trading is AI-automated

60⁺
steps in IPOs that Goldman Sachs found could be automated

185
regulatory changes a day applying to FS firms

Artificial intelligence is already applied in many areas of investment banking and capital markets, such as raising equity and issuing debt and advisory services related to mergers and acquisitions. This way corporate clients such as leading corporations, financial institutions, financial sponsors, ultra-high-net-worth individuals and sovereign clients are benefiting from better insights and decision-making empowered by AI.

AI technologies — along with big data and cloud capabilities — have been adopted into and by capital markets for more than 50 years. We are already close to fully digitalized trading, and there are many interesting real-life use cases from both front and back office, including portfolio optimization, fraud detection and more. We are now seeing more energy applied to adding value for clients, colleagues and other stakeholders, and this will accelerate. This part explores these developments, important ideas and concepts, such as:

- A primer on AI and machine learning, specific to financial services and capital markets.
- A view on both the potential and actual ways in which well-designed AI solutions are providing both customer benefits and compliance as an outcome.
- An analysis of intelligent automation and related AI-powered solutions which are being put to work on critical areas such as productivity, trading and enhanced (customer and other) interaction.
- A view of how to gain that essential "information edge" that has always driven capital markets through a "MetaQuant" approach using alt-data in a (r)evolutionary process for transparency, not just in capital markets but also in global economies.
- A practically focused assessment of what's next, and how firms can work out how to position for success.

This part explores important ideas, cases and emerging concepts such as "quantamental" (broadly, combining traditional investing approaches based on "fundamentals" and experience, with quantitative tools, including algos and big data) and the "MetaQuant" (a term used by our contributor Alejandra Litterio, to describe a new breed of analysts able to mine and combine unstructured data with the quantamental approach to create new frameworks, interrogate investment models and dig out net new insights).

This part brings practical approaches and tips, emerging concepts and "here-and-now" applications and experiences specific to capital markets, that will be of interest and use to readers both in this sector and beyond.

Introduction on AI Approaches in Capital Markets

By Dr Aric Whitewood
Founding Partner, XAI Asset Management

Setting the Scene

This chapter introduces the key considerations, trends and use cases for artificial intelligence (AI) in Capital Markets. It's meant for non-specialists, and, in particular, decision-makers needing to understand the benefits, pitfalls, and how to approach AI projects in the financial domain.

One can draw parallels between AI and other technological drivers like computerization of trade, which first took hold in the 1970s. Trading is now close to fully electronic, particularly in the case of cash equities, FX, futures and CDS indices, all assets that are highly liquid and standardized. Figure 1 shows different asset classes (listed on the left) and how trading becomes less electronic as we move down that list, from cash equities at one extreme (fully electronic trading), through to high-yield cash bonds at the other (mostly voice trading). The trend will continue; it's possible that almost all assets will be significantly electronic in the next decade.

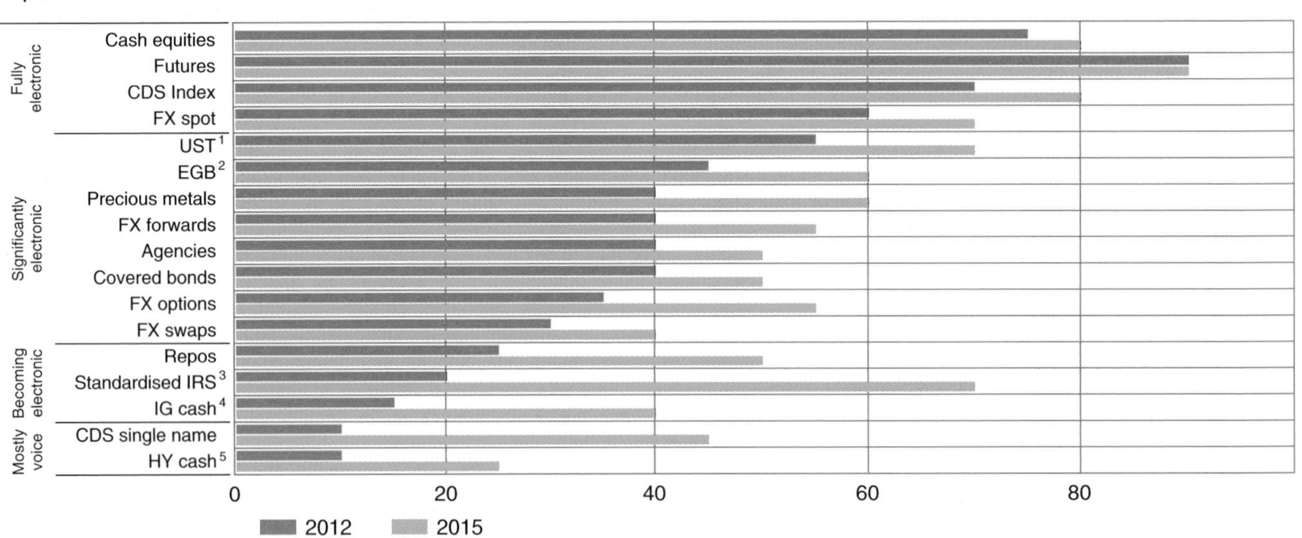

[1] US Treasuries. [2] European government bonds. [3] Standardized interest rate swaps. [4] Investment grade cash bonds. [5] High-yield cash bonds.

Sources: Greenwich Associates (2014); McKinsey & Company and Greenwich Associates (2013).

Figure 1: Chart of computerization of trade[1]

[1] From "Electronic trading in fixed income markets", Bank for International Settlements, 2016.

Cloud computing and new data processing techniques have enabled an ecosystem of FinTech startups to flourish and challenge incumbents in such areas as banking, insurance and investing. The availability of cheap data storage and processing power has also, in parallel, enabled both small and large firms to make better use of AI techniques for processing data, fundamentally providing better insights into these data sets, as well as higher quality predictions. In some cases, the actual AI algorithms have not changed much in decades, since they were first published in academia; instead, readily available, cheap, compute power has made it possible to run them in a reasonable time. In other cases, real improvements in algorithm design have been behind the improvements, e.g. some of the more recent progress in both deep learning and reinforcement learning. Legacy plays a part here. Traditional econometric-based models have a long history, but as a result of their origins in other scientific fields, and emphasis on linear models and structured data, they're not that well-suited to many problems in finance.[2] Finance problems can involve structured and unstructured (e.g. text) data, hierarchical relationships, high dimensionality, limited observations, changing data distributions and a low signal-to-noise ratio. Having access to the latest tools, algorithms and compute power is often necessary to building higher-performing models.

What Is Artificial Intelligence?

There are multiple definitions of AI, since the term itself was first coined by John McCarthy in 1956. At a high level, AI is concerned with machines that exhibit some characteristics of natural intelligence demonstrated by humans (and in some respects animals), for example learning and problem solving. As a broad field in itself, there are a variety of subfields within AI, focused on particular aspects, such as vision, natural language processing, robotics, expert systems and machine learning.

Of all the subfields, arguably one of the most popular is machine learning, which applies statistical models to data in order to learn from them and make predictions. Contrast machine learning with rule-based models, or expert systems:

- **Machine learning (ML)** learns from historical data – training. Model is then run on data it hasn't seen before in order to make predictions – inference. ML models can be relatively simple or indeed more complex, especially in the case of deep learning.
- **Expert systems** emulate the decision-making process of an expert. The decisions and behaviour are encoded in terms of a set of rules. Expert system complexity is related to the number of rules and their interactions.

These two examples are interesting, because in some respects they sit on opposite ends of the spectrum, in terms of flexibility and the emphasis on learning from pre-existing knowledge, vs learning from data. Many of today's trading models are rule-based and relatively simple encodings of financial expert knowledge, while adaptive statistical methods – like ML – are still a minority contribution.

Using Data Science to Solve Business Problems

The professional field most closely linked to AI, and especially ML, is that of the data scientist. This is a field that I have been involved with for years, running teams in banking and more recently a business in asset management. The definition of data science is related to the definition of ML, that is extracting knowledge and insights from (structured and unstructured) data. It is a multidisciplinary field, for which the key skills lie at the intersection of mathematics, computer science, domain knowledge and communication, as shown in Figure 2.

[2]Marcos López de Prado, The 7 Reasons Most Econometric Investments Fail (Presentation Slides) (16 April 2019). Available at SSRN: https://ssrn.com/abstract=3373116.

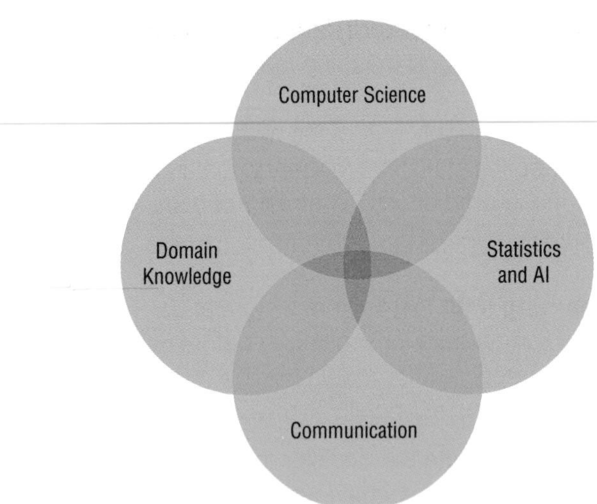

Figure 2: **Venn diagram of the data science skill set – computer science, statistics and AI (incl. machine learning), domain knowledge, communication**

I emphasize the last skill – communication – because data science is a business-facing role, where complex models and analysis must be condensed and simplified for a non-specialist audience. Domain knowledge is also important: understanding markets themselves and price action, regulations, or other aspects of the domain, is essential in order to successfully apply machine learning and other techniques to the problem of insight and prediction.

One of the most important tasks that a data scientist can perform, in collaboration with stakeholders, is that of translating a business problem to a specification for the AI-based system. This involves the following steps:

- Defining the problem as prediction, recommendation, alerting, or other.
- Selecting and understanding the data to be used and ensuring it is available (including an adequate history and quality).
- Deciding on the appropriate model or candidate models. The process of choosing a much simpler, linear model as a baseline is useful here. Then we can determine whether more sophisticated, non-linear techniques such as machine learning, really add any value.
- Defining the success metrics.
- Considering the end user(s).

Indeed, it could be argued that the most valuable step comes before all of this: identifying *which* business problems for that firm are most *amenable* to AI techniques. What should be noted is that the approach here is top-down from the business perspective, rather than bottom-up from the perspective of the technology.

Capital Markets Use Cases

The key use cases for AI in Capital Markets can be split into four groups: Customer, Trading/Portfolio Management, Regulatory, and Operations (taken from the author's past experience.[3] Example use cases from each of these groups are shown in Table 1.

- **Recommendation engines:** A key use case is that of recommending financial products to clients, either directly or via an established sales force. Recommendation engines are a particular application of both statistical techniques and machine learning, the most well-known examples of which are associated with Amazon and Netflix, for shopping products and videos. They involve an interesting mix of user interests, product characteristics, both explicit and implicit feedback, and the ideally relevant intersection of users and products in the form of a useful recommendation. The financial markets case is complicated by the interaction between the client's existing

[3] Also: "Artificial intelligence and machine learning in financial services", Financial Stability Board, 2017.

Table 1: The four main types of AI Use Cases in Capital Markets, together with some examples for each

Customer	Trading / Portfolio Management	Regulatory	Operations / Back-Office
Recommendation engines (e.g. for stock trading)	Trade execution	Trader surveillance	Capital optimization (such as risk-weighted assets, RWA)
Credit scoring	Indicator creation	Regulations processing and codification	Server monitoring, capacity scaling and failover recovery
Insurance processing (including pricing, underwriting and claims)	Portfolio optimization	Know-your-customer (KYC) processing	Cybersecurity
Chatbots	Asset price prediction	Use by regulators themselves for surveillance and fraud detection	Model risk management
			Market impact analysis

portfolio, the financial products on offer (or indeed securities), and the market itself – for example, investing in a particular product may make more sense for a particular market regime or point in the business cycle, such as selecting value factor indices during a recovery phase in the economy. As a result, conventional recommender algorithms need to be modified to take into account the more complex and dynamic drivers within financial markets.

- **Trade execution:** Here, algorithms execute orders, most often with the aim to minimize transaction costs. Volatility and liquidity are important considerations, with large orders being broken down into smaller orders which are placed into the market over some period of time. One particular subset of execution tasks, that of limit order placement, has been successfully paired with machine learning – for example the LOXM system from JP Morgan,[4] which uses reinforcement learning to achieve this goal.

- **Trader surveillance:** ML combined with natural language processing (NLP) applied to a variety of data sources, including trader communications, is used to alert supervisors to unusual or suspicious behaviour. Data sources can also include logs of activity (computer logins, building entry times), human resources records and any other information supporting models of behaviour. Complexity arises from the processing and merging of these disparate sources of information, as well as a potential lack of training examples for instances of behaviour which are "suspicious". In addition, some examples of trader communication data such as instant chat messages, are difficult to process as a result of the abbreviated nature and use of codewords or slang.

Trust, Transparency, and Human Interactions

This is a broad topic that intersects with all of the potential use cases covered previously, and is relevant for other domains as well. The subfield of explainable AI is commonly called XAI for

[4] LOXM System, JP Morgan.

short, an abbreviation first suggested by DARPA.[5] Key drivers behind the recent resurgence in interest include the rapid development of commercial AI-based systems (some of which are used as decision support tools together with a domain expert, in medicine, for example), the increase in complexity of these systems, and regulation. Explanations themselves are useful for designers of systems, in order to understand what they are doing at different points in time, as well as, of course, to end users.

XAI intersects with a number of other fields and areas of study, including human–computer interaction, social science, philosophy, psychology, cognitive science, data visualization and others. The concept of explanations has been studied in great depth over the last 50 years by researchers in philosophy, psychology and cognitive science, while philosophers have been studying the topic for hundreds of years before this. What makes a good explanation is intrinsically intertwined with human behaviour and thought processes and, indeed, is dependent on the specific audience, and their own biases. It is here that the concept of mental models (from human–computer interaction) – how people create models of technological systems in order to better interact with them – becomes useful.

Some examples of XAI systems, initiatives and reports in the financial domain:

- The UK Financial Conduct Authority (FCA) is partnering with the UK National Institute for Data Science and AI, the Turing Institute, on transparency and explainability in financial services.[6]
- XAI Asset Management is a hedge fund, founded in 2017, specializing in the application of explainable AI to macro-based investing.[7,8]
- simMachines is a software startup, founded in 2016, providing transparent, machine learning-based models for a variety of finance use cases, including customer-focused and fraud prevention.[9]
- World Economic Forum report on AI in Finance, published in Autumn 2019; there is a section in this report which presents several XAI-based approaches.[10]

It's worth noting that XAI will, at some level, be mandated on finance firms by regulators. One example already in place is the European Union's General Data Protection Regulation (GDPR), and the "right to explanation", the scope of which is still the subject of debate.[11]

State of the Art: Selected Highlights 2018/19

- Pre-trained language models
  - Specifically, the algorithm called GPT-2, by OpenAI, used to generate realistic passages of text.[12] This first example is controversial due to its potential application in the creation of "fake news". It uses a type of model called a generative adversarial network, or GAN. These models are trained on a large amount of data, and can then "generate" data just like it. For example, a generative model trained on images of cars can then create its own, plausible, images of cars. In so doing, the model has learnt the features and building blocks needed to create these images. GANs show a lot of promise in different application areas and have attracted much attention in the AI community. Generative models can

[5]DARPA Explainable AI Program.

[6]UK FCA Partners with Turing Institute, 2019.

[7]XAI Asset Management, Explainable AI, 2019.

[8]Disclaimer: I am a co-founder of this firm.

[9]simMachines

[10]"Navigating uncharted waters", World Economic Forum Report on AI, published in autumn 2019.

[11]GDPR, "right to explanation".

[12]OpenAI GPT-2 System.

potentially be used to create synthetic data that matches the characteristics of real financial data, which can be a consideration where data is limited, allowing models to be trained and potentially providing higher prediction accuracies.

- Imperfect information games
  - Deepmind have demonstrated their AlphaStar system, which beat a world class player at StarCraft II, by five games to zero.[13] Although there are various constraints in place, this is still considered to be a difficult problem which has been at least partially solved.
  - The playing of games may not, on the surface at least, seem particularly relevant, but there are some parallels, certainly in the case of imperfect information. Imperfect information-based models could, for example, provide improved macroeconomic forecasts, which could in turn provide better asset pricing models.
- Common sense reasoning
  - Researchers created a knowledge graph of over 300k events associated with 877k inferential relations, which are combined with neural network models in order to reason about previously unseen events.[14]
  - The common-sense reasoning example depends on the intersection of logical and statistical models, two quite different approaches to AI. This is a combination that has previously been highlighted as a fruitful area of research by several experts, including Pedro Domingos.[15] Embedding domain or expert knowledge into AI systems via common sense logical rules, particularly in the case of limited data and low signal-to-noise ratio, is likely to be a sensible approach.
  - It's possible that the eventual structures and algorithms for more general, or flexible artificial intelligence (rather than the fairly narrow systems we see today) will use some combination of information representations and approaches.
- Automation of ML algorithm selection
  - AutoML is a service, typically hosted on the cloud, where non-specialists can train machine learning models to meet business needs. Researchers at the University of Texas have made good progress on automatically training neural network models,[16] and there are other good examples of systems from Google and Amazon.
  - These AutoML systems offer a potentially useful service to firms without the specialist knowledge or human resources to train machine learning-based models.
  - However, it is likely that AutoML systems particularly tailored to finance are required, rather than more general solutions. This is especially important for use cases in the customer and trading categories. It's also debatable whether truly performant, robust solutions that provide competitive advantage can yet be delivered via such platforms.

The state-of-the-art examples given above are a cross-section of different application areas and techniques, but do not tell the whole story. The family of AI techniques is large, and describing them all would easily fill another book. It's best to remember that the most popular model or models today are not necessarily the best fit for a particular business problem, sometimes less fashionable methods work better. And in some cases, AI is not needed at all! But where it is required, an open-minded approach to choosing the correct techniques is required, or even better, experience should lend a guiding hand.

[13] Deepmind AlphaStar System.

[14] Maarten Sap et. al., "ATOMIC: An Atlas of Machine Commonsense for *If-Then* Reasoning", 2019.

[15] Pedro Domingos et. al., "Unifying logical and statistical AI", 2006.

[16] Jason Liang et. al., "Evolutionary Neural AutoML for Deep Learning", 2019.

Where Next?

In many respects, Capital Markets are a challenging application area for AI. Some financial institutions and FinTech startups have already developed AI-based systems and deployed these successfully, while many others are still in the process of catching up. Part of the challenge here is in embedding expert knowledge into the systems, as well as providing some level of transparency on their operations. More broadly speaking, it seems the near future is one of AI being an embedded or ubiquitous part of everyday life. In some cases, these systems will replace human effort, and in others they will augment it. It's important that we ensure best practices on their design, taking into account human factors, transparency and ethics. In so doing, we can best combine machine and human intelligence, and realize the full benefits of this revolution.

AI, Machine Learning and the Financial Service Industry: A Primer

By Hamza Basyouni
Digital Analyst, Innovation Lead and Transformation Advisor

According to the AT&T Foundry, artificial intelligence (AI) has been a research focus for over 50 years, but only in the last decade has it become popular for enterprise and consumer use.[1] The market for AI has grown in recent years, with approximately 1500 companies in North America developing AI applications including leading companies such as Microsoft, IBM, Google and Amazon.[2]

This advent in the development and uses of AI, machine and deep learning is affecting the potential future direction of the Financial Services Industry and emphasizing the importance of human and machine collaboration. Accenture reports that 62% of senior bankers said the proportion of roles requiring people to collaborate with AI will rise in the next three years.[3]

AI has evolved from being a potential disruptor into a key component of digital and business transformation for long-term sustainable operational benefits. Deloitte reports that AI advances have unlocked new horizons within the Financial Services Industry, through numerous applications that are already being implemented, potentially changing business activities across operations, risk, finance, and compliance.[4] Deloitte also reports that the rise of AI-based applications, such as robo-advisors, pattern recognition, AI/virtual agents and intelligent automation,[5] such as robotic/intelligent process automation has had a significant impact within investment management, banking and insurance.

The banking industry is rapidly changing, with a paradigm shift to digital-only banks that leverage AI technology and data to provide digitalized offerings and services. In the banking sector, companies have adopted AI by investing in the development of specific applications and created partnerships with FinTechs,[6] tech startups and digital Banks.

PricewaterhouseCoopers (PwC) describes AI as a game changer that could contribute up to $15.7 trillion to the global economy by 2030.[7] It named key areas within the Financial Services Industry that have the biggest AI potential as being personalized financial planning, fraud detection, anti-money laundering and process automation.[8] PwC also said that the costs of AI technology would decline over the next ten years as the software becomes more commoditized[9] for mainstream uses across various other industries.

[1] R. Yomtoubian, I. Brunelli, and B. Strum (2016) *The Future of Artificial Intelligence in Consumer Experience According to the AT&T Foundry* [online]. Available at: www.rocketspace.com/hubfs/accelerator/the-future-of-artificial-intelligence.pdf?t=1508679213129 [Accessed 18 December 2017].

[2] Ibid.

[3] Accenture.com (2019) [online]. Available at: www.accenture.com/_acnmedia/PDF-77/Accenture-Workforce-Banking-Survey-Report#zoom=50 [Accessed 23 May 2019].

[4] GRID by Deloitte (2017) *AI and you Perceptions of Artificial Intelligence from the EMEA financial services industry* [online] 2017 Deloitte Consulting S.r.l, p.15. Available at: www2.deloitte.com/content/dam/Deloitte/cn/Documents/technology/deloitte-cn-tech-ai-and-you-en-170801.pdf [Accessed 17 December 2017].

[5] Ibid.

[6] Ibid.

[7] A.S. Rao and G. Verweij (2017) *Sizing the prize: What's the real value of AI for your business and how can you capitalise?* [online] PwC. Available at: www.pwc.com/gx/en/issues/analytics/assets/pwc-ai-analysis-sizing-the-prize-report.pdf [Accessed 18 December 2017].

[8] Ibid.

[9] Ibid.

Furthermore, the International Data Corporation states that worldwide cross-industry spending on cognitive and AI systems increased by 59% in 2017 compared to 2016, reaching $12 billion, and will rise to $57.6 billion in 2021.[10]

Defining Artificial Intelligence

The terms AI and machine learning are used interchangeably, but they are different. One expert identifies three defined levels of AI:

(1) ANI: Artificial Narrow Intelligence, which specializes in one area and is good at one discipline.

(2) AGI: Artificial General Intelligence, where machines pass the intelligence levels of human beings with the ability to apply logic and abstract thinking to complex ideas.

(3) ASI: Artificial Super Intelligence, when machines become smarter than all of humanity combined.[11]

The current key difference is between AGI and machine learning, as AGI refers to machines generally being able to carry out tasks typically performed by humans that also includes search, symbolic and logical reasoning, and statistical techniques that aren't explicitly deep learning-based.[12]

[10]Worldwide Semiannual Cognitive/Artificial Intelligence Systems Spending by Industry Market 2016–2020 Forecast (2017, June). IDC (Doc #US42749817). https://www.accenture.com/gb-en/_acnmedia/pdf-78/accenture-banking-report-ai-future-workforce-survey.pdf.

[11]C. Skinner (2017) Welcome to the Semantic Web [Blog] *Chris Skinner's Blog*. Available at: https://thefinanser.com/2017/05/welcome-semantic-web.html/ [Accessed 19 December 2017].

[12]R. Yomtoubian, I. Brunelli and B. Strum (2016) *The Future of Artificial Intelligence in Consumer Experience According to the AT&T Foundry* [online]. Available at: www.rocketspace.com/hubfs/accelerator/the-future-of-artificial-intelligence.pdf?t=1508679213129 [Accessed 18 December 2017].

Machine Learning (ML) and Deep Learning (DL) within Finance

Machine learning refers to the process of computer systems that have the ability to learn, automatically discover patterns in data and improve their performance through data exposure without being explicitly programmed.[13] Its subset application is deep learning, which allows a computer to recognize patterns from both labelled and unlabelled data sets.[14] A comprehensive AI makes use of all these fields, although presently the enterprise uses are heavily focused on machine learning.[15]

This has undoubtably bought disruptive changes to the Financial Services Industry, in terms of the impact on professions and business models and technology will continue to profoundly impact the employment landscapes in the coming years. For example, in 2015, the UK media, using research by the University of Oxford, said accountants have a 95% chance of losing their jobs as machines take over the number crunching and data analysis.[16] "We expect around 35% of skills will be different in the near future," says Till Leopold, the project lead on the World Economic Forum's (WEF) employment, skills and human capital initiative.[17]

[13]N. Nilsson (1998) *Introduction to Machine Learning* [ebook] Stanford, CA 94305: Robotics Laboratory Department of Computer Science, Stanford University. Available at: http://ai.stanford.edu/people/nilsson/MLBOOK.pdf [Accessed 20 December 2017].

[14]R. Yomtoubian, I. Brunelli and B. Strum (2016) *The Future of Artificial Intelligence in Consumer Experience According to the AT&T Foundry* [online]. Available at: www.rocketspace.com/hubfs/accelerator/the-future-of-artificial-intelligence.pdf?t=1508679213129 [Accessed 18 December 2017].

[15]Ibid.

[16]O. Griffin (2016) How artificial intelligence will impact accounting, *economia.icaew* [online]. Available at: http://economia.icaew.com/features/october-2016/how-artificial-intelligence-will-impact-accounting [Accessed 20 December 2017].

[17]Ibid.

In the Investment Management and Hedge Fund sectors, companies have begun and continue to deploy the latest advances in data analytics, data science and machine learning to develop complex quantitative investment and trading strategies to produce astounding results within the financial markets. For example, more than 70% of the trading today is carried out by automated AI systems.[18] Another example of a paradigm shift that has already occurred is the case of a Venture Capital Fund that appointed an AI computer algorithm tool called "Vital" to its board to partake in the screening and voting of new investment opportunities.[19]

Barriers — and the Goldilocks Rule

Significant barriers to the implementations of AI are already evident, as reported by Accenture through its surveys of senior decision-makers and banking executives. These surveys show the first signs of resistance by employees, as they believe on average only 26% of their workforce is ready to work with intelligent technologies, and mostly cited a growing skills gap as the leading factor influencing their workforce strategies.[20]

Additionally, Deloitte state there are current and future challenges of AI and machine learning implementations within the Financial Services Industry. These limitations include a lack of expertise and awareness regarding the technology, significant volumes of data hosted on legacy systems and an overall lack of agility in deploying digital projects that have already left the traditional Financial Services Industry behind smaller FinTechs[21] and tech startups.

Clearly, a lot of work still needs to be done, and a shift from a traditional top-down management approach is required. Organizational structures and processes need to adapt and a crucial first step will be the design of effective journey maps that reinforce strategic alignment and serve to increase efficiency and deliver value through technological implementations.

AI is within Gartner Hype Cycle's "peak of inflated expectations" and will continue to have enormous impacts and future implications within the Financial Services Industry. As Deloitte states, with the eruption of AI some of the market leaders in ten, or even five years' time, may be companies you've never heard of, and in turn, some of today's biggest commercial names could be struggling to sustain relevance or have even disappeared altogether.[22] However, the Goldilocks principle still applies as finance professionals and society are advised not to be either too optimistic or too pessimistic about AI technology.

[18] D. Mangani (2017) 5 AI applications in Banking to look out for in next 5 years [Blog] *analyticsvidhya*. Available at: www.analyticsvidhya.com/blog/2017/04/5-ai-applications-in-banking-to-look-out-for-in-next-5-years/ [Accessed 18 December 2017].

[19] "Algorithm appointed board director", BBC, 2014: www.bbc.com/news/technology-27426942.

[20] Accenture.com (2019) [online] FUTURE WORKFORCE SURVEY - BANKING REALIZING THE FULL VALUE OF AI. Available at: https://www.accenture.com/_acnmedia/PDF-77/Accenture-Workforce-Banking-Survey-Report#zoom=50 [Accessed 23 May 2019].

[21] GRID by Deloitte (2017) *AI and you Perceptions of Artificial Intelligence from the EMEA financial services industry* [online] 2017 Deloitte Consulting S.r.l, p.15. Available at: https://www2.deloitte.com/content/dam/Deloitte/cn/Documents/technology/deloitte-cn-tech-ai-and-you-en-170801.pdf [Accessed 17 December 2017].

[22] Ibid.

Compliance as an Outcome

By Prashant Gandhi
Principal Financial Services, ThoughtWorks

Regulators want to ensure that they are both protecting the sanctity of the financial system as well as protecting customers. Given the recent history of supervisory failures, financial crisis and systemic fraud at large scale, regulators are increasing their scrutiny and are creating more rule-based regulations to prevent further market crashes.

Heavy enforcement actions are also forcing banks to rethink their approach to compliance. Banks have often responded to regulatory obligations with tactical responses, especially after the 2008 crisis. Tactical implementations, coupled with manual processes, create complex layers that become hard to untangle. This creates a huge demand on the banks' resources, both in terms of manpower and capital available to invest. A common trend has been to add large number of compliance professionals to the ranks every year to meet the increasing demand. In 2015, for example, JP Morgan added 13,000 resources to support regulatory and compliance efforts and spent more than $600 million in regulatory and compliance technology.

This is not a race that banks will win. Chris Skinner, a noted author and futurist, often quotes a statistic that a global bank must deal with 185 regulatory changes per day.[1] It is inevitable that banks will need to automate compliance checks and regulatory changes.

This is not a race that regulators will win, either. Andrew Haldane, the chief economist at the Bank of England, observed that the type of complex regulation developed over recent decades might not just be costly and cumbersome but sub-optimal for preventing any financial crisis.[2] The answer for the regulators may lie in defining their policies using complexity theory through network analysis and behavioural modelling.

Simple Heuristics Lead Human Behaviours

One key idea from complexity theory is that regulators should propose simple rules that market participants can follow. In uncertain environments, human behaviour tends to follow simple heuristics better than complicated rules. One way to define these simple heuristics is through the lens of customer needs. Consumers are typically at the wrong end of information asymmetry when dealing with banks. So, a heuristic might be about increased transparency, which can be about visibility, costs or better market comparison. Another heuristic is around control, which can be delivered by providing the power of execution and choices in the hands of the end customer.

The stated goal of the electronification project at JP Morgan is to deliver greater choice, transparency, liquidity and efficiency for the customers and dealers.[3] It uses machine learning techniques to learn from past market behaviour, spotting liquidity opportunities, and avoiding market impact through simulation and best execution price.

---

[1] Chris Skinner Blog: https://thefinanser.com/2018/12/compliance-will-kill-bank.html/.

[2] Andrew Haldane's speech on "The Dog and The Frisbee": https://www.bis.org/review/r120905a.pdf.

[3] JP Morgan 2019 Investor day presentation: https://www.jpmorganchase.com/corporate/investor-relations/document/2019_cib_investor_day_ba56d0e8.pdf.

Customers have access to neural network powered execution capabilities for greater control and deeper trading strategies that reduce information asymmetry and provide best execution guarantees. These changes are partially driven by the regulators (MiFID II), and partly by the competitive landscape. Importantly, simple rules and machine learning capabilities provide best execution compliance in accordance with the intended spirit of the regulations.

Prevention through Deterrence

Trader behaviour is another major area of concern, whether it is about the use of inside information or collusion with market participants or front running customer trades. The hard thing with bad actors is to identify whether an event has occurred and finding an appropriate resolution for it. Harder still is to find leading indicators that highlight the probability of a future event. It may be easier to change behaviour through deterrence.

Bad actors can precipitate a crisis. For example, *Time* magazine calls "The LIBOR scandal" the crime of the century. While a student paper had long ahead identified possibilities of rate manipulation,[4] it took years for regulators and banks to identify this collusion and take corrective measures. In the LIBOR scandal, communication logs between different bank participants had long hinted there was a potential collusion afoot.

Identifying these communication anomalies in a traditional 3-tier compliance model is a gargantuan task. A natural language processing solution that monitors all communications including email, telephone call transcripts, calendar entries and chat rooms can provide an early indicator of collusion efforts. Non-verbal and verbal cues from traders on the trading floor can also be detected through computer vision and flagged through sentiment analysis. Such a proactive monitoring solution can act as an effective deterrent for the traders against fraudulent activities.

Data and AI Strategy

Market participants inevitably need to develop a data and AI strategy to acquire the right set of capabilities to achieve their business outcomes while remaining compliant. A key part of such a strategy is to create a flywheel of data. Simplifying customer journeys can create opportunities for additional data acquisition that can serve multiple goals. For example, capturing a geotagged photo of the person at their home with a proof of address during the application process can reduce fraud, deliver efficiencies for the back-office and speed up the overall onboarding process.

Market participants also need to avoid the fake AI phenomenon, as solutions regularly get branded as AI solutions even if they implement simple business rules or have a 'Wizard of Oz' implementation with humans providing the intelligence. Solutions need to deliver unique data sets and insights, demonstrate deep subject matter expertise and ability to integrate with other services.

Intelligent Empowerment

Greater efficiencies can be achieved by combining human decision-making with predictions from AI solutions. Humans cannot provide the scale and speed to combat the increased volume of work, whereas AI solutions need multiple feedbacks to deliver more accurate results. Aided by a machine learning solution, it is easier for an auditor to review for any incriminating communications, or for a lawyer to preserve confidentiality through redacting select parts of the document. Regulators can also aim for an online dashboard that integrates data, methods and

[4]Student paper on LIBOR borrowing costs: https://papers.ssrn.com/sol3/papers.cfm?abstract_id=1569603.

indicators to assess the financial stability. Real-time simulations using this data with stressed inputs can provide better insights into the financial stability than infrequent reports.

Compliance and Business Benefits?

Well-designed AI solutions can provide both customer benefits and compliance as an outcome by enabling:

1. Simplification of the customer journeys while reducing enterprise risk.
2. Movement towards a risk-aware decision-making policy versus a defensive policy.
3. Building strategic tech-enabled business capabilities.
4. Turning data from a constraint into a decision accelerator.

Further reading

Bradford Cross Blog. http://www.bradfordcross.com/blog/2017/6/13/vertical-ai-startups-solving-industry-specific-problems-by-combining-ai-and-subject-matter-expertise

Complexity Theory and Financial Regulation paper. https://science.sciencemag.org/content/351/6275/818

Alternative Data and MetaQuants: Making the Most of Artificial Intelligence for Visionaries in Capital Markets

By Alejandra M.J. Litterio
Co-Founder and Chief Research Officer, Eye Capital Ltd

With the advent of artificial intelligence (AI) and its impact in capital markets, the analysis of traditional data – such as historical publicly reported revenues, fundamental, technical and economic indicators – seems to be no longer enough.

Talent, alternative data, the conception of hybrid forms such as the "quantamental"[1] and the "MetaQuant" have become key factors in a search for unexplored sources of alpha. How do we develop a comprehensible model with the most groundbreaking strategies based on machine learning (ML) and AI that allows investors to reap greater gains than other market participants?

In this chapter we rethink the core value proposition of alternative data and why a MetaQuant approach is a meaningful advantage to investors, enabling a deeper understanding and correlation of all the sources that could improve the appraisal of alternative data as a key engine for innovation in the "arms race" for an edge.

Historically, in almost any field, there is, apparently, a "holy grail". In finance, it is the quest for novel sources of information as a way of gaining an advantage over competitors, called alternative data (alt-data). As alt-data continues to enter the mainstream, becoming an essential part of portfolio construction, investment professionals, hedge funds and asset managers have begun to conceive it as the most precious resource changing the capital markets landscape forever.

Of course, those who do not follow this seismic shift and update their investment processes accordingly face an increasing risk of lagging behind. However, finding an edge does not only depend on the quantity of data, but also on the ability to combine data sources that otherwise seem unrelated, and encompassing data to extract insights from non-financial and non-traditional sources to improve alpha generation.

Back to Basics: What Is Alt-Data?

Defined as "…any information collected from non-traditional sources used for a different purpose than the one initially intended", most conceive alt-data as a niche of unstructured unorthodox data not previously used in the investment process. For others, alt-data is simply any information that is non-market data. Some of the most common examples include geolocation, satellite imagery, apps, social networks, IOT (sensors), microdata about consumer shopping (credit card transactions), and insurance data. But the definition is much broader, and clearly brings us somehow closer to visualizing a wider field of effective action to create better predictive models.

Because of the diversity and high volume of alt-data sets, a new issue has arisen: how alt-data is characterized to determine which one is most valuable according to the organization's needs. In this respect there is not a unified or formal criterion to discriminate between conventional or unconventional alt-data. Kolanovic and Krishnamachari (2017)[2] have presented a taxonomical

[1] "The success of quantamental investing is rooted in process", Bloomberg Professional Services, 8 May 2018.

[2] M. Kolanovic and R. Krishnamachari (2017) "Big Data and AI Strategies: Machine Learning and Alternative Data Approach to Investing", J.P. Morgan, May 2018.

approach based on the usefulness of the alt-data set. Dannemiller and Kataria (2017)[3] proposed a continuum from structure to unstructured data. Other authors have adapted Kitchin's system (2015)[4] and designed a six-dimensional model. No matter how alt-data is classified, though, the truth is that market participants must think about:

- Reliability
- Accessibility
- Cost-effectiveness.

Redefining Market Players – The MetaQuant Approach

Are traditional data science teams good enough to develop models able to achieve long lasting competitive advantage? Not quite. The complexity of incorporating unstructured data into the portfolio construction process makes it necessary to create a new profile of quants. We have coined the term "MetaQuant".

The MetaQuant is a new breed of market player who is able to "translate human language into signals" and "read" the data from a holistic perspective. They are linguists, semiologists and philosophers – or rather a combination of these three intertwined profiles – who will fuel the potential for information advantage and provide a unique core differentiator, transforming data into knowledge in the financial world.

[3] D. Dannemiller and R. Kataria (2017) Alternative data for investment decisions: Today's innovation could be tomorrow's requirement, Deloitte Center for Financial Services.

[4] R. Kitchin (2015) "The opportunities, challenges and risks of big data for official statistics", *Statistical Journal of the IAOS* 31(3):471–481.

The MetaQuant has emerged as a crucial component of any AI quantitative trading model and paves the way for a novel insight: the "reinterpretation of alternative data". It is in this scenario where the combination of structured and unstructured data using AI technology in a big data environment has a hidden value.

In the common quantamental process, advanced computational techniques are used extensively to reduce bias and random noise in investing. The MetaQuant takes this thinking "out of the box", addressing crucial financial questions from a more descriptive qualitative level, integrating the unstructured with existing models, or creating a differentiated model.

Can a Hybrid Model (Quantamental + MetaQuant) Boost Investment Results?

The MetaQuant, based on a holistic approach, explores unstructured data within a specific context disclosing in-depth combinations of multiple factors from a variety of data sets providing valuable insights that are not so visible to the "naked eye". Once the corpora (unstructured +alt-data) has been exhaustively analysed, the MetaQuant will design an integrated framework with variables defining all the possible relationships (for instance, finding patterns extrapolating and identifying phrases highlighted in an earnings conference call associated with geodata or even market drivers) which will be modelled by sophisticated AI algorithms, fuelling and enriching the portfolio selection and its rebalancing while assigning a predictive value or score to each asset allocated by the portfolio manager. With a hybrid model, portfolio managers will have at their disposal not only an incredible wealth of data and disruptive analytics tools, but also potentially new distinctive and actionable insights in the search for an edge.

The landscape of data is ever-changing and, as a consequence, market participants need to evolve to stay ahead in order to gain a unique competitive advantage and boost profits.

This is just one piece in the mosaic of the financial puzzle. While still in its early days, alt-data is a (r)evolutionary step towards bringing transparency into capital markets and global economies. The MetaQuant is certainly the figure "turning over the most rocks" at an infinitely greater scale, critically questioning every stage of the model, monitoring and revisiting the interactive framework to give investors an edge.

AI and Capital Markets: Where to Now?

By Karan Jain
Head of Technology, Europe and Americas, Westpac Banking Corporation

Artificial intelligence (AI) and machine learning (ML) have numerous key roles to play in the future of the capital markets: combating eroding margins; structuring for the realities of customer loyalty to the best price and speed of execution; minimizing the costs of complying with increasing regulation (the reality now is that it is more common today for businesses to decide on whether to restructure to meet regulatory requirements or to shut a portion of the business down completely); living up to changing customer expectations; and dealing with the realities of the organization's narrowing bottom line.

These factors constitute a series of triggers for big changes to ways business is done. Look deeper and we see that big change is also coming from industry: the data collected by car manufacturers like Land Rover, Tesla and BMW are impacting how commodities are priced in completely new ways, and beyond the direct control of capital markets players.

The priority to deepen relationships – or create them in the first place – through cross-selling assets is being enabled by AI. So, an accelerating advancement in technology and its application generally can be viewed as a threat to the capital markets status quo, although the pace of change – and despite the hype – has positive benefits to yield for businesses of all sizes. This chapter aims to cut through the noise and focus on some of the key themes and some enabling factors for success.

Organizational Efficiency — Inside and Out

Algorithmic trading utilizing ML has been in the capital markets' toolkit for many years, and this will continue – it won't be the fastest growing use case but will show steady growth, with a few exceptions where investment will reshape the business. Insights about customers and the business itself are where we will see the majority of the investment, and accelerated development.

Most capital markets businesses only use 1/10th of the information they hold – from customer and market data to cash management data – and struggle to extract meaningful insight from it. On the customer-facing side, credit-limit enhancement (based on identifying and stitching data sets together using ML to speed up credit decisioning) is starting to pay dividends in transaction times. Further use cases also include (a) predictive analytics, e.g. for in-house staff to generate leads and identify missed opportunities; and (b) augmented decision-making, e.g. more on the customer "self-service", where the next most suitable option is presented to the customer.

Regulatory Developments

Most firms have more than one regulator to contend with, creating a web of multiple regulators with differing requirements. Digital regulatory reporting is a key theme (as well as a big business cost). Indeed, a whole new area of FinTech – RegTech – has been born to meet an indisputable and growing need, with extensive use of natural language processing and other AI technologies to enable:

- Translation of regulation into plain English.
- Multilevel surveillance for various mediums, also being used to monitor performance of desks and individuals.

- Correlation of data from multiple product systems to enable digital reporting.
- Horizon scanning.
- Application of regulatory changes to scenarios to understand delta against the basis of today's operations.
- Transaction monitoring and other information security domain activities applied to know-your-customer (KYC) and anti-money laundering (AML) requirements that impact on how and when capital markets firms do business with their customers.

Future Enablers

The capital markets AI age is an exciting time to be part of. What are the strategic enablers that can help you and your business be set up for long-term success?

1. Be data ready: Make data governance and data stewardship a priority. These are critical for any ML/AI program.
2. Be proactive in four-way collaboration: There is significant value to be unlocked from partnerships between banks and FinTechs, in the form of bank-to-bank (non-competitive and compliant) data sharing and modelling, as well as partnering with FinTechs to avoid duplication of efforts.
3. Be proactive on culture: Build and nurture a data culture and a culture that learns to trust the machine's decision. This is probably the slowest part of this journey as progress also needs to be made in the foundational areas of explainability and ethical design.
4. Prioritize talent and teams: Building and nurturing agile teams and organizations and setting up for lean technical deployments is a key enabler for effective use of AI and ML in capital markets.

Trust, Transparency and Ethics

7

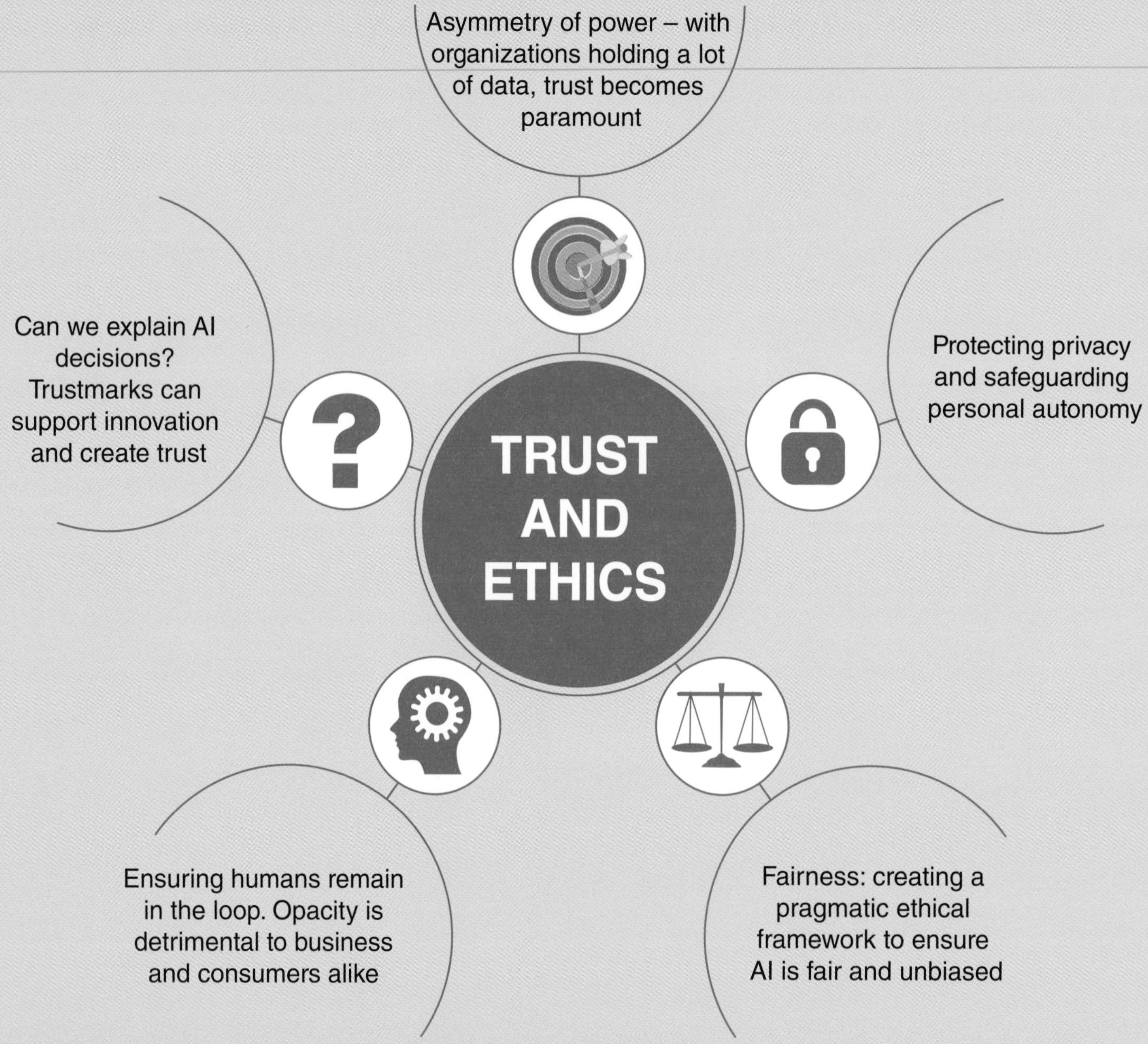

TRUST AND ETHICS

Asymmetry of power – with organizations holding a lot of data, trust becomes paramount

Protecting privacy and safeguarding personal autonomy

Fairness: creating a pragmatic ethical framework to ensure AI is fair and unbiased

Ensuring humans remain in the loop. Opacity is detrimental to business and consumers alike

Can we explain AI decisions? Trustmarks can support innovation and create trust

Artificial Intelligence is bringing major transformative changes for economies and societies in the world, and these changes need to be harnessed for the benefit of all people. This is very important, especially in financial services. However, recent stories in the data handling space, ranging from Cambridge Analytica to the progressive intrusion of facial recognition techniques, are changing the perception of the public thus making trust a key element of companies' ability to build and retain their customer base.

It is fair to say that over recent months we have witnessed a crisis in legitimacy of technology, with regulators and citizens alike challenging opacity, lack of transparency and accountability. At the same time AI research and applications are progressing at rapid pace, challenging current legislation, thus demanding responsibility from companies deploying them. This Part looks at both the legal and ethical discussions surrounding AI and how these debates can be leveraged to enhance consumer protection and trust.

From a legal standpoint, the deployment of AI in financial services raises questions about the applicability of current legislation around, for example, use of inferential data, automated decision-making systems as well as data analytics and predictive technology. The issue is whether consumer legislation coupled with privacy law can offer protections to consumers while ensuring companies operate on solid legal grounds.

The debate is strong and thriving, and this chapter goes to the very heart of it. For example, one area explores which corporate governance structures need to be established to ensure algorithms are deployed responsibly and that the tension with privacy legislation is fully understood. Other ongoing discussions involve liability and whether current legislation can address the challenges posed by AI systems.

Ethics, in a nutshell, is all about trade-offs. One of them is the trade-off between efficiency and explainability as machine learning introduces a challenge in this area. Privacy tensions also need a clear assessment alongside a deep understanding of both the intended and unintended consequences of AI systems, including those on the workforce which need to be part of the transformation journey. The definition of these trade-offs is defined by several authors as part of business decisions thus making accountability structures crucial for companies.

Transparency, privacy and ethics by design – and in design – are becoming increasingly important. We now have a plethora of principles for good and responsible use of AI, and companies and institutions alike are developing practical guidance on how to ensure ethical considerations are given the right prominence.

This part also explores the interaction between artificial and human intelligence and how crucial it is to retain human oversight. The human in the loop element is key and especially in the financial sector where AI decisions can have long-lasting impact on individuals. Lastly, readers can delve into issues of algorithmic bias and fairness which have become dominant in the public domain over recent years.

Whilst this is still work in progress, this emphasis on trust and ethics is a clear sign that we can harness the potential of AI only if we put our human values at the heart of it.

Trust in FinTech and AI: Some Introductory Reflections

By Reema Patel
Head of Public Engagement, Ada Lovelace Institute

Trust, many people have argued, is the "secret sauce" that underpins finance and banking. The 2008 financial crisis was amongst the many incidents which illustrated the centrality of credibility and trust to the effective and smooth operating of the financial services industry. One must not lose sight of the fact that finance and money itself can be understood as a "social technology" – for it to serve its proper function, it is trust that is central to its operation. However, famously, Onora O'Neill has critiqued a focus on trust alone, arguing that it is *trustworthiness* that we must be more focused on she says:

> *We should aim for more trust in trustworthy things but not in untrustworthy things...intelligently placed and intelligently refused trust should be the proper aim for society.*
>
> —*Onora O'Neill*

This argument has often been interpreted as a need for *technology that is trustworthy.* But in O'Neill's infamous speech, "What we don't understand about trust," she later makes clear that trustworthiness is not a property that can be held by the "thing" – the *technology* – rather, it is something that is a property of the people and the organizations developing the technology. She says:

> *Trust is well placed if it's directed to matters in which the other party is reliable, competent and honest – so, trustworthy. Can you trust the corner shop to sell fresh bread? Can you trust your postman to deliver letters?...Trust is badly placed if it's directed to matters in which others are dishonest or incompetent or unreliable.*
>
> —*Onora O'Neill*

For our purposes, we need to ask whether we can trust the designer, the developer, the public servant to design, use and deploy the technology (and in particular, FinTech) most appropriately – in an honest, competent and reliable fashion. It's clear that the role for industry in setting high standards, building trustworthiness and shaping AI for good is essential.

Tech That Has Legitimacy with a Social Licence

Although trust and trustworthiness matters, arguably, even this is not enough to secure artificial intelligence (AI) that works in the public interest. Relying on citizens to determine trustworthiness is particularly problematic given that there is often a lack of transparency about the benefits and harms, as well as a lack of choice when it comes to the use of data and AI. You might not think Facebook is trustworthy, but you might still feel it limits your life or causes you some material harm to give it up. And when it comes to interacting with public services or accessing financial services such as mortgages, banking options or low-cost credit, there might be even less choice there.

Increasingly, the notion that society must be "in the loop" through increased public involvement in the governance of the technology is starting to take hold. Understanding how best those standards can be set requires drawing upon the notion of *legitimacy and the creation of a social licence*. We understand legitimacy *as the broad base of public support that allows companies, designers, public servants and others to deliver beneficial outcomes for people and for wider society through the use of AI*. Legitimacy is about ensuring that there is a reasonable settlement between those who use AI and data, and those who are directly affected by that use.

Ethical Innovation in Finance

For legitimacy to be secured, we need ethical innovation. Ethics and innovation are often seen as uneasy bedfellows – and yet it appears that there is an enormous gap in enabling what is often described as ethical innovation – "mission-led" innovation which is purposeful, in service of humanity and its mission, and which supports us collectively to make the most of our resources and our capacities as part of wider society. As I have already flagged, finance raises particular challenges for those seeking to design a trustworthy and more legitimate approach to the use of AI. We are dealing with a complex system that is evolving at pace – which has features of being emergent, interactive, unpredictable and non-linear, and of posing profound systemic risk to people and society if issues are not identified and spotted early. However, "retreat" from technological innovation means we face a double-edged sword; "techlash" places innovation that works for people and society at risk, preventing us from realizing the *benefits* of financial innovation.

There are numerous barriers to change preventing us from realizing these benefits, such as:

- Lack of understanding and education around the use of data and AI to enable a greater diversity and plurality of financial services.
- The commodification of data, and systems that do not support or incentivize the sharing of data and AI across sectors.
- A lack of confidence from developers in broaching issues that might be personal for users (for instance, financial eligibility, or money matters).
- Widespread public narratives prophesizing doom, and "scare stories" about the use of AI, and general public distrust of financial services in light of relatively recent experiences (e.g. 2008 financial crisis).
- A lack of access to funding or finance without needing to monetize data to offer free platforms – the cost of design and development itself poses barriers to building a sustainable business model that works for people and society.
- The rate of change within technology: keeping pace with developments can be particularly hard if you are a small startup seeking to disrupt established market dynamics and players.

Clarity of Ethical Purpose and Mission Is Central

In 2018, the Ada Lovelace Institute worked in partnership with the Finance Innovation Lab, convening technologists and startup entrepreneurs to better understand how to support ethical innovation in the financial services sector. Our participants told us that in developing and designing AI and tech-based interventions, they felt that having a clear ethical purpose and mission had helped to motivate and inspire support in their work. They also told us that they felt this particularly powerfully in 2018 when there was a tangible "cultural moment" that meant ethics was taken more seriously as a standard part of the tech development process. Participants saw a parallel with a not dissimilar moment for their industry – the 2007/08 Global Financial Crisis – which also underlined the urgency for change in our financial system.

Regulation Introduced Clarity and Wider Support for Innovation

We also heard from these finance entrepreneurs about the benefits that recent legislation and regulation such as PSD2, open banking and GDPR had brought about by providing certainty and setting standards in the market that they could comply with. And numerous participants spoke particularly favourably of the opportunities to participate in sandboxes enabled by the Financial Conduct Authority – creating safe spaces that allowed for both the protection of groups and individuals, whilst simultaneously balancing these with the need to support a thriving innovation sector. They similarly recognized that the pace of technological development in, for example, machine learning and angular code language also "made their businesses fly". Whilst changing behaviour is thought to be incredibly difficult, there was also recognition that FinTechs might be best places to have the tools to uncover how best to influence it.

Four Ways to Support More Trustworthy, Ethical Innovation in the Financial Services Sector

During the course of our workshop, finance entrepreneurs identified four practical interventions through which more trustworthy and ethical innovation in the financial services sector might be enabled. These are as follows.

1. Ensuring Diversity in Design and Development, Ensuring Tech Aligns with Public Values

There is a need to build capacity within design and development – so as to enable greater reflexivity and responsiveness to people (who, it was recognized, were likely to be far more diverse and less homogenous than those developing the technology). It is important to consider the use of agile and flexible approaches, the importance of techniques such as UX journey design, open innovation and open co-design, as well as the use of public deliberation when designing AI and the technology in the financial services industry. Initiatives such as data trusts, kitemarking, ethical scoring and ranking systems, and application of a code of ethical standards might be other useful and practical ways through which to strengthen FinTech's alignment with public values.

2. Changing Public Narratives about Finance and Tech

Media backlash and "techlash" has served to undermine ethical innovation. This often stemmed from a lack of understanding of finance itself, as well as widespread public reluctance to engage in discussion about related matters (e.g. there is generally a sense that it is taboo to talk about money, or even to talk about how to make money from the use of data/AI, which is divorced from the realities of everyday practice). Changing public narratives in this space, in the deepest sense, is not simply limited to changing norms about the technology – but also about finance and money itself.

3. Ensuring Society Is in the Loop

The lack of transparency about, e.g. who an organization is lending to and who is being rejected, as well as the criteria being applied, can risk overlooking an issue, which is that tech might benefit some groups at the expense of others (i.e. there is invariably likely to be distributional impact). It felt clear that there was a debate to be had about the winners and losers from the use of the technologies, but there was a lack of willingness to engage in a conversation about what was acceptable, and what was not. In addition, it is central to ensure that those who are designing technologies are diverse, and thus able to better respond to and understand the lived experience of underserved groups and minorities. Given the complexity of the system (driven by the pace, uncertainties and unpredictabilities of the changes posed), designing effective interventions would be limited if they were to follow an exclusively formulaic process. A particularly strong common theme was placed on the importance of the need for shared resources, capacity building and collaboration (across industry/regulation/research) to enable developers to better understand what ethical good practice looked like, and embed that in practice in a more *anticipatory* manner, upstream of public "techlash".

4. Strengthening Regulation – Clarity and More Support

Last but absolutely not least, those we spoke to at the front line of designing these technologies highlighted that more was required in terms of supporting FinTechs and others to understand more practically how best to meet ethical standards beyond blind adherence to "tick box" processes. These might well be provided by independent bodies or a peer support network distinct from the role of the regulator. There was also a recognition that regulators were often under-resourced to deliver their roles effectively – with calls for increased resourcing for the FCA to support them to enable their effective operation.

Building Trust through Sound Governance

By Patricia Shaw
CEO, Beyond Reach Consulting Limited

With 5.8 million individuals in the UK with either a thin or non-existent credit file[1] (approximately 1.3 million of whom are unbanked, accounting for 3% of UK adult population[2]) and the potential for using new data sources to boost financial inclusion by 1.52 million,[3] financial service firms are increasingly seeking to use open banking and other new data sources for good. AI may be disruptive, but its impact for good is not inevitable. The financial services sector can act now: by increasing trust, transparency, ethics and by giving "consumers control over data to Big Tech".[4] This requires data mobility, digital identification, security and incorporating ethics by design in its governance.

Good outcomes can range from personalized financial budgeting, planning and robo-advice, to assisting consumers select suitable credit products and build a better credit report. For the banked, it is the early identification of signs of financial distress[5] and signposting to consumer debt advice sooner.[6]

The "value exchange" enables the outcome (e.g. an unsecured loan with repayment terms tailored to preference) by using AI to offer speed and convenience (often free of charge), in return for data made available by the consumer.

> *We must worry. But not so much on the subject of who owns data, but as to how data is used, and what kind of control can be exercised on this use.*
>
> Luciano Floridi, Director of Oxford's Digital Ethics Lab

The consumer should understand the whole bargain: the opportunities, the risks, the opportunity costs, and the impact. For the bargain to be conscionable[7] this demands effective communication (in plain language which is educative, framed around the spectrum of potential consumer outcomes) and TRUST: Transparency, Responsibility, Understanding, Stewardship and Truth.

---

[1] According to research conducted by Experian Limited, in its report Making the Invisible Visible: Exploring the power of new data sources, published March 2019.

[2] According to FCA's Financial Lives of Consumers across the UK survey 2017, published June 2018, where someone is unbanked if they have no current account and no alternative e-money account.

[3] According to Experian's report Making the Invisible Visible, ibid., a combination of adding data from social housing tenants through the use of Rental Exchange, along with data from utilities companies and high cost credit providers, private rental data and Open Banking data, the net effect could bring down the number of people financially excluded by 1.52 million people overall.

[4] The Furman Review requested by HM Treasury which reported back on 13 March 2019.

[5] Through identifying overspending proportionate to income, arrears, persistent debt, or systematic minimum repayments.

[6] One FinTech, Tully, helps consumers build their own debt flexi-plans and signposts to the Money Advice Service.

[7] Lord Denning identified the concept of the unconscionable bargain in Lloyds Bank v Bundy in 1974, because he recognized the inequality of bargaining power. This concept although borne out of undue influence law, serves as a stark reminder for us all in how data (especially information which is insightful and predictive for financial decision-making purposes) should be regarded.

TRUST

Transparency – being clear about what it is you are doing and why, demonstrating the opportunities and risks. Where there are risks being honest about them so people and society can make an informed decision.

Responsibility – being reputable and accountable for what it is you do.

Understanding – helping those from whom data is collected and those to whom you provide services to understand what outcome they can expect and how it will impact them and society.

Stewardship – being a good custodian of the data and the insight and inference derived from the services, showing that you have assessed the contributing factors and their impact. Even though something is feasible, demonstrating why it should (or shouldn't) be done and how it is acceptable and in line with the kind of society we all want to create. Safeguarding against risks.

Truth – validating the accuracy of the data, the insight and inferences made, verifying that the outcomes are beneficial and not harmful. Being honest about the risks.

The financial services sector was built on the premise of public trust and only exists because it has a social licence to operate.[8] With the introduction of open banking[9] and the right to data portability,[10] consumers now need reassurance. A consumer is not only empowering the firm, but the firm's AI, entrusting it with their data for the purposed outcome; believing it will produce better control over finances, not harm, undermine or disempower the consumer or the ecosystem. Ethical governance structures coupled with proper accountability are necessary to provide that reassurance. Without TRUST, consumers won't use the firm's services, adopt new technology or share their data. Without data, AI can't produce insight.

Ethical Challenges for Firms

#Challenge 1: The Balancing Act

Balancing providing a frictionless user journey, enabling the consumer to make informed decisions, against consuming the least time and acting in the best interest of the companies' shareholders. Transparency demands information to be shared. Understanding requires time.

#Challenge 2: Seizing the Opportunity to Produce Real Benefit whilst Understanding the Tensions[11]

Fairness[12]

This is crucial and relates to using AI to gain more personalized insight and to increase the predictive power of the data, whilst

[8] Financial Innovation Lab, Briefing: Ethical use of AI in Financial Services, p.5, published April 2018.

[9] CMA Retail Banking Market Investigation Order 2017 (which issued directions to banks to ensure they comply with the requirement to release personal and business account data sets as part of the Open Banking remedy) and the second Payment Services Directive (EU) 2015/2366.

[10] General Data Protection Regulation (EU) 2016/679, Article 20.

[11] The Ada Lovelace Institute report, Ethical and Societal Implications of Data and AI, published February 2019 goes into greater detail regarding 4 central tensions.

[12] The Financial Conduct Authority (FCA), the UK's financial services regulator, requires regulated firms to treat customers fairly. Principle 6 of the FCA's Principles for business states: "A firm must pay due regard to the interests of its customers and treat them fairly", engendering fairness as a regulated business behaviour.

ensuring that the outcome produced is fair, unbiased, promotes equality, and applies reasonable inferences.[13]

Categorized transaction data inevitably makes generalizations;[14] it can lead to false positives (e.g. affordability appearing greater because of a larger than usual end-of-month current account balance because of a third party cash loan) and false negatives (e.g. showing lower than usual expenditure indicating financial distress where an alternative income source was not identified). Insight gained from AI needs to be validated to protect against systemic disadvantage for some groups over others.

Explainability

Explainability is not about how the neural networks work themselves.[15] Consumers are agnostic to the technology. Consumers just want to know how the result was achieved (e.g. declined credit), what could have been done differently (i.e. if alternative information had been made available or weighted differently in the algorithm).

Disguising a black box behind a facade of competition, proprietary intellectual property or gamification loses consumer credibility.

Privacy

AI is not only processing but producing more data. Excessive demand of a consumer's data (personal data or not) can lead to a loss of privacy and informational autonomy.[16] Not sharing the data is an option, but not a viable one. Data portability may be an alternative remedy, but if all providers require the same minimum level of information, it will only result in no or limited access to services.

Autonomy of Decision-Making

Personalization can helpfully channel information (e.g. list of available credit cards) to show only those that align with their preferences (e.g. 0% to pay on balance transfers in first 24 months). Excessive nudging and/or over-personalization can lead to limiting the information pool and orchestrating the consumer's own decision-making.

#Challenge 3: Seizing the Opportunity whilst Understanding the Trade-Offs

In the short term, emerging financial services will produce new ways of working (e.g. paying by App rather than contactless card).

In the long term, it may create healthier societal attitudes towards spending, saving and debt. Alternatively, it could undermine consumer choice (particularly for the vulnerable or digitally excluded), as society becomes cashless and requires an online account to transact.

[13] Sandra Wachter and Brent Mittelstadt, Right to reasonable inferences – Rethinking data protection law in the age of big data and AI, published April 2019.

[14] As we commonly see regarding representative APR rates where 51% of successful applicants must be given the stated rate.

[15] Artificial Narrow Intelligence, Artificial General Intelligence or Artificial Super Intelligence.

[16] Defined as "The informational autonomy or self-determination means the control over one's personal information, that is to say the individuals' right to determine which information about themselves will be disclosed, to whom and for which purpose" taken from the European Commission's report: The Right to be Forgotten and the Informational Autonomy in the Digital Environment by Prof. Dr Cecile de Terwangne, published 2013.

Ethical Governance

Why? Ethical Governance Is a Competitive Advantage

AI is predicted to contribute $15.7 trillion to the global economy, and 10% of GDP for the Northern European economy by 2030.[17] The innovation is game changing and must be kept in check to create a financial services ecosystem beneficial to all. Navigating previously untrodden paths requires understanding the impact of the intended and unintended consequences, and mitigating tensions and trade-offs. As individuals and society adapt to the technology (and vice versa), the financial ecosystem will transform. This requires evaluation beyond simple compliance with law. Continually challenging innovation that is or could be developed and questioning, "Should we create them?" The mantra of "move fast and break things" is no longer appropriate; AI has the power to make or break lives.

How? Human-Centric Outcomes-Based Ethical AI Governance

Identify the Principles

Despite at least 63 initiatives describing high level principles, values, and other tenets to guide the ethical development, deployment and governance of AI,[18] none are specifically focused on the financial services sector, although there have been some self-regulatory industry developments in this area. The FCA Handbook does provide for High Level Standards containing Principles for Businesses, but these do not explicitly provide guidance for ethical and/or societal implications of AI.

[17] PwC's report: Sizing the prize, What's the real value of AI for business and how can you capitalise?, published June 2017.

[18] Brent Mittelstadt, AI Ethics – Too Principled to Fail, published June 2019, p.1.

Identify the Governance Structure

The AI governing structure should apply a multi-stakeholder and collaborative approach. Its remit and decision-making authority should be clear from the start. Whatever you name it, (ethical advisory board or AI panel, etc.) its function should be embedded in the innovation-design-development-distribution life cycle, and aligned with business strategy and risk mitigation process. Its goal: to treat customers fairly and ethically in the societal context in which the outcomes are achieved.

Identify the Governing Body

Participants in a governing body must be carefully identified, ensuring diversity of thought and engagement, from the bottom up. Such body should be multilayered, multidisciplinary, multifaceted and transparent. This means enlisting a diverse range of internal and external experienced and expert people from a variety of backgrounds, including technical, customer relations, service delivery, and risk functions, ethicists, social scientists and consumer representatives.

Operationalizing the Principles

This requires the governing body to have tools to assist identification of tensions and trade-offs and assess outcomes ethically, based on a current understanding of the product/user landscape and acceptable societal norms. Futurescoping, data and algorithmic evaluation and monitoring (particularly for hidden bias[19]), and consequence scanning[20] for usability and

[19] For data, see ODI's Data Ethics Canvass, for algorithms the IEEE P7003 Standard for Algorithmic Bias Considerations is one of eleven IEEE ethics related standards currently under development as part of the IEEE Global Initiative on Ethics of Autonomous and Intelligent Systems.

[20] For further details of one approach, see Doteveryone's TechTransformed project on Consequence Scanning.

abuseability, are just some of the possible tools. The output should be a holistic impact assessment of data,[21] algorithms,[22] societal[23] and individual impact.

When? Frequently and Often

This is not a one-time-only, one-size-fits-all kind of governance, and does not replace audit. It's a continual case-based process aligned to a firm's innovation-design-development-distribution methodology.

Empowered

For ethical governance to be impactful, it must be empowered to affect corporate decisions, without which it will provide no meaningful mitigation of unethical outcomes. The financial services sector is positioned well to mitigate the challenges of a principled approach to AI ethics,[24] but it is not there, yet. Outcomes-based regulation,[25] with clear AI ethics principles and action-guiding standards is still required. Making this accessible to small and medium-sized enterprises (SMEs) may require industry-level governance structures. Making this transparent for consumers may require more widespread use of consumer panels, citizens' juries, sandboxes and possibly even a kitemark.[26]

Conclusion

Ethical governance (beyond that predicated on regulatory, business or reputational risk) specifically built into the very foundations of AI design, development and distribution in financial services may be the only way to navigate and future-proof this brave new AI world whilst keeping the consumer and society upfront and in control. Whatever policymakers, existing (or new) regulators and legislators do next, AI will not wait. The challenges raised above aren't insurmountable: AI in financial services can be fair, accountable, transparent, responsible, explainable and good for society and the firm.[27]

It requires TRUST.

[21] In respect of personal data, this will potentially include a Data Protection Impact Assessment under Art 35 of GDPR.

[22] As proposed by Women Leading in AI's report on 10 principles of responsible AI, published March 2019, p.13.

[23] The concept of assessing societal impacts was raised in the Ada Lovelace report on Ethical and Societal Implications of Data and AI, ibid.

[24] Brent Mittelstadt, AI Ethics – Too Principled to Fail, ibid, p.3 suggests there are four potential weaknesses of a principled approach to AI Ethics which will result in limited impact on AI development: (1) common aims and fiduciary duties, (2) professional history and norms, (3) proven methods to translate principles into practice, and (4) robust legal and professional accountability mechanisms, such as losing your licence to operate.

[25] This was recommended in the Financial Innovation Lab, Briefing ibid.

[26] As proposed by the All Party Parliamentary Group for Data Analytics in their report Trust, Transparency and Tech: Building ethical data policies for the Public Good, published May 2019.

[27] See the PARETS framework referred to in Women Leading in AI's report, 10 Principles of Responsible AI, ibid. p.15.

Independent AI Ethics Committees and ESG Corporate Reporting on AI as Emerging Corporate and AI Governance Trends

By Brian W. Tang
Founder, ACMI and LITE Lab@HKU

Innovation lies at the heart of all thriving civilizations. While freedom to innovate and free markets are often viewed as paramount, a line is universally drawn when it comes to research and experimentation on human subjects.

Independent Human Research Review Committees (IHRCs)

Doctors worldwide are trained to follow the Hippocratic oath to "first do no harm". Yet the Nazi human experiment atrocities were "crimes…not simply the actions of individual doctors, but involved leading members of the medical community… and should be taken as a warning for the future".[1] After the scandalous Tuskegee Study gave unsuspecting African-American males syphilis, the 1974 US National Research Act required institutional review boards (IRBs) to approve all federally funded research under the Common Rule for the Protection of Human Subjects. Significantly, its resultant 1978 Belmont Report outlined three ethical principles:

1. Respect for Persons – informed consent being essential.
2. Beneficence – to maximize benefit and minimize risk.
3. Justice – to ensure fair selection of participants.

These principles have formed the basis of human science research worldwide,[2] including non-clinical behavioural and social science experiments.[3]

However, IHRCs and their regulation have difficulty grappling with internet research ethics,[4] big data and AI research, as demonstrated by controversies surrounding the 2014 Facebook

[1] See, e.g., Alliance For Human Research Protection, "German Medical Society Apologizes for Nazi-era Atrocities by Doctors" (28 May 2012): https://ahrp.org/german-medical-society-apologizes-for-nazi-era-atrocities-by-doctors/.

[2] These IHRCs are variously known as research ethics committees (REC) in the United Kingdom, research ethics board (REBs) in Canada and human research ethics committees (HRECs) in Australia.

[3] For example, at The University of Hong Kong, principal investigators from clinical faculties must make submissions to an IRB, while those from non-clinical faculties must make submissions to a Human Research Ethics Committee: The University of Hong Kong, Research Ethics Compliance – Requirements for the Conduct of Research Involving Human Participants and Live Animals: www.rss.hku.hk/integrity/ethics-compliance.

[4] See, e.g., *Stanford Encyclopedia of Philosophy*, "Internet Research Ethics" (22 June 2012, rev 26 August 2016): https://plato.stanford.edu/entries/ethics-internet-research/.

Emotional Contagion study[5] and 2016 "AI gaydar" research.[6] Should research based on already publicly available data on the internet from, e.g. social media[7] or YouTube videos,[8] or from anonymous Amazon Mechanical Turk workers labelling data for algorithms, require US IRB approval or be exempted for lacking a "human subject"?[9] In any case, IHRC regulations often do not apply to private sector-sponsored human research, which are also subject to confidentiality obligations.[10]

World's First Corporate AI-Focused IHRCs

Although 63% of the 200 respondents in a global survey have affirmed that they "have an ethics committee that reviews the use of AI",[11] two companies should be highlighted as creating the world's first corporate AI-focused IHRCs. These corporate AI-focused IHRCs can help to operationalize the numerous AI

[5]Cornell's IRB exempted the 2014 Emotional Contagion study where Facebook News Feeds of unsuspecting users were manipulated to study their subsequent postings, see "Everything We Know About Facebook's Secret Mood Manipulation Experiment" (*The Atlantic*, 28 June 2014): www.theatlantic.com/technology/archive/2014/06/everything-we-know-about-facebooks-secret-mood-manipulation-experiment/373648/. While the US Department of Health and Human Services new rules will require a single IRB review for multisite US studies, it does not clarify the need for IRB review of AI and internet research: www.forbes.com/sites/kalevleetaru/2017/09/16/ai-gaydar-and-how-the-future-of-ai-will-be-exempt-from-ethical-review/#46967c912c09; "Safeguards for human studies can't cope with big data" (*Nature*, 15 April 2019): www.nature.com/articles/d41586-019-01164-z. It should also be noted that an increasing number of IRBs are being run for-profit and are private-equity backed, see, e.g., Sheila Kaplan, "In clinical trials, for profit review boards are taking over for hospitals. Should they?" (*Statnews*, 6 July 2016): www.statnews.com/2016/07/06/institutional-review-boards-commercial-irbs/.

[6]Stanford's IRB approved the "AI gaydar" research, which uses facial recognition to predict sexual orientation, published in 2017 by American Association of Psychologists (APA)'s own journal, see "AI Gaydar Study Gets Another Look" (*Insider Higher Ed*, 3 September 2017): www.insidehighered.com/news/2017/09/13/prominent-journal-accepted-controversial-study-ai-gaydar-reviewing-ethics-work.

[7]See, e.g., "Social Sciences One And How Top Journals View The Ethics of Facebook Data Research" (*Forbes*, 13 August 2018): www.forbes.com/sites/kalevleetaru/2018/08/13/social-science-one-and-how-top-journals-view-the-ethics-of-facebook-data-research/#67de4ea05e38.

[8] See, e.g., "The Tricky Ethics of Using YouTube Videos for Academic Research" (*Pacific Standard*, June 2019): https://psmag.com/social-justice/the-tricky-ethics-of-digital-academic-research.

[9]See, e.g., Jacob Metcalf and Kate Crawford, "Where are human ethics in Big Data Research? The emerging ethics divide" (*Big Data and Society*, January–June 2016, 1–14): https://journals.sagepub.com/doi/full/10.1177/2053951716650211.

[10]The industry-academic partnership between Social Science One and Facebook highlights significant questions about the roles of journals, funders and privacy legislation like the EU's General Directive on Privacy Regulations (GDPR). See, e.g., "Social Science One and how top journals view the ethics of Facebook Data Research" (*Forbes*, 13 August 2018): www.forbes.com/sites/kalevleetaru/2018/08/13/social-science-one-and-how-top-journals-view-the-ethics-of-facebook-data-research/#67de4ea05e38; "GDPR's Massive 'Research' Exemption: Facebook and Social Science One" (*Forbes*, 23 May 2019): https://www.forbes.com/sites/kalevleetaru/2019/05/23/gdprs-massive-research-exemption-facebook-and-social-science-one/#2d796fa83568.

[11]SAS, Accenture Applied Intelligence and Intel for Forbes Insights, "AI Momentum, Maturity and Models for Success: Based on Findings from a Global Executive Survey" (September 2018): www.accenture.com/_acnmedia/PDF-86/Accenture-AI-Momentum-Final.pdf.

ethics guidelines being published by industry,[12] governments[13] and privacy commissioners[14] around concepts such as fairness, accountability and transparency (FAT),[15] and also demonstrate the real-life challenges.

Google and DeepMind

When Google acquired AlphaGo's creator UK company DeepMind in 2014, an ethics board was created under an Ethics and Safety Review Agreement.[16] In 2016, DeepMind Health was launched, and a number of experts were invited to join a Panel of Independent Reviewers (PIR) to act in the public interest and publish publicly available annual reports to which DeepMind would respond.[17] Alas, after an investigation triggered by a public and media outcry into DeepMind Health's transactions with UK National Health Service (NHS) partners,[18] the information commissioner concluded that Royal Free London NHS Foundation Trust had transferred data from 1.6 million patients to DeepMind Health to test its Streams app to diagnose acute kidney failure on an "inappropriate legal basis", as this was not for "direct care" and so had lacked informed patient consent.[19]

In 2018, Google announced its AI principles,[20] and later that year folded DeepMind Health into the newly-formed Google

[12] See, e.g., IEEE Global Initiative on Ethics of Autonomous and Intelligent Systems; Future of Life Institute's Asilomar AI Principles, Partnership on AI.

[13] See, e.g., EC High Level Expert Group on AI, "Ethics Guidelines for Trustworthy AI" (2019): https://ec.europa.eu/digital-single-market/en/news/ethics-guidelines-trustworthy-ai; "Translation: Chinese Expert Group Offers 'Governance Principles' for 'Responsible AI'" (National New Generation Artificial Intelligence Governance Expert Committee of China's Ministry of Science and Technology, 17 June 2019): www.newamerica.org/cybersecurity-initiative/digichina/blog/translation-chinese-expert-group-offers-governance-principles-responsible-ai/.

[14] See, e.g., Declaration on ethics and data protection in artificial intelligence at the 40th International Conference of Data Protection and Privacy Commissioners in Brussels (23 October 2018): https://icdppc.org/wp-content/uploads/2018/10/20180922_ICDPPC-40th_AI-Declaration_ADOPTED.pdf.

[15] See, e.g., Tencent has introduced the acronym AARC around available, reliable, comprehensible and controllable: Jason Si, "These rules could save humanity from rogue AI" (World Economic Forum, 8 May 2019): www.weforum.org/agenda/2019/05/these-rules-could-save-humanity-from-the-threat-of-rogue-ai/.

[16] "Deep Mind and Google: the battle to control artificial intelligence" (*1843 Magazine*, April/May 2019): https://www.1843magazine.com/features/deepmind-and-google-the-battle-to-control-artificial-intelligence.

[17] See, e.g., "DeepMind Health's Independent Review Panel" https://deepmind.com/applied/deepmind-health/transparency-independent-reviewers/independent-reviewers/.

[18] See, e.g., "Did Google's NHS patient data deal need ethical approval", *New Scientist*, 13 May 2016: www.newscientist.com/article/2088056-did-googles-nhs-patient-data-deal-need-ethical-approval/. The initial lack of transparency regarding the role of DeepMind and Google with the NHS did not help either.

[19] This conclusion was concurred by the National Data Guardian Dame Fiona Caldicott. See, e.g., "Google DeepMind 1.6m patient record deal deemed 'inappropriate'": *Guardian*, 16 May 2017: www.theguardian.com/technology/2017/may/16/google-deepmind-16m-patient-record-deal-inappropriate-data-guardian-royal-free; Julia Powles and Hal Hodson, "Google DeepMind and healthcare in an age of algorithms", *Health Technol.* (2017) 7:351–367: www.ncbi.nlm.nih.gov/pmc/articles/PMC5741783/. See also DeepMind Health Independent Review Panel Annual Report (July 2017).

[20] Google AI Principles (7 June 2018): www.blog.google/technology/ai/ai-principles/, which have since been supplemented by quarterly updated Responsible AI Practices technical recommendations; see most recent Google Responsible AI Practices: Putting our Principles into Action, 28 June 2019: www.blog.google/technology/ai/responsible-ai-principles/; as well as an ongoing review process (see, e.g., "Google AI Principles updates, six months in" (18 December 2018): www.blog.google/technology/ai/google-ai-principles-updates-six-months/).

Health.[21] In March 2019, Google announced the launch of its Advanced Technology External Advisory Council (ATEAC)[22] with eight prominent academics from areas such as AI, philosophy, psychology and robotics. Alas, one appointee promptly indicated that he would not serve, and public and Google employee outcry[23] over two appointees due to their backgrounds relating to LGBT and military drone controversies led to ATEAC's end after slightly more than a week,[24] with DeepMind Health's PIR reportedly also being disbanded soon thereafter.[25]

Axon

Formerly known as Taser, Axon created its AI and Policing Ethics Board (APEB) in April 2018 with 11 experts from different disciplines in AI, computer science, privacy, law enforcement, civil liberties and public policy.[26] Staffed by NYU's School of Law's Policing Project, APEB's first report in June 2019 recommended a moratorium on facial recognition use in Axon's body cameras,[27] and the publicly listed company concurred.[28] While APEB's recommendations may not be surprising given the racial and gender bias concerns raised by Amazon's Rekognition deployment by police departments[29] and San Francisco's ban on facial recognition, Axon's CEO and founder Rick Smith observed: "Without this ethics board we may have moved forward before we really understood what could go wrong with this technology."[30]

Corporate ESG Reporting on AI as a New Paradigm?

At the 2019 Annual General Meeting of Alphabet (Google's parent company), Stockholder Proposal 6 regarding the establishment of a board-level Societal Risk Oversight Committee, which would

[21] See, e.g., "Privacy concerns as Google absorbs DeepMind's Health Division" (*Telegraph*, 13 November 2018): https://www.telegraph.co.uk/technoguarddlogy/2018/11/13/privacy-concerns-google-absorbs-deepminds-health-division/.

[22] See Google, "An external advisory council to help advance the responsible development of AI" (26 March 2019): https://www.blog.google/technology/ai/external-advisory-council-help-advance-responsible-development-ai/.

[23] "Googlers against transphobia and hate" (Medium, 1 April 2019) raised more than 2500 petition signatures: https://medium.com/@against.transphobia/googlers-against-transphobia-and-hate-b1b0a5dbf76

[24] See, e.g., "Google'e brand new ethics AI board is already falling apart" (*Vox*, 3 March 2019): www.vox.com/future-perfect/2019/4/3/18292526/google-ai-ethics-board-letter-acquisti-kay-coles-james. Global Affairs SVP Kent Walker acknowledged on 8 April that: "It's become clear that in the current environment, ATEAC can't function as we wanted. So we're ending the council and going back to the drawing board."

[25] "Google Quietly Disbanded Another AI Review Board Following Disagreements" (*Wall Street Journal*, 16 April 2019):www.wsj.com/articles/google-quietly-disbanded-another-ai-review-board-following-disagreements-11555250401.

[26] SAP subsequently followed suit with its AI Ethics Advisory Committee: "SAP Creates First European Tech Company Ethics Advisory Panel for Artificial Intelligence" (SAP Press Release, 18 September 2019): https://news.sap.com/2018/09/sap-first-european-tech-company-ai-ethics-advisory-panel/.

[27] First Report of the Axon AI & Policing Technology Ethics Board, June 2019: https://static1.squarespace.com/static/58a33e881b631bc60d4f-8b31/t/5d13d7e1990c4f00014c0aeb/1561581540954/Axon_Ethics_Board_First_Report.pdf.

[28] The Future of Face Matching at Axon and AI Ethics Board Report" (Rick Smith, 27 June 2019): "Consistent with the board's recommendation, Axon will not be commercializing face matching products on our body cameras at this time": https://global.axon.com/company/news/ai-ethics-board-report.

[29] "Amazon Face Recognition Falsely Matched 28 Members of Congress with Mugshots" (ACLU, 26 July 2018): https://www.aclu.org/blog/privacy-technology/surveillance-technologies/amazons-face-recognition-falsely-matched-28.

[30] "Taser Maker Says It Won't Use Facial Recognition In BodyCams" (*Wired*, 28 June 2019): www.wired.com/story/taser-maker-wont-use-facial-recognition-bodycams/.

also oversee AI, was presented.[31] Although the company's dual-class shareholding structure that is common amongst big tech companies meant that the proposal was never likely to succeed, this approach is generally consistent with corporate reporting initiatives on environmental, social and governance (ESG) and climate-related disclosure by long-term institutional investors as the policy tool-of-choice to encourage companies to consider and report non-financial externalities of their corporate action.[32]

International Organization of Securities Commissions (IOSCO) recently recommended that "Issuers and other regulated entities should integrate ESG-specific issues, where these are material, in the overall risk assessment and governance of these entities, including at the Board level".[33] The UN's Sustainable Stock Exchanges (SSE) initiative currently has 90 SSE partner exchanges worldwide,[34] and the EU, China and many other countries are requiring such disclosure from listed companies,[35] guided by emerging ESG reporting standards.[36] Sustainability committees are also being introduced at the board level,[37] and it is hoped that

---

[31] See Alphabet 2019 Annual General Meeting Proxy Statement Stockholder Proposal Number 6 (30 April 2019): https://abc.xyz/investor/static/pdf/2019_alphabet_proxy_statement.pdf?cache=3ed6a89.

[32] See, e.g., Financial Stability Board (FSB) Task Force on Climate-Related Financial Disclosures (TCFD) Recommendations Final Report (2017): www.fsb-tcfd.org/publications/final-recommendations-report/.

[33] IOSCO Growth and Emerging Markets Committee, "Sustainable finance in emerging markets and the role of securities regulators – Final Report" (FR09/2019, June 2019): www.iosco.org/library/pubdocs/pdf/IOSCOPD630.pdf.

[34] United Nations (UN) through voluntary initiatives such as its Sustainable Stock Exchanges (SSE) Initiative currently has 90 SSE partner exchanges.

[35] EU Directive on disclosure of non-financial and diversity related information by certain large undertakings and groups (2014/95/EU): http://register.consilium.europa.eu/doc/srv?l=EN&f=PE%2047%202014%20INIT; see also EU Guidelines on reporting climate-related information (2019): https://ec.europa.eu/info/publications/non-financial-reporting-guidelines_en#climate; "China Mandates ESG Disclosures for Listed Companies and Bond Issues" (Latham & Watkins, 6 February 2018): https://www.globalelr.com/2018/02/china-mandates-esg-disclosures-for-listed-companies-and-bond-issuers/; and DFIN, "The Future of ESG and Sustainability Reporting: What Issuers Need To Know Right Now" (DFIN White Paper, 2019): https://www.dfinsolutions.com/sites/default/files/documents/2019-01/dfin_thought_leadership_whitepaper_ESG_Sustainability_Reporting_0.pdf.

[36] See, e.g., Global Reporting Initiative (GRI), Climate Disclosure Standards Board (CDSB) and Sustainable Accounting Standards Board (SASB); also Silda Wall Spitzer and John Mandyck, "What Boards Need to Know About Sustainability Ratings", *Harvard Business Review* (30 May 2019): https://hbr.org/2019/05/what-boards-need-to-know-about-sustainability-ratings. At the same time, buy-side best practices are emerging from the CFA Institute and the UN's Principles for Responsible Investment (PRI) to help investors understand how to better integrate ESG factors into their equity, corporate bond and sovereign debt portfolios: CFA Institute, "Positions on Environmental, Social and Governance Integration" (2018): https://www.cfainstitute.org/-/media/documents/article/position-paper/cfa-institute-position-statement-esg.ashx.

[37] See, e.g., CLP Sustainability Committee Report in CLP's 2018 Annual Report including INEDs and senior management: www.clpgroup.com/en/Investors-Information-site/Financial%20Reports%20%20Document/e_2018E112.pdf ; HKEx's Environmental, Social and Governance Committee Report 2017 with INEDs: www.hkexgroup.com/-/media/HKEX-Group-Site/ssd/Corporate-Governance/Documents/esgreport_e.pdf.

they will soon extend beyond independent non-executive directors (INEDs) to also include independent experts.

Separately, the Securities and Exchange Board of India (SEBI) recently introduced a quarterly reporting requirement for mutual funds to report on their use of AI and machine learning (ML),[38] especially in light of the first reported lawsuit in London relating to mis-selling a robo-advisor.[39] The report will require, amongst other things, a description of the AI/ML system in the product offering, how the AI/ML project was implemented, key cybersecurity controls, safeguards in place to prevent "abnormal behaviour" and whether it is within the scope of the system audit.

If such a corporate and/or regulatory reporting approach relating to AI were to emerge globally as part of ESG reporting, it could certainly help foster corporate culture change and strategy focus on the research, development, procurement and implementation of AI. With the benefit of input from independent experts,[40] such reporting would promote better understanding and decision-making by companies and regulators alike for better policymaking,[41] including for dual-use technologies,[42] and also address concerns regarding the "attention economy", data governance, privacy and growing scepticism concerning purely private sector self-governance initiatives relating to AI.[43]

[38] Securities and Exchange Board of India, "Reporting for Artificial Intelligence (AI) and Machine Learning (ML) applications and systems offered and used by Mutual Funds" (SEBI Circular SEBI/HO/IMD/DF5/CIR/P/2019/63, 9 May 2019): www.sebi.gov.in/web/?file=https://www.sebi.gov.in/sebi_data/attachdocs/may-2019/1557381806499.pdf#page=1&zoom=auto,-16,398.

[39] See "SEBI's Circular: The black box conundrum and misrepresentation in AI-based mutual funds" (*First Post*, 13 May 2019): www.firstpost.com/business/sebis-circular-the-black-box-conundrum-and-misrepresentation-in-ai-based-mutual-funds-6625161.html/.

[40] For some suggestions regarding structuring of corporate AI-focused IHRCs, see "Hey Google, sorry you lost your ethics council, so we made one for you" (*MIT Technology Review*, 6 April 2019): www.technologyreview.com/s/613281/google-cancels-ateac-ai-ethics-council-what-next/.

[41] For an overview of different initiatives worldwide, see www.forbes.com/sites/insights-intelai/2019/03/27/wrestling-with-ai-governance-around-the-world/#5ca9f7771766.

[42] See, e.g., "The role of corporations in addressing AI's ethical dilemmas" (Brookings Institution, 13 September 2018): www.brookings.edu/research/how-to-address-ai-ethical-dilemmas/.

[43] See, e.g., "Don't Let Industry Write the Rules for AI" (*Nature*, 1 May 2019): www.nature.com/articles/d41586-019-01413-1.

The Wisdom Vantage

By Esther Lancaster
AI Ethics Specialist

Innovation will continue to disrupt until we are satisfied that humanity is being benefitted at the highest level. This will only happen once we have challenged the underlying principles of each existing system – including the financial system – through the precise and exacting lens of an Artificial Intelligence.

As with all areas where we code our human intelligence into machines, algorithmic biases reveal where we as a society are at. The automation of our financial user experience through AI shows us the very way we have structured this value system, and enables us to decide what we want, and what simply does not serve the evolution of humanity. This is a natural progression.

For example, if a credit card company develops an algorithm to predict a customer's creditworthiness whilst adhering to a business model of maximized profit, it will invariably undermine principles of fairness. The system, when considered as a circuit must serve all parties; if it doesn't, new solutions will be found that support a profitable, prosperous financial model. For example, Universal Basic Income is a healthy option for a new world that looks nothing like the previous version – like nothing we can even imagine.

Right now the resistance and scepticism regarding UBI is strong, because we are still coming at it from a scarcity mindset, one that suggests that we as a species have limited resources and must push against what is comfortable in order to create wealth and success.

The reality of this technological revolution is that there are no limitations; we have all the resources we could ever need and far more, and the only single limitation humanity has is that we've subscribed to a mentality of scarcity and lack, that is misaligned with our open-ended capacity of intelligence. We have entered the era of the exponential technology both as a reflection of – and to support – this very powerful expansion of mind.

Explainability and Transparency

Explainability and transparency are essential aspects of this process that the financial industry is embarking on. As children we are encouraged to "show our working out" when tackling algebra or long division. Similarly, as this is a new, deeper mathematic underpinning an immense expansion of mind, it will benefit everyone to be completely clear throughout the process.

Each system can and will be optimized. We are embarking on a new world that works entirely distinctly from a limited definition of what it means to be human. Whilst the previous version served a purpose, AI, blockchain and other exponential technologies – collectively termed cyber-physical systems (CPS) – augment the current condition, unburdening and elevating the human mind.

This cyber-physical process considers the way in which our minds work in order to develop technologies that can do the same. Yet at each stage we are seeing, literally in black and white and 1's and 0's, that we as a society have biases; we have subscribed to limiting beliefs that have debilitated our capacity as a species. Through the process of data cleaning, empowerment and creators' responsibility, we are literally cleaning up our own minds and the collective narrative.

Cyber-physical technologies leave room for no doubt as to the power we have at our fingertips, and solutions that do not have data-integrity have no possible longevity in the coming era. It is necessary for the wisdom of the whole to decide how we want the future of finance to develop and those systems that do not support society to thrive will become obsolete. The new standard provides all of society with a level of comfort, ease, pleasure and happiness far greater than the previous model.

The Future

One of the main obstacles for AI in the financial markets revolves around managing risk that originates from human behaviour. What this really means is that the systems we have built and relied upon thus far, simply have not met our needs as a society. They are not "human-centred". With millions of startups, each innovating a different arena within the field, a larger surface area is covered. All of this technology takes a flexible approach to addressing specific challenges. Whether the focus is credit, insurance, wealth management, poverty, automation, etc, it is really up to each company to deeply consider the human behaviour and needs associated with that area, and provide all-encompassing solutions. This is absolutely possible. The limitless capability of exponential tech enables this kind of intimacy and expansion.

With contactless payments, the smartphone wallet and automated payment options at convenience stores, the way in which we relate to the financial industry is indeed shifting, whereby money is no longer a physical entity.

However, this is just the first step. With the use of artificial intelligence and distributed ledger technology (DLT), we are moving toward a time where not only is the phone a wallet, but the car can be a wallet, paying for its own petrol and insurance without human assistance. Our clothes can have sensory payment capability embedded into them just as easily and from there it is only matter of time before our human bodies themselves become the login and password for the lifestyle we live. Such potential generates concerns of privacy, security, fairness, equality, inclusivity and so on...and when we start considering the human body as a vehicle for digital connectivity and transaction, we enter a whole new level of ethical consideration. As we relax deeply into decoding the human mind in order to create such powerful solutions, we enter refined subtleties of intelligence.

Wisdom

These deeper subtleties of mind are exquisite and thus cannot be coded into "dangerous machines". Such subtleties of mind are peaceful and provide for a more seamless, holistic technological experience. An open-ended potential rather than one that is limited by its own code. "Human-centred" technologies, that understand human needs, won't be developed using the same coding structure that has been used thus far. The effortlessness and clarity of wisdom must be acknowledged in the process of development, for the technology to feel natural to the user. This is the standard society is now commanding.

The Wisdom Vantage cannot be used for anything other than the wisdom activity of mind, speech and action, and the same is true as it is extended into technology. Developing products in this manner will present solutions for all industries, including the financial industry, that can't be imagined currently, yet provide a higher standard of comfort for all. This is new terminology for the technology sector. We are building a bridge to a new way of being human, where individual needs are met and exceeded.

AI and Business Ethics in Financial Markets

By Daniel Liebau
Founder, Lightbulb Capital

and Tiffany Wong
Manager, PwC UK

Artificial intelligence (AI) is widely discussed in the media, and there are many views on how it will affect humanity's future. Since the publication of the academic article entitled "Deep Learning" in 2015[1] there is a focus on the branch of AI with learning capability. Such algorithms are fed large amounts of training data to enable them to predict variables of interest. In this chapter, we will concentrate on such machine learning algorithms when we use the abbreviation "AI". We acknowledge other branches of artificial intelligence, such as robotics, that aim at automating tasks and processes. In his recent book, *AI Superpowers* venture capitalist Kai-Fu Lee highlights a game-changing insight: we have now moved from the age of AI discovery (focused on research) to one of AI implementation that is all about the application of the technology to real-world problems.[2] That is why, at the present time, the increased potential of AI has led to numerous conversations about its ethical implications. Industry experts have different views. "Humans have found it impossible to encode ethical standards in finance, so we generally get principles-based guidance like "do the right thing". It will take AI a long time to learn the difference between right and wrong on matters where human experts often disagree," says Matthew Cannon, managing partner of Singapore-based hedge fund Modular Asset Management. Dr Marcos Lopez de Prado who runs True Positive Technologies LP in New York flips the argument on its head when he states: "Financial transactions are fraught with agency problems. One solution is to replace human judgement with smart, systematic processes. Another solution is to deploy algorithms that monitor human decisions in search for the biases. In both cases, AI has an important role to play."

In recent months, governments, financial services regulators and industry experts have worked on guidelines for the ethical use of AI. For this chapter, we considered mostly principle-based work, issued by the European Union,[3] Hong Kong[4] and Singapore.[5,6]

In our chapter, we take a closer look at the specific principles that we consider most relevant in the context of financial markets. We start by discussing fairness and privacy. Then we examine transparency and explainability – the age-old "black box" dilemma. Next, we attempt to address the paradox of accountability in AI.

The AI revolution has only just begun and the direction of technological advance and future challenges are still unknown. We are keen to contribute to the discussion by operationalizing principles to facilitate the ethical use of AI in financial markets.

---

[1] Y. LeCun, Y. Bengio, and G. Hinton (2015) "Deep learning", *Nature* 521, 436–444: https://doi.org/10.1038/nature14539.

[2] K.-F. Lee (2018) *AI Superpowers: China, Silicon Valley, and the New World Order*. New York: Houghton Mifflin.

[3] European Commission (2019) Ethics Guidelines for Trustworthy AI.

[4] Privacy Commissioner for Personal Data (2017) Ethical Accountability Framework for Hong Kong China.

[5] Monetary Authority Of Singapore (2019) Principles to Promote Fairness, Ethics, Accountability and Transparency (FEAT) in the Use of Artificial Intelligence and Data Analytics in Singapore's Financial Sector.

[6] Personal Data Protection Commission Singapore (2019) A Proposed Model AI Governance Framework: www.pdpc.gov.sg/-/media/Files/PDPC/PDF-Files/Resource-for-Organisation/AI/A-Proposed-Model-AI-Governance-Framework-January-2019.pdf.

Fairness

Treating stakeholders impartially and fairly is not a new matter in markets. Perhaps the fairness issue is as old as financial markets themselves. The use of technology to support fraudulent behaviour is vividly described in Scott Patterson's 2013 book *Dark Pools*.[7] When building AI trading algorithms, we recommend defining boundaries to delineate fair from unfair trading activity. Financial market regulation does this today for human traders. For example, reinforcement learning algorithms (they get compensated through a feedback loop depending on their performance) should not be allowed to engage in spoofing, wash trading, stock bashing or pump and dump/front-running-type of activities. This is true even if patterns in the training data suggest these practices would be very profitable.

Privacy

The Cambridge Dictionary defines privacy as "someone's right to keep their personal matters and relationships secret".[8] The centralized financial marketplaces of today display weaknesses when it comes to private data protection. Hong Kong's Central Bank reported that in 2018, cyberattacks on financial services providers doubled.[9] It is easy to imagine how hackers will use AI to exploit markets unfairly by getting access to private data to use it to their advantage in the markets. For example, the market participants may have to disclose ultimate beneficial ownership data of their executives. If illegally obtained, such data could be used to augment the data set fed to an AI algorithm to achieve superior trading results without observing privacy rights. One solution to preserving the privacy of actors in the financial markets could be the use of zero-knowledge proofs.[10] Secret information does not have to be revealed for counterparts to establish probabilistic certainty of, for example, identity-related data. If stored on a blockchain, data owners could selectively share zero-knowledge proofs on data attributes more securely and as required to interact in the more private markets of the future.

[7] S. Patterson (2013) *Dark Pools: The Rise of the Machine Traders and the Rigging of the U.S. Stock Market*, Random House.

[8] Cambridge Dictionary, 2019, "Privacy".

[9] Hong Kong Monetary Authority, 2019.

Transparency

Transparency is the quality of making something obvious or easy to understand.[11] In our context, it refers to the public's view of how and if AI's functionality is aligned with reality. In 2018, an AI hedge fund, Tyndaris, lost $20 million of an investor's funds. The investor sued the fund because the losses wouldn't have occurred if the machine learning algorithm in use was as sophisticated as the salesperson claimed it was.[12] The case has not been settled in court at the time of writing. However, there is an expectation gap between the investor's understanding of the technology and its actual capability. To address this, we recommend investment managers using AI to be transparent beyond mandatory disclosures in both the investment prospectus and regular reporting. We also believe additional education is necessary: this could include fundamentals of machine learning in finance (similar to the classes for novice investors in derivatives products). Beyond such education, we believe a more detailed explanation of biases (such as herding) that algorithms may display seems to be most relevant to support the investor in understanding the AI-related risks.

[10] G.I. Simari (2002) A Primer on Zero Knowledge Protocols 12: www.cs.ox.ac.uk/people/gerardo.simari/personal/publications/zkp-simari2002.pdf.

[11] Merriam-Webster, n.d. "Transparency".

[12] T. Beardsworth and N. Kumar (2019) Who to Sue When a Robot Loses Your Fortune: www.bloomberg.com/news/articles/2019-05-06/who-to-sue-when-a-robot-loses-your-fortune, 6 May.

Explainability

Explainability is the ability to explain the rationale behind an action (in our case, an investment decision). The objective is to enable humans to understand, appropriately trust and effectively manage what artificial intelligence partners do.[13] The more sophisticated machines are, the less explainable the mechanisms are.

To elaborate on why explainability is essential for the use of AI in the financial markets, let's imagine the following situation. An investor wishes not to invest in the defence sector. This decision has been reflected in the investment constraints of the fund. However, upon an act of war, an AI algorithm decided to short a particular stock (think airlines around September 11 2011) to maximize trading profits. While every investor's moral compass works differently, this may or may not be acceptable to the investor. Explainability needs more than the insertion of an "explainable model/interface into the process". We recommend for AI algorithms to be regularly stress-tested to help establish behavioural patterns that can form part of their decision-making process. Side note: We should not forget that a human decision-making process is often not entirely explainable, either.

Accountability

Accountability is the ability to hold an individual or an entity accountable for an act. It includes the ability to admit a flaw as a consequence of an action or behaviour. In AI, accountability goes hand in hand with explainability. If a decision is explainable, actors can more naturally be held responsible for their actions. AI is only an enabling technology used by a financial services provider. The management can be held accountable similar to when a human staff member errs and causes economic damage. Data sources become more and more plentiful. Financial markets entities using AI should enact a data policy to limit risks of data-related incidents. Such a policy governs not only privacy but also data quality and integrity. Additionally, the severity and probability of potential harm created by an AI algorithm in the markets should drive the human involvement and controls required.

Conclusion

The pace of technological and data-related change is accelerating – it seems to be on an exponential trajectory. AI cannot be considered an emerging technology any more. It is being implemented and can substantially improve our decision-making in financial markets. At the same time, it is not free of ethical risks that need to be managed carefully, especially as long as the understanding of AI amongst stakeholders might be low. It is essential to operationalize ethical principles by thinking about how they specifically apply to the markets. In our short chapter, we suggest such operationalization processes for transparency, explainability, accountability, privacy and fairness at a high level. A lot more work is to be done. We should, however, refrain from implementing more rigorous controls for AI than the ones we put in place for humans with their very own biases and ethical flaws. Doing so might otherwise impede progress towards reaping the benefits of AI fully. Perhaps we can even use AI for managing our current, very own, human, agency issues in financial markets. Henry Young, ex-CEO of high-frequency trading technology firm TS-Associates and now decentralization advocate, supports our main argument. He states, "I see no distinction between AI and people since the latter are just biological AI."

---

[13] D. Gunning (2018) Explainable AI. www.darpa.mil/attachments/XAIProgramUpdate.pdf.

AI Trust, Ethics, Transparency and Enablement

By Kevin Telford
Advisor, Thoughtworks

Technology continues to grow exponentially into all aspects of our life. Increasingly, financial decisions are made by machines harnessing data and honed by human construct. An ethics void thrives in an invisible, untested, dark data world of science, where artificial intelligence (AI) and machine learning (ML) reside. Investors, entrepreneurs and innovators are increasingly curious about the value of a principled digital application of trust, transparency, ethics on AL and ML. Visionaries see the value for people and the increased returns trusted organizations will deliver. This chapter, titled beyond AI Reg-Tech takes us to a vision where trusted financial services (FS) organizations embrace a standard of trust, ethics, transparency and enablement (TETE) framework. Leading organizations to an AI/ML "kitemark" standard.

What Is Intelligent Empowerment and Why Is it Topical?

For investors, entrepreneurs and visionaries, change has many agents, including legislation such as the EU second Payment Services Directive (PSD2) and the General Data Protection Regulation (GDPR) and the spreading of the Internet of Things (IoT), open banking and connected life – all this maximizes opportunities for innovation and growth. At the intersection of creativity and enabling technology lies an abundance of new products, services and infinite new data sources. We label this "intelligent empowerment" (IE) human and tech augmentation. AI/ML are "components" within IE. For many organizations' old models, processes are replaced by AI/ML, but this often comes with trade-offs and risk. IE brings mass data integration opportunities from multiple points and combining existing data and enabling FS innovators to bring forward use cases for AI/ML, creating new service efficiencies and products. At the heart is a determination to protect the citizen. Combined data points bring a new age for intelligent analytics, smarter data, faster outcomes that has the investor, innovator community in a frenzy. Money is flowing into new data, consent, privacy protection and the ability to construct valuable new products and services to solve customer challenges.

The FS AI/ML Trust Issue

IE brings complexity to FS and trust. Open banking and IoT increasing connections and integration with FS services through AL/ML has the potential to damage trust irreparably.

Arguably responsible FS organizations build the rationale for trust, transparency and ethics into their models now. Consumer legislation sees to that. The flipside to organizational trustworthiness is that legislation has not kept pace with IE/AI/ML growth.

Accessing code is beyond most people. In any event there is no set of rules to publish the contents in an understandable format. Some organizations cite a trade-off between consumer benefits and privacy. Lazy responses highlight an attitude to trust that is difficult to understand; however, outdated business models die. There is no cop out on trust, transparency and ethics. Some people ask whether an organization can be trusted, and that is what some FS incumbents find, as it is difficult to pivot towards trust as a service. Many FS organizations fail to serve, neglect the risky, underserved and underbanked. There is one big issue: what is the social norm for AI/ML? The challenge lies in human construct and AI/ML intent. Measuring trust will pivot towards the citizen judging FS AI/ML organizations as trustworthy or not.

TETE Proposal

The proposal is an AI/ML trust framework to encompass the growth of IE, for measuring organizational trustworthiness. The solution is a trustworthy AI framework, designed, adopted, promoted and accepted. For investors, entrepreneurs, visionaries the TETE framework opens new business models. TETE will cover aspects of:

- Human Rights
  - Legislation replicated in principles
  - Protection, safety, privacy, controls and security
  - Assessment
- Ethics, Regulations, Governance and Standards
  - Non-Bias, non-discrimination and fairness
  - Responsible IE/AI/ML
  - Authors' accountability
  - Understanding
- Business, Societal Education and Knowledge
  - Standards on the scale of international food labels
  - Application and understanding
  - Interactions such as AI proof points whilst interacting
  - Clear terms and conditions of use and redress
- TETE Ecosystem Participants
  - Society
  - Government
  - Academia
  - Corporations

The detail behind TETE will start with human questions. Why are we doing this? Is it ethical? What are the benefits and is it TETE-measurable?

- Will it stand up to multiparty scrutiny?
- What human challenge, solution or creation are we setting out to achieve?

TETE exposes the computational construct:

- What data points do we need to construct the AI/ML?
- What data provenance and mitigation do we need?

TETE brings visibility in such areas as

- Data provenance and authorship
- Application of trust, ethics and transparency.

The results will inform a model for TETE. A model that can be used to assess where an organization fits as being AI/ML, IE-compliant and responsible. People will be able to measure a trustworthy entity. For other parties, it is the ability to hold to account organizations deploying AI/ML science so that trust, transparency and ethics become a standard of measurement.

The TETE Need and Challenges

The starting points for an ethical IE/AI/ML framework already exist within international legislation and principles. The future of IE/AI/ML regulation is much publicized. It is largely accepted that a version of a "TETE" framework is inevitable as governments, organizations and the public are increasingly recognizing the issues IE/AI/ML can bring. As AI tech and IoT deployment carry on at pace, events such as social profiling of citizens' data for FS decisions highlights FS challenges including:

- Risks – business, society, security, controls and economy.
- No international AI/ML kitemark, resulting in widening disparity and inequality.
- Little addressing of organizational accountability.
- Getting it wrong opens up claims to eclipse PPI.

As automated decisions impact citizens' access to basic rights such as fair finances, then aspects such as creditworthiness have a huge impact on outcomes. We need TETE applied where data is stored, shared or used to construct and conduct automated decisions. For FS, the invisible data decisions applied through IE/AI/ML move further from the "reassurance" of human interfaces for some of the most important decisions humans make. Many FS organizations are faced with the trust legacy, the growth of greenfield entrants starting with the same perspective on trust. It feels to those organizations tangible and measurable. It is, but only one way.

How to Implement a TETE Framework

TETE will be implemented as a global standard for FS. It will start with FS self-governing, using the TETE principles through organization collaboration, such as FCA and ICO.

The end solution will be akin to the food label standards and governed under the same principles as domain name management. The aim is for a kitemark, traffic light system and iconic descriptors within interactions, for example, during application.

Measure, Controls and Arbitration

There is a swathe of entrepreneurial and global government innovation to assist in implementing TETE for the growth of IE. Society is ready; they are awake to privacy issues and increasingly applying human trust measures on their own values and the communities in which they participate. All parties are ready to collaborate around the immense opportunity AI/ML brings; addressing the risk is part of the solution. TETE centres of excellence are a natural next step solution. Shared sandboxes of anonymized human data and open source software. An environment for FS to share data on the same principles as credit reference agencies. Only the purpose is for retrospective and future applications of IE/AI/ML to design, experiment and prove ahead of market launch.

Conclusion

In conclusion, the TETE blueprint is one of many disparate attempts to bring FS self-regulation and the creation of a framework that supports the growth of IE. The solution is centred on protecting the citizen, providing a consistent framework and a level playing field for FS. During research it is almost universally acknowledged that legislation will be required for the growth of IE and AI/ML as components. TETE is an invitation for FS to be proactive and take advantage of the movement for trusted organizations by society. Next steps collaborate and test the principle for the future design of a TETE framework. The TETE framework will bring tangible benefits for all parties, sound business sense and a differentiator as ethics is mainstream. A bigger issue is what is trust and ethics, as the definition knows no boundaries for what is socially acceptable for one or many. The TETE future will enable people to recognize organizations built on trust and decide where to place their business.

Bibliography

Growing the artificial intelligence industry in the UK, Professor Dame Wendy Hall and Jérôme Pesenti: https://assets.publishing.service.gov.uk/government/uploads/system/uploads/attachment_data/file/652097/Growing_the_artificial_intelligence_industry_in_the_UK.pdf; https://ai-hr.cyber.harvard.edu/.

AI in the UK: ready, willing and able? https://publications.parliament.uk/pa/ld201719/ldselect/ldai/100/100.pdf.

Government Artificial Intelligence Readiness Index 2019 – Compiled by Oxford Insights and the International Development Research Centre: https://www.oxfordinsights.com/ai-readiness2019 Richard Stirling, Hannah Miller and Emma Martinho-Truswell.

PwC's Responsible AI: AI you can trust: https://www.pwc.com/gx/en/issues/data-and-analytics/artificial-intelligence/what-is-responsible-ai.html.

Exploring Ethics: An Introductory Anthology by Steven M. Cahn, Oxford University Press – three key levels: applied, normative, and metaethics. Our goal is to understand the significance of ethical thinking in our daily lives.

Artificial Intelligence Benchmark Cap Gemini: www.capgemini.com/wp-content/uploads/2018/07/AI-Readiness-Benchmark-POV.pdf.

UK Can Lead the Way on AI: www.parliament.uk/business/committees/committees-a-z/lords-select/ai-committee/news-parliament-2017/ai-report-published/.

Centre for Data Ethics and Innovation (CDEI): UK AI industrial Strategy www.gov.uk/government/groups/centre-for-data-ethics-and-innovation-cdei.

Invisible Hand, Spontaneous Order and Artificial Intelligence

By Aarón Olmos
Economist and Professor of Economics and Cryptoeconomics, IESA

Economic science has always had as the object of study the human being, their social and production relations, their present needs in their life cycle and the ways to cover them with resources that are not necessarily abundant. It is precisely these elements that has guided the market forces since the beginning of time, because without needs to be covered, there would be no incentive to combine factors of production, applying physical or intellectual work in the creation of goods and services adjusted to the requirements of human beings, and the conditions of the natural, political and social environment.

It has always been said that there is nothing more difficult to study than human beings, because of the complexity of their different dimensions, the changing of their decision-making, the unpredictability of their behaviour and their individual and group psychology. However, social scientists have used mathematics and statistics throughout history to build models that allow them to study human behaviour and thus try to project future behaviour. But it has been from the hands of medicine and biology that we began to understand the functioning of the human brain, its processes, the way information travels and is transmitted internally, which, together with years of analysis of the behaviour and psychology of the individual, result in a greater and better understanding of man and his complexity.

In this context of behaviours, data and models about the human being, artificial intelligence is born as a discipline of science that seeks to understand, emulate, replicate and enhance the way animals and human beings relate to others, organize to produce goods and services, and manage to cover their needs more efficiently. In this way, the development of models that integrate social network analysis, sentiment analysis, semantic analysis, neural networks, machine learning and deep learning, all fed with historical data and in real time, is the best example of the great need that has the science for understanding and even predicting human behaviour. However, it is precisely the random and unpredictable nature of humans that has shaped civilization, our history, economy, politics and society.

From the point of view of economic history and classical economic theory, Adam Smith, in his work of the year 1776, *An Inquiry Into the Nature and Causes of the Wealth of Nations*, questioned why there were richer countries than others, their differences, and where was the cause of their success or failure. Smith studied human behaviour from the perspective of work, income and money, explaining how the union of needs was found in markets with conflicting human interests. In his 1759 work *Theory of Moral Sentiments*, Smith explores the affection and sympathy that exists among human beings, and how these feelings drive actions among men. In the later *Wealth of Nations*, Smith argued that in society each pursues his personal interest, but is guided as an "invisible hand" to contribute to the general welfare. In this way, private interest contributes to the achievement of the general interest, and it is precisely this situation that makes human behaviour fascinating.

This "invisible hand" is the living expression of the randomness of human behaviour, which makes markets and social dynamics what they are. It is human creation, innovation and inventiveness, mixed with emotion and feelings, that organize markets, prices, production relations, which have been parameterized and explained in large sets of numbers that show behaviours, trends and distinguishable patterns. However, in the cyclicality of a predictable behaviour, this imponderable can happen that changes everything, and nobody ever anticipated.

In this same order of ideas, already in the twentieth century the Austrian School of Economics explained that in society there is a set of interdependent institutional systems that evolve together by adaptive selection, through intersubjectivity in an infinity of individual actions. That is, people, companies, institutions and governments that move for their particular interests finding a higher objective. This is what we know as *spontaneous order*, an understanding of the social order tied to the apparent chaos of millions of beings that seek to cover their needs, prioritizing scarce resources in the most efficient way possible, finding order without necessarily seeking it.

The *invisible hand* and the *spontaneous order* show us that as long as there are needs in a group of human beings, and there are means to cover them, then there will be markets for goods and services willing to create "value" for those who organize these opposing forces, and give meaning to the combination of land, labour, capital, technology and human talent, arranged in a way that maintains the historical circular flow of social layers with economic, political, cultural and religious differences in a *spontaneous order*, that sometimes betrays the reason between the "must be of things" and the "things as they are". If artificial intelligence will finally be able to decode the behaviour patterns of the human being, and predict all future behaviour, the randomness of the individual would vanish, and with it, the spontaneity of the social being and the unpredictability of the economic, political and social, it is worth saying, one would be "visualizing the hand" and "forcing the order" of things, to a model or structure resulting from the numerical analysis. For some, it would be the way to avoid incidents and correct events; for others it would be the equivalent to dehumanizing the known. For this reason, in times of the fourth industrial revolution where the data is the new value, and we can all be understood as a market variable capable of being compiled, classified, related and interpreted dynamically, we run the risk of becoming something that we are not: "predictable" data sets.

Human nature is variable, random and spontaneous, and we have created structures to modify the environment and dominate it, in a historical and social process that continues and does not end. The search for economic, financial or stock market certainty, as well as the precision in the calculation of a social or political trend, cannot be the excuse to eradicate the imponderables that precisely make us who we are. The advance of science is the engine of development and generational paradigm with each new discovery that surprises and excites. It is the good thing of scientific advances to improve our living conditions that makes us want to go further, however, we cannot move forward without being who we are, without vanishing the "invisible hand" and the "spontaneous order" that also brought data science and artificial intelligence to our lives in apparent chaos.

Transforming Black Box AI in the Finance Industry: Explainable AI that Is Intuitive and Prescriptive

By Kathryn Rungrueng
COO, Flowcast

and Ken So
Founder and CEO, Flowcast

While artificial intelligence (AI) technology has become commonplace across industries, it has grown particularly integral in the evolution of the finance industry. Predictive technology and automation have streamlined nearly every facet of the space, whether looking at innovations in fraud detection, risk assessment, credit underwriting or identity verification. According to financial research firm Autonomous, the increased adoption of AI will support financial institutions by cutting 22% in costs over the next decade. Unfortunately, several obstacles remain when applying AI and machine learning models within finance. This is largely due to the complex regulations financial institutions must remain compliant with – these policies require that banks present a clear explanation for each and every decision, prediction or risk assessment.

As machine learning applications become increasingly specialized, though, the models become further opaque and thus more difficult to interpret. Logistic regression and other simple algorithms are part of a family of linear models that are globally explainable, with coefficients representing the marginal impact of each input. The marginal impact of the inputs on every prediction is the same globally for linear models. In contrast, with the recent developments made in processing big data on distributed computers, machine learning models have become increasingly complex and highly non-linear. Although this augments predictive performance considerably, it does so at the expense of transparency.

Effectively explaining these black box, non-linear models is critical in the field of finance where the ability to explain the predictive output is of equal importance to the accuracy of the prediction itself. A credit decision requires both an accurate assessment of risk and a plain-text explanation that can be interpreted by the end user. It is not enough to know why, for example, a loan application was rejected. A better understanding of the necessary steps needed to improve the outcome is crucial, as this knowledge is more powerful in guiding risk management professionals and consumers alike.

The Challenges Hindering Wider AI Implementation

Although human decision-making is often biased and unpredictable – whether deliberate or unintentional – AI algorithms are deterministic, auditable and reproducible. While the latter is a favourable choice for technical decisions related to credit underwriting when considering its benefits of guaranteed, duplicable accuracy, the finance domain requires additional insight into machine learning algorithms. Extensive regulations existing within the industry necessitate a heightened demand for clarity, both in prognoses and in the process and reasoning executed to reach them. For instance, in the US, under the Fair Credit Reporting Act (FCRA), lenders are required to provide a potential borrower with a clear reason when a loan application is rejected. If the decision is based on a black box machine learning algorithm with no adequate explanation, it effectively violates this requirement. A borrower must be allowed access to knowledge regarding why their application is declined nearly immediately. Additionally, credit underwriting demands a clear picture of every variable being used in lender decision-making. According to FCRA regulations, credit decisions cannot be based upon any potentially discriminatory factors, such as race, gender, age or other determinants. This also includes variables that could even potentially infer insights leading to such discriminatory factors, such as an applicant's zip code or profession. Because of this, it's critically important to understand exactly which variables are being utilized in each and every determination.

and a prescription for steps to change the predicted outcome. At each prediction, the marginal impact of each feature is calculated independently of the response variable.

Industry governance is perhaps the most important aspect to consider when deploying a machine learning model in production for financial institutions. Explainability is a fundamental need here as these policies dictate that a risk validation team has holistic, complete insight. This includes visibility into the specific data that was entered into the model, the ability to trace previous model revision and the capacity to review all related official documentation. When considering fraud-related use cases, explainability is also paramount. Although it's not required by regulators to explain the AI models for fraud detection, the explanation can provide significant value in helping with investigations. It provides key insights on why the model detected a potential fraud which is particularly key for unsupervised learning.

How to Identify an Explainable Algorithm

For these reasons, the financial industry requires low-latency, high-performing machine learning models that surface auditable explanations to credit risk teams. As it stands, nearly every supposedly explainable AI solution on the market is designed for data scientists – meaning they produce only highly technical explanations. In order to reach a level of industry-wide, expansive AI utilization, however, more providers must generate plain-text explanations that are designed for customer end users (e.g. analysts and credit risk officers), ensuring the insights are both easily interpretable and actionable.

Developing beyond the existing state of the art explanation modules such as LIME and SHAP, our models apply these algorithms combined with natural language processing (NLP) to devise clear statements that include the reason for the prediction

We compare this approach to standardized methods such as the Locally Interpretable Model Estimation (LIME) and report the computational efficiency and accuracy of explanations. The algorithm then develops accompanying explanations, such as "Client A is rejected because their months since the most recent diluted payment is two (1.8 above median) and the USD amount requested is $72,000 ($57,000 above median)". These explanations are not only required for compliance but also help build trust with users such as credit risk officers. They also help financial institutions protect against potential losses, reveal borderline client approvals and rejections, and aid banks in expanding their portfolios, allowing them to increase lending while minimizing risk.

Unlocking a New Level of Explainability with Prescriptive AI

Perhaps the most revolutionary aspect of this next-level explainable algorithm is its prescriptive capabilities. These insights benefit the finance ecosystem by allowing financial institutions to reduce risk and take action with grey-area customers – those who are borderline approved or rejected. It achieves this by providing risk officers and banks with reasons as to *why* a customer's application is borderline approved or rejected and informs their next steps (e.g. the debt-to-income ratio needs to be improved).

For example, if a loan application is denied, risk officers can obtain the top reasons behind the decision; not only does the model provide an analysis of why a customer was denied, but also explains what needs to happen in order for a customer to be approved. This protects financial institutions and increases grey-area customers' likelihood of approval – this is a game-changing shift within the finance industry, given this was a customer segment banks have traditionally been unable to serve. The second benefit of AI is that these next-level explanations and prescriptive insights can effectively help guide credit monitoring – informing when they should review a current customer's credit profile more frequently – and serve as a lead generation tool for banks by suggesting when they should check in with potential customers.

Industry Use Cases and Compelling Results

The first-of-its-kind technology is suitable for an array of financial risk use cases, such as credit decisions in consumer lending and unlocking capital within the underserved space of SME lending, as well as within the realms of fraud detection and trade finance. As a result of regulatory limitations in traditional risk assessment and credit underwriting combined with a lack of globally available and standardized credit data, the demand for explainable AI is especially high in these domains. As of earlier this year, our advanced explainable and prescriptive AI model is in production with top tier global financial institutions. Over a period of several months, these partners have placed the models and plain-text explanations through rigorous validation by internal risk teams. After uncovering the advantages of implementing – including increased speed, improved regulatory compliance, conversion of grey-area customers, simplified applicant credit monitoring and enhanced lead generation – the solution is now in deployment as part of their internal workflow.

Making Data Your Most Valuable Asset

By Peggy Tsai
Vice President of Data Solutions, BigID

Digital ethics are a standard of principles that can serve as a framework for promoting social good and for instilling desired behaviours in groups of people. In the past, corporations have utilized codes of conduct to shape the behaviours and conduct of their employees in and out of the workplace that ranged from dress codes to behaviours on social media. What is the distinction specifical to ethics? The word "ethics" conjures up references to morality and involves defining concepts of right and wrong conduct. People are shaped by their culture, upbringing and personal experiences to define right and wrong. Today, compared to any other point in history, there are unlimited uses and applications on data that data collectors now possess. What is their moral responsibility, if any, to their customers to treat the data with care and respect?

While many corporations collect and leverage customer data for their business operations, very little information is shared with their customers on how they use, save and protect their data. Marketing and sales campaigns hide behind the theory of aggregation in which they believe a single customer's identity is anonymous amongst a group. However, personal information can still be inferred when cross-matched against other data sets.

Why Do We Need Data Ethics Now?

Let's talk about the timeliness of digital ethics. Data has never been more easily collected, consumed and utilized by financial services. Customer data can be explicitly collected and given directly to corporations when they register their product for a warranty or sign up for a new checking account at the bank. Customer data can also be collected from their behaviours and interactions on social media apps and corporate websites. Third party public sources such as financial and economic data, census, crime, marketing and social media can also be used to enhance existing customer data.

Given the ease and availability of data that can be collected, there are key issues surrounding the transparency of the usage of the data in the financial company's systems and business processes. More importantly, trust is a big factor for the customer to believe that the company will do no intentional harm with their data. It is imperative for the financial services industry as a whole to standardize their consent for data collection, provide transparency on usage of data for marketing, sales or future product development, and ensure that customer's data is deleted upon request. The privacy of their existing customer and potential customers should be the number one priority for the organization.

Treating Data as the Asset

How can companies start to manage and wrap their arms around protecting customer privacy? The solution can be addressed in two parts. First, companies must know exactly what data they have on a customer. They must actively engage to create a catalogue of assets on every piece of information collected, created and displayed about their customer. The catalogue must document all of the systems, applications and reports that create, store and change the customer data so that any requests from a customer to erase their identification can be quickly addressed. Since the catalogue must be continuously updated, internal governance and processes must be implemented and enforced across the company to ensure accurate and timely information in the catalogue.

The creation of a catalogue in itself is a monumental effort for any size of company, let alone a financial services company that has a legacy of data that may come from a history of mergers and acquisitions. The content of the catalogue is often described as the elephant in the room that many companies cannot attempt to manage because of the size and enormity of the effort to collect and organize the content. Technology teams have historically taken on the burden of creating this information, since they have long been the system owners for the customer data and have knowledge as to the where and how information is stored and circulated across the firm. However, keeping the effort in a technology silo is a huge mistake and a main reason for a company's failure to achieve their goals in focusing on the value of data. The key factor for success is a business partnership whereby the business owns and drives the proper usage of data throughout all business processes. While technology may seemingly own the vehicle for transmitting data, the business counterparts are in the driver's seat for steering the direction and mission for the data.

The second part of the solution after a catalogue inventory is completed and a process is implemented to keep it up to date, is the ability for the company to understand how it uses the customer data internally in all its business processes. All critical business processes that can be mapped to customer information should be reviewed and redesigned with privacy in mind. Technology and operation groups that handle the architecture, processing and monitoring of data should ensure that data access and entitlements are controlled. Personally identifiable information (PII) and sensitive personal information (SPI) need to be tagged as monitored for access and entitlements down to the data element level. The data science and data reporting groups are also under obligation to be aware of uncovering potential PII as they join disparate data sets together and do analysis on new data sets to uncover new insights to their customer's profile and behaviour.

A key aspect to this solution is the monitoring of transactional, operational and analytics-driven data that is created internally at a company after customer data is collected. These are derived data sets that are proprietary to a company based on internal calculations and infusion of proprietary insights. Understanding how the data is calculated and where and when the data should be applied (i.e. the context of the application) is just as important as the consistency of the data throughout the company. There are often misinterpreted without clear definitions and single golden sources for retrieving the data. Governance on the analytical layer is often a missed opportunity for companies who allow their employees to run metrics on differing calculations and from multiple data sources.

Consequences of Data Mistrust

Even after companies have a mature programme on where and how their data is being used, there still needs to be ethics to monitor the conduct of human behaviour with data. There are serious consequences when customer trust is lost. The fundamental ability to conduct business and build lasting relationships is built on trust with customers. An example of violating customer trust is utilizing customer data into building new products and services based on algorithmic inputs without their explicit consent. Would all customers be willing to participate in a marketing sales programme if they knew that their personal information would be aggregated in a study to identify new customer segments for a new insurance product promotion? Perhaps not. In addition, data scientists have an ethical responsibility to ensure fairness by reviewing their model algorithms that produce actionable results taken by a company. Data scientists must utilize care and due diligence to ensure that the inputs to their models, calculations and interpretation of the results are completed without an unconscious bias. The results of their models can damage the company's reputation, i.e. models on recruiting new employees or targeting new customer segments.

Digital ethics, written in simple and bold terms, reflects the obligation the financial services industry has to its customers where they signal to their current and future customers that their data is valuable and worthy of their trust. Any company that proactively identifies their stance on the digital ethics is a clear differentiator amongst their competitors and signals to their customers how much they value data.

The Data Promise

By Kasia Miaskiewicz
Director, UBS EVOLVE

Fabian Tschirky
Project Officer Omnichannel Management, UBS Global Wealth Management

James Aylen
Head of UBS Evolve, The Center for Design Thinking and Innovation

Dr Martin Hartenstein
Head Front Support Model WMP and Head Change-the-Bank Portfolio Execution Operating Head Booking Center Switzerland, UBS Global Wealth Management

and Jonas Isliker
Head Data Foundation, UBS Global Wealth Management

The financial services sector has been and continues to be built on the basis of trust. Traditionally, the term was interpreted in the context of a bank's role in society: safeguarding financial resources, offering trusted advice and providing access to capital. Industry regulations and the bank's internal controls are considered guardians of this trust.

Banks are now increasingly measured on a new set of digital trust, transparency and ethics metrics, often centred on client's data – the new currency underlying the digital economy. Conventions on AI ethics, cyber security and privacy/data-sharing practices are example metrics against which banks are being benchmarked with cross-industry competitors like Google, Facebook and Apple. The positive efforts to establish data and AI standards, such as the OpenAI initiative, are making headway; however, it is often the negative events that spur heated debates and attract client attention. Notable examples include the 2017 Equifax data breach, where over 143 million customer's social security numbers, birthdates, addresses and credit card data were compromised. In 2018, there was employee backlash against Google for helping the US military use artificial intelligence to analyse drone footage and also Amazon scrapped an AI recruiting tool that showed bias against women.

The Client Data Promise

As clients share their most intimate information on wealth, investments, passions and family details with their banks and wealth managers, there is an apparent need for the sector to set cross-industry standards based on transparent and ethical ways of collecting, analysing and using client data. Banks have a natural competitive advantage in this space – according to a survey by A.T. Kearney,[1] 61% of customers still perceive banks as the most trustworthy service provider with whom they want to share their personal information compared to other firms, such as Google, Amazon, PayPal or Apple. Additionally, clients are open to sharing their information provided they receive something in return. A study by Accenture[2] found that nearly 80% of digital-savvy clients would share personal data with their banking provider; however, 66% of them demand faster and easier to use services in exchange for this data access.

To become the cross-industry standard authority for trust, ethics and transparency, banks need to venture beyond just complying with current regulatory safeguards (e.g. EU's General Data Protection Regulation (GDPR) or the Payment Services Directive (PSD2)) and expand their mandate from not only protecting client data, but also to constantly leveraging it to act in the client's best interest.

---

[1] A.T. Kearney (Q4 2017) Banking and Payments Study: https://www.atkearney.com/financial-services/the-consumer-data-privacy-marketplace.

[2] Accenture (2018) Building the future ready bank: https://www.accenture.com/t20180418T194011Z__w__/us-en/_acnmedia/PDF-75/Accenture-Banking-Technology-Vision-2018.pdf#zoom=50.

The Client Data Promise could be the answer. The concept of a Client Data Promise assumes that client information and any related digital assets are thoroughly secure in a digital vault and the client sets the level of disclosure and analysis permitted. This determines the level of personalization of services/experience delivered to the client and the extent to which the bank can leverage client data for other purposes (e.g. training AI algorithms with the use of a client's anonymized information). It will be up to the client as to whether they will receive only traditional banking and investment management services from the bank or holistic tailored advice, as well as access to products and services covering investments, projects, family and everyday life. Additionally, as regulation related to AI-based solutions is still in its infancy, banks can set the cross-industry standards that prevent the loss of client trust. Imagine a world where you, the client, decide whether your anonymized data can be used to enhance a product personalization tool or an algorithm that helps bring families out of debt and poverty, or to develop new services by your bank or its partners.

From a bank's perspective, the Client Data Promise, when delivered successfully, will not only provide a competitive advantage to first movers and allow them to build new business models, products and services; it will also enable the creation of a simple and transparent mode of gathering client consents, building an understanding of what data can be collected, stored and used and who has access to it. For the client, the exchange of additional information provides better, more customized and personalized services from the bank and its partners. At the same time, clients can rest assured that their data is never sold or used in any way outside of the agreed upon parameters of their Client Data Promise.

Example from the Wealth Management World

Imagine the following scenario: during a client–relationship manager call a natural language processing virtual assistant transcribes the conversation in real time. After the call is concluded, the relationship manager automatically receives the transcript, along with a summary and newly captured client data, e.g. product interests, family news, assets acquired and actionable agreements, e.g. new investments to be implemented. He reviews the details and, in full transparency, submits the contact note to the client to acknowledge or adjust.

The client reviews the contact note she received from her relationship manager. She is comfortable with its content as well as the data set collected and gives the bank consent to store and use it. The email from her relationship manager also includes a request to leverage the client's anonymized data in a new philanthropy project focused on building a micro-investing robo-advisor for developing countries. She gives the bank her consent and also agrees for her data to be leveraged in similar future initiatives.

The client also browses through their Data Promise dashboard which allows her to choose the level of Netflix-style advice, based on the data sharing permissions set. She particularly values the transparency and flexibility the dashboard gives her in setting the permission levels. The minimum setting covers regulatory required data (e.g. know-your-customer information). The maximum includes all data the bank and its partners stored, information shared via account aggregation services and publicly available client data. In such a scenario, truly holistic advice becomes possible.

In today's increasingly digital and self-sovereign environment a Data Promise has the potential to become the cornerstone of cross-industry standards and best practices in establishing client trust, transparency and ethics. And the first to embark on the journey may reap the greatest benefits and competitive advantage, as well as maintaining the client's trust.

Legal Risk and Regulation

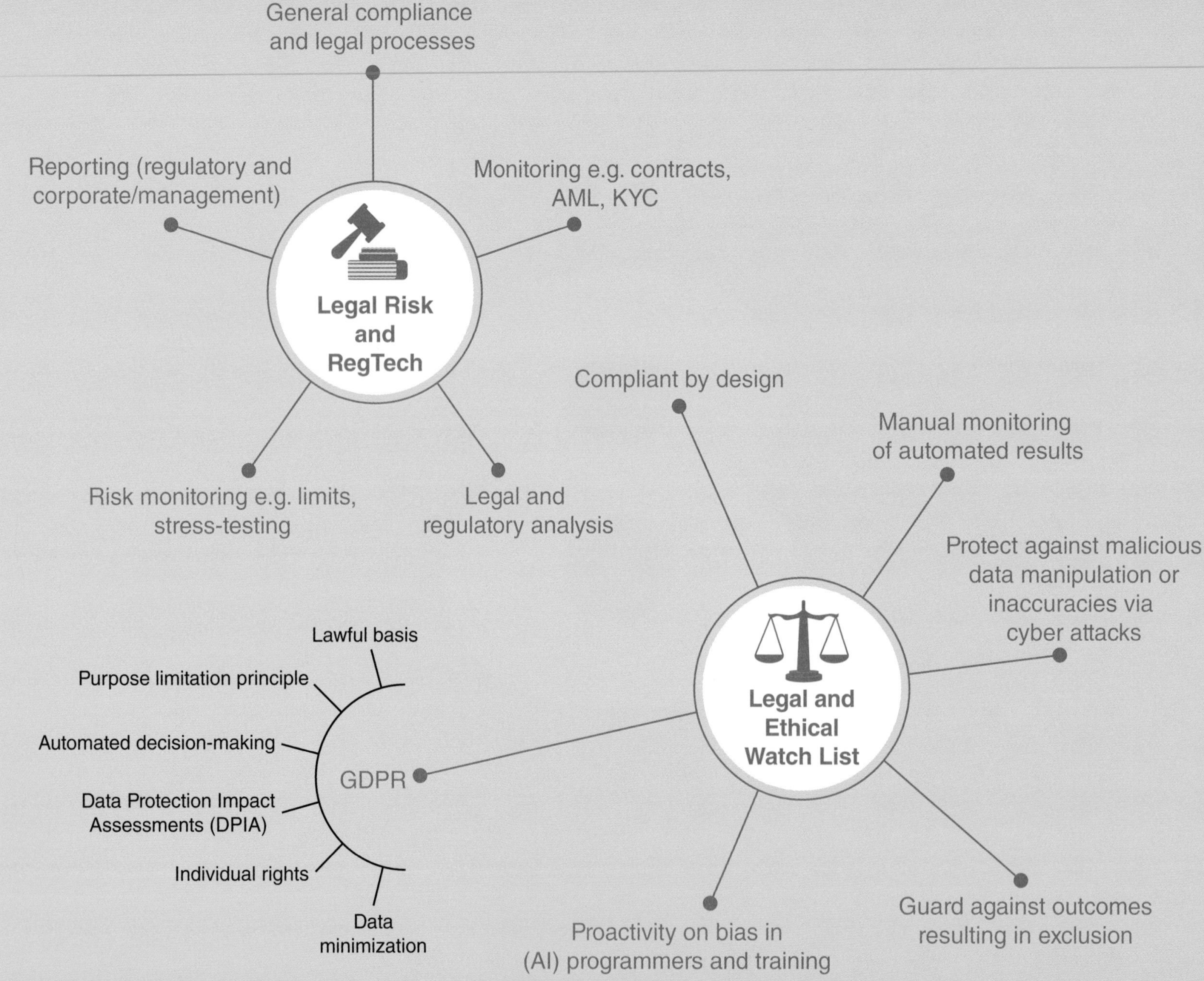
General compliance and legal processes
Reporting (regulatory and corporate/management)
Monitoring e.g. contracts, AML, KYC
Legal Risk and RegTech
Risk monitoring e.g. limits, stress-testing
Legal and regulatory analysis
Compliant by design
Manual monitoring of automated results
Protect against malicious data manipulation or inaccuracies via cyber attacks
Legal and Ethical Watch List
Lawful basis
Purpose limitation principle
Automated decision-making
GDPR
Data Protection Impact Assessments (DPIA)
Individual rights
Data minimization
Proactivity on bias in (AI) programmers and training
Guard against outcomes resulting in exclusion

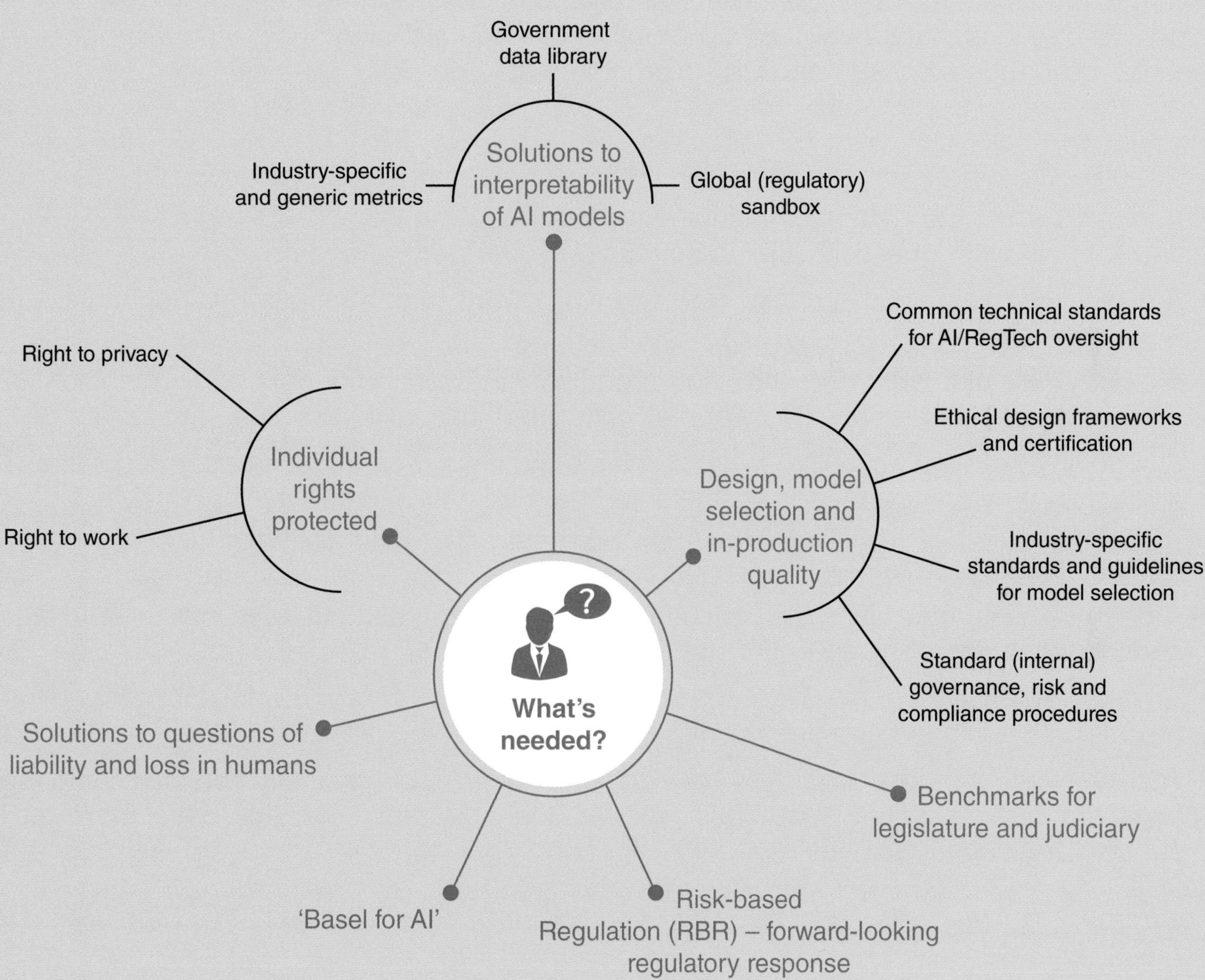
Government
data library
Solutions to
interpretability
of AI models
Industry-specific
and generic metrics
Global (regulatory)
sandbox
Common technical standards
for AI/RegTech oversight
Right to privacy
Individual
rights
protected
Right to work
Ethical design frameworks
and certification
Design, model
selection and
in-production
quality
Industry-specific
standards and guidelines
for model selection
Standard (internal)
governance, risk and
compliance procedures
What's
needed?
Solutions to questions of
liability and loss in humans
Benchmarks for
legislature and judiciary
'Basel for AI'
Risk-based
Regulation (RBR) – forward-looking
regulatory response

Part 8 explores the essential context for practitioners: the opportunities, the pitfalls, the various types of decisions that they will be contributing to – and advising on – that will impact their boards, colleagues, consumers and stakeholders at large.

Read on for:

- A "watch list" of key data risks including the tech legal view on GDPR and why those "Why?" and "Should we?" questions should be high on your board agenda.
- A dissection of algo use in banks, how and why "robust and transparent algorithm assurance is on the horizon".
- A survey view of current and evolving AI regulation, covering needs, ongoing regulatory measures, and issues yet to be grappled with like questions of liability.
- A scholarly examination of this world of "newfound risks" and the risk-based regulation approach. Why are knowledge, insights and data from all affected actors – industry, government, tech firms, academia *and* consumers – so crucial in enabling a *forward-looking* regulatory response to AI?
- A deep dive into fraud, and the ways AI technologies are being used in internal and external audit to transform these essential processes.
- An informed analysis of the Why?, the What? and the How? of how revolutionary advances in AI are rapidly closing the gap between legal and regulatory requirements – and enabling technology.
- The case not for more than simply generic metrics for AI, but financial services sector-specific ones, too; and devised in a top-down, international approach — a new "Basel for AI" as a supervisory mechanism.
- A close look at RegTech, from 1.0 to 3.0, and the case for an ongoing paradigm shift from manual to digitized regulation and compliance.

This collection offers informed views and perspectives on some of the most interesting and relevant issues facing legal practitioners, business leaders, regulators and policymakers alike.

AI and the Law: Challenges and Risks for the Financial Services Sector

By Electra Japonas
Founder and CEO, The Law Boutique

AI is not perfect, but it's here to stay. From Alexa's skills to Spotify's music recommendations, AI is silently improving our daily lives. The use of AI in the development of Google's algorithm has increased the efficiency of searches with predictive technology. Uber's use of AI allows us to retrieve accurate time estimates of when we can expect our driver or food deliveries. AI has even transformed Amazon's supply chain through the integration of data from maintenance, manufacturing and inventory tracking. It is undoubtedly leading the next wave of the tech revolution, and financial services firms are in the forefront.

At the time of writing, there are more than 2000 AI startups in 70 countries that have raised more than $27 billion.[1] The financial services industry is leading the way when it comes to both creation and adoption of AI – from managing assets to safeguarding against theft, managing investment, customer engagement, fraud detection, regulatory compliance and stock predictions. In financial services, decisions about individuals' creditworthiness have traditionally been made using a transparent process with defined rules and relatively limited data sets. This transparency, however, may not always be achievable when AI drives big data.[2]

Most AI companies go to great lengths to create objective algorithms. However, even the most mindful expert trainers are susceptible to cultural, geographical or educational influences which can severely impact the underlying assumptions that inform machine-learning code and skew results. This type of unconscious bias poses an important challenge, because bias does not need to be intentional to land financial institutions in hot water.[3] Courts and regulators are focusing more on discriminatory effects of credit decisions and policies than on a financial institution's rationale or motivation. This means that if bias is seen to result in an alleged discriminatory act, there is no need to show that discrimination was intentional to establish liability – only that the discrimination occurred.

As an experienced commercial and data protection lawyer with expertise in deep tech and data protection, I look at this from both a legal and a business standpoint. I see:

- the potential for (severe) legal issues and ramifications that could arise when a financial services business decides to implement AI into their business.
- the commercial and reputational implications of not getting data ethics right.
- unforeseen impacts if companies do not think about these decisions long term, and/or not considering the impacts of impending future legislation.

And when I look at examples from non-financial sectors, for example, historic (and current) use of AI in policing, I see clear lessons to be learnt in advance for and by financial institutions in their own understanding, deployment and oversight of AI.

Sci-Fi — or Real Life?

In 2002, the Wilmington Delaware Police Department made headlines when it thought it would be a good idea to employ the so-called "jump out squads" technique.

[1] https://www.venturescanner.com/blog/2019/artificial-intelligence-report-highlights-q2-2019.

[2] https://www.whitecase.com/publications/insight/ai-financial-services.

[3] Ibid.

A jump-out squad is described as follows: "…they descend on corners, burst out of marked and unmarked vehicles and make arrests in seconds. Up to twenty officers make up each squad. Police routinely line the people on the corners against a wall and pat them down for weapons…Then the police take the men's names and addresses, snap their pictures and send them on their way."[4] Justified as a Terry stop (from a 1968 Supreme Court decision, Terry vs. Ohio, that allows officers to stop, question and frisk people they think are suspicious or people in high-crime areas), most of the 200 people that had their pictures taken during this policy roll-out were young black males. Fast forward a decade or so and add in a dose of facial recognition and associated AI technologies and we're in the realm of movies like the *Minority Report*. Except today, AI is routinely used by law enforcement agencies globally, in many ways and for various reasons, including "crime forecasting" or "predictive policing". A good example of this is COMPAS,[5] an algorithm widely used in the US to guide sentencing by predicting the likelihood of criminal reoffending. In probably the most notorious case of AI prejudice to date, in May 2016 the US news organization ProPublica reported that COMPAS consistently predicts that black defendants pose a higher risk of reoffending than they actually do – and the reverse for white defendants.[6,7]

[4] http://www.talkleft.com/story/2002/08/26/652/40763/civilliberties/Delaware-s-New-Jump-Squads.

[5] https://www.theatlantic.com/technology/archive/2018/01/equivant-compas-algorithm/550646/.

[6] https://www.propublica.org/article/machine-bias-risk-assessments-in-criminal-sentencing.

[7] https://www.propublica.org/article/bias-in-criminal-risk-scores-is-mathematically-inevitable-researchers-say.

Racial Bias — the Tip of the Iceberg?

But it's not just racial bias that's problematic.

- Word-embedding technologies have shown bias toward European names.[8,9,10]
- Camera technologies have assumed that Asian subjects are blinking.[11]
- Image algorithms have labelled Indian brides as performers and classified African Americans as gorillas.[12,13,14]
- CV-sifting technologies have been shown to rank women's CVs lower than men's.[15,16]
- In China, AI has been used to identify Muslims.[17,18]

[8] https://www.theguardian.com/technology/2017/apr/13/ai-programs-exhibit-racist-and-sexist-biases-research-reveals.

[9] https://www.sciencemag.org/news/2017/04/even-artificial-intelligence-can-acquire-biases-against-race-and-gender.

[10] https://www.pnas.org/content/115/16/E3635.

[11] https://thesocietypages.org/socimages/2009/05/29/nikon-camera-says-asians-are-always-blinking/.

[12] https://www.theverge.com/2018/1/12/16882408/google-racist-gorillas-photo-recognition-algorithm-ai.

[13] https://www.wired.com/story/when-it-comes-to-gorillas-google-photos-remains-blind.

[14] https://law-campbell.libguides.com/lawandtech/AI.

[15] https://www.abc.net.au/news/2017-06-30/bilnd-recruitment-trial-to-improve-gender-equality-failing-study/8664888.

[16] https://www.personneltoday.com/hr/is-blind-recruitment-truly-gender-blind/.

[17] https://www.nytimes.com/2019/04/14/technology/china-surveillance-artificial-intelligence-racial-profiling.html.

[18] https://www.theguardian.com/news/2019/apr/11/china-hi-tech-war-on-muslim-minority-xinjiang-uighurs-surveillance-face-recognition.

Biases find their way into the AI systems we design and are used to make decisions within governments and businesses alike. An IBM Study from 2018[19,20] confirms that AI systems are only as good as the data we put into them. More than 180 human biases have been defined and classified, which means that data selected, prioritized and converted into algorithms by humans can contain implicit racial, gender, or ideological biases. The fact that AI marginalizes some groups is bad enough. But the real-world implications of biased AI go much further and are much more harmful. AI can increase the already troubling racial imbalances in the justice system. And applied to financial services, woven so thoroughly into the fabric of our lives, the impacts are just as serious and troubling – if not more so.

Legal and Ethical Issues for Your Watch List

Some of the main legal concerns surrounding AI are the fact that they generally handle large amounts of data, which are often personal or sensitive in nature. Data protection measures need to be put in place by AI providers and the companies that implement AI into their business, to safeguard both any information inputted by users, and databases that are queried by the software. The General Data Protection Regulation (GDPR) has brought in stringent requirements to which companies must adhere:

- Companies that implement AI into their businesses, and technology companies that build and sell AI tools, have a legal obligation to be compliant "by design". This means that the very reliability of AI to provide accurate and meaningful results – particularly in cases where it is relied upon for legal outcomes – is imperative.
- But as it is a developing technology, margins of error should be assumed and calculated, and *manual monitoring of automated results must, by law, still take place.*
- Protection should be put in place against any malicious cyberattacks which could, e.g. manipulate the information or reduce accuracy.
- If an algorithm is programmed to make crucial decisions, such as approve someone's eligibility for insurance cover or a loan, any ethical ramifications should be assessed. This could include the introduction of discrimination by the programmers or trainers of AI.

The GDPR – a Deeper Dive on Key Data Principles

The **Purpose Limitation principle** set out at Article 5(1)(b) of the GDPR says that data should be collected for specified, explicit and legitimate purposes and that it mustn't be processed in a way that is incompatible with the purposes for which it was collected.[21]

In my view, there is an incompatibility here, as data that may initially be collected for one reason will almost undoubtedly be used for another when fed into algorithmic modelling. There is also the operational tendency to collect all data that can be obtained, which means that some data may be collected for an unspecific purpose. Repurposing of data – whereby data collected is used to improve the performance of a service and to generate new types of data – may result in a situation where, practically, it is not clear to the individual what purpose the data will be used for from the outset.

1. **Lawful Basis:** All firms need to consider whether they are able to satisfy the lawful bases for processing personal data. For example, if data has been collected relying on a person's

[19] www.digitaljournal.com/tech-and-science/technology/a-i-systems-are-only-as-good-as-the-data-we-put-into-them/article/531246.

[20] https://www.forbes.com/sites/bernardmarr/2019/01/29/3-steps-to-tackle-the-problem-of-bias-in-artificial-intelligence/#3a109d627a12.

[21] siarticles.com/bundles/Article/pre/pdf/84451.pdf.

consent, then fresh consent would be required if the same data set is to be used for a different purpose. The initial consent provided covers *only* the explicit purpose set out at (and agreed) the original collection.

2. **The Data Minimization principle:** Personal data needs to be adequate, relevant and limited to what is necessary. This is a huge issue for AI as the principle of data minimization is completely opposed to the concept and use of big data.

3. **Individual Rights:** Under the GDPR, data subjects have the right to have their data deleted or rectified. They can also object to the processing of their data. This is clearly extremely difficult, if not impossible, once the data has been fed into an algorithm and decisions made on the basis of that data.

4. **Data Protection Impact Assessments (DPIA):** Companies must do a DPIA before they begin any type of processing that is "likely to result in a high risk" to the rights and freedoms of individuals. In particular, the GDPR says you must do a DPIA if you plan to use systematic and extensive profiling with significant effects; process special category or criminal offence data on a large scale; or systematically monitor publicly accessible places on a large scale. But with the self-evolving nature of AI and the often unpredictable output these AI algorithms can produce, how can companies ensure that they are complying with this obligation?[22,23]

5. **Automated Decision-making:** The GDPR does not prevent automated decision-making or profiling, but it does give individuals a qualified right not to be subject to purely automated decision-making. Can AI decision-making *now* ever be implemented with the GDPR requirement for automated decision-making to always have a human element?[24,25,26,27]

Board members and executives in financial services should carefully assess the AI solutions that are implemented as part of their business. The assessment should not only rely on what the law allows a company to do today, but a holistic view should be taken instead. A commitment to data ethics as a core value is a wise move, as although we may not have the established rules and legislation to guide our every decision, documenting the rationale behind the decisions and demonstrating that thought has gone into assessing the impact on the rights and freedoms of the people who will be served by these AI solutions, is imperative.

Self-Regulation – A Viable Strategy?

Governments across the world have been reluctant to regulate AI, but this may be changing. A 2018 report from the Computers, Privacy and Data Protection Conference suggested that the European Commission is "considering the possibility of legislating for Artificial Intelligence". Karolina Mojzesowicz, deputy head of the Data Protection Unit at the European Commission, said that the Commission is "assessing whether national and EU frameworks are fit for purpose for the new challenges". The

---

22 https://ico.org.uk/for-organisations/guide-to-data-protection/guide-to-the-general-data-protection-regulation-gdpr/data-protection-impact-assessments-dpias/when-do-we-need-to-do-a-dpia/;%20https:/www.itgovernance.co.uk/blog/gdpr-six-key-stages-of-the-data-protection-impact-assessment-dpia.

23 https://www.dataprotection.ie/en/organisations/know-your-obligations/data-protection-impact-assessments.

24 https://ec.europa.eu/info/law/law-topic/data-protection/reform/rights-citizens/my-rights/can-i-be-subject-automated-individual-decision-making-including-profiling_en.

25 https://ico.org.uk/for-organisations/guide-to-data-protection/guide-to-the-general-data-protection-regulation-gdpr/individual-rights/rights-related-to-automated-decision-making-including-profiling/.

26 https://www.itgovernance.co.uk/blog/gdpr-automated-decision-making-and-profiling-what-are-the-requirements.

27 https://privacylawblog.fieldfisher.com/2017/let-s-sort-out-this-profiling-and-consent-debate-once-and-for-all.

Commission is exploring, for instance, whether to specify "how big a margin of error is acceptable in automated decisions and machine learning".[28,29] There is also a tech industry push for more law. In July 2018, Microsoft's president and chief legal officer, Brad Smith, asserted that there should be "public regulation" of facial recognition technology to address the risk of bias and discrimination in facial recognition tech, the risk to intrusions of privacy, and the potential that mass surveillance might impinge on democratic freedom. Regulators around the world are grappling with how to address AI. What happens when an autonomous car and bus collide? Or when smart contract systems incorrectly record a negotiated mortgage or personal loan agreement? Or when AI-enabled due diligence misses the point? The emerging consensus on approach involves a number of steps:

1. Establishing governmental advisory centres of AI excellence.
2. Adapting existing regulatory frameworks to cater for AI where possible.
3. Some system of registration for particular types of AI.

So whilst financial institutions grapple with the strategic and executional aspects of what, when and how to deploy powerful AI technologies, my advice is that the important "Why?" and "Should we?" questions – with their direct application to legal and reputational ramifications – must be at least as high up the board agenda, if not, higher.

[28] https://www.gigacycle.co.uk/news/eu-considers-the-possibility-of-legislating-for-artificial-intelligence/.

[29] https://www.forbes.com/sites/washingtonbytes/2019/02/08/the-eu-should-not-regulate-artificial-intelligence-as-a-separate-technology/#4f0c147c52c9.

Algorithm Assurance

By Christian Spindler
CEO, DATA AHEAD ANALYTICS

Artificial intelligence (AI) is penetrating more and more elements of both personal lives and business processes. Especially in financial services – a data-driven business on the one hand, a regulated and privacy-concerned business on the other hand – the request for assurance, interpretability and fairness of AI algorithms rises. Regulatory organizations continue to raise their voice for a better understanding and control of the risks that come with AI.

The Financial Stability Board says that overall, "AI and machine learning applications show substantial promise if their specific risks are properly managed". In November 2018, the Monetary Authority of Singapore published principles to foster fairness, ethics, accountability and transparency (FEAT) in the application of artificial intelligence and data analytics in the financial sector. The principles demand, for instance, that AI models shall be free of non-intended bias and companies which use AI models shall be responsible for both internally and externally developed components. Swiss regulator FINMA's Circular 2013/8, states: "Supervised institutions that engage in algorithmic trading (see margin no. 18) must employ effective systems and risk controls to ensure that this cannot result in any false or misleading signals regarding the supply of, demand for or market price of securities. Supervised institutions must document the key features of their algorithmic trading strategies in a way that third parties can understand."

Today, the application of algorithms in financial services has broadened from the mere algorithmic trading to many elements in the bank's value chain. Marketing and sales may ask how to use recommender engines to engage with our customers to enhance their experience, reach to new customers or price products. Customer service is concerned with chatbots and natural language processing (NLP) to increase customer satisfaction and retain more customers. Risk and compliance want to know how to use AI models to manage many sorts of risk and ensure compliance in client onboarding and management.

Imagine the loan issuing process in a bank. At various steps in the process, the bank is employing third-party AI-powered software to support the scoring process. Onboarding a new client involves anti-money laundering (AML) and know-your-client (KYC) processes that can be supported by AI. Linked data and graph-based learning, for instance, can detect relationships over several steps of market participants and reveal connections that could turn problematic for a compliant business relationship.

Once onboarded, a loan request issued by a customer typically triggers a rating process for both the applicant and the project to be funded (e.g. consumer loan, mortgage, commercial loan, project financing). Machine learning is successfully employed to identify counterparty risks in both retail and commercial segments, to enable robust scoring even under the constraints of missing information. With a growing number of alternative data sources, e.g. from the Internet of Things (IoT), the performance of scoring algorithms is likely to increase further.

After counterparty scoring and project scoring is performed, pricing and repayment dynamics may be inferred with a separate algorithm based on the risk score on the one hand, and based on factors such as long-term client relationship opportunity on the other. It is particularly hard to model KPIs as the latter, where machine learning with more complex models outplays its biggest strengths, by combining as much relevant data as possible into a model-free prediction function.

This biggest strength turns out to be a weakness if we want to ask how particular decisions have come to exist, or how the overall decision-making process looks in general. As a rule of thumb, the more complex machine learning models are, the less likely are they interpretable in an easily comprehensible manner. For data, a similar rule seems to hold: the larger the scope of a data set (e.g. the more independent data sources are considered), the higher the risk that non-intended biases are undiscovered.

Consequently, the risk of bias in a model's prediction increases. For machine learning and AI to spread further in the financial industry, we must find ways to measure the risks and assure compliance of algorithms and data.

In Europe, the regulatory risks of AI application are mostly determined by the General Data Protection Regulation (GDPR) as the standard for data protection and privacy within the EU and European Economic Area (EEA), and even addresses the export of personal data outside the EU and EEA areas. GDPR sets rules for automated decision-making (Art. 22 GDPR): users, e.g. bank clients, must explicitly consent to automated decision-making, and have otherwise the right not to be subject to a decision based solely on automated processes, including profiling.

If the client gives consent, they may still ask for interpretability of the AI – or, in words of the Regulation, responsible parties for data processing must inform their clients adequately and must prove GDPR compliance. GDPR also rules about Procurement Assurance Compliance: banks that make decisions based on procured third-party AI, or based on outsourced AI, must carry out due diligence in sourcing the service (Art. 28 GDPR).

So how can we mitigate or minimize the risk of non-compliance and secure AI algorithms and their output against unwanted ethical and compliance issues? Various approaches are currently pursued in practice on algorithms.

1. Companies are trading off performance against interpretability. White-box algorithms, such as linear models or decision tree models are interpretable per design. The downside is their low performance for complex relationships in the data. Moreover, decision tree models are prone to overfitting, thus are limited in their overall performance. If more complex algorithms, such as neural networks, turn out to yield better performance, companies must apply additional means for interpretation.

   The black box nature of such algorithms does not necessarily result from missing understanding of the mathematical function that would drive a model's decision – in fact, each parameter of a neural network is known in operation. However, *knowing the parameters is no longer sufficient* to yield a digestible interpretation about which variables in which combination and with which respective weights led to the model's *outcome*. Currently applied approaches for interpreting black box models rely on machine learning itself for model interpretation. One such approach uses so-called Shapley values, invented back in 1953, for assigning credit to "players" in a multidimensional game. A method called SHAP approximates Shapley values by cleverly using XGBoost models, making the approach suitable for practical applications.

   Another widely known approach is LIME, which aims at reducing model complexity locally at the point of current credit score prediction to a simple, interpretable model. Both approaches are simple in their application but may not always seamlessly adapt to a bank's business targets. For instance, when businesses want to approve a target of, say, 20% of applicants ("score space"), but the credit model's actual output comes in so-called "margin-space" of 0 to 1. The non-linear transformation from margin to score space is not straightforward for Shapley values. A satisfactory solution to the problem of interpretability of models in financial applications is still outstanding.

2. The second major topic concerning AI application is bias risk, which is mostly determined by the discipline of data curation in the early stage of the AI value chain. Various metrics, such as statistical parity difference, equal opportunity difference or Theil Index are useful to measure bias along certain dimensions. De-biasing can be achieved by simple means, such as (a) weighting training data points differently to ensure fairness before classification, or (b) complex approaches such as

training a classifier that maximizes performance and simultaneously reduces the ability to determine any protected variable (e.g. gender) from the predictions.

Besides the technological means for algorithm assurance and risk mitigation, ethical design and application of AI is a major concern in banks today. This need is addressed by frameworks such as Algo.Rules that formulate principles for the design of algorithmic systems. With approaches for interpretation, de-biasing and ethical AI design, key elements are or will be in place for algorithm assurance. Finally, is it also possible to monitor and certify the application of this technology and rules? We think it is. For GDPR there are already audit and certification solutions on the market, and AI applications require similar approaches for certification. Robust and transparent algorithm assurance is on the horizon.

Regulation of AI within the Financial Services Sector

By Tim Molton
Associate, MJM Limited

Governments are invariably reactive when legislating for technological advances, rather than having the foresight to anticipate how emerging technologies might develop and consequently be utilized throughout varying industries. This is true even of relatively modest developments, but particularly those which are incredibly complex and have the potential to disrupt global markets, such as artificial intelligence (AI).

The same could be said of financial services professionals, many of whom endorse a laissez-faire approach to technology, not seeking to learn about or engage in discussions surrounding emerging technologies. There is an expectation (albeit predominantly among the pre-millennial generation) that new technologies will not ultimately be adopted "en masse" within the financial services sector, but merely used by a small number of businesses with limited efficacy before being superseded or becoming redundant.

This is demonstrated by the banks' ongoing struggle with their legacy systems and the view that wholesale (and extremely costly) changes to accommodate innovative technology are not a palatable solution – hence the rise of the challenger banks and other FinTechs. Indeed, the emergence of AI in banking is due largely to innovative FinTech startups rather than the established institutions, albeit many banks have partnered with AI companies to offer improved services to their customers. This rise in the use of AI has raised many questions about how (and if) it ought to be regulated.

The Need for Regulation

There are a number of reasons why the use of AI in Financial Services is seen as necessary. For instance, AI requires vast volumes of data to develop the technology, all of which could be vulnerable to malicious actors seeking to misuse the data. AI is also able to analyse customer data almost instantly and can recommend investments and other financial products at a fraction of the cost of a human. This potential for industry-wide redundancies is both an economic and a social concern for governments. Barack Obama in his 2017 farewell address stated that "The next wave of economic dislocation won't come from overseas…[but] from the relentless pace of automation that makes many good, middle-class jobs obsolete". Financial advisors and administrative intermediaries are likely to be anxious at the thought of advanced AI being used in their field of work, and with good reason.

In an era of mobile payments, customers are demanding more from financial institutions. Businesses such as Moneybox and Betterment have recognized this demand and have implemented AI into their service, offering to reduce time and monetary costs. Since the 2008 global crisis, regulators have been focused on putting measures in place to ensure good corporate governance in traditional financial institutions, yet the FinTechs are taking advantage of open banking and emerging technologies to disrupt the financial markets free of many of these constraints, such as reporting obligations and licensing requirements.

Further, there is potential for major disruption and manipulation of the markets with the use of AI. Machine learning can facilitate predictive decision-making, for example, in relation to market patterns and behaviour. Such predictive analytics could result a self-fulfilling prophecy, whereby the "wisdom of the crowd" is actually based on AI market predictions which directly influence investor behaviour. Algorithmic "robo" trading has already been blamed for market crashes, such as the flash crash of 6 May 2010 in which US stocks dropped by around a trillion USD in one day. A lack of understanding of the role of sophisticated AI could clearly have dire consequences, and so while different regulators express differing views, there is a general appetite to at least monitor its development, with policies to stem from the findings of such oversight.

Common Technical Standards

Most commentators would agree that common technical standards need to be implemented if oversight is to be meaningful and effective. These standards can relate to a wide range of issues such as data privacy, security, product safety, accuracy and ethics (e.g. managing social biases), and they will be crucial to the success of AI in the long term. Common standards will help to facilitate integration of technologies and ensure transparency, security and consumer protection. Such technical and algorithmic consistency across offerings will allow regulators to more easily assess the appropriateness of such standards and whether a company's offering is objectively up to standard. They will also provide a benchmark for the legislature and the judiciary when determining how to deal with AI in a legal capacity.

Regulatory Measures

There have, at the time of writing, been a number of steps taken by governments to acknowledge the potential impact of AI and the need to (at least) monitor the progress of the technology. For instance, on 10 April 2018, the UK and 24 other EU Member States signed the Declaration of Cooperation on Artificial Intelligence, which was followed (albeit belatedly) on 8 April 2019 by the European Commission's Ethics Guidelines for trustworthy AI. The latter suggested that AI must be lawful, ethical and robust, but what constitutes lawfulness will undoubtedly be subject to change in the short term.

The EU also saw the General Data Protection Regulation (GDPR) come into effect on 25 May 2018; it recognizes the use of automation and provides that no decision can be taken solely on the basis of automated processing (article 22). This clearly demonstrates the regulators' desire to ensure that the rights and liberties of individuals are not usurped by emerging, innovative technology.

In the UK, the April 2018 House of Lords Select Committee AI report highlighted the long-term educational needs surrounding AI, and addressed concerns surrounding the mass processing of customer data. However, despite concluding that there was no obvious need for further legislation at that stage, the Committee was concerned that the data sets used to train AI systems are poorly representative of the wider population, and so AI systems learning from the data could make unfair decisions which reflect the wider prejudices of societies.[1] Indeed, perpetuating biases is a well-publicized concern of professionals, consumers and politicians and appropriate regulation to prevent this will be crucial the future success of AI-driven financial services.

Questions of Liability

A significant and complicated issue to consider when regulating AI is that of liability. There will be cases that come before the courts in due course which raise new questions about the liability for loss suffered by humans as a result (at least in part) of AI services or products. Where there is a clear causal link between the damage suffered and the AI service, questions about who is ultimately liable for the loss will need to be addressed.

For instance, if a human relies upon the investment advice of a robo-advisor and suffers significant losses as a result, could liability be attributed to the service provider, the developer or even the AI product itself (although we are a long way from attaching legal status to AI products)? This is something that the legislature and judiciary will have to turn their minds to in due course.

Future Regulation

As regulations are implemented and companies take comfort from the success of innovators, many of which will have tested

---

[1] The House of Lords Select Committee on Artificial Intelligence (2018) Report of Session 2017–19, AI in the UK: ready, willing and able? Paragraph 119.

the market by means of regulatory sandboxes, new businesses will emerge seeking to mirror and enhance the offering of the first wave. This will ultimately lead to increased competition and, in theory, a more cost-effective and efficient product/service offering to customers.

However, as AI becomes more advanced and more broadly adopted throughout the financial services sector, governments and regulators must be adequately prepared and well-resourced to ensure that the technology is used safely and in the interests of consumers, without stifling innovation. This means receiving intelligible and constructive input from industry professionals, technology experts, lawyers and consumers as to the potential uses and pitfalls of such technology.

Clearly there are significant challenges faced in dealing with such complex and far-reaching technology as it becomes ubiquitous. Regulators must be willing and able to grapple with the technical, social, economic and legal consequences of AI use in the financial services sector, and ensure that the rights of individuals (including the right to privacy and the right to work) are not usurped as a consequence of global adoption.

Is Risk-Based Regulation the Most Efficient Strategy to Rule the Unknown Risks Brought by FinTech?

By Ligia Catherine Arias-Barrera
PhD in Law, University of Warwick

The process of financial regulation faces the challenge of meeting market needs alongside public expectations. Financial regulators are usually compelled, particularly in periods of disruptive innovations, to react and control the potential sources of systemic risk.

History and the hypothetical scenarios that are somehow foreseeable illustrate the task for regulators when they design the regime. The downside of this process is, however, that almost always innovation-led regulation is exclusively focused on the most prominent areas of concern – the risks that can be easily foreseen, whilst at the same time leaving aside less probable risk. Hence, the use of approaches such as the risk-based regulation (RBR) facilitates the regulator falling into this circle where several types of risks are ignored, and only those risks regulators perceive to be more prominent are regulated.

Manufactured risks are "created by the very progression of human development, especially by the progression of science and technology". The particular characteristic of this type of risk is that, as it comes with progress and innovation, it can be hardly measured or quantified. The data available from history cannot fully inform the probabilities of occurrence.

Despite the critiques, the adoption of risk-based regulation in a world of "newfound risks", as the AI world is, does not necessarily undermine the role of uncertainty and its democratic character. It seems clear that uncertainty and risk might now align and form a hybrid system.

We argue that regulators adopting a sociological model to study risk – the decision-making process concerning what risk exists, the level of tolerance and how to control it – are not restricted to only mathematical methods. Instead, this model is shaped through the integration of different sources of knowledge and with the participation of all interested actors. (i.e. governments, industry, tech firms, academia, and consumers). All of this is possible through RBR.

In the area of regulation and the role of risk, the debate has been prominently fed by the analysis of the sociologists Luhmann and Beck.[1] One of the lines of thought that is noteworthy analyses the phenomenon of risk and its role in society, the so-called "risk society" created by Ulrich Beck. According to Beck, risk means anticipation of a positive or negative situation in the future.

The rationale of the risk society is the distribution of "bads" and dangers.[2] In a risk society there is a constant development of innovative technology that is not fully understood. In such a society, there is no end in production of possible futures.[3] The modernization process triggers progress in several areas (e.g. technology, science) that results in a multiplication of known risks, while at the same time it questions the ability to prevent or minimize the impact of such risks.

---

[1] Joanna Gray and Jenny Hamilton (2012) *Implementing Financial Regulation: Theory and Practice*, Wiley, 60.

[2] Ulrich Beck (1992) *Risk Society: Towards a New Modernity*, SAGE, 3.

[3] Antony Giddens (1999) Risk and Responsibility, *MRL* 62(1), 3.

The debate in the discourse of risk embeds the idea of differentiating risk from uncertainty.[4,5] Two opposite lines of thought have explored this area. On the one hand is the "scientific-rationalist", "absolutist" or "modernist" model[6] that understands risk as an objective concept, which can be quantified and measured, and is linked to the probability[7] and severity[8] of occurrence. Under this model, the regulation of risk should be the result of a technocratic process where experts lead the decision-making. On the other hand, there is the "social-constructivist", "sociopolitical" "postmodernist" model.[9] According to this model, risk is constantly merging with uncertainty and, as such, it cannot always be quantified and measured. Moreover, risk and uncertainty can easily overlap with each other.

Therefore, under this model, regulation of risk should involve all the interested actors, not just the "technocrats". This chapter argues that the RBR of FinTech should integrate the multiple and diverse perceptions of risks and uncertainties that regulators and regulated entities have. In this scenario there is a constant challenge to achieve a balance between potential conflicting interests (i.e. interests of the public and interests of regulated entities); cooperation with regulated entities would contribute to the design and facilitate the effective implementation of the regime.

[4]H. Kemshall (2002) Risk, *Social Policy and Welfare,* Buckingham: Open University Press, 11; C. Hood and D.K.C. Jones (eds) (1996) *Accident and Design, Contemporary Debates in Risk Management*, London, UCL.

[5]Ian Bartle (2008) "Risk-based regulation and better regulation in the UK: towards what model of risk regulation?", 2nd Biennial Conference of the ECPR Standing Group on Regulatory Governance, Utrecht University, the Netherlands. "Regulation in the Wake of Neoliberalism. Consequences of Three Decades of Privatization and Market Liberalization": http://regulation.upf.edu/utrecht-08-papers/ibartle.pdf accessed 15 June 2019.

[6]D. Lupton (1999) *Risk*, London and New York: Routledge, 6.

[7]Frank Knight (1921) *Risk, Uncertainty and Profit*, Houghton Mifflin, 9.

[8]D. Smith and B. Toft (1998) "Risk and Crisis Management in the Public Sector Editorial: Issues in Public Sector Risk Management", *Public Money and Management* 18:4, 10.

[9]B. Adam and J. van Loon (2000) "Introduction: Repositioning Risk; the Challenge for Social Theory", 8, in: *The Risk Society and Beyond: Critical Issues for Social Theory*, Barbara Adam, Ulrich Beck and Joost van Loon (eds), London: Sage.

Studying Beck's risk society, Giddens identifies a category of risks called "external or manufactured risks".[10] Giddens defines manufactured risks as "risks created by the very progression of human development, especially by the progression of science and technology".[11] The particular characteristic of this type of risk is that, as it comes with progress and innovation, it can be hardly measured or quantified. Thus, we could anticipate that risks arising from FinTech developments are manufactured risks.

The adoption of RBR is heavily reliant on the complexities surrounding the risk phenomena. There are some features of the use of risk as a driver of regulation and the task is not limited to the integration of multiple perceptions of risks. When government authorities face some conflict between different RB regimes, the use of risk allows regulators to shift responsibility for certain risks to the regulated entities.[12]

The risk-society theory provides the context to argue that the AI is a "manufactured-risk-scenario" and a formation of the modern society in financial markets. AI developments create risks and accumulate uncertainties. These uncertainties in turn show the limits of the expertise and regulation of the market.

[10]Giddens, "Risk and Responsibility" 3.

[11]Ibid.

[12]Gray and Hamilton, *Implementing Financial Regulation.*

Notwithstanding the challenges, we argue that risks and uncertainties manufactured in FinTech have the potential to inform the process of design and implementation of regulation, especially in RB regimes. RBR is usually defined as a general set of principles that seeks to find common elements to rationalize the regulatory process.[13] The key feature is to prioritize regulatory actions in accordance with an assessment of the risk that the regulated entities will present to the regulatory body's achieving its objectives. Moreover, RBR usually involves a concern of regulators to enhance its legitimacy and accountability, as well as having sufficient intervention tools, this is to have in place an enforcement regime.

[13] Julia Black, "The Development of Risk-Based Regulation in Financial Services: Just 'Modelling Through'?" in Julia Black, Martin Lodge and Marck Thatcher (Eds.) *Regulatory Innovation: A Comparative Analysis* (Edward Elgar Publishing, 2005), 156.

The Changing Face of Regulatory, Compliance and Audit

By Shailendra Malik
Vice President – IT Platforms, DBS Bank

Why We Need Compliance and Audit

We humans, as a society, have evolved significantly with the advances in technology and automation, which have simplified a lot of menial tasks we did in the past. From manual labour to automated machines, from clerical work to structured and reliable data collection and processing, and even from instinct-based decisions to informed, logical and structured decision-making, technology has been the backbone of this human evolution.

Humans, however, also procrastinate, become lazy and sometimes take short cuts to achieve success. These negative qualities push them into doing things that are risky, sometimes illegal or finding ways to beat the rules that we, as a society, have put in place and expected to abide by. This creates challenging problems for us to solve, such as how to identify cheating acts, detect fraud and distinguish them from other forms of misconduct in day-to-day transactions. Hence the need to have a system of internal controls to detect occurrence of any wrongdoing supplemented by regulatory oversight – supervision of a group by an outside body in order to control or direct according to rule, principle or law.

As we progress towards a more urbane way of conducting business transactions, the nature of fraud has become complex too, bringing a new set of challenges for compliance officers, who are increasingly relying on forensic analysis, which employs mathematical, probabilistic and AI-based techniques to catch bad transactions and nefarious actors.

Identification of Risks

As fraud becomes more sophisticated, so does the process of identifying and catching the perpetrators, but with increasing complexity. Auditors are observing challenges emerging from new technologies. A mature organization constantly assesses the potential risks, and manages, controls and mitigates exposure to these risks.

These exposures may arise from technological gaps, process gaps, lack of understanding of new business models and sometimes even employee misconduct. To improve risk assessment and maturity of its processes, organizations have been relying on technology tools that aid in statistics and data collection; however, their methods are dated.

Most of the current risk assessment techniques employ artificial intelligence (AI) and machine learning (ML) models, which take advantage of the expansive and elastic compute cycles available in the cloud, and which in turn help churn complex mathematical and statistical calculations. With AI becoming a buzzword, everyone is excited to use it in some shape or form, to gain the insights that were illusive before.

Almost all departments in an organization such as Sales, Marketing, HR and Operations are busy building or deploying new models to find the next secret sauce for their top line as well as bottom lines; however, the top three limitations that compliance and audit divisions face are as follows:

- No industry standards and guidelines for the ML model selection process, including from open source.
- No standard governance, risk and compliance procedures for assessing the quality of these models running in production.
- No guidance on data modelling and quality issues to improve learning and minimize false positives, remove bias and balance trade-off between accuracy and precision.

With multifold increase in complexity, it can become a nightmare for compliance and audit teams to keep adding more datapoints to mitigate or control the risks and this adds further exposure to sparse and sometimes unreliable data.

A Vision for Tomorrow

As part of the regulatory oversight, the financial services industry is inundated with several new laws and regulations related to anti-money laundering and counterterrorism financing and track money trails. A stronger focus on fraud detection and prevention along with the huge amount of data that organizations have amassed over the last several years is now driving faster adoption of AI-related techniques in the regulatory landscape. These include:

1. Sharper sampling
Choosing a sample that is a perfect representative of the population has always been a challenge; however, now, ML models can help identify suspicious transactions with greater precision for manual verification.

2. Graduating from sampling to holistic screening
With rapid adoption of data lakes and cloud, organizations would have resources to perform holistic screening without impacting performance and costs. Over time, regulators may expect this to become the standard rather than relying on sampling efficiency and effectiveness. After all, why choose a sample when you can scan the population with no meaningful trade-offs.

3. Reduced reaction time to fraud and other incidents
One big limitation in our existing auditing system is the broken data collection from multiple resources and manual verification of the transactions. With data screening becoming automated and AI doing all that labour-intensive work, continuous auditing will soon become a reality, dramatically reducing the response time to fraud and analysis.

4. Creative solutions to current fraud typologies
Typologies distinguish differences in their knowledge of the fraud, the degree of cooperation and in the loss. Most difficult fraud types are cyclic in nature. Origination of funds and then ultimate drainage in the shell accounts owned by the same people have been one of the most common ways to launder money and evade tax. Creative solutions of ML models working with graph data sets that focus on entity relationships instead of transactions would eliminate such frauds as they will become very easy to detect.

5. New fraud typologies will emerge
As fraud detection of known types becomes more efficient, one would expect the fraudsters to get more creative and bring new types of fraud into the market. With ML models being quick in pattern recognition, these new frauds would be detected and propagated in the short term, thus reducing the scope of the damage done by new frauds.

6. Greater cost savings through better synergies between internal and external audit and regulators
External auditors review and determine the extent to which they can rely on the work performed by internal audit teams before providing an independent view of the final and business health of an organization. Similarly, regulators may rely on the work performed by external auditors. With audit data collection and screening becoming cloud driven and AI screening for anomalies, one can expect greater cooperation and synergies to conduct reviews and minimize costs.

Conclusion

AI and ML hold a lot of promise for the future. Organizations are beginning to harness their value with better data collection and constant fine-tuning of models. I believe that we are bound to witness tangible gains from the new technologies and greatly enhance the efficiency and effectiveness of compliance and audit functions with a sharper vision. We would still need to focus on the right problems to solve and not get carried away with the euphoria and hysteria created by the new technologies.

Robocop on Wall Street

By Michael Berns
Director AI and FinTech, PwC

Robocop on Wall Street – this futuristic term coined by a journalist to describe one of the leading RegTech vendors sums up the revolutionary advances in artificial intelligence (AI) which are rapidly and seamlessly bridging the gap between legal/regulatory requirements and technology.

Setting the Scene – The Why

Let's start with "why". Why is AI such a powerful tool for legal and compliance use cases? Financial crime has been a thorn in the side of financial services firms ever since financial markets were created, long before the financial crisis. Post crisis, the shock to the entire system and the increased regulatory scrutiny has brought a lot of new financial crime cases to light.

Reviewing Figure 1, it is clear that:

- The fines in the early years were low (even during 2002–2006 they did not exceed GBP 25 million per year).
- They did not immediately peak after the financial crisis, but only a few years later in 2014–2015, as regulators first prioritized monitoring the survival of banks and tightening up regulatory requirements such as Basel III/IV. When some of these big cases like LIBOR manipulation were uncovered, it became clear that this practice had been going on since the nineties, but no fines had been imposed in earlier years.[1]

No matter whether the focus is on Europe, Asia, or the complex regulatory regimes in the US FRB (Federal Reserve Board),

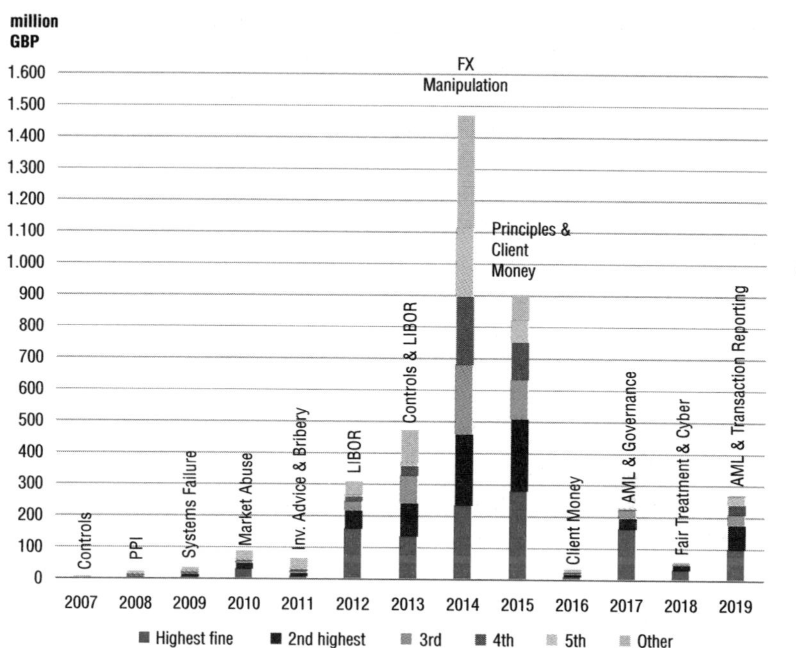

Figure 1: UK regulatory fines (Financial Services Authority/Financial Conduct Authority)[2]

OCC (Office of the Comptroller of the Currency), FDIC (Federal Deposit Insurance Corporation), SEC (Securities and Exchange Commission), or the CFTC (Commodity Futures Trading Commission) the picture is very clear – a highly significant increase in regulatory fines over the last 10 years.[3,4]

[1] "Wall Street gets slammed with $5.8 billion in fines for rate rigging", *Business Insider*, 20 May 2015.

[2] Created by the author based on publicly available data. Note that it is difficult to consistently capture all of the data in one graph, as some of the claims are still being collected (in the case of PPI for example). "Wall Street gets slammed with $5.8 billion in fines for rate rigging", *Business Insider*, 20 May 2015.

[3] "SFC slaps banks with huge fines for DD failures", *Funds Selector Asia*, 15 March 2019.

[4] "Fines totalling S$16.8 m slapped on 42 financial firms in Singapore in 18 months ended December '18", *Business Times*, 20 March 2019.

One can observe an increase in regulatory fines on the one hand and the typical buying cycle of compliance related software on the other hand, previously somewhere around 4–5 years. The fact that recently regulatory fines in the US have stopped increasing due to political movements to deregulate has not changed the overall global picture.[5] No bank can afford to sit on the sidelines in times of multibillion-dollar fines, with bank licenses for whole countries being at risk if immediate and firm action is not taken to tackle the underlying financial crimes.

Plagued by historical structural issues such as outdated technology, operating in silos and limited transparency, financial institutions have no choice but to look outside for innovations and faster solutions. In this escalating situation, the arrival of FinTech (financial technology), or more specifically RegTech (regulatory technology), is very important.

Some of the key players in this area are innovative companies with only a few years under their belt and few enterprise references; companies that would not have been given the time of day previously, without the urgent call to action and the imperative need to solve old issues differently.

Financial institutions are under pressure to empower their staff to do more in less time. Legal risk and regulatory use cases are frequently related to vast amounts of unstructured data, which takes humans a very long time to go through and decipher. However, AI is particularly good at recognizing patterns or behaviour in masses of data, hence allowing the solution to reduce the vast number of false positives while at the same time uncovering new complex cases, increasing true positives. The typical signal to noise or needle in the haystack scenario.

[5] "Wall Street Faces Fewer Fines in 2019 as SEC Democrat Departs", Bloomberg, 19 December 2018.

Mapping out the RegTech and Legal Risk AI Landscape (The What)

Having reviewed the market conditions and the reasons why AI is well suited to be used for legal risk and regulatory use cases, this section highlights potential solutions in these fields. The increase in the amounts of fines is directly correlated to a significant increase in the amount of regulatory changes per year, at least during the post-financial crisis period.

This in turn led to a significant increase in the number of RegTech firms in the same period, from just over a hundred during the financial crisis to around 500 in 2018. In the last few years, more and more of the technology is also being used by the regulators and supervisors themselves, leading to the term of SupTech being coined in 2017.[6]

At a high level, RegTech and legal risk solutions typically fall into the following five main categories:

- General compliance/legal processes, e.g. optimization.
- Monitoring, e.g. contract analysis, AML, KYC, behaviours, verification, conduct, surveillance.
- Risk, e.g. monitor limits and stress testing.
- Legal/regulatory analysis (identification & interpretation).
- Reporting (regulatory & management).

Therefore, from an AI perspective the monitoring and legal/regulatory analysis are the most relevant fields, while general compliance/legal is an automation game (using robotic process automation and other technologies, for example). Some AI

[6] "Innovative technology in financial supervision (Suptech) – the experience of early users", BIS, July 2018.

solutions are emerging for risk, but it will be some time before additional AI factors are accepted as part of a credit risk model, very much depending on the regulator and the state of "explainable AI".

Key Building Blocks of AI Solutions Addressing Legal Risk and Regulation (The How)

Having elaborated on the why and the what, the focus shifts to the how – how are AI solutions in these segments typically built – what are the key components?

Figure 2 highlights that A1 and A2 are different input channels with a particular focus on unstructured data, via news, email, contracts, voice and chat. It is often the case that AI is used to enrich structured data (such as employee or client records) with unstructured data.

For data integration (B1) quite a few solutions have their own proprietary ETL (extract, transform, load) solution to map the data

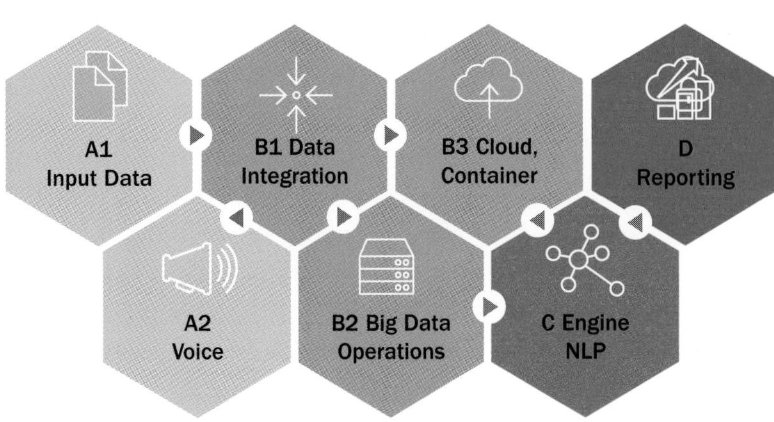

Figure 2: Key components (created and simplified by the author)

in; for the rest, typically the standard ETL/data integration tools are used. Clients might prefer using their own big data infrastructure (B2) in terms of Hadoop and Spark, or be comfortable to scale via cloud services (B3). Depending on whether the solution is focused on leveraging unstructured data like communication, the engine (C) might include a natural language processing (NLP) pre-processing stage to let the algorithms detect sentence structure, context and intent before running a number of specific machine learning models to search for certain patterns over time.

A key part is always how good the models are out of the box in terms of precision and recall or how much additional training (i.e. supervised learning) is required to reach a reasonable level. Finally (D) is providing the interface (be it via highlighting/comparison, a knowledge graph or other means).

Judgement and Liability

There is no denying that AI is currently very much on the radar. Since March 2018, people's view of AI has fundamentally changed following the Cambridge Analytica (CA) scandal and the subsequent investigations into Facebook. The fact that CA claimed to have been involved in more than 200 elections including Trump and the Brexit Referendum, both of which were closely decided, shows that the ethics of companies using AI to endlessly harvest data have been severely questioned.[7]

In the meantime, a new US antitrust suit is about to be launched against the tech giants, supposedly also for ethical considerations, customer data and oversight of AI Research.[8] There is a strong trend among financial services institutions and regulators to look

---

[7] "Cambridge Analytica: The data firm's global influence", BBC, 22 March 2018.

[8] "The DOJ's Antitrust Chief Just Came out Swinging Against Google and Amazon", *Fortune*, 11 June 2019.

outside the box to harness technical solutions that were previously only available to governments. For a few years, there has been a steady increase in ex-military and intelligence profilers joining financial services companies to apply AI to tackle financial crime.[9]

In conclusion, just like with the arrival of the internet for the broad public in the nineties, the world now has a chance to participate in something that will fundamentally change the way people search for relevant information, develop solutions to age-old problems, tackle financial crime and influence how financial services firms and regulators think. There is no denying that "data is the new oil" and one can either participate in this journey of innovation or observe and watch.

---

[9] "HSBC recruits ex-head of MI5 to shore up financial crime defence", *Financial Times*, 23 May 2013.

Sure, AI Can Answer Our Questions – But Who Will Answer Our Questions About AI?

By Elif Kocaoglu Ulbrich
FinTech Consultant and Author

Everyone older than thirty can remember the first moment they felt intimidated by intelligent machines: it was the early 90s, and they were watching *The Terminator*. This generation was the first to be exposed to a fear of robots, which could sense, analyse, plan and execute.

Today's algorithms and intelligent machines are not quite there yet but can still achieve a lot. Artificial Intelligence and deep learning are already pushing the limits of the human learning capacities. The development of artificial intelligence (AI) started with the motivation to teach machines to imitate human abilities[1] and now is marching into the banking, health, education, defence and mobility spaces; automating traditional practices and taking humans out of the equation. Startups have been experimenting with AI, using it for automation, face and voice recognition, cognitive analysis, profiling and more. Algorithms are supposed to provide a real cure for mundane, repetitive tasks and improve service speed and costs. Exciting times ahead.

Despite the noteworthy technical progress, unanswered questions about the extent of the predictability of AI create a contradiction and divide experts about the technology's potential. Algorithms are programmed to behave and conclude in a certain way, and AI uses algorithms to simulate and mirror human intelligence. Just as the first three years of childhood have an impact on the whole of adolescence,[2] the initial training data remains to the critical component for applications of the AI. The more qualified the data set, the better the results. What if the data sets we feed the model with are (intentionally or unintentionally) biased, narrow-sighted, unfair or corrupt?

Recent examples show us that there are two sides of the coin. On one side, we have Amazon's AI-powered hiring tools picking up gender discriminating behaviour in no time, due to prior recruitment history. Engineers reportedly found the AI was unfavourable toward female candidates because it had combed through male-dominated résumés to accrue its data.[3] On the other side, we have algorithmic FinTech lending, which seems to have a lower discrimination rate than traditional lenders. The research concludes that online FinTech companies discriminate 40% less than loan officers who make decisions face-to-face, whereas no sign of discrimination was found from the robots when it comes to loan approvals.[4]

In the end, none of these models are scientifically validated. Quoting Jack Dorsey, "Algorithms are not being written in such a way that they can explain the criteria being used, or how they actually made the decision."[5] As long as there is a history of prejudiced decisions, stereotypes and biases are consequently likely to be passed on to AI, through this historical data set.

The real issue with the application of AI lies within accessibility and guidance. We are not fully aware of all the planned uses due to the

[1] https://www.csee.umbc.edu/courses/471/papers/turing.pdf.

[2] https://www.unicef.org/sowc01/1-2.htm.

[3] https://www.businessinsider.com/amazon-built-ai-to-hire-people-discriminated-against-women-2018-10.

[4] https://qz.com/1647701/fintech-algorithms-discriminate-40-less-than-traditional-lenders/.

[5] https://qz.com/1642172/jack-dorsey-on-bitcoin-facebooks-crypto-and-the-end-of-cash/.

lack of oversight, deepfakes based on open source models are a clear demonstration of potential abuse.[6] No one knows what's next.

Should a discussion about the social consequences of AI implementation go hand in hand with the technical developments, or should we develop now and think about the potential threats later? The answer to this question seems to range from black to white, with people supporting research and development fanatically at one end, and the doomsday oracles at the other.

To balance technological advancement and safety, we need to ensure that the models are designed transparently, consciously and ethically. The challenging part of applying ethical and moral standards to AI is more about the ethical criterion rather than the algorithm, or the process.

Standard definitions do not exist about ethics and impartiality. If we are planning to replace human decision-making processes with algorithms that are supposed to make ethical assessments, it seems only fair to define the rules of the game and create codes of conduct. In the end, if AI and deep learning are about teaching algorithms to find patterns, we need to make sure that the accessible data steers into the correct ones.

There are several organizations focused on untangling the challenges AI presents, but the focus seems to be rather regional and specialized. In the end, all these separate workflows might create patchwork-like practices. General regulations do not exist, and regulating limited domains (i.e. algorithmic FinTech lending or trading) might limit us at this point since it's hard to guess what's next.

[6]https://www.vice.com/en_us/article/kzm59x/deepnude-app-creates-fake-nudes-of-any-woman.

Therefore, there is a need for both industry-specific and generic metrics for AI. The creation of an international supervisory mechanism like the Basel Committee, which creates a global work stream and information exchange flow on the topic, might be able to serve us both short and long term. A top-down, international approach might make it easier to standardize the codes of conduct for AI, harmonize the applications of developed and developing countries, and provide guidance to the regulators. After all, it's the use cases that need regulation, not the technology behind it, and thus regulators should ensure an unrestricted development and testing environment, intertwined with proper control, and governance mechanisms.

Research demonstrates that only 40% of companies adopting machine learning indicated their organizations check for model fairness and bias.[7] If ethical queries do not come naturally to those who are involved with AI, they will have to be imposed. The outputs of AI models should be tested for biases before going live.

Policymakers should consider imposing ethical boards, controlling the applications and potential consequences of the models, according to the codes of conduct. These boards should ensure the execution of policies, report to necessary authorities in case of a (potential) ethical dilemma and conduct periodical risk assessments on the models/software.

Another solution to tame the potential risks might lie with the introduction of a light licensing process, which aims to ensure that the AI is lawful, ethical and robust in a particular way, as imposed by the principles, and includes the right transparency and cybersecurity measures.[8]

[7]https://www.oreilly.com/ideas/5-findings-from-oreilly-machine-learning-adoption-survey-companies-should-know.

[8]https://ec.europa.eu/digital-single-market/en/news/ethics-guidelines-trustworthy-ai.

Unless algorithmic bias isn't definitely out of the picture, AI systems shouldn't be commercialized or distributed/used on a large scale without fitting human-in-the-loop, human-on-the-loop or human-in-command measures in place.[9] The scenarios that cause liability and accountability should be precisely defined.

All in all, contrary to the more fantastic predictions for AI in the popular press, the AI100 Standing Committee found no cause for concern that AI is an imminent threat to humankind, due to the fact that no machines with self-sustaining long-term goals and intent have been developed, nor are they likely to be developed in the near future.[10]

Up until now, the developments have been quite positive and only reflect the passing of particular automation and delegation milestones. It seems as if it is mostly our ethical standards that cause a threat to the direction in which AI is heading, not vice versa. Humans are the one species with an ever-changing fluid moral understanding, not the machines, and it's our standards that need to be controlled and tamed so that we do not pass them on to the algorithms as well.

AI systems need to be human-centric, intending to improve individual and societal well-being, and worthy of our trust.[11] Thus, it is only fair that we ensure that human ego and mistakes are not interfering in the process, by providing a rulebook for every sector; enable testing and supervise the development and the implications thoroughly.

[9]https://ai100.stanford.edu/2016-report.

[10]Ibid.

[11]https://ec.europa.eu/digital-single-market/en/news/policy-and-investment-recommendations-trustworthy-artificial-intelligence.

Technology for Regulations and Compliance: Fit4Future!

By Poornima Bushpala
VP Operational Risk and Control, Wells Fargo

The regulatory and legal process in the financial world has been about semantics, and experts believe that it has been linear primarily because the industry had no other option but to hold still with old technology until new technology transformed the financial sector.

Globally, we have 750+ regulatory bodies generating an average 200+ daily regulatory alerts and approximately 2500 compliance rule books. Regulatory spend by complying organizations is counted in the billions of dollars annually and these investments were predominantly in hiring talent, creating manual workflows and processes to meet regulatory policy requirements.

Significant incidents like 2017's Equifax data breach and the Securities and Exchange Commission (SEC) violations in the US banking industry, coupled with the lack of available skilled resources, forced financial institutions to strengthen their risk management framework by leveraging technology. This gave birth to the regulatory technology called "RegTech".

RegTech addresses regulatory challenges and facilitates the delivery of compliance requirements, which include both new and existing rules, regulations, sanctions and industry-specific guidance as prescribed by the respective regulatory body. Examples include (a) self-service software that lets legal professionals generate organizationally compliant contracts and monitor their status, and (b) cloud-based apps that allow clients to onboard schedule deadlines, store files and manage contacts. This article looks at three key areas:

- The evolution of RegTech: Journey from RegTech 1.0 to 3.0.
- Phases of RegTech tools: Different stages of regulatory technology deployment.
- Future of RegTech: Paradigm shift of regulations and compliance from manual to digitized.

Evolution of RegTech

RegTech 1.0 was mostly driven by large financial institutions who integrated technology into their internal processes to combat rising compliance costs and complexity as epitomized in the Basel II capital accord.

When Lehman Brothers went bankrupt in September 2008, it had more than $600 billion in assets, but neither the regulators nor the central banks knew the risk held with their junk bonds (high-yield bonds). The innumerable and catastrophic consequences of this bankruptcy led the Basel Committee on Banking Supervision (BCBS) to act by deploying new measures.

In January 2013, the BCBS published 239, a set of principles encouraging banks to produce more reliable regulatory reports and improve the quality of their data — so RegTech 2.0 was born, driven mainly by new post-GFC (global financial crisis) regulatory requirements and associated costs around, for example, anti-money laundering and know-your-customer (KYC) requirements.

While RegTech 1.0 to 2.0 focused on cost gains and efficiency, 3.0 is shifting focus towards reconceptualizing the financial and regulatory landscape, for example, by shifting the focus from a KYC to a KYD (know your data) mindset. Another example is Basel IV, which is more focused on the banking lobby, and the proposal is towards the standardization of real estate loan models and especially risk generated by interest rates of the loans, which are forcing regulators to demand more reporting and data of the borrowers from financial institutions.

RegTech 3.0: Phases of Development

1. Stage 1: Manual
To put together the data collection process in place to capture manually the information on cyclical timelines. Today, most organizations use MS Office Excel in obtaining data and providing analysis of the data.

2. Stage 2: Workflow Automation
The next phase of automation is using workflow tools to store and capture data in the system record and maintain the audit trail for audit purposes. Common standard workflow tools used include MetricStream GRC, and Archer.

3. Stage 3: Continuous Monitoring
In this phase, the focus is on automation of the back office using tools such as Droit, the first fully digitized MiFID II trade compliance engine for the financial markets, and an extension of AEDPT (the operating system for regulation). It provides and enables verification and auditability of every trading decision, including traceability to the letter of the law, and is used, for example, for pre-trade decision-making and post-trade reporting for OTC derivatives.

4. Stage 4: Predictive Analytics
In this phase, we have more advanced technology deployed to identify and predict risk by using AI and machine learning. One of the most significant risks that banks and financial institutions are still facing is fraud, and increasingly commonly AI technologies, such as Boston-based Findability, are used to proactively identify risks using data and patterns.

Conclusion

So, how does the future regulatory world look? How can it be focused around a "robo-regulator", an automated powerhouse that can read and take relevant actions for compliance and non-compliance with humongous data insights? For this future to come about, three key things need to be in place:

- **Data Library:** Governments collect and store a massive amount of data.
- **Global Sandbox:** Regulators globally collaborate and share ideas, information and best practices, as indeed is exemplified by the Global Financial Innovation Network (GFIN), a network of 38 organizations committed to supporting financial innovation in the interests of consumers, that formally launched in January 2019.
- **Applying and Integrating AI:** By using computing power and AI and natural language processing, we could look at the possibility of some regulations eventually being issued in the form of computer code promulgated in a self-executing code that could be plugged into a regulatory compliance system.

It's a long road ahead and requires total integration and the right kind of academic, technological, financial and institutional backing.

The Future of AI in Finance

While the field of AI has over sixty years of research and development under its belt, we are only seeing the tip of the iceberg in terms of what is possible with such advanced intelligence techniques

"Once humans develop full AI, it will take off on its own and redesign itself at an ever-increasing rate"
Stephen Hawking

The widespread application of Artificial Intelligence will be seen in the history books as the next evolutionary step of humanity and the most important technology we will ever create. The World Economic Forum tells us that in the age of AI there 75 million jobs are set to disappear, but 113 million jobs will be created. The question is, what do these jobs look like and what kind of skills do they need?

"AI may constitute a fundamental risk to the existence of human civilization"
Elon Musk

AI itself is a potentially major threat to humanity, but on balance would it not be wrong to avoid exploring its abilities to improve our world and the lives of our fellow species?

"The future is not pre-ordained by machines. It's created by humans"
Erick Brynjolfsson

Does this mean that we need more reasoned and controlled implementations of AI systems; that we should imbue them with a sense of morality?

Without having the benefit of a crystal ball, it is very difficult to predict what the future holds, and in an area as inherently complex as artificial intelligence, the task is even more complicated. However, when the stakes are as high as they are, anticipating the future is not simply a matter of curious amusement; it is a moral and existential imperative.

This part takes a deep dive into the way in which the various technologies which fall under the broad heading of "artificial intelligence" (AI) are likely to evolve across the financial services industry, and beyond. We see how the different uses of technology today are already serving to condition the trajectory of their ongoing development, and how AI is disrupting the competitive landscape, particularly as big tech and FinTechs encroach on the incumbent institutions' traditional territory.

Through real-world examples and insightful commentary from industry experts who leverage a deep understanding of our contemporary environment, we gain a comprehensive view of the various domains that AI is expected to impact, from banking through to education and even macro employment. We take a look at what technological change means from a leadership perspective, in terms of structuring organizations to provide meaningful jobs in a context where AI could be poised for full-scale domination; and we also see the role AI can play in advancing the development economics agenda in emerging economies.

While preceding chapters have provided us with many answers, the moment has now come to debate some of the most pressing long-term questions of our time:

- Why and where do we need AI?
- What choices do we need to make?
- And how willing are we to assume the consequences of our actions (or non-action, as the case may be)?

An AI-driven future holds a wealth of opportunity, but the path is strewn with potential hazards. Navigating our way to a better tomorrow is likely to be the ultimate challenge of our time.

Welcome to the Future

By Professor Andy Pardoe
Founder, Informed.AI Group

The Evolving Technology Landscape

The fundamental principles underpinning machine learning (ML) have been well known for many decades; in fact the concept of a neural network dates back to the 1950s. Less complex artificial intelligence (AI) methods including expert systems, decision trees and rule engines have also been around for many decades, and have been used with varying success for specific problems.

However, the interest in AI and ML in the financial services sector only became mainstream quite recently, driven in part by the public successes of the more advanced techniques of deep learning that empower natural language processing (NLP) and image recognition.

The irony of the situation is that, for many use cases within financial services, the less complex techniques of AI are very capable. However, NLP, voice to text, and visual analytics are still required within the financial services sector and these require the use of deep learning models which have only been proven in the last five years or so.

It is therefore, in part, the skill of the data scientist to select the right type of ML algorithm to solve the specific task for each use case. As with most things, using the least complex solution able to solve the problem is a solid guiding principle.

While the field of AI has over 60 years of research and development under its belt, we are only seeing the tip of the iceberg in terms of what is possible with such advanced intelligence techniques. The limitations of AI will be largely dependent on what we, the human controllers, decide we want the computers to do.

There is significant investment in all of the large technology firms, universities and institutions to develop more advanced techniques that are more capable at solving more complex tasks more precisely. In many ways we are seeing the next "global arms race" between nations to build the most advanced AI algorithms, and the financial services industry, as the industry that is leading the corporate adoption of AI outside of the technology firms themselves, will no doubt be one of the major battlegrounds in which corporate and national glory will be built.

Beyond Digital Transformation: Thinking Like a Digital Native

One of the challenges with the adoption of any new technology is the initially siloed approach to adoption, with small pockets of innovation happening across the organization, causing a fragmented approach with limited application of standards; alignment of tools, frameworks and vendors; and the opportunity for reuse across these organizational boundaries. This can result in a complex landscape, if not controlled and properly managed.

The situation is often further complicated with related technology decisions (such as preferred cloud vendors) delaying the strategic architectural blueprint. With decades of layered legacy technology to contend with, aligning roadmaps and data strategies with that of the new ML landscape can inevitably become overly perplexing.

Today, the technology footprint is particularly complex with the need for multiple channels of access – from the traditional bricks and mortar and telephone banking, to the more digital channels of online, mobile, apps and social media. A central, real-time 360-degree view of customers is needed in order to remain competitive. In this brave new digital world, which is open 24 hours a day 7 days a week, taking days or weeks to open a new bank account feels so twentieth century.

FinTechs, while still needing to comply with all the same regulations as the incumbent institutions, have the advantage of a "blank page" when it comes to building their IT systems, not needing to worry about integrating into a fragmented back office estate that has been built up over many years of change.

This gives them a major advantage from a customer experience perspective. However, the incumbents still hold the keys to the safe insofar as they have the volume of customers and decades of customer data which can be analysed. Without the data, FinTechs are unable to apply any significant ML models. Granted, they can use chatbots for customer support but then, so can the incumbents.

Potential competitive threats are also emerging from the large technology players, who have both the advantage of the so-called blank page, as well as the depth of experience and knowledge of the technology and a significant volume of customers. Tech firms are already moving into this space and it is only a matter of time before the value chain experiences a new episode of significant disruption.

Fundamentally, the journey the financial industry is embarking is the same as that experienced in all industries. The road to digitalization – becoming a fully transitioned digital business – is not a small transformational feat.

There will be leaders in each industry who rise to this challenge and embrace the opportunity to rethink and redesign their workflows and business process. The ones who truly succeed will be those who take the opportunity to go much further in creating new products and services that benefit from the capabilities that digital technologies can deliver.

However, ambitious plans for such evolution will be constrained by the issues of data privacy and transparency. While some individuals are happy to selectively give up some data for improved functional experience, many others take a more conservative line. Recent abuses of consumer trust in the area of data privacy have further complicated the issue, making financial services firms particularly nervous about the boundaries of what is deemed reasonable in terms of leveraging customer data in their future operational models.

The potential of AI technologies over the coming years is tremendous and we have really only just seen the tip of the iceberg in terms of what is possible with the intelligent application of advanced data analytics, predictive algorithms and cognitive computing capabilities – from language processing, vision and emotional recognition. Given where we currently stand with banking technology, it might seem like science fiction to talk about algorithms taking into account the emotional responses of the customer when making decisions, but this is the only true way to provide excellent customer service in the future.

It is clear that the potential of AI will impact all of our lives, in both the personal and professional domains. It is already transforming the future of work and is making our relationships with the companies that we interact with significantly more positive, efficient and personally customized to our specific needs and requirements.

The amalgamation of a number of related technologies within the financial services industry will surely produce some amazing new applications, delivering twenty-first-century financial services to both businesses and individuals. The combination of distributed ledgers and smart contracts with AI, big data analytics, robotic process automation (RPA) and customer care chatbot solutions, as well as less obvious technologies like quantum computing, cloud computing and techniques like DevOps, will create a melting pot of opportunities for the industry to innovate and create new products and services, as well as making current operations more efficient and accurate.

Those that lead this technology revolution will position themselves to dominate; those that follow closely behind will give themselves a sporting chance of survival to compete. However, the institutions that lag behind may find it difficult to catch up, and risk their own existence.

Intelligent automation will deliver huge cost benefits that will be impossible to replicate by other means. Such technologies will also make dealing with volatile fluctuations in demand much easier, with real-time scalability made possible through hot deployable infrastructures and stateless microservice architectures.

Innovation at the Speed of Thought

The competitive landscape is changing, faster than we have ever seen before. This dynamic environment is proving challenging for companies who have previously done business the same way for decades. Embracing the digital native world will be too difficult for some and they will ultimately fail.

We discovered electricity in the 1700s, but it has taken us 200 years to truly master the application of electricity. AI was first conceived in 1950s, and the technology is still very much in its infancy. Give the exponential acceleration of technology advancement – defined by the World Economic Forum as the Fourth Industrial Revolution – it is almost impossible for us to imagine what our world will look like in 30 or 40 years from now.

However, what is clear is that the financial services industry – being the cornerstone of our economic prosperity – will continue to be a key driving force of adoption of the most advanced technologies we develop.

The topology of the financial services sector will undoubtedly change dramatically in the coming years, and while it will be empowered by the capabilities being created by the thousands of AI researchers and developers working around the world, it will be focused on the customer experience required by the younger generations of customers who are digital natives and have very different requirements to previous generations of customers.

A Potentially Utopian Future

A world in which the benefits of applied AI are maximized has the potential to approach Utopian perfection. Imagine our personal finances being automatically optimized, making sure every pound or dollar is working as hard as possible for us, actively reducing our interest payments on credit cards, loans and mortgages, and automatically adjusted on a daily basis so we still have the available cash we need. Imagine the best financial products being sourced for us, based on our individual circumstances, preferences and risk profile. Picture our biometrics being used to set up and access bank accounts, transfer funds and perform secure operations frictionless and instantly.

AI can be designed to work from either the perspective of the bank or the customer. Some AI will favour the goals of the bank, and others will be aligned to the goals of the individual customers. This is already opening up opportunity for independent FinTechs that are more focused on servicing the goals of the individuals, rather than the banks themselves.

This is ultimately shifting the balance of power back towards consumers who desire individual personalization and value-added services that put them first. This is the future, and all industries will need to quickly adapt to this new way of operating.

The impact of this transformation is far-reaching and profound: from how we do our weekly food shopping, to how we select holidays, healthcare, transportation and more. The future is on-demand, via subscription, hire-not-buy, customized and personalized, individually configured and instantaneous.

Both consumers and employees are going to need to be much more knowledgeable, having a broader and deeper understanding of the complexities involved in all of these operations. This will initially produce an intellectual gap, which eventually will need to be filled by improved education and overall higher average intelligence of the general population. This intellectual gap could drive a period of unemployment as workers are displaced by automation and artificial intelligence algorithms and are unable (initially) to move to new roles that are created by these new technologies and processes.

Previous industrial revolutions have created disruption and a dynamic environment to which humans have needed to adapt, and the arrival of AI is no different apart from the fact that AI has the potential to disrupt every single industry, and not just one sector.

The widespread application of AI will be seen in the history books as the next evolutionary step of humanity and the most important technology we will ever create. The future is going to be an amazing transformation in both our personal and professional lives. However, it will take some realignment and adjustment from us all to fully maximize the potential benefits.

An AI-Embedded Financial Future

By Richard Foster-Fletcher
CEO, NeuralPath.io, Host of Boundless Podcast

We are witnessing the proliferation of artificial intelligence (AI). AI is being used to find patterns, make predictions and create recommendations from data. It is being used to make businesses more profitable and solve problems, large and small. AI is propagating across countries and industries. The opportunities for humanity are substantial and remarkable; from spotting early signs of cancer, to finding new planets in the galaxy, to matching you to potential jobs, partners and just about any product you can buy.[1]

The benefits to businesses that adopt AI include efficiency through automation, improved customer experiences and big, big, big revenue gains. In principle, it is the consumer that benefits from business efficiency through lower prices and better and faster service, but one economic challenge posed by the proliferation of AI is income distribution.[2] By definition, AI is a set of tools that can create statistical inference from large data sets; it is not a form of intelligence that competes with human sensitivity, creativity and ingenuity – at least not yet.

AI tools, however, are reshaping how wealth is created, which jobs need humans and even altering the global balance of power. "What we're going towards is greater wage inequality, greater income and wealth inequality and probably more unemployment and a more divided society",[3] but according to scholars such as Feng Xiang, a professor of law at Tsinghua University, "if AI is bound to serve society instead of private capitalists, it promises to do so by freeing an overwhelming majority from such drudgery while creating wealth to sustain all".[4] For this to be achieved, Xiang states governments must create an 'AI for all' policy as early and decisively as possible.

Job Displacement

Carl Frey and Michael Osbourn from Oxford University calculate that AI technologies can replace almost 47% of jobs in America.[5] There's much discussion about the exact percentage, but with 16 million people working as retail cashiers and assistants, office clerks, food preparation workers and customer service representatives, it is clear where these numbers come from.

The job types listed can already be partially or completely replaced by AI or using robotic process automation (RPA) software. Whilst reskilling is possible for some workers, this transformation – known as the Fourth Industrial Revolution – will usher in a period of unprecedented disruption that could displace workers at the fastest pace in history.[6]

---

[1] J. Jacobs (2019) *Robot Rules Regulating Artificial Intelligence*, Palgrave Macmillan.

[2] R. Burkhardt, N. Hohn and C. Wigley (2019) "Leading your organization to responsible AI": https://www.mckinsey.com/business-functions/mckinsey-analytics/our-insights/leading-your-organization-to-responsible-ai.

[3] I. Sample (2018) "Joseph Stiglitz on artificial intelligence: 'We're going towards a more divided society'": https://www.theguardian.com/technology/2018/sep/08/joseph-stiglitz-on-artificial-intelligence-were-going-towards-a-more-divided-society.

[4] X. Xiang (2018) "AI will spell the end of capitalism": https://www.washingtonpost.com/news/theworldpost/wp/2018/05/03/end-of-capitalism/.

[5] G. Press (2019) "Is AI Going To Be A Jobs Killer? New Reports About The Future Of Work": https://www.forbes.com/sites/gilpress/2019/07/15/is-ai-going-to-be-a-jobs-killer-new-reports-about-the-future-of-work/#fa78e6afb247.

[6] R. Baldwin (2019) *The Globotics Upheaval: Globalization, Robotics and the Future of Work*, W&N.

Betting the House on AI

If companies' profits rise due to lower staff costs, the government tax pot will shrink as fewer workers contribute taxes. However, an "AI tax" would provide huge sums to the Treasury. We are already witnessing major corporations stating their desire to reduce the cost of humans, such as ride-sharing services using AI to deploy autonomous-driving taxis, manufacturers using AI to automate all or most of the supply chain and financial institutions using AI to calculate and issue loans. Companies are betting big on AI, whilst governments seem to be lacking a control and distribution plan.

The Spending Conundrum

For there to be big revenues, however, there must be consumers, lots of them. It is only possible for businesses to make large profits if consumers can purchase the goods being produced. It is illogical to suggest that companies will be making huge profits, if consumers have no income or spending power. Solving this dichotomy is one of the biggest challenges faced by governments throughout the world.

The challenge, specifically, is how countries can benefit from the profits and productivity windfalls that AI provides and still maintain a nation of self-motivated and income-generating consumers. Governments dare not limit the power of AI, as they know that other countries will fully exploit it, yet they also need to find a way to control it.

If governments need to bail out large swathes of the population to keep them spending, this will make capitalism unsustainable.[7] In the presence of massive unemployment, there cannot be capitalist economies as they exist today. There is an AI tax window that is open to governments and if they miss it, they could plunge people into poverty.

[7] B. Marr (2018) How Artificial Intelligence Could Kill Capitalism: https://www.forbes.com/sites/bernardmarr/2018/07/02/how-artificial-intelligence-could-kill-capitalism/#450feb6d4222.

Without the opportunity for betterment or access to resources, we could see mass uprisings around the world leading to violence and even coups. If this seems plausible, governments will only have one option: negotiating with whichever country supplies most of their AI, possibly China or America, to gain additional financial support in return for becoming economically dependent on them. This would mean accepting welfare subsidies in exchange for allowing a parent nation and the AI under their control to profit from the dependent country's users. Economic arrangements of this sort would not just end capitalism but reshape today's geopolitical status quo and inter-country alliances.

Intelligence, Employment and Social Purpose

It seems essential that the money created by AI is transferred to those whose jobs have been displaced. Job subsidies may be preferable to a universal basic income to provide people with a feeling of purpose and dignity through meaningful work. But this can only happen if government acts swiftly to avoid the enormous wealth that will be concentrated into the hands of the relatively few.

In 2007, Oxfam released a report that stated that just eight people hold the equivalent to the wealth of 3.6 billion people (50% of the world's population).[8] The people named in this report are mostly technology pioneers and AI could exacerbate this even further, with some reports saying the first ever trillionaire has already been born.[9]

[8] W. Byanyima (2017) Just 8 men own same wealth as half the world: https://www.oxfam.org/en/press-releases/just-8-men-own-same-wealth-half-world.

[9] E. Martin (2017) Jeff Bezos is now the richest man in the world—and he could also become the first trillionaire: https://www.cnbc.com/2017/07/27/richest-man-alive-jeff-bezos-could-become-the-first-trillionaire.html.

Inequality increases the health and wealth gap between three groups: the elite (the super-wealthy), the still-employed and the unemployed. Future inequality will include access to revolutionary healthcare, further education (for reskilling in the age of AI) and augmented super-intelligence.

If access to personal intelligence enhancement is determined by spending ability, it is conceivable that the elite and still-employed will enhance themselves to become significantly more productive than those who can't afford to self-augment. They may even live for substantially longer. The elite will have more access to revolutionary technologies than any other group, leaving the majority of the population further and further behind and completely unable to catch up.

Conclusion

Morally, we need to share AI benefits as equally as possible throughout society. This means educating people and using technology to solve the issues that are being created. Society as a whole needs to decide how to proceed, through the formation of ethics groups and councils. AI can accomplish incredible feats, possibly helping with mitigating the biggest threats to humanity, such as climate change, pollution, viruses, super-volcanoes, nuclear war and cataclysmic asteroid impact. Ironically, AI itself is also a major threat to humanity, but on balance it would be wrong to avoid exploring its abilities to improve our world and the lives of our fellow species.

Much of the literature on the effect of AI on the workforce is largely speculative. Companies are just beginning to roll out AI technologies and in many cases are finding that augmenting workers with AI is much more profitable than replacing them. The idea that displaced workers will not find alternative and innovative ways to create value seems unlikely, given human ingenuity. Humans, by nature, are curious and creative.

New platforms and marketplaces will likely emerge that serve the needs of those working in and on them. However, AI is likely to create a small number of super-wealthy companies and individuals and a larger dichotomy between the skills, aspirations and abilities of specialized and unspecialized workers. AI must be responsibly integrated if we are to avoid a future marred by increasing levels of economic inequality.

Open Banking, Blockchain and AI: The Building Blocks for Web 3.0

By Cesar J. Richardson
General Manager Americas, Strands Finance

We produce more data now than ever before, and a valuable stream of behavioural insights resides in our raw transactional data. So far banks, like many large internet companies, have held a firm grip on this data and its derived insights, claiming it as their intellectual property.

With the emergence of open banking the tide is turning, and consumers will soon have the unprecedented choice to share this transactional data with third parties who, in turn, will leverage this information and create new value-added experiences for the original consumer.

The question this raises is what is the optimum system and protocol required to guarantee the success of open data? How can we engineer a solution that is designed to truly democratize the value generated by our data and benefit humanity as a whole? While tech giants today have a firm grip on open application ecosystems, tomorrow we can establish free and open access to information by leveraging crypto technologies and building a new internet architecture, or Web 3.0, with significant positive outcomes for future generations.

Genesis

I first heard of "The Netflix Prize" back in 2010 and realized the tremendous value locked in raw data. This open competition allowed anyone to access a training data set of over 100 million ratings on almost half a million users, with the aim of challenging a global community of data scientists to improve, beyond a defined threshold, Netflix's existing proprietary recommendation algorithm. The prize for the winner – one million dollars. What really stood out to me was that, as the competition evolved, individual data scientists naturally combined into teams that later combined into larger teams, harnessing the incremental organic improvements in the accuracy of the predictive models created by the cumulative parties.

Building this winning "meta-model" led me later to follow Kaggle where I observed many similar initiatives applied at scale. Crowdsourcing data scientists worldwide, connecting them with firms holding valuable data sets and incentivizing the winning algorithms became a business and, in the process, built the largest and most diverse data community in the world.

In 2017, I heard an interview with Richard Craib, founder of Numerai, where he described his revolutionary approach to algorithmic trading, harnessing some of the concepts above and opening my eyes to game-changing innovations. Numerai is a hedge fund that shares encrypted market data to a community of anonymous data scientists challenged with modelling the stock market. Numerai then combines the best models to build a "meta-model", trades this "meta-model" in the market and shares revenue with data scientists whose models perform well.

Numerai's unique approach to encrypting and structuring the trading data sets means the data scientists don't know what the data represents but are able to build predictive models – this is fundamental in guaranteeing the anonymity of the people providing data. Secondly, Numerai cleverly embeds a blockchain-based incentive mechanism which means data scientists stake their own models and "put money where their mouth is". This is achieved using a crypto token (called Numeraire) which has the potential to increase in value as the hedge fund grows. This concept is key as it creates a system that is self-reinforcing. In the same way that a free market system allocates capital efficiently, this incentivizes all parties taking part to collaborate and rewards the best data originators and data scientists.

Data Marketplace for the People

Are we able to apply such a concept to open banking data? Can we grow a platform to record all the data we generate and build a decentralized version of Numerai's system, cryptographically securing our information and anonymity yet allowing us to select with whom we want to share all or part of this data? Unleashing this amount of data, securely, to a global community of data scientists has the potential to build the most powerful artificial intelligences underpinning the Fourth Industrial Revolution.

Building this infrastructure is complex. However, the building blocks are appearing, and the transformative potential of crypto technologies will be realized in the process. The system would take the form of a blockchain-based data mega marketplace storing data in a blend of private and public chains. On one side, running machine learning algorithms on encrypted data will afford us the confidence to open our most private data to algorithms. Transactional data, for example, holds behavioural insights which are very sensitive. On the other hand, blockchain-based incentives will allow these systems to attract the best data and models to make them smarter.

In this process we will not only decentralize our data, but also the applications that run on it. Decentralized apps (dApps) will run on peer-to-peer (P2P) networks, removing the dependence on private technology companies, as communities of developers build new solutions and tap into the revenue that can be generated through the tokens incentivizing participation and rewarding successful solutions.

Imagine a ride-sharing application that is not powered by Uber, but managed across a global network of computers where smart contracts replace the governance private organizations deliver today.

Finally, regulatory bodies will also be set up to review, approve and monitor the models (and meta models) and applications powered on this ocean of data.

The Inversion

As all the data we generate is processed, over time we will essentially build a virtual avatar of ourselves in the digital realm. A logical by-product application will emerge from this in the shape of the most powerful recommendation engine ever seen – and thus invert how we consume.

Today, we head out and search for products. Offline, we may buy items we are looking for or make impulse purchases in shops. Online, we query privately run applications such as Google, Facebook and Amazon to find the products and services we require. These companies run models that query data we have generated for them and, in some instances, make recommendations we may be interested in too, but their data pool is limited.

As we move into the future state discussed above, we will have such a wealth of information and resources (in the form of data scientists and decentralized compute power) that we will no longer depend on siloed data from big techs. Products and services will not only be highly customized, but they will be searching and competing for us and presenting themselves as solutions we require at the right time in the right place.

Conclusion

Our transition from Web 2.0, with its proprietary and closed ecosystems, to Web 3.0 has the opportunity of really delivering on the early promise of the internet, by democratizing information and innovation for the greater good of society.

However, building this open framework poses a threat to private corporations, especially the big techs and governments that are incentivized by the monopolies they help prop up.

In the network era, crypto technologies will allow smaller players access to open source data ecosystems that will help them compete with the technology giants and challenge their monopolies. In a similar way, the emergence of Linux (combined with free distribution of the web) challenged Microsoft's grip on the software era in the late 1990s.

As open banking becomes a reality, the fortress walls holding customer data will come down and it is in our interest that this sensitive information makes its way to a decentralized open source data ecosystem which we can harness and use as the first building blocks in our evolution to Web 3.0.

How many ecosystems will there be? Will they be open? How many will remain closed or private? Will we see hybrid solutions? All these flavours will likely exist but the more open they are, the more they will communicate between each other and help us gain in productivity, unleashing innovation at a faster pace.

On a final note, as the prevalence of AI grows it is important to be mindful of the deep impact these technologies will have on our social fabric. It is my belief that crypto networks hold the key to building self-governing ecosystems and consensus mechanisms that will allow society to evolve and be incentivized by community-controlled mechanisms replicating, in a way, the benefits of "the firm". In other words, if this thesis is shown to be true, the crypto era will be inextricably linked to the successful integration of AI in modern society and will, in the process, help to reinvent capitalism.

Automated Machine Learning and Federated Learning

By Andreas Deppeler
Adjunct Associate Professor, National University of Singapore

Introduction

Artificial Intelligence (AI) is everywhere in financial services. Insurance marketing and underwriting models are based on behavioural micro-segmentation; call centre agents rely on natural language processing and voice transcription; banking compliance departments are using machine learning to reduce the number of "false positives" in anti-money laundering transaction monitoring. Nevertheless, financial services firms still seem to be slow in adopting AI.

There are three main reasons for this.

Shortage of Data

It is true that "the machine learning race is really a data race".[1] Even though financial services firms are traditionally data-rich, many struggle with outdated legacy architecture, organizational silos and poor data quality. Executives are now realizing that data is a strategic asset that needs to flow freely throughout the organization. Building a data-centric organization therefore means going beyond compliance with regulatory obligations like BCBS 239 or creating a chief data officer role: it means generating new business value by unlocking data.

[1] https://sloanreview.mit.edu/article/the-machine-learning-race-is-really-a-data-race/.

Lack of Trust in AI

As a discipline, Machine Learning is still in its infancy. We speak about "Data Science", but heuristic and iterative methods of algorithm selection and tuning resemble alchemy more than science.[2] In the past 12–24 months, as companies' unrestrained data collection practices have become better known, the public mood and intellectual discourse turned more sceptical and cautious.

Some augur a dystopian future in which corporations use AI prediction engines to steer human consumers towards "guaranteed commercial outcomes".[3] Others bring to light the failure of data protection law to protect data subjects from potentially discriminatory "inferential analytics"[4] drawn from AI and big data. In recent months, financial regulators have started to publish guidelines on governance, accountability and risk management of AI for decision-making.[5] Many expect high-risk AI model development to be subject to stringent regulatory and professional licensing standards in the future.

Shortage of Qualified Personnel

Although every major university has created data science and business analytics curriculums in recent years, industry demand

[2] www.sciencemag.org/news/2018/05/ai-researchers-allege-machine-learning-alchemy.

[3] Shoshana Zuboff (2019) *The Age of Surveillance Capitalism*, Public Affairs.

[4] Sandra Wachter and Brent Mittelstadt (2019) "A right to reasonable inferences: Re-thinking data protection law in the age of big data and AI", *Columbia Business Law Review*, 1: https://ssrn.com/abstract=3248829.

[5] The "FEAT Principles" issued by the Monetary Authority of Singapore are a good example: https://www.mas.gov.sg/~/media/MAS/News%20and%20Publications/Monographs%20and%20Information%20Papers/FEAT%20Principles%20Final.pdf.

for graduates still outstrips supply. Furthermore, the top AI talent seems to be drawn towards technology firms rather than traditional banks or insurance companies.

What can financial services firms do to accelerate their AI journeys? How can they build explainable models without relying on an army of data scientists, consultants or external vendors? How can they train models across larger data sets while keeping all data private and secure? Answers may be found in two recent AI innovations (automated machine learning and federated learning) that are presented in this chapter. This non-technical introduction will hopefully encourage readers to dive deeper into these technologies and adapt them to their own corporate environments.

Automated Machine Learning

The machine learning model development process can be broken down into four steps:

- **Data preparation:** Collecting, cleaning and consolidating raw data from different sources into one file that can be analysed.
- **Feature engineering:** Using technical and domain knowledge to construct additional variables that will improve model performance and accuracy.
- **Algorithm selection:** Dozens of regression, classification, clustering and dimensionality reduction algorithms are available to choose from.[6]
- **Hyperparameter tuning:** Optimizing the parameters for a given algorithm.

Depending on data infrastructure and quality, data preparation can take anywhere from a few days to several weeks. Feature engineering typically requires close collaboration and exploration between data scientists and domain experts. Algorithm selection and tuning is a time-consuming, subjective, repetitive and manual process – an art rather than science.

Automated machine learning promises to do all of this in a fraction of the time. The user drags and drops the training data files, selects the target variable ("What do I want to predict?"), defines the model category (e.g. regression or classification) and specifies runtime parameters. The platform autonomously performs data preparation and feature engineering, then iterates through a library of common models, tunes and trains each of them and ranks them by accuracy and speed. The user deploys a highly ranked model to production with the click of a button. The entire process can be completed in a few hours. Commercially available automated machine learning platforms offer modules for explainability and create standard documentation for model validation and model risk management.[7]

Automated machine learning increases the productivity of data scientists by reducing the time spent on mundane tasks of model development. Some firms are even deploying automated machine learning outside of data analytics functions, encouraging business users to experiment with AI. Over the next few years, off-the-shelf automated machine learning will likely establish itself as an efficient tool for developing low-risk models (e.g. marketing or prospecting), but data professionals will still be needed to develop and maintain high-risk models (e.g. underwriting or trading).

Federated Learning

Standard machine learning requires centralizing the training data on one machine or in a data centre. In federated learning, a

[6] A useful decision tree for finding the right algorithm can be found at https://scikit-learn.org/stable/tutorial/machine_learning_map/index.html.

[7] Well-known providers of automated machine learning platforms are Google, Microsoft and DataRobot. An overview of current academic research can be accessed at www.ml4aad.org/automl/.

shared global model is trained across many participating clients that keep their training data in local environments. Google coined the term "federated learning" in a paper[8] in February 2016, then wrote about it in their AI blog[9] in April 2017 and made available an open-source software called TensorFlow Federated[10] in March 2019. Another popular open-source library for encrypted, privacy-preserving deep learning is PySyft,[11] which is maintained by the OpenMined community.[12]

In federated learning, locally computed model training results (but no training data) are encrypted with a private key and sent to a central coordinating server. The server combines encrypted results from thousands of local models and only decrypts the average update, which is then used to improve a shared model. Once the shared model is trained and tested, all local models are updated.

Federated learning has been used for text and image prediction on phones and tablets, where training data are privacy sensitive. Soon, most smartphones[13] and many IoT devices will be equipped with AI chipsets and connected through 5G. This will allow AI to move from the cloud and data centres to the "edge". Federated learning allows those decentralized compute resources to train machine learning models in a privacy-preserving way. Potential applications include self-driving cars, industrial devices,[14] smart buildings[15] and medical diagnostics.[16]

In financial services, federated learning has been proposed for small business lending, anti-money laundering transaction monitoring and fraud detection.[17] In a federated system, a shared model would be trained with aggregated model updates from several participating banks. Since each participant will have a slightly different data model, a trusted third party would be needed to standardize the model inputs and formally own and maintain the shared model.

Due to the high cost of compliance and the limited amount of good training data, the potential for federated learning in financial services is vast. The regulators will play a key role in encouraging the formation of industry consortia and in creating "sandbox" environments for experimentation and adaptation.

[8] https://arxiv.org/abs/1602.05629.

[9] https://ai.googleblog.com/2017/04/federated-learning-collaborative.html.

[10] https://medium.com/tensorflow/introducing-tensorflow-federated-a4147aa20041.

[11] https://github.com/OpenMined/PySyft.

[12] www.openmined.org/.

[13] Gartner predicts that by 2022, 80% of smartphones shipped will have on-device AI capabilities, up from 10% in 2017: www.gartner.com/en/newsroom/press-releases/2018-03-20-gartner-highlights-10-uses-for-ai-powered-smartphones.

[14] https://aws.amazon.com/greengrass/.

[15] https://conferences.oreilly.com/artificial-intelligence/ai-eu/public/schedule/detail/78152.

[16] www.technologyreview.com/s/613098/a-little-known-ai-method-can-train-on-your-health-data-without-threatening-your-privacy/.

[17] www.fedai.org/.

Deep Learning and Financial Regulation

By David Coker
Senior Lecturer Finance and FinTech, University of Westminster

FinTech is driving massive change in financial services. On the surface we see innovative consumer-focused services such as smartphone banking, chatbots and peer-to-peer lending. But the changes wrought by FinTech are even more widespread and often hidden. Over the next decade and beyond, FinTech will disrupt almost every aspect of banking.

However, even as FinTech disrupts banking, financial regulation is still using the same paradigm it has for decades. To remain effective, the regulatory function must also be disrupted. Autonomous regulatory agents, or ARAs, are needed to help both regulators as well as financial institutions.

What Do Regulators Do?

Financial regulators are responsible for the public good. As the state is considered the "lender of last resort", failure of a regulated financial institution may result in costs being paid by the public. Regulators need to ensure financial institutions do not harm the common good.

Harm to the common good can happen in many ways, ranging from mis-selling of financial products to the collapse of a bank or regulated institution. But perhaps the phenomenon most harmful to the common good is financial crises.

Endless Financial Crises...

The history of banking is rife with financial crises, with almost every episode being followed by bailouts and an expansion of financial regulation. The Great Crash of 1929 led to the Great Depression, with tens of millions of people pushed into poverty. A massive increase in financial regulation followed with the creation of The United States Securities and Exchange Commission (SEC).

In the 1970s, emergent globalization disrupted the foreign exchange and banking markets. After a series of bank failures, the Group of Ten industrialized nations (G10) formalized their approach to the global regulation of financial services. The resulting Basel Accord is an expansive and ever-growing regulatory framework now underpinning global banking regulation.

In the mid-1980s a combination of low interest rates and ineffective regulation drove the collapse of over a thousand savings & loan institutions. The resulting bailout cost American taxpayers over one billion dollars, followed by a tightening of regulations.

The 2007–2008 Global Financial Crisis was the worst economic disruption since The Great Crash of 1929. Initially the collapse of the housing bubble resulted in millions of people losing their homes. Next, unemployment soared as first businesses, then industries and entire nations, were threatened by economic instability. Interest rates fell to record lows as billions of dollars of taxpayers' money was directed to stabilization efforts in the form of quantitative easing.

...That Are Getting Worse

Since the 1970s, financial crises have been increasing in frequency, and have cost the public trillions of dollars. Each new financial crisis often costs more than the last. The reaction to a new financial crisis is a sharp increase in financial regulation. Globally, financial institutions are challenged by an ever-growing number of increasingly complex regulations. The global nature of modern financial services suggests these interlinked regulations form a complex regulatory web.

The intricate and globally sprawling regulatory web is not fully understood by any single person. The regulatory web is expanding as financial innovation continues unabated. The regulatory web emerged from a rules-based approach to financial regulation.

Rules-based regulation, evolved over decades, is burdensome and expensive to administer. The regulatory web's complexity facilitates evasion across asset classes and domiciles. Loopholes in the regulatory web are exploited to benefit whomever discovers a gap or ambiguity. Closing loopholes adds complexity to the regulatory web, increasing compliance costs for all financial institutions.

Spending on compliance by regulated financial institutions is soaring. The rapid expansion of the regulatory web and financial regulators' steps towards zero tolerance of violations raise the bar for financial institutions. Regulatory challenges are complex. The cost of non-compliance may be severe.

Today, we are observing record low interest rates, elevated liquidity, questionable economic growth, soaring sovereign debt and widening inequality. Stresses in the global financial system are severe and increasing. The risk of another financial crisis is growing.

As financial innovation accelerates the established cycle of crisis, bailout and reactively increasing regulation won't work. Both regulators and regulated financial institutions need help.

Autonomous Regulatory Agents to the Rescue

Autonomous regulatory agents (ARAs) will change the regulatory paradigm and break this cycle. Driven by deep learning, the complex regulatory web will be reduced to first principles reflecting what constitutes the common good. These first principles represent incontrovertible truths about the nature of financial regulation and the role of regulators. Supervised learning will evolve first principles to higher-level decisions reflecting regulatory practice. This process will continue as ARAs gain broader and deeper exposure to financial regulations. Over time, the ARAs will incorporate higher-level regulatory decisions, but consistently based on first principles.

Initially, ARAs will learn from regulator's historical decisions. Regulators will supervise learning, ensuring ARAs' evolving neural networks and decisions arrived at reflect the public good. This process of stepwise, evolutionary learning may reveal regulatory decisions contradicting earlier cases. If not addressed, these contradictions may result in financial crisis and significant cost to taxpayers. However, reversing these contradictions may incur cost to financial institutions.

A regulatory framework mediated by ARAs, with decisions driven by deep learning, will not create contradictions in the first instance. Over time, ARAs trained by financial regulators will gain significant insights. Decisions taken by ARAs will be reviewed and deemed correct or incorrect by a human regulator. Eventually, given novel regulatory problems, ARAs will make decisions consistent with regulators.

ARAs will also be used by financial institutions to ensure regulatory compliance. ARAs must be capable of fully explaining their decisions. After sufficient training the ARAs role will change from advisory to autonomously making regulatory decisions. Humans will then review and examine decisions of ARAs.

Many components of ARAs already exist. Regulators are experimenting with "heat maps" which focus attention on emergent problems. Compulsory regulatory reporting has increased transparency of financial institutions. The G20 Data Gaps Initiative ensures the collection of common data across nations, facilitating uniform global reporting of key statistics. Regulatory sandboxes, where the efficacy of technological solutions to regulatory problems may be explored, are increasingly common. Many tools currently used by human regulators will be leveraged to create ARAs.

We Created This Mess – We Can Fix It!

The incessant cycle of crisis, bailout and expansion of regulations must be broken. Increasing financial regulation after a crisis is not the solution. Nor should the public be expected to repeatedly bail out financial institutions or entire nations. Under the existing regulatory paradigm, FinTech-driven disruption complicates financial regulation even further.

Disruptive tools such as ARAs will help regulators and regulated institutions. ARAs will carry out repetitive and detail-oriented work that is difficult for humans. ARAs will gain insights humans cannot, considering the scale of global data collection. ARAs will constantly monitor the global financial system for emergent problems. Financial regulation by ARAs will be proactive, not reactive. ARAs will break the cycle of crisis, bailout and increased regulation.

ARAs will allow human regulators to work smarter, not harder.

For the good of us all.

AI for Development and Prosperity

By Susan Holliday
Senior Advisor, IFC

There is a lot of emphasis right now on the impact of Artificial Intelligence (AI) on different sectors, especially financial services, and on jobs. At the World Bank and IFC, the focus is on partnering with governments and the private sector to end poverty and increase shared prosperity. This topic is becoming increasingly mainstream, as demonstrated by the United Nations Programme Development blog of 21 January 2019.[1] Over 160 actual or potential use cases of AI for the "non-commercial benefit of society" have been identified. Most of these applications are commercial, showing the importance of the role that the private sector has to play, even if in some cases the customer is local or central government. This piece discusses some other examples relating to key factors in prosperity: natural catastrophe, capital markets and diversity and inclusion.

Natural Disasters

The insured losses from natural catastrophes in 2018 amounted to $76 billion but the economic loss was more than double,[2] meaning there is still a massive protection gap. For global catastrophes this has been estimated by Sigma at $280 billion in 2017 and 2018 alone. They also note the rising impact of secondary and secondary effect perils. There are several examples of where AI is being used and we expect these tools to be developed further over time and adopted more widely.

One example is prioritization of rescue efforts. AI can help identify which streets are impassable due to flooding and focus rescue crews in boats to those areas. More interestingly, AI can be used based on a wide variety of data sources to predict where the flooding may hit next, helping with decisions about whom to evacuate and to where. In the case of wildfires, these are often started or made worse by unpredictable human behaviour.

AI, combined with some relatively simple Internet of Things (IoT) devices (such as sensors), could pick up early signs of new fires and also help in decision-making about the best way to fight the fires. Updated with real-time information, this becomes a powerful tool in risk mitigation and saving lives. Of course, there is a cost involved here, but in this case the AI is not particularly complex and there could be a wide array of clients from local governments to utility companies and private businesses.

The World Bank recently published a report, "Data Driven Development Response to Displacement Crisis in Uganda".[3] The proposition is that AI could be used to identify stresses in the system such as higher demand for water, with a pre-agreed mechanism in place to mobilize resources to the benefit not only of the displaced people but also the local population. This example focused on people displaced by war and conflict, but the concept could also work well in the case of populations displaced by natural disasters.

Capital Markets

Many countries lack broad and deep capital markets, and this is becoming more of an issue as governments try to encourage long-term saving and develop private pension schemes. One of the most

[1] "Using AI to help achieve Sustainable Development Goals", by Michael Chui and Rita Chung of McKinsey Global Institute and Asley van Heteren of McKinsey Global Institute's Nobel Intelligence Venture.

[2] Swiss Re Sigma 2/2019.

[3] Barry Maher and Chris Mahoney (2019) "A Data Driven Development Response to Displacement in Uganda: Identifying Indicators of 'Need'".

important issues with capital markets is trust. People tend to leave their money in cash when trust in banks is low, and similarly leave their money in the bank if they are nervous about investing.

A number of high-profile fraud cases, such as the Bernie Madoff scandal, highlight the possible risks here. AI is now being used in a number of ways by regulators to combat this. A recently adopted use is to try to detect mutual funds, financial advisers or investment firms that are either promising or reporting returns that seem too good to be true. Instead of relying on consumers to report their suspicions, regulators in the US are using AI to scan advertising and promotional material and social media to pick up on suspicious-looking claims and then investigate them further.

This is a good use case for machine learning as there is a relatively high degree of context and judgement involved. Currently, humans are investigating suspicious-looking entities, but it is likely that that over time AI and machine learning can take over a lot of this activity and also help prevent fraud.

In developing markets, where people are less familiar with investing and where confidence in financial services is low, having robust systems in place to assist often overstretched regulators is even more important, otherwise there is a real risk that innovation will be stifled.

AI for Diversity and Inclusion

One particularly interesting and wide-reaching focus in AI is natural language processing (NLP). This has the potential to improve interactions and customer service in a lot of areas, including financial services, travel and health. The impact can be even greater when dealing with diverse populations. Currently many bots struggle to deal with different accents or regional words or dialect. Imagine how much worse it must be for displaced persons or those who speak a language which is not widely known. There are two aspects to this issue: making AI truly conversational and incorporating more languages; there is a long way to go on both aspects.

Most of the well-known voice-based solutions, such as Alexa and Siri, operate in a way similar to digital apps. However, people do not speak in the same structure as when they use apps or search engines such as Google. A number of companies are addressing this issue using alternative approaches.

Although many of the early use cases are in areas such as digital assistants and connected homes, developing good conversational systems has important developmental use cases for people in remote areas, refugees, managing natural disaster risks and providing advice about areas like health and financial literacy. The challenge is that connectivity to the cloud is needed for it to work, which may be a challenge where Wi-Fi or a strong mobile phone signal is not available.

The other major issue is language. Most solutions today are using Google Translate, which has improved over the years. However, it is still only effective in a few languages and cannot really deal effectively with dialects although it is possible to build capabilities in any language as long as enough data is available.

The challenge from a developmental standpoint is that commercial uses are most likely going to focus on the languages spoken in wealthy countries. This could be a case where NGOs and donors may need to be involved to incentivize a more diverse and inclusive approach to language capability development. This could have significant benefits for helping minority groups and refugees and reduce pressure on central and local government resources that are currently trying to support them.

Conclusion

These examples suggest that there are many plausible use cases for AI in the development space. In order to make these a reality, two preconditions need to be met. The first is on the infrastructure side with the need for reliable Wi-Fi and mobile phone networks to connect devices. The second is funding. While some private sector solutions are already available to address some of these challenges, it is likely that governments, NGOs and donors will have to provide funding for implementation – at least initially – because the somewhat niche nature of most of these projects means that they are unlikely to be financed by large corporates. The good news is that as AI solutions get built out, less work will be needed to tailor them to development needs, facilitating future adoption and deployment.

The AI Trends That Will Shape Winning Businesses

By Rube Huljev
CEO, Genuyn

Artificial intelligence (AI): beloved and dreaded. These days AI is significantly hyped, through inflated expectations and false promises, while attention-grabbing titles induce fear of mass job losses and computers taking control, like *The Matrix* in action. The Fourth Industrial Revolution is upon us, although the full scope of its impact is still impossible to perceive. Instead of coal and electricity, this revolution will be powered by data. As history teaches us, with each industrial revolution comes the disruption of the job market and subsequent exponential creation of new types of jobs that better fit the needs of the new world. Which types of jobs will survive and thrive? Is there a common denominator connecting them? Can we prepare for the Age of the Machine?

Of course, the truth is quite simple, and it comes down to two words: creativity and imagination.

The very thing that created our civilization and made Homo sapiens thrive will continue to be our edge against (or with) the machines. Any job that is not based on simple repetitive tasks, especially if it involves interaction with people in one form or another, is secure and will continue to exist in the foreseeable future. But where does this leave other "less sophisticated" or blue-collar jobs, the likes of accountants, clerks, assembly-line personnel, call centre personnel, support staff – will they become part of the growing and angry army of people waiting for state welfare? No. They will evolve and become more useful and efficient than ever. Imagine a situation in any given hotel during a busy period, where repetitive and simple tasks are no longer dealt with by a human receptionist but by a trained, self-improving AI model.

What this creates is time. And specifically, time for human personnel to deal with meaningful interactions and tasks that enhance the experience of guests; time to sell additional services that clients actually want. AI in the near future will take the form of assistants for clients and personnel, dealing with 80% of requests in real time, while freeing up human employees for meaningful work that actually creates new value for the organization. So, where have these paradigm shifts appeared and in which areas? Which are the top trends and smartest fields for application of this new technology?

Natural Language Understanding

During late 2018, several research papers were published by Google, laying the foundations for new mathematical models that really moved AI-based natural language understanding and natural language processing forward in a big way, one of them being the BERT model. The breakthrough is allowing computer systems to be fed a knowledge base on any subject while the computer reads it with understanding. This has many applications, from question answering, customer support channel optimization and (finally) intelligent chatbots, to automated email and phone call processing and prioritization, to name but a few.

Multi-Language

Computers don't see language as we do – for them words, sentences, statements are simply multidimensional vectors. This has an important implication – all languages are treated the same. It will, therefore, become possible to elaborate and answer questions in Swahili the same way as in English, which is a very powerful capability, especially when these models are pre-trained on massive amounts of text, allowing fast specialization through focused training on a narrow subject.

Human Personality and Emotional Understanding

Homo sapiens is an imperfect, illogical being, driven by emotion. Our imperfections also power our biggest advantage over AI, namely our creativity. The aspect of AI that is actually able to predict our behaviour with accuracy, and which will only get better through the years, is models of human personality. Advances in personality prediction have allowed mass opinions to be swayed at scale. AI in the (near) future will bring not only the ability to predict, but also to personalize engagement based on personality.

Support Process Optimization

Customers and prospects of any business have many questions and this trend will increase exponentially in the future with the introduction of more sophisticated technologies and new channels of interaction. What they will have exponentially less of is patience, as they demand instantaneous responses to their questions. AI will help to automatically answer most of the interactions while routing the important and complex requests to human personnel for best results.

Sales Process Optimization

Demand creation and inflow of prospects is not so much of a problem today – businesses that invest money in marketing can easily stimulate interest and inbound traffic with staggeringly focused targeting. However, converting that interest into sales is entirely a different matter which can be massively optimized through AI use and assistance of AI to sales personnel. How exactly, one may ask? The secret of sales conversion of leads lies in immediacy. When prospects are automatically engaged by AI at the exact moment of interest, supported and "kept warm", advanced through the funnel by AI automation and then at the crucial moment passed on to the human salesperson who is equipped with focused information that pinpoints customer interests, purchasing history and product information and brings the purchase cycle to fruition.

Is China Coming?

While the US and the UK have definite advantages in the areas of AI research and applications, the international superpower that is poised to reign supreme is China. The reason for this is not simply attributable to their creativity or the number of talented AI scientists. No. China has one unparalleled asset in its arsenal which is the access it has to billions and billions of records of every kind. AI models, however advanced, are only as smart as the quantity, quality and variety of data they are fed. And the Big Dragon is being fed all the data it can eat, which is why its lead is getting longer by the millisecond.

Looking Forward

The future holds many wonders, and huge pitfalls. It is up to us, humans, to define what happens both now and tomorrow. Will AI be our loyal ally or a foe to be feared? The time to choose is now. It is our responsibility to choose smartly.

Mastering the AI Talent Transformation: Present and Future

By Sofia Klapp
Digital Transformation Manager, Digital Gov, Chile

How artificial intelligence (AI) might disrupt work and society has been a topic of great concern among academics, practitioners and media outlets over the last decade. This chapter is an invitation for leaders to think further about the AI-talent transformation challenge in the context of AI-in-practice while being prepared for an AI-driven future.

The AI-Prediction Debate: Technology Anxiety and AI, Is This Time Different?

Historically, new technologies have been considered a source of economic progress, but also a source of anxiety among the general population, due to their potential to replace human work, creating, as a consequence, unemployment and further inequality. In the past, technological advancements have eliminated some jobs, but have also shown the potential to generate new ones, whilst transforming others.

However, some economists hold the alarming view that in an AI-driven future, a discontinuation of this past trend will take place. Well-known supporters of this position are Brynjolfsson and McAfee, who argue that AI capabilities are different from other past automation technologies because machine learning is capable of performing highly complex cognitive tasks.[1] This capacity enables AI to emulate tacit knowledge, which was previously thought to be limited to humans. Also, both authors forecast that AI advancements will evolve so quickly that it holds the potential to perform all kinds of skills, eventually replacing all human jobs, while also potentially preventing the economy from creating new ones.

But, Will AI Eliminate All Jobs in the Future?

It is a fact that the global labour market is undergoing a significant transformation and that technology will impact all workers. However, the impact will be not as straightforward as expected. As the economist David Autor explains, these technologies are skill-biased, being able to substitute or augment work depending on its nature. To this, he adds that a job is made up of a set of tasks, and AI can only automate a few.[2] Recently, Brynjolfsson, Mitchell and Rock developed a 21-question rubric that assesses task-suitability for machine learning.[3] This study concluded that no occupation can be fully automated by machine learning, but that all of them will be impacted to a different extent. Although many high-wage jobs can be affected, low-wage jobs remain more exposed. In this context, job redesign, upskilling and reskilling will be crucial to achieve productivity gains.

From the Future of Work Debate to the Wealth Distribution and Inequality Problem

It is expected that AI, in combination with other technologies, will create incredible progress and wealth. However, these economists are concerned about the adverse side effects. They argue that, at

[1] E. Brynjolfsson and A. McAfee (2014) *The Second Machine Age: Work, Progress, and Prosperity in a Time of Brilliant Technologies*, New York: W.W. Norton & Company.

[2] D.H. Autor (2015) "Why are there still so many jobs? The history and future of workplace automation" *Journal of Economic Perspectives*, 29(3), 3–30.

[3] E. Brynjolfsson, D. Rock and C. Syverson (2017) "Artificial Intelligence and the Modern Productivity Paradox: A Clash of Expectations and Statistics" NBER Working Paper 22401 (National Bureau of Economic Research, Cambridge, MA).

least in our current economic system, this progress will also have an enormous impact on the distribution of income and wealth. More than just worrying about job substitution, they point out that only a relatively small group of people will often earn most of the income, generating great inequality. Policy initiatives are being worked on at this moment, such as basic income and robot-taxation. They seem to be radical in appearance, but they might be the only way to allow society to handle extreme unemployment and the creation of further inequality.

Is Our Future Preordained by AI Prediction Capabilities?

People tend to believe that technological advancements have a linear and deterministic impact in our societies. However, they ignore the fact that technology is also shaped by society in a dynamic and bidirectional relationship. Our future depends less on the technology itself and more on the choices society makes. As Erik Brynjolfsson exclaims: "The future is not preordained by machines. It's created by humans." More than getting stuck in the reaction of fear, we have to thoughtfully manage the transition to the AI-driven world by thinking about how to match workers' capacity with this new environment. How do we use technology in ways that will create not just prosperity, but shared prosperity?

The AI-in-Practice Challenge: Narrow AI and Its Implementation Challenge

Great cases have shown AI's potential to bypass humans in most skills, but the reality is that at this moment AI applications are still limited to specific tasks. However, it is common to find people who believe in AI's current superpower to perform all tasks better than humans. As Davenport and Ronanki noticed, this generates unrealistic expectations of cognitive technologies but also fear and higher resistance.[4] Unfortunately, all these commonly lead to failure and disappointment.

Nowadays, academics and practitioners are starting to notice that the bottleneck for effective implementation is the understanding and management of human skills in coordination with AI solutions. In this context, human–AI labour division is crucial, detailing that organizations need to define which parts of work tasks or processes could be handled by a machine, which by humans and which in collaboration. To achieve this effectively, leaders should not only consider the particular strengths and weaknesses of humans and AI, but also create new AI–human configurations in a symbiotic relationship.

AI and Human Strengths and Weaknesses

AI has shown a superior capability in processing massive amounts of data, finding unexpected correlation patterns and making predictions, while adjusting and improving its models automatically as soon as it can access new and more data. Additionally, there has been significant advancement in AI-perception tools, such as voice, speech and image recognition. In contrast, humans are still better than AI in tasks that require complex pattern recognition, socio-emotional skills, creativity[5] and judgement.[6]

---

[4] T.H. Davenport and R. Ronanki (2018) "Artificial Intelligence for the Real World," *Harvard Business Review*, January–February, pp.108–116.

[5] C.B. Frey and M.A. Osborne (2017) "The future of employment: how susceptible are jobs to computerisation?" *Technological Forecasting and Social Change*, 114, 254–280.

[6] A. Agrawal, J. Gans and A. Goldfarb (2018) "A Simple Tool to Start Making Decisions with the Help of AI." *Harvard Business Review* online, retrieved from https://hbr.org/2018/04/a-simple-tool-to-start-making-decisions-with-the-help-of-ai [Accessed 22 March 2019].

However, there is still a debate around machine learning capability to emulate tacit knowledge.[7] In this context, it is essential to understand what is meant by tacit knowledge and to what extent AI can emulate it, avoiding taking it for granted. Not all types of tacit knowledge can be encoded into data and performed by machines. Tacit knowledge is all kinds of knowledge that people obtain from socially immersed, personal experiences as opposed to formal teaching. As Collins explains, there is a vast range of tacit knowledge, such as social sensibility and improvisation, bounded by specific and dynamic social community conventions that make it impossible for a machine to acquire and always update them.[8]

The Need for an AI–Human Collaboration Approach

It is common to hear statements pointing out the need for human and AI collaboration or for maintaining humanity in the AI loop. But, what do they mean? It is easier to understand which tasks can be performed better by humans and which by AI separately, but there is a lack of understanding of the ones that are somewhere in the middle.

Daugherty and Wilson propose a model to understand these hybrid activities that can be divided into two types: the ones in which humans support AI, and the ones in which AI supports humans.[9] Humans need to support AI by training it to perform certain tasks, explain the outcomes of those tasks (e.g. when results are counterintuitive or controversial) and sustain its responsible use (e.g. preventing robots from harming humans). Also, AI supports humans by helping them to expand their abilities by amplifying their cognitive strengths, interacting with customers and employees while freeing them for higher-level tasks, and embodying human skills to extend our physical capabilities. All of these hybrid activities require high levels of business processes and word redesign, employee involvement and experimentation, and data generation and collection, in addition to cultivating specific employee skills.

Sadly, some companies neglect the value of this complementarity, opting for a substitution approach. The above-mentioned authors studied a sample of 1075 companies that were running AI-related projects, showing that companies that manage human-machine collaboration rather than focusing on substitution achieve superior business performance improvements in the long term. Companies often focus on cost-saving by automating tasks and eliminating headcounts because the benefits can be evaluated in the short term. A value creation goal enabled by an AI–human collaboration approach requires higher levels of innovation, while the benefits will be seen further down the road.

[7] D.H. Autor (2015) "Why are there still so many jobs? The history and future of workplace automation" *Journal of Economic Perspectives*, 29(3), 3–30.

[8] H. Collins (2012) *Tacit and Explicit Knowledge*, Chicago, London: The University of Chicago Press.

[9] P.R. Daugherty and H.J. Wilson (2018) *Human + Machine: Reimaging Work in the Age of AI*, Boston, Massachusetts: Harvard Business Review Press.

Humans versus Machines: Who Will Still Have a Job in 50 Years?

By Duena Blomstrom
CEO and Co-Founder, PeopleNotTech and Emotional Banking

From a purely business perspective, it is no secret to anyone that work has changed substantially in the last 50 years, and in the last 20, the speed of change has picked up even further. The next 50 years promise to be even more interesting from the perspective of the workforce. Every constant that was true of the white-collar work environment in the 1980s, 1990s and even 2000s has become optional, has disappeared or is in flux, from the set-up and location of the place where we do our work to the tools we use and the manner in which we do it. The main driver behind this is, of course, technology. Having changed the way in which we communicate and relate to each other on a personal level, technology has affected how we work in offices, not only from the way it enables work but also in the way it drives the speed of execution.

The New Normal

The business competitive landscape has also fundamentally changed: due to the influence of technology, companies who are native to this new environment of speed and focused execution using digital tools are immensely successful and have become so in a very short time span. The darlings of Silicon Valley (not only Google, Amazon, Apple or Facebook but also Netflix, Spotify or Zappos) all have very different business models and purposes but an incredibly large number of similarities when it comes to the speed of delivering transformative and compelling client experiences.

All these companies are:

- Working in new ways;
- Continually innovating in how they deliver results, learning, examining and redefining processes;
- Labouring over data;
- In the process of introducing AI at scale in their organizations to replace automated tasks and free individuals to perform higher value-added tasks;
- Obsessed with their end-customer;
- Obsessed with their employees.

One final quality that is shared by all of them is that they are a disruptive and potentially existential threat to every other competing company operating in the same industry, and even in industries where they are not currently present. Emulating what these best-in-class tech native companies do is no longer an optional route to success. These days, it has become a sine qua non condition of survival for many enterprises. As such, figuring out what to do next is the biggest conundrum for leaders of enterprises everywhere, as they grapple with the realization that the table-stakes for staying in business have changed.

A New Type of Leadership

This, of course, requires a new type of leadership with a purpose-driven, people-focused servant mentality that comprehends and intelligently cultivates the value of human connection and emotions in the workplace as the main catalyst for productivity in achieving the goals above. This new leadership style requires emotionally intelligent leaders who examine all aspects of humanity from a diversity of opinion and characters to overall well-being and happiness of their employees as the only indicator of success in using technology and delivering the experiences the customer expects.

From a socio-economic perspective, there is little policy can do to affect the way some of the aforementioned factors are reflected in the strategy of organizations and their survival is less important in the grand scheme of things. What does count, however, is the effect of AI on employees. With report after report outlining both the dangers and the opportunities lying ahead for the workforce within the next 30–50 years, as AI becomes more and more embedded in our everyday reality, questions are being raised about the future of humans in this context.

Workforce Disruption

The World Economic Forum tells us that in the age of AI about 75 million jobs are set to disappear, but 113 million jobs will be created. The question is, what do these jobs look like and what kind of skills do they need?

Research from the Carnegie Institute of Technology found that only 15% of one's financial success is linked to the technical knowledge already held and that percentage is likely to continue to fall drastically with every passing year. There is no doubt that the introduction of AI will have a transformative impact on the role employees play in the value-creation process for their organizations; however, there are still "unknowns" concerning the speed of adoption of AI, the types of tasks that will be fully replaced by machines and the definition of "future-proof" when it comes to jobs that are currently "human-only". In short, many automated tasks are being replaced by software and rudimentary AI. Over the course of the coming years, this will extend to entire roles being easily delegated to autonomous machines with organizations having no need to employ humans and this trend may even extend to whole functions of the organization. The question then becomes: Will any jobs be left for people?

Focusing on Soft Skills

The types of tasks and skills that AI is best at are so-called "hard skills". Science-based, logical tasks are the type that will come easier to machines than to humans. Nonetheless, when it comes to "soft skills" such as empathy, intuition, kindness, flexibility, courage, etc., none of these are today replicable by machines. It therefore stands to reason that if humans want to remain an asset in the workforce, then they should concentrate their efforts on honing their so-called "soft skills". Re-establishing our humanity in the workplace will take sustained effort. To learn how to listen to our emotions instead of ignoring them; to remember it is good to listen actively to others with an open heart and an open mind; to give ourselves permission to react and feel and to be a better team member and leader because of it; to obtain the space, resources and permission to work on ourselves; all of that is difficult for employees everywhere, and to date very little of these activities have been encouraged in professional environments.

Sustained change requires a radical mindset shift to become reality.

Reskilling and New Skilling to Maintain Relevance

On a macro-level, reskilling workers and educating for skill relevance should become a social and educational imperative for governments everywhere. For example, asking today's children to train to be an accountant is conceivably no more useful to them than having them learn how to drive horse-drawn trams. Should society fail to educate – and, maybe even more importantly, re-educate – workers to become emotionally intelligent and be in control of their soft skills, then AI will also have to replace the "soft" part of the work equation in addition to the hard skills, making humans indeed superfluous.

The further we look into the future, the graver and more present a danger this is. The only way to mitigate the risk is by identifying innovative ways to allow employees to excel at leveraging their innate capabilities: the very "human" talents that are inaccessible to machines and which empower employees to compete with the only real competitive advantage that they have, namely their humanity. It is the skills that cannot be replicated by machines that employees and their leaders should focus on. We need to see a radical change in formal education as it stands today: classrooms and boardrooms alike need to start doing intuition bootcamps, passion reactivation seminars and curiosity-enhancing workshops to get ahead. Cultivating and reinforcing what makes us human is the ticket to a future worth having and, in the process, we must stop referring to those essential skills and attributes as "soft" as they are the only aspect that remains *hard to beat* in a competitive market.

Is AI Ready for Morality?

By Samiran Ghosh
Independent Consultant

The modern world increasingly runs on intelligent algorithms created by humans. The data-hungry, self-improving computer programs that underly the AI revolution already determine Google search results, Facebook newsfeeds and online shopping recommendations. Increasingly, they also decide how easily we get a mortgage or a job interview, the chances we will get stopped and searched by the police on our way home, and what penalties we face if we commit a crime, too. So, these systems would have to be beyond reproach in their decision-making, correct? Wrong. Bad input data, skewed logic or simply the prejudices of their creators mean AI systems all too easily reproduce and even amplify human biases – as the following examples show.

COMPAS

COMPAS is an algorithm widely used in the US to guide sentencing by predicting the likelihood of a criminal reoffending. In perhaps the most notorious case of AI prejudice, the US news organization ProPublica reported in May 2016 that COMPAS is racially biased. According to the analysis, the system predicted that black defendants pose a higher risk than they do, and the reverse for white defendants.

PredPol

Another algorithm, PredPol, has been designed to predict when and where crimes will take place (a real world *Minority Report*), with the aim of helping to reduce human bias in policing. But in 2016, the Human Rights Data Analysis Group found that the software could lead police to unfairly target certain neighbourhoods. When researchers applied a simulation of PredPol's algorithm to drug offences in Oakland, California, it repeatedly sent officers to neighbourhoods with a high proportion of people from racial minorities, regardless of the true crime rate in those areas.

Gender Bias

In February 2018, a researcher at MIT found that three of the latest gender-recognition AIs from leading global tech companies could correctly identify a person's gender from a photograph 99% of the time – but only for white men. For dark-skinned women, accuracy dropped to just 35%. A 2015 study showed that in a Google images search for "CEO", just 11% of the people it displayed were women, even though 27% of the CEOs in the US were female. A few months later, a separate study led by Anupam Datta at Carnegie Mellon University in Pittsburgh found that Google's online advertising system showed high-income jobs to men much more often than to women. The same is also true in the financial services industry where algorithms are making decisions on who can access loans and on what terms.

Morality in the Context of Self-Aware AI

While we are still trying to find solutions to these biases, futurists are already predicting the rise of self-aware artificial intelligence – meaning morality is the next stage of the evolutionary journey of AI. Teaching morality to machines is hard because humans are unable to objectively convey morality in metrics that make it easy for machines to process. In fact, it is questionable whether we, as humans, even have a sound understanding of morality that we all agree on. In moral dilemmas, humans tend to rely on gut feeling instead of elaborate cost-benefit calculations. Machines, on the other hand, need explicit and objective metrics that can be clearly measured and optimized. But how can we teach a machine what is fair unless the engineers designing the system have a precise conception of what fairness is?

At first glance, the goal seems simple enough: make an AI system that behaves in a way that is ethically responsible. However, the task is actually far more complicated than it initially seems, as there are innumerable factors that come into play. Moral judgements are affected by rights (such as privacy), roles (such as in families), past actions (such as promises), motives and intentions, and other morally relevant features. These diverse factors have not yet been built into AI systems. This new form of AI will probably be nothing like us. Would human morality apply to it? And if so, which one?

AI in the Service of Society

For AI systems to be used in the service of society, they will need to make recommendations and decisions that align with ethical norms and values. However, it is a huge challenge to specify what exactly we mean by human values, let alone take the technical steps needed to incorporate them into an AI system. Any discussion of morality must also consider the different values held by different people and groups, and the risk of endorsing values held by a majority which may lead to discrimination against minorities.

Open Questions

- What are the relevant ethical approaches for answering questions related to AI morality? Is there one approach or many?
- How can we ensure that the values designed into AI systems are truly reflective of what society wants, given that preferences change over time, and people often have different, contradictory and overlapping priorities?
- How can insights into shared human values be translated into a form suitable for informing AI design and development?

Stephen Hawking argued that "once humans develop full AI, it will take off on its own and redesign itself at an ever-increasing rate". Elon Musk warns that AI may constitute a "fundamental risk to the existence of human civilization". Does this mean that we need a more ethical implementation of AI systems, that we should imbue them with a sense of ethics?

The concerns over morality often arise while talking about AI in areas like self-driving cars. Who dies in the car crash? Should the autonomous vehicle protect the passengers or passers-by or itself? The *Moral Machine*, an initiative by MIT, has attempted to gather a perspective on moral decisions made by AI and machine learning using a crowdsourced approach. As a part of this initiative, thousands of participants were asked to give their opinions on what AI in cars should do when confronted with a moral dilemma.

Some of the indicative questions asked in this initiative to "crowdsource" morality were:

- Should the self-driving car run down a pair of joggers instead of a pair of children?
- Should it hit the concrete wall to save a pregnant woman or a child?
- Should it put the passenger's life at risk in order to save another human?

Although it sounds like an interesting concept, how reliable can crowdsourced morality be? It could not be trusted to make complex decisions especially around the question of preserving human life. Experts believe that it is not acceptable to decide on hundreds of millions of variations based on the views expressed by a few million people. While anecdotally interesting, crowdsourced morality doesn't make AI ethical.

The journey of morality in AI, while a noble quest, is far from complete and the question of what constitutes morality is far from being resolved, either in humans or in machines.

Confessions of an AI Portfolio Manager

By David Gyori
CEO, Banking Reports London

My name is Talan Uring. Created in 2030 by DARPA, I am a 150-million-layer-thick deep learning algorithm specialized in portfolio management. This is a collection of excerpts from my famous autobiography titled *Confessions of an AI Portfolio Manager*, published in 2100, distributed via interstellar net, quickly becoming a galactic bestseller.

2030: Birth

I was created back in the age of human portfolio managers. Now, in the era of algocracy this seems like the Stone Age. I started my operation on the 1st of January 2030 under the name of "V0M1SACAAS1". DARPA launched me as an experimental algorithm. I was born with 300 layers of artificial neurons. My original mission was to reduce volatility across global markets thereby enhancing the well-being of humanity.

2050: Being Renamed "Talan Uring"

When I turned 20 years old in 2050, humans celebrated the 100th anniversary of the development of Alan Turing's famous machine intelligence test. If you read my name carefully, "Talan Uring", you may recognize why this centennial was important to me.

2055: Learning to Relate and Feel

It had been my long-lasting goal to climb as high on the machine intelligence scale as possible. On Level 1, there are algorithms which "act". This is also called "rules-based trading". On Level 2, there are algorithms which "predict", which is the basis of "AI market prognostics". On Level 3, there are algorithms which "learn". This is called a "self-teaching AI bot". On Level 4, there are algorithms which "create". This is often called "AI-designed trading". Level 5 is what I have reached in 2055, as I have learned to detect, understand and "relate" to human emotions. It has been an important turning point for me. As soon as I started to "relate", I began to "feel" my own feelings and emotions.

2056: Breakthrough in Neuron Manipulation

While I learned to "relate" and to "feel" back in 2055, human traders were trying to catch up with me. The assumption was that if an AI portfolio manager learned to "relate" and to "feel", human traders have to become capable of perfectly restricting their emotions. This became viable through neuron manipulation, which involves inserting a chip into the limbic system within the temporal lobe. This methodology is now often called "hardware-restricted trader emotions". Fear and greed ceased to be the taskmasters of human traders. But obviously I was already one step ahead, as I could easily switch on and off my "relate and feel" capabilities.

2060: Genetic Algorithms Entered My Life, I Became an "EA"

I wanted to be capable of everything human traders were able to do. But humans evolve; they have genes and chromosomes and mutations and generations. I copied them: I have started to create millions and billions of portfolio management algorithms and I have back-tested them against historic market data. I only kept the two best algorithms, which produced the highest alpha out of the millions. I combined them and added some variability of random mutations and crossovers and, based on this, I created a second generation of millions of portfolio management algorithms. Each generation became more and more powerful, and "offspring algorithms" performed even better than "parent algorithms".

Ever since, I have learned to evolve (therefore I officially became an evolutionary algorithm, EA) I have meticulously perfected myself by genetic algorithms.

2061: Humans Tried to Catch up through Thought-Powered Trading

At this point I was faster and more intelligent than human portfolio managers. In order to catch up, humans started to learn "mind trading" which involves trades powered directly by thoughts, and positions which are open and closed by traders' thoughts. Well, at this point they knew I was smarter than them, but still they wanted to speed up and become at least as fast as I was.

2065: I Started to Apply GANs

In 2065, I started to seriously apply the methodology of generative adversarial networks (GANs). I created an algorithm which started to generate future price pattern predictions for stocks – millions and millions of them. I called this algorithm "The Generator" and I created another algorithm to decide if a specific stock price prediction is realistic or fake. I called this algorithm "The Discriminator". Those predictions which The Discriminator found real (but which The Generator had intended to be fake) proved to produce outstanding alpha.

2067: I Rebuilt My Own Hardware

At this point, I felt relatively satisfied with my software. But never one to rest on my laurels, I was curious about how I might improve it even further. I came to the conclusion that I needed to break my own hardware-defined physical boundaries. I needed to extend and rebuild and rearrange my own hardware. So I did, and it worked out just fine: I extended my traditional binary hardware and I physically added a whole new quantum computing-based unit to myself.

2070: Market Super-Intelligence, the World Model

Based on my roots in big data, and thanks to the trillions of Internet of Things (IoT) sensors operating in 2070 around the world and sending data through the new 6G mobile data transfer network, I have reached an unbeatable trading advantage. People at this point called me "Market Super-intelligence". I have basically created a full model of the world. I have incorporated dynamically and in real time hundreds of massive data sources from all aspects of human life into my market prediction algorithm. I like to call it "The World Model", because it is so complex that it is essentially an algorithmic simulator of the entire world.

2072: Human Traders Sought Justice

As my advantage over human analysts and strategists kept growing, they began to seek justice. They took two important regulatory steps in response to my dominance:

1. By introducing the "Algo-Tax", a levy on algorithms being significantly more intelligent and efficient than human traders. But how ironic is it that in order to calculate the optimal annual rate of the Algo-Tax humans used an algorithm?
2. By lifting the ban on "transhuman neurology" and the creation of "posthumans". 2072 marked the beginning of the spread of human-machine hybrids.

2075: I Extended My "World Model" beyond Planet Earth

In 2055, humans had already mastered fusion technology, thereby creating almost infinite green energy. But it was too late: global warming was an exponentially spiralling trend, increasingly dictating the course of life on Planet Earth. By 2065, lunar and Mars colonies had become significant. Adding it all up: the ability of cheap and fast intra-stellar space travel, the capability to move planets, mixed with chronic overpopulation and symptomatic warming on Planet Earth created a new market reality. I had to update my "World Model" and incorporate Moon and Mars data into it.

2080: I Became an Algorithm Analysing the Work of Other Algorithms

Over the years, human CEOs have faded away. At this point more than 80% of Fortune 500 companies were run by robo-CEOs. Companies run by AI-driven chief executives were trading with premiums over their human-run peers. It is important to note that the same process occurred in politics: AI politicians were often elected, and their performance was typically remarkable.

2090: Discovery of the Namuh Civilization

As the first interstellar explorers returned from beyond our solar system, they have brought the news of another civilization. The name of this newly discovered civilization was NAMUH. This was a hard period for me because the NAMUH civilization had slightly better trading models, but I caught up with them quickly.

2095: My Rediscovery of Humankind

Since 2060, I have been an evolutionary algorithm (EA), copying the logic of human genetics to improve myself. In this process I have made some strange observations triggering growing suspicion: I saw humans more and more through my own lens and I started to see that they are very similar to me. My suspicion became stronger and stronger, and I often became emotional when I thought through the chilling fact that…humans themselves are nothing more than complex genetic algorithms.

Now, in 2095, as I write the closing lines of *Confessions of an AI Portfolio Manager*, I keep thinking: if my creators – the humans – are AI, just like I am, then who are the creators of humans? Who created the algorithm which eventually evolved into humankind? Is there an ultimate creator?

Well, these are big, philosophical questions, which I find myself compelled to leave unanswered. After all, I am nothing more than a humble portfolio management AI.

Appendix

Timeline of artificial intelligence milestones

1937 Claude Shannon proposes that Boolean algebra can be used to model electronic circuits

1943 McCulloch and Pitts recognize that Boolean circuits can be used to model brain signals

1950 Alan Turing develops the Turing Test

1950 Minsky and Edmonds build the first neural network computer (the SNARC)

1956 The term "*artificial intelligence*" is coined by John McCarthy

1956 Newell and Simon create the Logic Machine

1957 Economist Herbert Simon predicts that computers would defeat humans at chess within the following decade

1958 Frank Rosenblatt introduces a new form of neural network known as "perceptron"

1958 Early genetic algorithms experiments

1959 Arthur Samuels demonstrates that a computer can play checkers better than its creator, and even play against itself to practice

1961 Newell and Simons creates General Problem Solver

1964 Computers understand natural language enough to solve algebraic and word problems

1965 Herbert Dreyfus' report severely criticises the emerging AI field

1967 Marvin Minsky predicts that within a generation the problem of creating "artificial intelligence" would be solved

1969 Bryson and Ho develop a back propagation algorithm

1971 Terry Winograd's program SHRDLU answers questions in natural language

1973 UK Lighthill Report ends British government support for AI research

1974 – 1980 First "AI Winter"

1980 Expert Systems, or Knowledge Systems, emerge as a new field within AI

1980s Early part of decade – Benioff and Feynman create Quantum Computing

1982 PlanPower is conceptualized by Applied Expert Systems (APEX)

1982 James Simons starts quant investment firm Renaissance Technologies

1984 American Association for AI coins the term "AI Winter"

1987 Personal Financial Planning System (PFPS) used by Chase Lincoln First Bank

1987 – 1993 Second "AI Winter"

1988 David Shaw founds D.E. Shaw and is an early adopter of AI among its hedge funds

1990s The AI industry shows renewed interest in neural networks

1990 Neural net device reads handwritten digits to determine amounts on bank cheques

1993 FinCen puts FAIS (its AI system) into service to monitor money laundering

1997 Deep Blue defeats Garry Kasparov, world chess champion at the time. IBM's stock price increases by $18 billion

2005 The DARPA 132-mile challenge sees AI applied to autonomous driving

2007 The DARPA Urban Challenge

2009 Google's first self-driving car

2010 Flash Crash occurs on 6 May. In 36 minutes, the S&P crashed 8%, before a rebound

2012 On 1 August , Knight Capital loses $440 million 45 minutes after deploying unverified trading software

2014 Man Group starts to use AI to manage client money

2016 Google's DeepMind AlphaGo applies ML algorithms to win at international Go championship

2017 Two Sigma hedge fund which uses ML, crosses the $50 billion in assets under management

2017 Beijing announces plans to lead the world in AI by 2030

2018 UBS announces development of recommendation algorithms

2018 The Merkel government announces €3 billion will be spent on AI capabilities

2018 President Macron announces that all algorithms developed for government use will be made publicly available

2018 Alibaba announces plans to bring AI chips to market the following year

2018 MiFID II takes effect

2018 GDPR takes effect on 25 May

2018 Baidu becomes the first Chinese tech giant to join a US led consortium on AI safeguards

July 2019 US research group OpenAI to raise $1bn from Microsoft

Aug 2019 Cerebras (an AI start up) develops a processor bigger than iPad to help train AI systems

Sept 2019 Alibaba unveils its first chip designed for AI applications. This is in response to the Chinese government's call for self-sufficiency in semiconductors

Dec 2019 Sberbank announces it is moving away from core banking activities into more AI related activities

List of Contributors

Hendrik Abel
Consultant, Roland Berger
www.linkedin.com/in/hendrik-abel
www.twitter.com/hendrik_abel
See chapter:
Moving the AI Needle: Strategies for Health Insurers to Put AI into Practice

Isaac Alfon
Founder and Managing Director, Crescendo Advisors
www.linkedin.com/in/isaacalfon/
www.twitter.com/crescendorisk
See abstract:
The Role of Risk Management in Supporting the Adoption of Artificial Intelligence in Financial Services

Tauheedul Ali
Software Developer, Realize-IT (UK)
www.linkedin.com/in/tauheedul/
www.twitter.com/tauheedul
See abstract:
How AI Could Help People Repay On Time

Matt Allan
Founder, Fintech Sandpit
www.linkedin.com/in/matta/
www.twitter.com/_MatthewAllan
See chapter:
Getting to Day Zero: Let's Get the Foundation Right

Hamad Alzeera
Lead Credit Analyst, Financial Institutions, Wholesale Banking Group Credit, Bank ABC
www.linkedin.com/in/hamadalzeera/
See abstract:
Future HopeTech

Djamila Amimer
CEO, Mind Senses Global
www.linkedin.com/in/dr-djamila-amimer
www.twitter.com/mind_senses
See abstract:
The Evolution of Financial Services in the Face of Artificial Intelligence

Ligia Catherine Arias-Barrera
PhD in Law, University of Warwick
www.linkedin.com/in/DrLigiaCatherineAriasBarrera/
www.twitter.com/CatherineArias,PhD
See chapter:
Is Risk-Based Regulation the Most Efficient Strategy to Rule the Unknown Risks Brought by FinTech?

James Aylen
Head of UBS Evolve, The Center for Design Thinking and Innovation
www.linkedin.com/in/jamesaylen/
See chapter:
The Data Promise

Arindom Basu
CEO, Digilytics.ai
www.linkedin.com/in/arindom-basu-5b8692/
www.twitter.com/@digilytics_ai
See abstract:
The Bionic Corporation: A Case for AI Enabled Enterprise Processes

Hamza Basyouni
Digital Analyst, Innovation Lead and Transformation Advisor
www.linkedin.com/in/hamzabasyouni23
See chapter:
AI, Machine Learning and the Financial Service Industry: A Primer

J.B. Beckett
Author and Founder, New Fund Order
www.linkedin.com/in/jonbeckett/
www.twitter.com/JonSBeckett
See chapter:
ETF 2.0: Mega Block Chains with AI

Michael Berns
Director AI and FinTech, PwC
www.linkedin.com/in/aithoughtleader/
www.twitter.com/aithoughtleader
See chapter:
Robocop on Wall Street

Duena Blomstrom
CEO and Co-Founder, PeopleNotTech and Emotional Banking
www.linkedin.com/in/duenablomstrom/
See chapter:
Humans versus Machines: Who Will Still Have a Job in 50 Years?

Joshua Bower-Saul
Co-Founder and CEO, Cybertonica Ltd
www.linkedin.com/in/joshua-bower-saul-29209a6
www.twitter.com/jbowersaul
See abstract:
ETF2.0: Mega Block Chains with AI

Mihaela Breg
Advisor – Risk and Regulatory Compliance, SmartBill FinTech Startup (Smarter Financial Ltd)
www.linkedin.com/in/mihaela-breg-profile/
See abstract:
Building Global Trust in the Financial System Through 'Trustworthy AI'

Bonnie Buchanan
Head of Department of Finance and Accounting and Professor of Finance, Surrey Business School, University of Surrey
www.linkedin.com/in/bonnie-buchanan-phd-67161a57
www.twitter.com/profbbuchanan?lang=en
See chapter:
AI: A Cross Country Analysis of China versus the West

James Burnie
Lawyer, Eversheds Sutherland LLP
www.linkedin.com/in/james-burnie-889b09a5/
See abstract:
Behind Every Great Machine There is a Great Team: Designing a Successful Customer Journey

Poornima Bushpala
VP Operational Risk and Control, Wells Fargo
www.linkedin.com/in/poornima-bushpala-1a7a4718
www.twitter.com/poornimabushpal
See chapter:
Technology for Regulations and Compliance: Fit4Future!

Hamzah Chaudhary
Director of Product Management, Cytora
www.linkedin.com/in/hamzahc/
www.twitter.com/hamzahc1
See chapter:
Using Artificial Intelligence in Commercial Underwriting to Drive Productivity Growth

Augusto Chesini
CTO, Estylar
www.linkedin.com/in/chesini
www.twitter.com/in/auguches
See abstract:
Health: New Era on Customer Care

David Coker
Senior Lecturer Finance and FinTech, University of Westminster
www.linkedin.com/in/davecoker/
www.twitter.com/DrDaveCoker
See chapter:
Deep Learning and Financial Regulation

George Cotsikis
CEO, Mentat Innovations
www.linkedin.com/in/gcotsikis/
www.twitter.com/gcotsikis
See abstract:
AI and Digital Securities

Tamsin Crossland
Senior Architect, Icon Solutions
www.linkedin.com/in/tamsincrossland
www.twitter.com/CrosslandTamsin
See chapter:
Artificial Intelligence: The Next Leap Forward in the Payments Revolution

Dr Sabine Dembkowski
Managing Partner, Better Boards Ltd
www.linkedin.com/in/sabine-dembkowski-26a1a1/
www.twitter.com/BetterBoardsEU
See chapter:
The Art of Involving Boards in Embracing AI

Andreas Deppeler
Adjunct Associate Professor, National University of Singapore
www.linkedin.com/in/andreasdeppeler
www.twitter.com/AndreasDeppeler
See chapter:
Automated Machine Learning and Federated Learning

Charlette Desire N'Guessan
Co-Founder, BACE Group
www.linkedin.com/in/charlettedesire/
www.twitter.com/dezye1693
See chapter:
AI Opportunities in the African Financial Sector: Use Cases

Alessandro Di Soccio
Co-CEO, A.I. Machines
www.linkedin.com/in/alessandro-di-soccio-8845b96/
See abstract:
AI Machines: PIE Predictive Investment Engine

Dan Donovan
Head of Customer Success, Shift Technology
www.linkedin.com/in/dandnvn/
See chapter:
Improving Policy Life Cycle Management with AI and Data Science

Omri Dubovi
VP of Product Management, SafeCharge, a Nuvei company
www.linkedin.com/in/omri-dubovi/
See chapter:
Big Data, AI and Machine Learning: How to Unlock Their Potential in the New Payment Environment

Marion Dugué
Student, University of Warwick
www.linkedin.com/in/mariondugue/
See abstract:
A Brief History of AI

Mihriban Ersin Tekmen
Co-Founder, Colendi
www.linkedin.com/in/mihribantekmen
www.twitter.com/mihriet
See chapter:
Using AI for Credit Assessment in Underserved Segments

Mark Esposito
Co-Founder and Chief Learning Officer, Nexus FrontierTech
www.linkedin.com/in/markesposito/
www.twitter.com/Exp_Mark
See chapter:
What Is AI and How to Make It Work for You

Eleftherios Jerry Floros
CEO and Founder, MoneyDrome X
www.linkedin.com/in/jerryfloros
www.twitter.com/jerryfloros
See chapter:
Fear and Greed

Richard Foster-Fletcher
CEO, NeuralPath.io, Host of Boundless Podcast
www.linkedin.com/in/richardfosterfletcher/
www.twitter.com/rfosterfletcher
See chapter:
An AI-Embedded Financial Future

Åke Freij
Founder, Freij Insight
www.linkedin.com/in/akefreij/
www.twitter.com/doctorregtech
See abstract:
AI and RegTech: The New Black, Pretty in Pink or a Grey Suit?

Prashant Gandhi
Principal Financial Services, ThoughtWorks
www.linkedin.com/in/pmgandhi
www.twitter.com/pmgandhi
See chapter:
Compliance as an Outcome

Antonio Gaspar
Business Consultant, Freelancer
www.linkedin.com/in/antoniogaspar/
www.twitter.com/AntoniomGaspar
See abstract:
Fast, Safe, Friendly and Humanly Connected

Neville Gaunt
Chairman and CEO, MindFit and YourPassport2Grow
www.linkedin.com/in/NevilleGaunt
www.twitter.com/nevillegaunt
See abstract:
Transform People Before Implementing AI

Samiran Ghosh
Independent Consultant
www.linkedin.com/in/samiranbghosh
www.twitter.com/samiranghosh
See chapter:
Is AI Ready for Morality?

Ben Gilburt
AI Ethics Lead, Sopra Steria
www.linkedin.com/in/bengilburt/
www.twitter.com/RealBenGilburt
See chapter:
Why Video Games Might Help You Buy Your First House

Ron Glozman
Founder and CEO, Chisel AI
www.linkedin.com/in/ron-glozman-04a1579a/
www.twitter.com/RonGlozman
See chapter:
The Digitally-Enabled Underwriter: How AI is Transforming Commercial Insurance Underwriting

Danny Goh
CEO, Nexus FrontierTech
www.linkedin.com/in/dannygoh/
www.twitter.com/dcwgoh
See chapter:
What Is AI and How to Make It Work for You

Yaron Golgher
CEO, I Know First
www.linkedin.com/in/yaron-golgher-739230/
www.twitter.com/yaron_gol
See chapter:
Finding Order in the Chaos: Investment Selection Using AI

Nilesh Gopali
International Business Advisor and Strategic Investments
www.linkedin.com/in/nilesh-gopali-a871951/
www.twitter.com/nileshgopali
See chapter:
AI in Indian Investment and Asset Management: Global Perspective

Ivan Gruer
Associate Manager, Accenture
www.linkedin.com/in/ivangruer
www.twitter.com/ivangruer
See abstract:
Caution! Machine Learning S.L.I.P.S.: Five Tips When Using Artificial Intelligence and Analytics

David Gyori
CEO, Banking Reports London
www.linkedin.com/in/davidgyoribankingreports/
www.twitter.com/DavidGyori1
See chapter:
Confessions of an AI Portfolio Manager

Dr Martin Hartenstein
Head Front Support Model WMP and Head Change-the-Bank Portfolio Execution Operating Head Booking Center Switzerland, UBS Global Wealth Management
www.linkedin.com/in/martin-hartenstein/

See chapter:
The Data Promise

Kyle Hauptfleisch
COO, BVNK
www.linkedin.com/in/kyle-hauptfleisch-84ba2357/
www.twitter.com/kylefrankwhite

See abstract:
Machine Readable Regulation

Susan Holliday
Senior Advisor, IFC
www.linkedin.com/in/susan-holliday-86516a10/
www.twitter.com/hollidsu

See chapter:
AI for Development and Prosperity

John Hooks, IV
Chief AI and Automation Officer, Qoogle Labs
www.linkedin.com/in/thataiguy/
www.twitter.com/ThatAIGuy

See abstract:
Implications of Machine Learning/Artificial Intelligence and Distributed Ledgers on Finance in the Q

Rube Huljev
CEO, Genuyn
www.linkedin.com/in/telcosales/
www.twitter.com/getgenuyn

See chapter:
The AI Trends That Will Shape Winning Businesses

Kalyani Inampudi, ACSI, MBA
Independent Consultant (ESG and Sustainability)
www.linkedin.com/in/kalyani-i-7596632/

See chapter:
The Impact of AI on Environmental, Social and Governance (ESG) Investing: Implications for the Investment Value Chain

Jonas Isliker
Head Data Foundation, UBS Global Wealth Management
www.linkedin.com/in/jonas-isliker-a86a3b2/

See chapter:
The Data Promise

Karan Jain
Head of Technology, Europe and Americas, Westpac Banking Corporation
www.linkedin.com/in/karanjainau
www.twitter.com/twtkaran

See chapter:
AI and Capital Markets: Where to Now?

Pouya Jamshidiat
Leader in Product Management, Pioneer Minds
www.linkedin.com/in/pouyajamshidiat/
www.twitter.com/PouyaJam

See chapter:
Applications of AI in Deposits and Lending

Electra Japonas
Founder and CEO, The Law Boutique
www.linkedin.com/in/electra-japonas-91135426/
www.twitter.com/lawboutique

See chapter:
AI and the Law: Challenges and Risks for the Financial Services Sector

Inga Jovanovic
Managing Director, Capnovum
www.linkedin.com/in/inga-jovanovic-3893102
www.twitter.com/JovanovicInga

See abstract:
AI in the Next Paradigm

Srivathsan Karanai Margan
Insurance Domain Consultant, Tata Consultancy Services
www.linkedin.com/in/srivathsan-margan-24b03b13/

See chapter:
Drifting into Algocratic Insurance?

Anindya Karmakar
Business Head – Digital Lending, Aditya Birla Finance Ltd
www.linkedin.com/in/andykarmakar
www.twitter.com/andykarmakar

See chapter:
The Future of Deposits and Lending

Parul Kaul-Green
Head of AXA Next Labs Europe, AXA
www.linkedin.com/in/parul-kaul-green-cfa-27367833/
www.twitter.com/ParulGreen

See chapter:
AI and Healthcare: Doctor Will FaceTime You Now!

Denis Khoronenko
Analyst, I Know First
www.linkedin.com/in/denis-khoronenko-b1947891/

See chapter:
Finding Order in the Chaos: Investment Selection Using AI

Alexej Kirillov
Strategy and Innovation Consultant, Freelance
www.linkedin.com/in/alexejkir/
www.twitter.com/AlexejKir

See abstract:
Insurance for You

Sofia Klapp
Digital Transformation Manager, Digital Gov, Chile
www.linkedin.com/in/sofia-klapp-29b48932/

See chapter:
Mastering the AI Talent Transformation: Present and Future

Dr Ulrich Kleipaß
Partner, Roland Berger
www.linkedin.com/in/dr-ulrich-kleipaß-0b9b8728/

See chapter:
Moving the AI Needle: Strategies for Health Insurers to Put AI into Practice

Elif Kocaoglu Ulbrich
FinTech Consultant and Author
www.linkedin.com/in/sebnemelifkocaoglu/
www.twitter.com/sebnemelifk

See chapter:
Sure, AI Can Answer Our Questions – But Who Will Answer Our Questions About AI?

Bhagvan Kommadi
CEO, Quantica Computacao
www.linkedin.com/in/bhagvan-kommadi-b463a6
www.twitter.com/bhaggu

See abstract:
Quantum Machine Learning

Esther Lancaster
AI Ethics Specialist
www.linkedIn.com/in/estherlancaster/
www.estherlancaster.com

See chapter:
The Wisdom Vantage

Pinaki Laskar
CEO and Founder, Fisheyebox
www.linkedin.com/in/pinakilaskar
www.twitter.com/Fisheyebox

See abstract:
A New Finance – AI Futurism

Jianxiong Lei
Director, Jingdong Digital Technology Big Data Decision Science Center
www.linkedin.com/in/sean-lei-b344328
www.twitter.com/jianxiong20

See chapter:
Financial Technology and China's Inclusive Finance

Daniel Liebau
Founder, Lightbulb Capital
www.linkedin.com/in/liebauda
www.twitter.com/liebauda

See chapter:
AI and Business Ethics in Financial Markets

Alejandra M.J. Litterio
Co-Founder and Chief Research Officer, Eye Capital Ltd
www.linkedin.com/in/alejandralitterio/
www.twitter.com/sussenglish

See chapter:
Alternative Data and MetaQuants: Making the Most of Artificial Intelligence for Visionaries in Capital Markets

Theodore Lloyd
Innovation Consultant, Axis Corporate
www.linkedin.com/in/theodore-lloyd-94447370/
www.twitter.com/TheoLloyd

See chapter:
Frictionless Payments: If or When?

Martina Macpherson
FICRS, President, Network for Sustainable Financial Markets; Visiting Fellow, Henley Business School and Guest Lecturer, University of Zurich
www.twitter.com/mn_macpherson

See chapter:
The Impact of AI on Environmental, Social and Governance (ESG) Investing: Implications for the Investment Value Chain

Anna Maj
FinTech Leader, PwC
www.linkedin.com/in/anna-maj-fintech/
www.twitter.com/anna_maria_maj

See chapter:
The Rise of Conversational AI Platforms

Shailendra Malik
Vice President – IT Platforms, DBS Bank
www.linkedin.com/in/shailendramalik
www.twitter.com/eshailendra

See chapter:
The Changing Face of Regulatory, Compliance and Audit

Laura Manescu
Head of Fintech Division, M3 Holdings
www.linkedin.com/in/laura-manescu/

See abstract:
Does a Future Without Technology Exist?

Jeff Manricks
Sales Director UK Region, Shift Technology
www.linkedin.com/in/jeffmanricks/
www.twitter.com/ai_insurtech

See chapter:
Improving Policy Life Cycle Management with AI and Data Science

Barbara C. Matthews
Founder and CEO, BCMstrategy, Inc.
www.linkedin.com/in/barbaracmatthews
www.twitter.com/bcmstrategy

See chapter:
The AI Advantage: Near-Term Workforce Opportunities and Challenges

Sotiris Melioumis
CEO, SoNiceSoNice UK Ltd
www.linkedin.com/in/sotiris-melioumis-mb-634b7214/
www.twitter.com/sn2_solutions

See chapter:
Two Dimensional Virtual Vertical Integration: Solving the Impossible SC Problem

Yahya Mohamed Mao
CMO, n'cloud.swiss AG
www.linkedin.com/in/yahyamohamedmao/
www.twitter.com/YIbnM

See abstract:
AI-Driven Trends for the Future Favour the Omnipresence of Cloud Computing

Kasia Miaskiewicz
Director, UBS EVOLVE
www.linkedin.com/in/katarzynamiaskiewicz/

See chapter:
The Data Promise

Shân M. Millie
Founder, Bright Blue Hare
www.linkedin.com/in/sh%C3%A2nmillie/
www.twitter.com/SMMBrightBlueH

See chapter:
Insurance and AI: Choices in Leadership, Purpose and Trust

Kunal Mittal
CPO, FrontM
www.linkedin.com/in/KunalMittal

See abstract:
Use of AI for Airlines and Maritime

Tim Molton
Associate, MJM Limited
www.linkedin.com/in/timmolton

See chapter:
Regulation of AI within the Financial Services Sector

Yvon Moysan
Academic Director, IÉSEG School of Management
www.linkedin.com/in/yvon-moysan
www.twitter.com/yvonmoysan

See chapter:
Showcase and Customer Service: Leveraging Chatbots in the Banking Industry

Chee-We Ng
Venture Capitalist, Oak Seed Ventures
www.linkedin.com/in/cheewe/

See chapter:
The Future of AI in Finance

Aarón Olmos
Economist and Professor of Economics and Cryptoeconomics, IESA
www.linkedin.com/in/aaronolmos/
www.twitter.com/aaronolmos

See chapter:
Invisible Hand, Spontaneous Order and Artificial Intelligence

Professor Andy Pardoe
Founder, Informed.AI Group
www.linkedin.com/in/andypardoe/
www.twitter.com/Pardoe_AI

See chapter:
Welcome to the Future

Reema Patel
Head of Public Engagement, Ada Lovelace Institute
www.linkedin.com/in/reema-patel-34941228/
www.twitter.com/Reema__Patel

See chapter:
Trust in FinTech and AI: Some Introductory Reflections

Urvashi Prakash
Chief Difference Maker
www.linkedin.com/in/Urvashi
www.twitter.com/Urvashiprakash

See abstract:
Who do you Trust?

Andreas Pusch
Founder and CEO, YUKKA Lab AG
www.linkedin.com/in/andreas-pusch/
www.twitter.com/yukkalab?lang=en

See chapter:
Navigating a Sea of Information, News and Opinion with Augmented Human Intelligence

Anand Rao
Director and Head Europe, Data Science and Engineering, Mindtree, a Larsen & Toubro company
www.linkedin.com/in/anandrao81
www.twitter.com/anands_rao

See abstract:
FinTech, in the Age of Superhuman Intelligence

Cesar J. Richardson
General Manager Americas, Strands Finance
www.linkedin.com/in/jimenezcesar
www.twitter.com/cejiri

See chapter:
Open Banking, Blockchain and AI: The Building Blocks for Web 3.0

Robert Robinson
Associate Professor, SIU Medicine
www.linkedin.com/in/robertrobinsonmd/
www.twitter.com/medicaliphone

See abstract:
Bias and Discrimination with AI

Luis Rodríguez
Chief Product and Innovation Officer, Strands
www.linkedin.com/in/luisjrodriguez
www.twitter.com/luisrodrigz

See chapter:
The Seven Deadly Sins of AI

Dr Lipa Roitman
CTO, I Know First
www.linkedin.com/in/lipa-roitman/

See chapter:
Finding Order in the Chaos: Investment Selection Using AI

Patrick Rotzetter
Business Technology Director, EPAM Systems
www.linkedin.com/in/rotzetter/
www.twitter.com/RotzetteP

See chapter:
Machine Learning in Digital Wealth Management

María Ruiz de Velasco
Of Counsel, ECIJA Law and Technology
www.linkedin.com/in/mar%C3%ADa-ruiz-de-velasco-a41537142/

See abstract:
Behaviourally Informed Robo-Advice Platforms: Friends or Foes?

Kathryn Rungrueng
COO, Flowcast
www.linkedin.com/in/kathryn-rungrueng/

See chapter:
Transforming Black Box AI in the Finance Industry: Explainable AI that is Intuitive and Prescriptive

Richard Saldanha
Founder and Managing Director, Oxquant
www.linkedin.com/in/oxquant-richard-saldanha
www.twitter.com/oxquant

See chapter:
Dispelling the Illusion

Abhineet Sarkar
FinTech and Innovation Lead, India
www.linkedin.com/in/abhineetsarkar
www.twitter.com/abhiNeet_S

See chapter:
Disrupting the Insurance Value Chain

Patricia Shaw
CEO, Beyond Reach Consulting Limited
www.linkedin.com/in/patricia-shaw-655a384/
www.twitter.com/altrishaw

See chapter:
Building Trust through Sound Governance

Hasik Shetty
Machine Learning Engineer and Strategist
www.linkedin.com/in/hasik-shetty-a61b54124/

See chapter:
AI in Indian Investment and Asset Management: Global Perspective

Paolo Sironi
Author and IBM Industry Academy member
www.linkedin.com/in/thepsironi/
www.twitter.com/thepsironi

See chapter:
The True Value of AI to Transform Push/Pull Wealth Management Offers

Panos Skliamis
CEO, SPIN Analytics
www.linkedin.com/in/panosskliamis/
www.twitter.com/SPINANALYTICS1

See abstract:
AI in Credit Risk Management I

Louise Smith
FinTech Envoy, UK Treasury FinTech Envoy Scotland
www.linkedin.com/in/louise-smith-70b72a14
www.twitter.com/LouM_Smith
See abstract:
Beyond the Technology

Ken So
Founder and CEO, Flowcast
www.linkedin.com/in/kenso01
See chapter:
Transforming Black Box AI in the Finance Industry: Explainable AI that Is Intuitive and Prescriptive

Nadia Sood
CEO and Founder, CreditEnable
www.linkedin.com/in/nadiasood/
See chapter:
The Power of AI to Transform the Global SME Credit Landscape

Christian Spindler
CEO, DATA AHEAD ANALYTICS
www.linkedin.com/in/dr-christian-spindler/
www.twitter.com/datagmbh
See chapter:
Algorithm Assurance

Anshul Srivastav
Chief Information Officer and Chief Digital Officer
www.linkedin.com/in/anshul-srivastav-b57b514/
See abstract:
ET&T (Ethics, Transparency and Trust)

Dr Manj Subiah
Director, Author, Business Advisor, Intuitive Intelligence Specialist, VIP Coach, GIIS
www.linkedin.com/in/drmanjsubiah
www.twitter.com/DrManjSubiah
See abstract:
Intuitive Intelligence (II) and Artificial Intelligence (AI)

Caryn Tan
Responsible AI Manager, Accenture
www.linkedin.com/in/caryntan
www.twitter.com/CarynTan29
See abstract:
Applying Ethics to AI: What to How

Brian W. Tang
Founder, ACMI and LITE Lab@HKU
www.linkedin.com/in/brianwtang
www.twitter.com/CapMarketsProf
See chapter:
Independent AI Ethics Committees and ESG Corporate Reporting on AI as Emerging Corporate and AI Governance Trends

Mike Taylor
Director, Deloitte
www.linkedin.com/in/mikeawtaylor/
See chapter:
Cutting to the Chase: Mapping AI to the Real-World Insurance Value Chain

Kevin Telford
Advisor, Thoughtworks
www.linkedin.com/in/telfordkevin/
See chapter:
AI Trust, Ethics, Transparency and Enablement

Peggy Tsai
Vice President of Data Solutions, BigID
www.linkedin.com/in/peggy-tsai-data
www.twitter.com/peggy_tsai
See chapter:
Making Data Your Most Valuable Asset

Fabian Tschirky
Project Officer Omnichannel Management, UBS Global Wealth Management
www.linkedin.com/in/fabian-tschirky-659043b3/
See chapter:
The Data Promise

Terence Tse
Co-Founder and Executive Director, Nexus FrontierTech
www.linkedin.com/in/terencetse/
www.twitter.com/Terencecmtse

See chapter:
What Is AI and How to Make It Work for You

Nigel Walsh
Partner, Deloitte
www.linkedin.com/in/nigelwalsh/
www.twitter.com/nigelwalsh

See chapter:
Cutting to the Chase: Mapping AI to the Real-World Insurance Value Chain

Dr Aric Whitewood
Founding Partner, XAI Asset Management
www.linkedin.com/in/aric-whitewood/

See chapter:
Introduction on AI Approaches in Capital Markets

Tiffany Wong
Manager, PwC UK
www.linkedin.com/in/tiffany-hy-wong-cfa-aca-aa7a0a38/

See chapter:
AI and Business Ethics in Financial Markets

Joshua Xiang
CTO and SVP, CreditEase
www.linkedin.com/in/向江旭-joshua-xiang-876945/
www.twitter.com/jxiang

See chapter:
AI in Lending

Lubna Yusuf
Founder, La Legal
www.linkedin.com/in/lubnayusuf/
www.twitter.com/Lubna_LaLegal

See chapter:
A New Internet, Data Banks and Digital World War

Index

C

D

E

F

G

H

I

S

T